THINKING
TUNA FISH,
TALKING
DEATH

Other books by Robert Scheer

With Enough Shovels: Reagan, Bush and Nuclear War (1982)

America After Nixon: The Age of the Multinationals (1974)

Diaries of Che Guevara (editor) (1968)

How the U.S. Got Involved in Vietnam (1965)

Cuba: Tragedy in Our Hemisphere
(with Maurice Zeitlin) (1963)

THINKING TUNA FISH, TALKING DEATH

❧ ❧ ❧

*Essays on the Pornography
of Power*

❧

ROBERT SCHEER

HILL AND WANG

A division of Farrar, Straus and Giroux
NEW YORK

Library of Congress Cataloging-in-Publication Data
Scheer, Robert.
   Thinking tuna fish, talking death: essays on the pornography of power/
Robert Scheer.—1st ed.
   p. cm.
1. United States—Politics and government—1945–   2. Vietnamese
Conflict, 1962–1975.   I. Title.
E839.5.S28 1988   973.92—dc19   88-9735

Grateful acknowledgment is made to the following publications for permission to reprint previously published material, some of which appears in this book in a slightly different form:
Esquire, "Pepsi Takes Moscow" (originally titled "The Doctrine of Multinational Sell," April
1975) and "Scoop: The Hawk That Haunts" (originally titled "Why You Should Think About
Scoop again and again and again," September 1975); Los Angeles Times, "The Bronx: A Poisoned
Flower" (originally titled "Bronx: Landscape of Urban Cancer," August 6, 1978), "Unterberger
the Hero" (originally titled "Old Schools Survive and Thrive," July 10, 1986), "The Jews of Los
Angeles" (originally published as a three-part series titled "Pursuing the American Dream,"
January 29, 1978, "Line Drawn Between Two Worlds," January 30, 1978, and "New Set of
Values for the Middle Class," January 31, 1978), "The Making of Joan Lunden" (originally
titled "The Rise of Joan Lunden: News Sense Unimportant," May 29, 1977), "The Hoax of
Tonkin" (originally titled "Tonkin—Dubious Premise for a War," April 29, 1985), "The Sham-
bles of Star Wars" (originally published as a three-part series titled " 'Star Wars': A Program in
Disarray," September 22, 1985, "Flaws Peril Pivotal 'Star Wars' Laser," September 23, 1985,
and "Scientists Split Over 'Star Wars,' " September 24, 1985), "Thinking Tuna Fish, Talking
Death" (originally titled "Thinking Tuna Fish, Talking Death: Inside the Nuclear Establish-
ment," October 4, 1981), "And Then Came Gorbachev" (of which Parts 2 and 3 were originally
titled "Gorbachev in College: Bold and Critical," December 4, 1987, and "The Gorbachev
Manifesto," November 15, 1987); New Times, "Zombies of the Left" (originally titled "Enough
Already," January 8, 1979); Playboy, "Ed Meese's Dirty Pictures" (originally titled "Inside the
Meese Commission," August 1986), "Nelson Rockefeller Takes Care of Everybody" (October
1975), "Jimmy, We Hardly Know Y'All" (November 1976), "Reagan Country" (originally titled
"The Reagan Question," August 1980), "Sparring with Fallaci: The Playboy Interview" (originally
titled "Playboy Interview: Oriana Fallaci," November 1981), "With Enough Shovels" (December
1982), "And Then Came Gorbachev" (of which Part 1 was originally titled "Then Came Gorbachev," August 1988); Ramparts, "A Warning from Phnom Penh" (originally titled "A View
from Phnom Penh," July 1965), "The Winner's War" (December 1965), "Lord Russell and the
B-52s" (originally titled "Lord Russell," May 1967); SunDance, "The Language of Torturers"
(August–September 1972).

To my wife, Narda Zacchino,
who reminds me that without her
I'd be "an alcoholic has-been with VD."
What a gal

Acknowledgments

A collection of articles previously published in well-edited journals obviously owes much to the editors who helped conceive, edit, and push for their publication. Let's not kid: good editors make good writers.

At *Ramparts* that meant Warren Hinckle and Dugald Stermer, who were often bewildered by my political preoccupations but said what the hell. The three of us became co-conspirators in reshaping a Catholic literary quarterly into the magazine of the sixties. I still think of it as the best ever.

And then came *Playboy*. Arthur Kretchmer bailed me out during the Nixon years when my kind of journalism was no longer in vogue and assignments were hard to come by. I was in hock for expenses incurred on a piece for the *Saturday Review* when it went belly up and Kretchmer took me on. "Yeah, you're on, but I don't have time to talk" was the inspiring literary sentiment he uttered. We haven't talked much since, but like everyone else who has taken his magazine down the garden path of controversy, I've known he's there and on the high road. For more than fifteen years, Kretchmer never once chickened out, cheapened a story, or in any other way failed to do what I thought was the right thing, which is no small achievement for the boss of a T-and-A mag.

Generous editors at *Playboy* like Geoff Norman helped to see that my rent was finally getting paid on time. Then one rainy day in Bolinas, California, shouting into a phone in an open-air booth, I encountered this schmuck Yalie, Barry Golson, the new editor on the block, who told me that the piece they had already bought was no good and they couldn't send the check. "Can't send the check?" I shouted over and over, my words becoming increasingly incoherent as the expletives created too much static and Golson hung up. He was right, as he almost always has been. I rewrote the piece under protest, and many more. Golson is simply the most gifted editor in the magazine business. He also reinvented the *Playboy* interview and has cut me in on some of the action, often becoming crazed trying to keep me and our subject in the same room. He's been my collaborator as well as editor and friend, and I am grateful, as I am for Thia Golson who kept us both in the ball park.

As for my adult-world employer, the ever-solid *Los Angeles Times*, the credit for my work goes to a number of fine editors. I was hired at the *Times* by Mark Murphy, a gruff ex-Mormon, and Bill Thomas, the paper's straight-arrow editor-in-chief, two golfing nuts who looked like Republicans to me. I never could figure out why they took a flyer on a bearded character whom they must have thought of as some sort of pinko. But they did, and never pulled back. Never, and the heat from a couple of the stories reprinted here was more than they needed. To have both the Jewish and the born-again Christian communities picketing your building may be more than they bargained for, but they never let me think that they feared controversy. I also want to thank Bill Boyarsky, Dennis Britton, George Cotliar, John Foley, Tom Johnson, Rick Meyer, and Mike Miller for their support. And, of course, Nina Green, researcher extraordinaire and good friend, whose help in coming up with facts and sources has been invaluable.

My immediate editor at the *Times*, Tim Rutten, could edit anything anywhere with grace and intelligence. Never when I left the Bronx did I think that I would find myself so trusting and respectful of the sensibilities and intelligence of an Irish Catholic. I saw his dignity erode only once, when we jointly interviewed the new Archbishop of Los Angeles and I gently inquired as to whether they still think we killed their Lord. They don't, but Rutten almost killed me.

Steve Wasserman, today the publisher of Hill and Wang, edited this book with infectious enthusiasm and remarkable persistence, and was, in another life, virtually my co-author on its most controversial article—"The Jews of Los Angeles." Together we sat at the home of a Doberman-guarded gangster who assured us there was no Jewish Mafia, and together we fielded the thousands of angry phone calls and letters demanding that we restore our foreskins. I knew that Wasserman would do better than me in life, and he has. But if he is going to be a hotshot publisher, it's better that he throw a few bucks my way.

Jason Epstein, my editor at Random House, is, as many people who know him say, the smartest person in New York, but he doesn't suffer fools lightly and lets me know when I'm being one. His criticisms, notions, and facts shaped several of these articles.

Stanley Sheinbaum has been a clipping service and a guru and, along with his wife Betty, has thoughtfully harassed me with a steady stream of story ideas. Not to make the list too long, but Alex Cockburn, Liz Familian, Jules Feiffer, Frances FitzGerald, Elaine Kaufman, John Larsen, Susan Lyne, Jean Stein, Anne Weills, Barry Weiss, and Helen Zacchino always came through. As did Ed Sorel, who has honored this book with his inimitable genius. Most of all I want to remember my late cousin Rachel Nitzberg, who made the trip with me from the Bronx to L.A. and was always my alter ego, critic, and conscience.

My two youngest sons were a constant nuisance in the writing of many of these pieces and deserve no credit whatsoever except as great distracting entertainment. And those conversations at day care and the Cub Scouts . . . don't tell me I don't know about America; I raise kids in Orange County two miles from John Wayne Airport. Have you any idea of the number of hands of bridge I have played with Bruce and Chris Baron, two schoolteachers here who amazingly enough founded the county's Amnesty International chapter, which is something akin to favoring Armenian nationalism in Istanbul.

My eldest son, Christopher, has influenced me greatly by putting me down when I get snotty and lifting me up when I lose hope. I talk to this extraordinary kid, who looks like a surfer, the way I did to my immigrant parents. We have taken many trips together, sometimes literally, as in 1987 to the Soviet Union, and my most interesting and humorous discussions are with him. However, he writes much better than I do, and I'm not sure how I feel about that.

Finally, a word about the Sicilian influence. I didn't know they went to college, but I now find myself married to a daughter of Palermo—Narda Zacchino—who outranks me not only at home but in the corporate structure of the *Los Angeles Times* as well. No matter—as long as she continues to find time to make sense of my scribbling. Happiness is having a warm editor in bed to wake up when you can't find the lead. Yes, she made me. No question, so don't break my legs. Look, she got the dedication.

R.S.

CONTENTS

THINKING TUNA FISH, TALKING DEATH

Introduction

When I was a kid I killed Krauts. I bring it up now only because my editor insists that it partly explains my journalism, which is admittedly a little offbeat and not overly respectful of God and country. I have never been a dispassionate accountant auditing the news. We are all products of our history and we would be zombie-like to deny its place in our work. I never have.

I was five in 1940 when Hitler went to war and ten when he lost it, and during those formative years my friends and I used to kill Germans—back then everybody called them Krauts—and I was very good at it. I killed them in the basement when I went to throw out the trash, and I killed them on the subway when they sat mysteriously across the aisle plotting to steal our nation's secrets. They could look huge and mean, but sometimes they were posing as just ordinary American people on subway ads screaming their warning that "loose lips sink ships."

I feared the Krauts because they wanted to conquer the world, and I hated them because they killed Jewish and Russian people. My mother, whom I loved, was both. The only problem was that my father, whom I also loved, was a Kraut. "No," my Jewish mother insisted proudly, "he's a socialist."

True enough. But there was also no denying that he was a Kraut. Despite coming over from Germany on his own hook at fourteen and looking, everybody said, just like Dick Tracy, he unmistakably retained a trace of the accent made famous by the villains in the movies we watched at the old Allerton Avenue Theater, where the other kids in the audience were either Jewish or Italian. The Italians, on the rare occasion when I talked to them (which means on the rare occasion when they were willing to overlook their claim that "you kikes killed da Lord"), didn't seem particularly troubled by their connection with Mussolini, who anyway soon became a joke.

I didn't know any other Kraut's kids except my cousins on Myrtle Avenue in Brooklyn, and while they also hated Hitler, they didn't seem to take it personally. They didn't have Jewish guilt. Which in my quarter of the Bronx was palpable, and never a joke.

At the war's end, when we learned more fully about the crimes of the Germans, I was grateful that my hero Franklin Delano Roosevelt was working with the Russians to make sure that there would never be a Germany again. In my child's mind I had finally worked it out. My father remained a good guy because he had denounced his native land and renounced the patriotism of his birthright. He had even transformed his German language into Yiddish and sold subscriptions to left-wing Yiddish papers, beginning with the Social Democratic *Forward* and later the Communist *Freiheit*. He would not go to German restaurants, and chose to live in a Jewish neighborhood. He knew that all Germans were not genetically evil, but he had lost patience with them.

Then an amazing thing happened. Germans were suddenly the good guys and the Russians were bad. Not to my father, who nursed his sense of betrayal, but that's the way it was on the radio and in the newspapers. German scientists were going to save us from the Bolsheviks and Germany was now a bastion of the free world. We heard that our relatives in Germany were working for the American Air Force base in Kaiserslautern.

I was dumbfounded. "No," I challenged my teachers, who embraced red-baiting and McCarthyism as fervently as only months before they had embraced Joseph Stalin, the hero of *Time* and *Life* magazine covers. I failed every class in the seventh grade. But I learned journalism. I was at war with the Cold War. I would go down to the Forty-second Street Public Library to get facts and arguments to hurl at these teachers before they hustled me down to the principal's office. I came to love libraries more than schools. I went to hear speakers like I. F. Stone and started devouring Murray Kempton's columns in the *New York Post* as if they were holy grail. My teachers, when they knew better, were silent and afraid. The International Communist Conspiracy and its timetable for the takeover of the world seemed the expected answer to most multiple-choice quizzes.

Books were thrown out to make landfill when they weren't burned. I lived near a housing project built by leftist trade unions, and some of the old Communists panicked when the FBI cars started swarming about. People went underground with the Smith Act indictments, and their books went into the trash. At the time I was delivering milk for Meyerovitch's grocery and often, on my early-morning rounds, I would find a political treasure trove. My parents, bless them, let me bring the orphan books home.

My Jewish mother—who is now eighty-eight and sleeping gently upstairs, where she lives with the children, the turtle, and the dog, all of whom snore the peace of the innocent—does not understand to this day that being half a Kraut can be traumatic. She thinks my occasional propensity to churn out somewhat provocative articles that result in angry letters in the newspaper is just the lot of the writer, and that I asked for it when I left engineering school over her objections. Writers, she would tell me, citing the troubles of Itsik Fefer, her favorite Yiddish writer, who was killed by the Soviet powers, are always in trouble. Nor does she think it has anything to do with my illegitimate birth or her being an illegal alien and a Communist.

Now, my mother is not really illegal or a Communist. She slipped through Ellis Island in 1921, having left Russia after the Bolshevik Revolution because the Jewish Socialist Bund, the organization for which she carried secrets in her hair, was crushed by Lenin. But she had been a revolutionary, and her sister was killed in the 1905 uprising against the czar, so she didn't tell them *everything* at Ellis Island.

Right away she started organizing for the union in her first months as a garment worker in the New York City sweatshops, and was distinguished for being arrested six times in one day on various picket lines. She never applied for citizenship because of her arrest record and to this day expects to be deported. As I write this, yet another form letter arrives from the INS in Los Angeles demanding that she report for a hearing. I once again call the office and tell them to come and get her, inquiring sweetly as to whether the Reagan Administration really wants to send this Jewish dissident back to Russia.

But I digress, which is not unusual, since my mother is, after all, upstairs. And she has been upstairs or downstairs for some twenty-five years now, having outlived three specialists in Parkinson's disease who predicted her imminent demise. If she is still around to read this book and her eyes hold up, she may like parts of it, but that's not what she will focus on. It will be the errors. "Too soft here and how come you didn't mention that . . ." But worst of all: "How could you call your father a Kraut?"

He *was* a Kraut, Ma, don't you remember? He came over from Germany on the eve of World War I, and his brother Edward came ten years later. They drank beer, played soccer, and blew the clarinet in a German oompah band. Pure Kraut stuff. I was a kid in the car hearing my Uncle Edward and my father yelling over my father's refusal to go down to North Carolina to visit their cousin Karl Weismann, who was being held in a POW camp there. I'll never forget the chill in that car when my father announced that, for him, all the *landsmen* were dead.

My father wrote off the Germans, even long after the war was over, because he had once respected them so. At the height of my Kraut killing, I had asked my father about his personal connection with Germany, and he made me sit down and listen to a scratchy record of Beethoven. Not a word passed between us until the music ended.

My father loved music. He came from a town where every male child was required to learn an instrument, and if they were any good, they would go off and get a job with the circus and send money back home to support, in his case, the other eleven children. He played oompah for money before records came in and live music went out. After that, he turned to repairing knitting machines at the New York Knitting Mills on West Twelfth Street. But while he played oompah for a living, he jammed on Beethoven after hours, and when he thought of Germany, it was not of the barren southwest German farmland he had worked and escaped but, rather, of its music.

Then the songs soured and my father was enraged.

What did my father believe? Not in God; he was one of those freethinkers who came to America in part to get away from the Lutheran Church. I have been to that little brick church in Mackenbach with my father's youngest brother, who was wounded on the Russian front during the war. He told me that the minister of the church wore a Nazi uniform while preaching his Sunday sermon. He said that in those days Hitler was a voice on the radio, and you were either red or brown in their neck of the woods, a scraggly poor farming area—the Pfalz section of southwest Germany, which runs into France. Erich Honecker was a red who lived nearby in Saarbrücken, and he spent the war in a Nazi prison camp. After the war, he became the head of East Germany. My uncle made it clear that none of our relatives in Germany was a red, but they all knew that my father and uncle in the States were.

My father had been a Wobbly, and a YPSYL follower of Eugene Victor Debs, and sometime in the darkest days of the thirties, he had joined the Communist Party. He was thrown out a year later on the testimony of my Uncle Leon's sister, Lily Nitzberg. My father had led a bloody strike at the New York Knitting Mills under the banner of the Communist-run Industrial Union. When the union leadership sold out with what used to be called a sweetheart contract giving the bosses too much, my father wouldn't go along and led a wildcat strike. He blasted the union leaders in front of the workers; Lily turned him in and he was kicked out of the Party. Lily remained a close family friend, and what I remember most about her is her attempts to wash the dirt off my face with the spit on her handkerchief. That, and her endlessly straightening her seamed stockings. It was my first introduction to erotica. Not my last, thank God; but once again I digress.

In my last years in high school, and for a time even in college, I worked as a cashier at S. Klein's, the huge department store on Union Square. That was an education—not so much in the store as across the street, where leftist organizers and nuts competed with religious proselytizers and anarchists for the possession of my mind. Sometimes I was the only audience. But nuts or not, they had literature, and I came to love pamphleteering.

I was also forced to come to grips with the horrors of Stalinism, which my father, not my mother, tended to overlook. The Union Square speakers could be merciless in their denunciations of the crimes of the left.

During my City College days, I fell in with a group of leftists who had it in for any government anywhere in the world, as if the mere act of assuming power inevitably led to betrayal of all that is decent. I would sit in small apartments and meeting halls in Greenwich Village soaking up the acerbic words of a Bayard Rustin in his War Resister days, before he became famous as an aide to Martin Luther King, Jr., or a Michael Harrington, my first Catholic radical, no small feat in the days of Cardinal Spellman. This was in the fifties, before the New Left, when anti-intellectualism was still considered a sin. And in this world the printed word was revered even as it was denounced. Writing was purposeful.

By then I was a smartass kid at CCNY, working my way through the great ideological alcoves of the old Shepard Hall dining room, from Trotskyist to vegetarian, with some Ayn Randists thrown in for good measure. Now, Abe Rosenthal of *The New York Times* went to City, and he's pretty conservative, and Ed Kosner of *Newsweek* and *New York* magazine was in my class, and he's as centrist and trendy as it is possible to be. So I shouldn't blame City for the way I am. But I do celebrate City in one of the essays in this book, and one thing many of us got from the place was confidence. How do you get people to tell you those things? City College. Why do you argue so much? City College. Who told you you're so smart? City College.

We're all smart. We're all as smart as "they" are, and where have you been if I have to tell you who they are? They had names like Binky and Missy, and inheritances. They assumed that opportunity would present itself and that positions of power and influence were theirs for the asking. And in this period before widespread financial aid, they went to private schools and we went to City College. And we felt superior for it. But not an automatic superiority, as in a birthright. My last years at City were financed by full shifts in the post office, and I knew I could end up there. But I also knew that I could get out.

"Class" is the unspoken word of American journalism, and class divisions are presumed to be the preoccupations of malcontents, not reporters. But somewhere between my parents and City College I developed an unshakable habit of thinking about social problems in class terms. Nobody seems to know who said "The role of the press is to comfort the afflicted and afflict the comfortable." The quote is attributed variously to Liebling, Mencken, and

Marx, but I believe it and cherish the moment at a *Los Angeles Times* awards dinner when I shared the sentiment with my employers.

To put it bluntly, I want in any story to know who's getting screwed and who's doing the screwing. I don't accept the idea that "common people," be they Palestinians in Gaza or Puerto Ricans in the Bronx, don't or shouldn't mind being on the receiving end. And if I ever tended to forget this, my mother was there, reading every word, ready to denounce me. She never went to high school and she worked for more than forty years in a sweatshop, but she and my Uncle Leon, the fruit peddler, and my Uncle Edward, the welder, were as capable of grappling with the toughest political problems as anyone I ever interviewed.

In the thirty years since City College, I have hustled after, queried, stalked, befriended, and name-dropped a long list of those who, like myself, presume to have answers for others. From Nelson Rockefeller to Fidel Castro, from Richard Nixon to Jimmy Carter, with various diversionary treks into the world of the Jerry Falwells and Jesse Jacksons. Very few women, but that is not of my doing. And it's not a bad bunch of guys. Most, like Ronald Reagan and Fidel Castro, were friendly, smart, and earnest. Most. Not George Bush or Edwin Meese. Others, like Richard Nixon, turned out to be surprisingly brilliant, if quirky. But they were also, as a group, quite often wrong, and in ways so obvious as to call into question the very exercise of power. What is revealed in the reporting that follows is not the stuff of evil conspiracy or even serious avarice. It is rather a loose compendium of poses of the powerful driven by fickle ambition, giddiness of purpose, and preening arrogance. The exercise of power is often pornographic, if I may define that word, which Attorney General Meese's commission was unable to define, because it aims at titillation rather than fulfillment. Look to the Bronx or to Vietnam and one finds the same dismal, gauzy striptease in which the audience is always kept at a safe distance from the truth.

The truth is a bitch. And capturing it is not so straightforward as journalism professors and media heavies sometimes suggest. This is often a scuzzy business. You want a story; they want their story told their way. So you play a smarmy game—cajoling, courting, humoring, stroking, berating each other, till you've got something as close to the truth as you can get and still make deadline. It's not the Boy Scouts or even *Dragnet*. Anyway, I prefer Peter Falk in the old *Columbo* TV series as a model: persistent, rumpled, modest.

The tricks of the trade are obvious. Never do an important interview without visiting the library first. I know it sounds like urging people to floss regularly, but this is the basic rule for journalistic health. Most issues have been thought about by someone before. The person being interviewed will know that and you had better. Bring your experience to bear, you weren't born yesterday, but finally go with what is and not with what ought to be. News is news. And know what you're talking about before you write, no matter what the editor demands. Finally, I have one standard. I want my take on a story to hold up after it's been moved off the front page to make way for the late final and after the pages are an unreadable yellow.

Looking back on these pieces, I realize that I wrote them the way I was taught to do term papers at CCNY by Stanley Feingold, that reed-thin, bespectacled, pockmarked genius with the ready smile who never got tenure but who knew that facts are not academic. This fanatic democrat, underpaid teacher of government, climbed out of the 125th Street subway station for decades, striding purposefully up Amsterdam Avenue, to convince succeeding generations of the unwashed that the secret of America lay in the assumption that nothing important is ever fully resolved. That we all have a duty to debate, as loudly and provocatively as we feel, and that we may all be wrong. But sometimes we are right and we ought not to keep such perceptions to ourselves.

In the Feingold religion the Bill of Rights was Torah, and he could be the fundamentalist fanatic as he held the line against modern reformers, of the left or right, who would substitute the expediency of their cause for the safeguards of a democratic process, which for him was as necessary as air. I have had my causes, but I would hope that Feingold, wherever he went after they forced him out of City, would not judge me a polluter.

After City I sobered up, got married, went to graduate school, and tried to become a professor. It didn't work. I wanted to write to have an impact, not to diddle. And I wanted to see things beyond the library. While in graduate school at Berkeley, I went to Cuba during summer vacation, saw and heard things not being reported in the mass media, and teamed up with Maurice Zeitlin to write a book. He went on to become a professor, a very good one, and I became a book clerk at City Lights Books, where I got a Ph.D. from Lawrence Ferlinghetti and eventually became a journalist.

My speech on journalism is simple. Be honest, be fair, but don't be indifferent. There is nothing morally superior about the stance of the voyeur. Yes, good journalism begins and ends with respect for fact over prejudice, and in the heat of the chase one must nurture an ability to be surprised and to go after and fairly report that which confounds one's preconception. Otherwise, why make the schlepp through libraries and airports?

I didn't fly around for weeks with Jerry Falwell in a scary little plane while he talked about Armageddon for the fun of it. An interview works when you think you might learn something. Open to Falwell? Yes. Suspicious? You bet. Particularly when he told me how the Cold War was simply the playing out of biblical prophecy which foretold that the Russians were the bad guys.

I knew better, because I had killed Krauts as a kid when the Russians were the good guys and the Germans were evil. Could those categories not get reversed again? Could we not be the bad guys and then good again? Falwell's perspective could not countenance such thoughts, and mine required them. His view may be better for a preacher, but mine is essential for a writer.

Lots of other things happened around me to etch my tablet, like living on home relief for the first five years of my life, my father having lost his job to the Depression the day I was born. I saw my mother push the gas company guy out the door so he couldn't cut off the heat. That experience leaves a journalist feeling a bit suspicious about charges of welfare fraud. Baggage, yes. But why travel light in this world? With baggage you may veer, perhaps in the wrong direction, but that is also interesting. And anyway, everyone has got baggage; they just don't all admit it. I can't recall the last journalist who didn't have the whole world figured out on the basis of something someone once told him back where he came from. Well, I also heard a few things back there where I came from.

ROBERT SCHEER
May 1988

PURSUING THE AMERICAN DREAM

The Bronx: A Poisoned Flower

The Good Humor truck circles aimlessly through silent blocks of burned-out buildings hunting the occasional waif still playing in the rubble who might yet desire a Popsicle. This time, there is no sign of life and the ice-cream truck departs with a last ring of its merry chimes, leaving a still life of the South Bronx warscape dotted by garbage lakes, dunes of litter, and beached hulks of abandoned cars. The streets are dead, as if locusts had descended and slurped up the ring-a-levio and stickball games, the philosophers of the benches, the checker kings and loud-music boys, the girls with fishnet stockings and stiletto heels, and the young studs with bodies some said were good for nothing but dancing. Gone the wild, chaotic, noisy cosmopolitan life of a borough that for decades belched up life continuously as its very mission. The bedroom borough where young hardworking couples returned in crammed cars of the D or the Lex from dark garment shops in Manhattan, exhausted but suddenly come to life as they emerged from their subway station to the babble of child-play noises which was the incessant hum of the Bronx.

These were couples who had left Manhattan to spend an hour each way in the subway crunch, marking the first grand suburban exodus to make and raise babies. The Bronx had space—farms, even parks, and plentiful empty lots on which to grow vegetables or build a hut. But it also had the civilization of apartment-dwelling and universities, of botanical gardens, libraries, and sufficient numbers of people so that one was not sentenced to the forced company of boring neighbors, as was assumed to be the case in the suburban housing tracts of Long Island, which was generally regarded as a cultural wasteland.

The Bronx—birthplace of Lauren Bacall, Herman Wouk, George Meany, Anne Bancroft, Jules Feiffer, Paddy Chayefsky, Burt Lancaster, Jonas Salk,

Diahann Carroll, and Carroll O'Connor. Where Edgar Allan Poe lived and worked in a little cottage on the Grand Concourse off Fordham Road. And where Leon Trotsky, in exile, lived on the fifth floor of a tenement and composed tracts in Yiddish and Russian that helped inspire the Russian Revolution. Because of its history, and despite the signs of rot that now appear as far north as the Yonkers line, it is still possible to love the Bronx and remain loyal to its heritage. The endless benches that surround each park and playground are shorn of their wooden slats. And as one passes the concrete bench arms, there remain only memories of past endless arguments about revolution and God and Bertrand Russell and who is the most offensive yenta on the block.

To those who remember, life around the Bronx benches once represented a high point of American civilization. Now there are fat, loud transistor radios blasting out music that numbs one's sensibilities, a fit accompaniment only for the daydreams of junkies and thieves. Or so it seems until a lone Anglo reporter squeezes into People's Park near St. Ann's Episcopal Church to hear Tito Puente play for thousands of kids, mothers, fathers—people—and suddenly the music, like the people, is mysterious, complex, poetic, and, in all other ways, alive. This is, of course, one of the better moments, but that's what we focus on in recalling the history of any ethnic group. Why not the same for the Puerto Ricans of the South Bronx? When in this century did the Bronx not have poverty, uncollected garbage, street gangs, and crime? Remember when the Irish gang, the Fordham Baldies, and the Italian Guinea Dukes—1,000 strong—battled each other for borough supremacy? Yet it was never quite the way it is today, not even close. But what about the Lower East Side, Hell's Kitchen, and East Harlem? The slums have moved north; the problems are the same.

That is why those who strive to save the Bronx are filled with a righteous indignation, for the problems of the Bronx did not germinate there. The Bronx was forced to import the problems of the rural American South, Puerto Rico, and East Harlem. The poor came to New York from all over, and the Bronx paid the price for the efforts to "save" Manhattan as the nation's commercial capital and playground for the rich.

The poor are being pushed out of the entire East Side of Manhattan from the East Village up through Yorkville, freeing the professional elite—the Bloomingdale's/New York magazine crowd—from having to associate with the poverty class. On the West Side, the Lincoln Center complex created another sanctuary for the upper classes. The poor, almost all black and Puerto Rican, were to be contained throughout the Bronx in the massive low-rent housing projects built for that purpose and in the tenements that remained. The insertion of those high-rise housing projects has ripped apart the fabric of the tenement neighborhood life in the Bronx. The projects in the short run have turned out to be viable holding cells for the minority poor, who barely are noticed by commuters on fast-track expressways from Westchester to Wall Street. But the high-rise tenements also have proved to be festering sores—centers of alienation, crime, joblessness.

We think now of these problems of the Bronx because President Carter stood in the midst of the desolation on Charlotte Street one day in the fall of 1977 to underscore his commitment to solving America's urban problems. No one seems to know for certain why he bothered to make this gesture of concern. Some say it was to get back at New York City's Democratic mayoral candidate, Edward Koch, who was giving Carter a hard time on his Mideast policy. Carter wanted to show Koch, according to one White House staffer, that he had "best tend to the problems in his own back yard." Carter had been at the United Nations that day, and another account has it that he went to the Bronx on a whim inspired by Patricia Roberts Harris, Secretary of Housing and Urban Development, to demonstrate that the President is as much concerned with domestic problems as with international ones.

Well, he wasn't. The dry rot of the Bronx has continued to accelerate up the Grand Concourse, the once-proud central artery of the borough. It would now be most accurate to think of the entire borough of 1.5 million people as being part of the "South Bronx problem."

The Bronx is now a poisoned flower.

The parks—Van Cortlandt on the northern boundary, Crotona in the center, and of course Bronx Park with its fabled zoo—are now seedy affairs neglected by the city, stained indelibly by perverse graffiti artists and incessant violence. They were once the perfect, green, refreshing counterpoint to urban life, a vacationland for hundreds of thousands of picnickers with their blankets, Sunday newspapers, mandolins, chess, and kids. Now they are empty, scary places. So, too, the miniparks and benches around the playgrounds that formerly functioned as neighborhood plazas—the heart of a freewheeling child-care, communications, dating network. There was a balance to the life of the Bronx. Now there is madness and the time of the bully.

As S. Robert Wilner, seventy-two, a retired engineer who now teaches meditation techniques to seniors at the Young Men's Hebrew Association, describes his tormentor: "I walk on the Grand Concourse and this regal person—must be seven feet tall—strides up. I didn't get out of his way fast enough, and his elbow strikes me on the head." Wilner's encounter with the giant of the Grand Concourse resulted in his hospitalization, as had two previous incidents, once when he and an eighty-year-old companion were brutally beaten by teenagers at a bus stop.

As Wilner attempts to complete his accounting, scores of elderly people crowd in to relate the details of multiple muggings that have marked the twilight of their lives. Their complaints mostly are against the violent young, who make street corners near schools so inhospitable that bus drivers will not stop to pick up the seniors. They live in apartments with two and three locks on the door, but burglaries occur regularly. Not one in the crowd would dare venture out at night. These are sweet people who say they love the Bronx and don't want to leave it. Some can't and are there because rent control provides them with the only place they can afford. These are people who worked all of their lives and now must subsist on $300 or $400 a month.

Here with the Jewish senior citizens it is the same as it is elsewhere with the blacks, Puerto Ricans, Irish, Italians, in the tenants' meetings or on the street corners—a sense of being cut off from power. Anyone who bears the marks of the outside—a camera, tape recorder, necktie—is seized upon as an antenna for messages of desperation. And the desperation cuts across all racial and ethnic lines. The sense of abandonment is pervasive. These people feel cut off and isolated in a world that no longer abides by any recognizable rules. They are too weak to play by the new rules of the jungle, yet feel that that is what the city has left them with.

There were harsh words for President Carter, who came around that once and who was the recipient of most of their votes. "Carter hasn't helped at all," said Ruth Ballan, whose house has been burgled five times. "Have you driven around here and seen all of those burned-out buildings? It's *schrechlich*—you know what *schrechlich* means? It's terrible, it's horrible. People used to be able to sit in this park; it was a haven for the elderly. It was just magnificent. The plants are gone, the benches are all broken up. There were statues. The kids cut off the heads. The filth is terrible." Representative Robert Garcia, a Democrat of Puerto Rican descent, has his arm wrapped around Mrs. Ballan, who owned the Snow White food store around the corner on Brook Avenue when "little Bobby [Garcia] used to come in." Garcia, who represents the South Bronx, shared Mrs. Ballan's despair. He recalled campaigning in the park. "In the old days it was bumper to bumper on those benches. You could not get a spot there. Now the park is empty." The kids in the area, mostly black and Puerto Rican, are not the way Mrs. Ballan recalls Bobby Garcia's group in the old days. The new breed, in her view, is wild beyond belief. "These kids that pull old ladies' pocketbooks—some of those they see are infirm and can't fend for themselves, they go after them. Sometimes just for sheer nastiness. Even the buses are a danger to travel on. There are regular pickpockets there."

Two floors below the senior center at the YMHA, hundreds of kids, almost all black and brown, are lined up to apply for federally funded summer jobs. They don't look like muggers or rowdies, and indeed must suffer considerable bureaucratic discipline to land these jobs. The director of the program, a twenty-seven-year-old Puerto Rican, Miguel Montez, who grew up in the South Bronx, feels the lack of jobs is at the root of the problem. In Montez's view: "We don't have enough jobs for the kids in the summer. It gets hot. And you're seventeen or eighteen and you don't have any money in your pocket, so you go out looking for some money. I'm not saying it is correct. We've got to get jobs for the kids, keep them occupied."

Welfare has been the alternative to jobs, and as Montez notes the shift, "I was born in the South Bronx, but it's changed. When I was a kid, I don't remember too many people being on welfare. We were poor, but I don't remember any of my friends being on welfare. When you don't have to go out and work and they just give it to you, it has to affect your attitude. You might try and go out to two or three places to get a job and then you give up. First, strike one because you're black. In my desk I have resumés of 250 [minority] people with bachelor's [degrees], a couple of people with master's [degrees]. And I can't get them jobs. Nobody wants them."

The South Bronx is a maintenance culture hooked on welfare and government-subsidized housing. It exists as apart from the mainstream economy as does the life of a methadone addict from straight society. The maintenance economy of the South Bronx is obviously made necessary by the fact that it has been easier for the government to house and feed people minimally than to provide them with jobs. It may be that when people are maintained too long, they are no longer fit for, or desirous of, gainful employment. But there is ample evidence of a large army of involuntarily unemployed people in the Bronx—and an overwhelming lack of jobs. The unskilled jobs that were the entry point into the economy for past generations of immigrants were replaced by mechanization or are now located in the non-unionized American South and abroad. Community organizers say the Puerto Ricans and blacks of the South Bronx are no less willing to work than were their predecessors, but the jobs are not there.

A recent notice of work to restore the Woolworth Building produced 5,000 applicants on short and limited notice. Thousands of young people went begging for the jobs provided this summer under the federal Comprehensive Employment and Training Act. The demand from the minority poor was so high that Koch, now the mayor, instituted a lottery. The announcement of a few security jobs paying $3 to $4 an hour at a newly opened housing project attracted hundreds of serious and enthusiastic applicants from the immediate neighborhood. But it is also true that it is less horrifying to be jobless in the welfare age than previously. With a bit of hustling, one need not go hungry often or sleep on park benches. With a bit more hustling, it is possible to score drugs or alcohol and forget temporarily that one is not doing anything with one's life except spacing out.

In the South Bronx, life is sustained by welfare—but just barely. At one tenants' meeting, a couple of middle-aged women encircled by children burst in to drag Garcia across the street to witness the squalor in which they are forced to live. These women, who live in a dilapidated five-story tenement, dream of being admitted to a municipal housing project which, despite its flaws, is blessed with concrete walls that neither burn nor leak. Their names are on a long waiting list. Most of the apartments in their tenement have burned out, and the "lucky" tenants who had occupied them were permitted to move into the projects ahead of the others. At least in the projects, there is some semblance of police security and landlord services. Here there is excrement, piles of it left by junkies who have turned the hallways of the Bronx tenements into public latrines. Here there are rats as big as cats that move boldly through the mounds of rubbish in the hallway in the daylight, even when a U.S. congressman is present. Here, in the midst of broken glass, rotting fruit, and the acrid and ever-present stench of urine, little children play jacks in their hallway playground of filth that is yet cleaner and safer than the dreaded streets.

Garcia grew up in this neighborhood. His father headed a small evangelical church for thirty-seven years, around the corner from the once prestigious St. Ann's. And he remembers this as a stable and safe mixed neighborhood—Puerto Rican, Italian, Jewish, Irish—going back to the 1930s. At times, Garcia seems like a Puerto Rican "Marty," who would rather attend a Yankee baseball game than lead a social crusade. But he moves easily on the streets of the South Bronx, and he obviously enjoys the close company of its people. The playful Garcia becomes deadly serious and near tears as the middle-aged women take him on a tour of the "apartment," which has been turned into a rain forest due to the broken pipes in the abandoned apartments above. It is necessary to use umbrellas to pass through the hallway. The congressman spies a school workbook in the midst of a clutter of fallen plaster and asks a ten-year-old girl if she has been doing her homework. Amazingly enough, she has. The congressman points out that he went to the same school. But things were better then.

Back on the streets, Garcia encounters teenage pigeon fanciers guarding the front of a boarded-up, burned-out tenement. They are concerned that the congressman will tear down this building, thereby depriving them and their pigeons of a home. These kids dropped out of school in the seventh grade and have tried to get into the Army since, but they have failed the test three times. One of them, a genial, bright kid whose father died of a drug overdose on a nearby roof, has old hypodermic needle marks all over his arms. He tells the congressman he is now off the stuff, thanks to Dr. Mike Smith. Garcia knows that means the acupuncture doctor at Lincoln Hospital detox, who uses pressure points and tiny needles as an alternative to methadone and big needles.

Smith, who does tenant organizing when he's not saving heroin addicts, insists that it's the landlords who hire the addicts to burn down the buildings in order to collect the insurance. There are few landlords left on the scene to dispute this. According to Smith: "Cultural institutions don't burn down, libraries haven't burned down, the churches haven't burned down, the private little houses—have they burned down? No—You know why all the other stuff burned down? For the profit motive. Let's face it, if you had that kind of investment and you saw that you couldn't come out of it any other way, you would buy the torch." There is a consensus among community organizers like Smith that the people of the South Bronx are not inclined to burn down their own homes and possessions and endanger their children. Whether they are Maoists or Episcopalians, there is an apparent unity among those who would save the Bronx from the bottom up, as opposed to the outside missionaries from Washington, think tanks, and developers. The people who work the streets love the life and the potential they find there in abundance, while the outside saviors feel it barely exists.

The Bronx is not dead. The situation is tragic precisely because there is so much potential, so much life despite the harsh realities. Buildings burn, track marks appear on ten-year-old arms, a four-year-old kid falls out of a tenement window because the landlord neglected to put up a window guard. But life goes on. The shopping hubs at 149th Street and Fordham Road are busier than ever. The Venice restaurant at 149th Street is still one of the best Italian restaurants in New York, and Jahn's, on Kingsbridge Road, serves the finest homemade ice cream. Pioneers are restoring row houses on Alexander Street, and small and successful "sweat equity" ventures, in which tenants rebuild their houses, abound.

Senior citizens in the Mitchel Houses housing project staff their own twenty-four-hour security patrol, which has eliminated crime in their racially integrated and cheerful building plunked down in the roughest neighborhood in the South Bronx. At the YMHA on the Concourse, seventy-two-year-old cartoonist Sam Goldin, who has been mugged four times, says that people are basically good and that all groups have a few bad apples. Up near 182nd Street in the Central Bronx, where the Puerto Ricans have encroached on the outer limits of Little Italy, there have been annual gang killings and threatened retaliations. But a tenants' group—led by two products of local Catholic education, Fran Fucelli, who is half-Puerto Rican and half-Italian, and Josephine Perrella, along with the Reverend Edmund Parrakow, a Catholic priest—has organized the neighborhood against the landlords and banks whom they judge to be the central problem.

Fifty blocks south, at St. Ann's Episcopal Church, where Gouverneur Morris, a signer of the Constitution, lies buried, the Reverend James Snodgrass, of proper Wasp bearing, acts in concert with Milton (Karate) Morales, a tough but cheerful Puerto Rican off the streets, and Roy Howard, who speaks in the cadences of a black minister, organizing tenants. These community organizers are particularly critical of the banks, which they charge with abandoning the economy of the Bronx. In their view, disinvestment by the banks has contributed to the creation of an economy based on welfare rather than jobs.

The big bank in the Bronx is the Dollar Savings Bank. For decades, Bronx children learned about saving, banking community ethics, and responsibility from a savings program sponsored by the Dollar and the Bronx public schools. Children saved their dimes, and when five dollars was accumulated, the teacher would assist in depositing the funds with the bank. Officers from the bank would regularly visit the schools to provide homilies on the role of banking and saving in building for a better tomorrow by investing in the community. Yet a report issued by the Bronx borough president's office in 1977 found the Dollar Savings and the other four largest banks in the Bronx "unquestionably guilty of red-lining the borough." This report defined red-lining as "a policy under which lenders decide to refuse mortgage loan requests in certain communities regardless of the qualifications of individual mortgage applicants and the inherent value of the property in question."

In a study of the 1975 data, the latest available, the borough president's office reported that of each dollar deposited by Bronxites in their local banks, "only 12.6 cents was plowed back into the borough in the form of residential mortgages." In that year, Dollar Savings made nearly $60 million in mortgage loans, but only $4 million were in the Bronx. In general, the report found that while 80 percent of the deposits in the five largest Bronx banks came from Bronxites, only 10 percent of these banks' assets were invested in the borough. The report concluded that one large bank, Eastern Savings, granted only ten mortgages that year in the Bronx, for a total of $260,000, while it invested more than $3 million out of the state, "mostly in the Deep South." Dollar Savings Board Chairman Henry Waltemade denied that his bank practices red-lining, and he cited his obligation to depositors to make sound investments.

But the borough president's office insisted that investment in the Bronx can be profitable, pointing to the example of a smaller bank, Yorkville Savings and Loan, with only 3 percent of the assets of the six largest Bronx banks combined. The report noted: "Dollar Savings has over twenty-five times as much in assets as Yorkville, and yet Yorkville made 197 Bronx loans in 1975, while Dollar made only thirty-two."

Community organizer Fran Fucelli, who refers to a file of hundreds of rejected mortgage and home-improvement-loan applications, charged that Dollar "has been the leader in red-lining this community out of existence.

They won't even give mortgages in Central Bronx neighborhoods that are still considered good. It's become the self-fulfilling prophecy, with the bank saying the neighborhood is going downhill and therefore not worthy of investment, and that in fact becomes a reality."

Community organizers are critical of the President's plans to save the Bronx because, in their eyes, it does not come to grips with the issue of red-lining. This was confirmed by one close adviser to the President who, when asked if Carter really is going to be able to save the Bronx said, "Of course not. How's his plan going to save the Bronx when the insurance companies and the banks are red-lining the hell out of it?"

The community organizers were also critical of sensationalist reporting on the Bronx which fails to discuss such mundane matters as red-lining, insurance payments for burned-out buildings, lapses in landlord services, etc. Members of one group, the Morris Heights Neighborhood Improvement Association, claim that they spent dozens of hours with representatives of *CBS Reports* for its feature "The Fire Next Door," which termed the Bronx the arson capital of the world. They insist that they took crews from the network to tenants' meetings, outlined the economic problems, and showed positive alternatives of tenants organizing to retain and maintain their own buildings. They are disappointed that none of this material was used in the program. Tenants' organizer Debby Smith, mother of two, said she was told by one CBS vice president that "positive stuff doesn't sell" and that red-lining was too complicated to go into.

There is no doubt that a great deal of "positive stuff" does go on in the Bronx. But compared to the dimensions of the problems, it often seems forlorn. The thousands of tenant organizations, neighborhood councils, dedicated church people, shopkeeper associations, community-run medical programs are real enough. But they are, in the main, efforts to spit against the wind. Big power in the Bronx—the banks, developers, government programmers—has proved indifferent to such activities. Those people, when interviewed, tended to look upon community organizers as rip-off artists who must have some sort of scam going, or else why would they do it? While there are, no doubt, poverty pimps—hustlers making a fast buck off programs to aid the poor—it is absurd to deny the obvious depth of idealism that persists, perhaps undeservedly, in the Bronx. There are endless tenants' meetings and subsequent agitation over such seemingly minor matters as obtaining a promised buzzer system, a locked front door and locks on all doors, mailboxes that close, and lights in the hallway. But for many of these tenants, such small improvements are perceived as representing the margin between life and death. And unhappily, the crime statistics back up those perceptions.

The community organizers hurl the rip-off artist charge right back at the developers and banks who, they claim, are acting in concert with government agencies to make profit off the poverty that abounds. In a recent article in the New York *Daily News*, one such activist, the Reverend John J. Jenik of the Bronx Church Coalition, charged that the announcement of Carter's South Bronx plan had unleashed a modern day "gold rush" to mine the poverty of the Bronx. Organizer Debby Smith said, "The only thing that will come out of this is another housing project that doesn't work and a campaign poster for Carter."

Gilberto Genera-Valentin, a New York City councilman who represents the South Bronx area, strongly denounced what he considers Carter's hypocrisy: "The South Bronx plan is part of the whole situation where people are being used and misused and promises are made which are not fulfilled . . . The plan doesn't mean anything. The plan is just a gimmick to get people riled up . . . The plan is one that is going to take seven years, and the first three years all they are going to do is build a little 100 units of housing over here and 200 over there. Imagine, you have almost 65 percent unemployed and you need at least 30,000 new apartments. So I guess poverty is the haven for those who are making the money . . . Those developers and the contractors and the banks—they're laughing."

But Carter did go to Charlotte Street. He was there, for however brief a time, when most of us would rather not have known about the problems of the South Bronx. Carter is the first President to formulate an explicit urban program. He cares, but at the same time, he is a consummate politician who believes he cannot afford to care too much. Because of that contradiction, it seems sadly ordained that he will once again raise expectations only to ultimately betray them.

Congressman Garcia has a wait-and-see attitude toward Carter's South Bronx plan. But time is running out. He points out that there are 1.5 million U.S. citizens living in the Bronx and they are entitled to the same rights to life, liberty, and the pursuit of happiness as anyone.

But in the Bronx, civil rights are seriously in question. There has been a breakdown of those ordinary social services that one would have thought were the birthright of any American citizen. The right to have one's mail delivered, for instance. It is commonplace for tenants who expect a Social Security check to line up at the mailbox on the appropriate day to abort a highly likely theft. Many mailboxes are inoperative, punched out by thieves and vandals and left unrepaired by landlords. It is assumed in many neighborhoods that the police will not enter, even if called. So people stop calling. Normal housing code inspections have been suspended or half-heartedly enforced because the relevant bureaucracy is undermanned and totally cynical about the prospects for improvement. Perhaps the most serious deprivation derives from the fact that many people in the Bronx no longer believe in the possibility of public education. Josephine Perrella, a welfare specialist in the Central Bronx, reports that even non-Catholic welfare recipients manage to scrounge up the $300 a year necessary to send their children to parochial schools. It is difficult to find a schoolteacher who believes that the Bronx public-school system can accomplish much. Discipline is lax, academic standards are virtually nonexistent, and teachers are cynical. One well-intentioned Puerto Rican teacher in the South Bronx referred to some classes at her school as being "headed straight for Sing Sing"—which is "tracking" with a vengeance.

The blame is cast everywhere—on unruly students, parents who don't care, teachers who live in the suburbs and flee at three o'clock, unions concerned only about higher wages, administrators who are incompetent and without hope. The blame is so widespread and the cynicism so pervasive that it is easy to lose sight of the fact that a child in the Bronx, particularly south of Fordham Road, no longer has the full right to a public education.

So what?

"They're defined by the elite as an underclass—more up-front racists would say spics, niggers, welfare cheats—any subhuman category will do that makes this desperate poverty seem naturally ordained," says Mike Smith, the physician. He explains how the elite of Manhattan manage to drive from Westchester past this cross between Calcutta and bombed-out Dresden and yet live with it. "They don't see it. That's why they built the freeways cutting through here, so you can go fast enough not to have to see the people stuck here. Minutes from here, they sit in posh offices and dine at elegant restaurants as if none of this has anything to do with the decisions they have made for this city. It's troublesome to notice it; it's best ignored." Smith spends his days finding pressure points in the ears of heroin addicts, an acupuncture technique, to calm them down. Perhaps he sees too much at Lincoln Hospital. Perhaps he should be more reasonable, more circumspect in his indictment, put things in perspective. But the perspective of the South Bronx obliterates any such sensibility. As Father Snodgrass of the Episcopal church put it, "These kids are sentenced before they are grown."

Around the corner from his St. Ann's Church, Snodgrass and Garcia wander through what was to have been a showcase housing project for the poor—the José de Diego-Beekman housing project. Next door stands the half-vacated, burned-out Mott Haven housing project that rivals Diego-Beekman as a disaster area. There on 139th Street, twelve-year-old Alfred Dennis is talking about the knifing on that very spot the day before. Young Dennis has been accepted at the elite Brooklyn Tech High School for the fall. He beat out thousands of other applicants from far more privileged backgrounds. No street bum, Dennis is a sound and sensible kid who wants to get ahead. But the daily world that he must deal with is grotesque beyond description, and the chances are great it will drag him under before he graduates from Brooklyn Tech.

The knifing the day before was a routine affair, as Dennis and his friends tell it. There was an older guy who had recently moved into one of the projects—despite management's boast of tenant screening—who had a history of raping little girls. He continued this practice once in the neighborhood, and the father of one of his victims took matters into his own hands, confronted the rapist, and ordered him to get out. The rapist pulled a knife and slit the throat of the father. This was too much—even for this neighborhood—and the other residents pummeled the rapist nearly to death. The blood from all this stains the sidewalk, but it is only one stain. Soon the rapist is forgotten, and dozens of sadder, more miserable escapades are related, as if the murders, rapes, knifings have become a village rite for marking the passage of calendar time.

Life is cheap. Perhaps not Dennis's—anyone who met him would want to hug him and save him. But life is cheap because we have never been properly introduced to the victims.

(*Los Angeles Times*, August 6, 1978)

Unterberger the Hero

Unterberger the hero. Unterberger who did not go to Los Angeles.

I think of him while negotiating the sidewalks of my old Bronx neighborhood, threading carefully among the drug addicts, derelicts, and the quiet majority of scared but decent people. Victims and future victims of the ever-present juvenile delinquents, the least of whose crimes is the graffiti that climb over the schools like kudzu vines determined to strangle the willow trees. But, surprisingly, they have not killed my old schools—P.S. 96, Christopher Columbus High School, and once proud City College. Education, that great rope ladder up for the immigrant and minority poor, lives against terrible odds in this northeast corner of the Bronx, thanks to teachers and parents who refuse to give up. People like Unterberger.

Of course, it's not the same as in the forties and fifties, when I went to these schools, when the world looked to this city's system as a model for what free, universal education could achieve. Then democracy meant first of all quality education for everyone, the poor, minorities, immigrants included, with New York showing the way. Now public education almost everywhere is perceived more as a problem than a promise. In New York, as in many urban areas, people who can afford it turn to private schools and starve the schools left to the rest. Others, like me, pull up in station wagons depositing their children at carefully selected suburban schools, eager to make sure their kids profit from the inequality in public education.

So I go back to the Bronx to check on what is left of an important dream and am startled out of my pessimism by P.S. 96 principal Martin Unterberger, who is quick to point out that he is no different from many other overworked and underpaid teachers around the country, L.A. included, who have refused to give up.

Unterberger the improbable hero.

How else to describe him? And what does that make me, a coward? What makes Unterberger so tough that he is still in the Bronx serving, while I am in Huntington Beach shopping? Didn't we both go to "City," City College of New York, uptown, to be precise, where we majored in social commitment before we majored in anything else? And what is social commitment if not staying where you are when it's become a mess and helping your own? Nothing against Huntington Beach, mind you, but it's not my village, and try as I might, the surfers will never be my *landsmen.* So why am I there while Unterberger is here in the Bronx? Did I leave out of fear? No, it was too long ago, and all I wanted was the sun. The Bronx was good, but California has been great. But could I live here? Today, I think not.

Sure, L.A. has problems. At night you only have to wander a few blocks from the *Los Angeles Times* building downtown to enter a no-man's-land of terror softened only by the pathos of hundreds of wasted humans sleeping in cardboard condos delineated by stolen shopping carts and garbage bags. The Bronx has no franchise on despair.

What's changed is that in the good old days—and they were not so hot— the Bronx was not as important for what it was as for what it believed. It was unique not as a state of being but as a state of mind—the borough of unreasonable hope. That is no more. Let me not exaggerate. On the main street, Allerton Avenue, there are cops and life is not, in the daytime, menacing. And three blocks up the avenue, across the IRT White Plains elevated line, where the Sicilians have dug in, life goes on somewhat like before. Gino's bar has expanded and serves the best prawns *diavolo* in New York, and the Koreans, who have moved into the sacred domain of fresh-produce marketing, do a better job of stacking, squeezing, and hawking than their fabled Italian predecessors.

But there is fear and the merchants complain about constant theft and harassment. They are not alone. Prowling these ruins of a civilization that once fascinated me, I, too, become an object of fear when I spot Normie's mother and she scurries away because a stranger can only be trouble. Normie's mother, who used to chase me down the street with a jar of milk she wanted me to drink. Milk for the brain, always the brain, on this, the Jewish side of Allerton Avenue.

I never knew much about the other world up Allerton on the other side of the "El" where the Italians lived and still live. Now theirs is the safe stable world and the world of the Bronx neighborhood Jews is no more. In the old days this part of the Bronx was a sanctuary from the sweat, boredom, and despair of the dead-end garment shops. A happy place, bustling with intellectual energy, ambition, and the pursuit of excellence. No one expected to have their kids work at their parents' job. All was possible through the magic of learning—and the palaces of magic were the schools. Now they are often, at best, temporary sanctuaries from child abuse, drunkenness, street gangs, and the other ingredients of a pervasive fear.

The question of fear is not irrelevant to the life of a Bronx principal. Imagine this demure man, who is shorter than some of the sixth-graders walking past him in the school's still institutional green halls, who will go outside to confront the vandals that appear to be twice his size. He will play Edward G. Robinson (who, I can't resist noting, also went to City) and stare down or call the cops, whatever works to protect this little garden of learning. Unterberger wants his school to be a garden: "Many of our children come from depressed areas, the South Bronx, Harlem, and when they first come here they are overwhelmed, they have never seen such a beautiful tranquil place." Unterberger cannot use the word "children" without implying treasure the way others might speak of their stocks or jewelry.

And the treasure is secured, at least for the hours of the day that he controls. The heavyset female guard at the front door comes around quickly from her desk to give the too energetic visitor something of a flying tackle until he produces a visitor's permission slip. In the principal's office there is the button to summon the police who seem to circle Bronx schools with some regularity. Unterberger's car, parked a block from the school, was stolen one day this past winter. But whatever the chaos outside, every morning at a quarter of an hour before the first class, the leather-covered doors of the old auditorium are opened and kids file in to collect themselves and remember where they are. In a school. Unterberger got the district to remodel the auditorium but preserved the old chandeliers and the leather trim on the doors. "Imagine, they wanted to put plastic doors, but these are beautiful. So I held out." One senses that the leather doors are a mark of excellence and this principal insists that kids in the Bronx have the right to know excellence. Not just to get by. Not just to be parked here. The classrooms are quiet and purposeful, hallway traffic bustles but is orderly, and the taxed resources of a tiny cafeteria serving shifts of hungry youngsters prove adequate to provide what is for many their best meal of the day. Despite enormous differences of language and prior education, most of the kids seem to come through.

Unterberger, ever prowling the halls, points to some older youngsters, ten- and eleven-year-old recent immigrants from Jamaica: "No schooling at all; they can speak but can't write English." And a knot of Cambodians who can do neither: "For some reason they are attracted to this neighborhood," Unterberger says with a trace of pride. As to their lack of skills? So what? There are solutions and Unterberger begins to tick off the details of the phonics program, the work of the two special reading teachers the district has assigned, and the poetry written by one kid a few years after entering as a functional illiterate.

We thought we had a melting pot with our mostly Jewish and Italian base and a few Puerto Ricans and blacks thrown in for some additional spice. But it was nothing like this. The Jews and Italians together now make up less than 20 percent of enrollment, whereas only ten years ago they numbered more than 90 percent, mostly Jewish. Their place has been taken by blacks, Puerto Ricans, Yugoslavs, Cubans, Vietnamese, Afghans, and representatives from virtually every South American and Caribbean country. At least ten languages are used in informal cafeteria conversation along with English.

This crazy choir, including Cambodians, Iranians, and Ukrainians, is welded together by a variety of techniques. While stressing that P.S. 96 is a "traditional school with great emphasis on academic skills and disciplines," Unterberger adds that "we try to build in certain values: concern for fellow students and other people besides themselves. We try to tell them what we expect when they come in from other outlying school districts and from the Caribbean and think they can do what they want. They soon find they can't. We have standards and they fall in line rather nicely because we are interested in them." (It is not unusual in the Bronx to refer to the Caribbean as an outlying school district.)

There is discipline. Children are suspended for various infractions, and Unterberger sets an example wandering the halls to calm the wilder outbursts with his mere presence which, while genial on the edges, can also be stern. But most of all, he takes pride in tales of peer group pressure, as when a kid taps the shoulder of a newcomer who is pulling a crayon along the wall and says, "We don't do that here."

But there is also experimentation: "We experiment all the time with new approaches, linguistic, phonetic, anything that works with the children. We have to try new things all the time to meet the needs of these children who come in with all these new needs. I'm hopeful that we find solutions; this is not a school that's stagnant." One solution that Unterberger has found is music. When he arrived at the school he hung up a picture of Richard Rodgers and renamed the school and its auditorium after the musical half of the Rodgers and Hammerstein team. The hand-bell choir is the only one in the city. There is the school symphony orchestra, which instructs in almost the full range of classical instruments. And to top it all, there is the annual musically driven theatrical production, which is taken very seriously. This year it was Gilbert and Sullivan's *The Mikado*, with a cast like a UNICEF poster come alive.

Why music? Unterberger looked annoyed with a question only an obvious Philistine would pose. It was particularly surprising coming, as it did, from a P.S. 96 graduate. At first he said simply that music is "wonderful." But then, perhaps sensing that in a time of budgetary restraints something more than wonderful is required, he ventured his own theory of music as an aid to reading: "Music, it's a form of decoding. To really learn to read music one has to learn to decode, and what is reading if not a form of decoding?"

And Unterberger has test scores to prove that his methods work. Seventy-five percent of his students read on or above grade level on the last New York statewide reading tests. Not bad, considering that a significant minority of them, Unterberger estimates 20 percent, knew little or no English when they first showed up.

He is a realist about what befalls many of these kids each day after school and after they graduate. The lurid graffiti on the outer walls which frame the schoolyard provide a grim reminder of the chaotic streets these kids return to when the last bell of the day rings. One corner of the schoolyard was intended for a garden, but that project had to be abandoned because neighborhood derelicts turned it into a hobo camp, sleeping and defecating there at night.

After graduation from P.S. 96, life quickly gets rougher. The folklore among some older residents in the streets is that families with children pack up and move out when their oldest kid passes the sixth grade. Some choose parochial schools and seem reassured. Others who must or want to use the public schools seem to have mixed feelings about the high school. It was named after Christopher Columbus because, as the surely inaccurate legend of my childhood had it, the Mafia wouldn't allow anything but an Italian name. The word "Mafia," then as now, was used loosely to mean anyone who had a private house and wasn't Jewish or Irish.

Whereas P.S. 96 used to be in a solidly Jewish area, Columbus, only ten blocks away, seemed as distant as Palermo, Sicily, a town that seemed to come up more often in cafeteria conversation than did Washington, D.C. We never talked about Vilna or those other funny places in Eastern Europe that our parents were determined to forget, but the Italian kids had strong ties that were often reinforced by new arrivals from the old country and the vacations they took there. And still take.

The whites who are Jewish, and who, in my day, provided 50 percent of the student body, have left, and those who remain, most of them recent immigrants from Russia, now make up only about 3 or 4 percent of the Columbus population. Jews do remain a majority of the teaching staff, although most commute from New Jersey or upstate New York to their jobs. It is the Italians from the rows of private homes built and owned primarily by contractors, construction workers, garbage collectors, and small merchants who have stayed rooted. But even their closely guarded world has been invaded. Whereas they also once provided 50 percent of the high-school students, it has now dwindled to 12 percent. Some grumble that St. Lucy's Catholic Church now features Spanish Masses, and its famous grotto, which struck me as a bit medieval back in the good old days when some of the more pugnacious Italian kids insisted rather pointedly that the Jews had killed Christ, is now locked up to prevent vandalism. There are still Italian toughs around— the fabled Arthur Avenue Italians have replaced the once legendary Guinea Dukes as arbiters of the faith—and their ranks are augmented by even tougher Albanians and Yugoslavs, who seem to bear particular animosity toward blacks. Not that all Italians and Albanians are so inclined, but the small minority that is casts quite a shadow in the school. For that reason, a number of teachers interviewed at Columbus scoffed at the idea of white flight from black violence. Columbus does have a large black and Puerto Rican population, but, again contrary to white folklore, it is mostly from the neighborhood, the logical result of huge public-housing projects planted in the midst of the Italian haven over the years.

But Mrs. Rosa, the Columbus principal, wouldn't like this kind of talk. She denies that there were Italian gangs in the old days or that there is ethnic and racial hostility now. I have to call her Mrs. Rosa, just like it's Mr. Unterberger, because I will go to my grave unable to call the principals of my old schools by their first names even though they have invited me to. Saying anything negative about Columbus would cross Grace Rosa, who has put in long days to turn a floundering school into a showcase of Bronx education. And it is. Crime is lower than at surrounding schools, test scores are better. This is largely due to Mrs. Rosa, who fought to get this job against what she perceived as prejudice against a woman and an Italian-American. She had a mission to restore Columbus to what she still perceives as its days of glory, when she was a student there in the late forties. "When I returned here seven years ago, I can't tell you how many seventeen-year-olds we had wandering around the halls with less than ten credits toward graduation. We started a remedial program, and another program to help kids pass the graduate equivalency exam." Her personal commitment was crucial, and now, having waged the good fight, she will retire this summer, at the age of fifty-five, after thirty-two years of teaching. She will live in upstate New York, a bit removed from the battle.

Columbus's success is relative. In 1985 it made the list of one of the worst schools in New York State, as did almost all of the New York City schools. Such is the state of public education at the high-school level in a city that once set the national standard for free education. Most of the other schools in the city failed to meet statewide standards in math, reading, writing, and dropout rates. Mrs. Rosa is quick to point out that Columbus flunked on only one count, its 10 percent dropout rate. But even there she can claim improvement, since the rate was a whopping 23 percent when she first took over.

As vivacious as Anne Bancroft—née Anna Marie Louise Italiano—the school's most illustrious graduate, who preceded her by a year, Mrs. Rosa throws off sparks as she lays low Columbus's detractors. "The whole city had an increase of just one regents scholar last year, while we went up 63 percent from twenty-seven to forty-four, and 79 percent of our kids now go on to college. Let me get the list here, Sarah Lawrence, Columbia, and a place out there where you are, Irvine something." Mrs. Rosa is proud of the fact that seven of the forty-four recent regents scholars—New York's statewide scholarship program to subsidize qualified graduates—were black, and another seven Puerto Rican, which is nonetheless an underrepresentation, given that the two groups account for 50 percent of the student body. Like Unterberger, she thrills to the ethnic diversity of the school. "You name it, we got it," she said, "it's like the United Nations."

But there isn't much ethnic mixing in the cafeteria, which seems modeled on the Balkans at the turn of the century, and which is the focus of terror and opportunity, depending upon one's strength and willingness to employ it as well as the restraining efforts of the lunchroom teacher guards. "It's not nice down here," Myrna Laracuente, dean of the cafeteria, noted with some understatement as two young ladies shot by without passes, pausing only to observe that the dean was in their estimation a "bitch." "At least I understand their language. Much of the time these kids can only make themselves understood in a language I don't recognize," Laracuente, a jovial woman in her forties, observed. And as if to punctuate her point, a Cambodian student in command of a handful of English words appeared to translate for his cousin, who knew none. They were not hostile, merely totally perplexed as to where they were supposed to be at that given time. She didn't know, and they melted quietly into an onrushing mass of students eager to eat or carry on food fights in the next cafeteria period.

In this, the world's most powerful and richest city, the schools that are expected to solve the most intractable of social problems are starved for resources. In the case of Columbus there is money to support only the barest athletic program, which means a bit of soccer and no football, which might relieve some of the tension. The cafeteria is pitifully small, the food starchy and uninteresting, and the schoolyard rocky and unkempt. Teachers' salaries have gone up a bit in recent years, but they are still miserable by comparison to the city's cost of living. Downtown, where I retreated at night, the yuppies in advertising and on Wall Street chortle happily about loving the Big Apple, while here, in one of the best schools, despite the best efforts of a highly motivated principal and staff, a teacher could speak of this "human garbage pit."

That is an exaggeration. But what does it say about the expectations for the young from so many nations who have been entrusted to this school? A resident New York City police officer assisted by eight security officers from the Board of Education have made Columbus secure, but what else is it?

What has been lost in the thirty-five years since my class graduated? It can be summarized as a vanished expectation of excellence. Perhaps I remember incorrectly or rely too much on the experience of my crowd of friends, but I can still sense that excitement, walking out of the Loew's Paradise movie house on the Grand Concourse, on graduation day, that I and most of my classmates could learn to do and be anything no matter how difficult or exalted. We were in awe of no elite. We were products of a public-education milieu that gave us the confidence to feel the equal of graduates of any private, parochial, or public school in the land. The Paradise is now closed, the Grand Concourse is a slum, and while some successful graduates from Columbus may feel that way, most have been educated to be graceful losers. Excellence in education for the masses had been at the core of the democratic dream, and excellence, even in a good school in the Bronx, seems to have gone under in the wake of budgetary cuts and severe urban decay.

And what's true for the high schools applies sadly enough to that once great network of free municipal colleges that at one time provided a fantastic education for hundreds of thousands of the best of New York's high-school graduates, some of whom became the next generation of schoolteachers. This process still goes on; most of the teachers are still trained at one of the city colleges, but it can no longer be assumed that the best students go there or that the education is any longer fantastic. To understand what went before, consider the sight in my neighborhood, when two months after graduating from Columbus we turn up one fall morning to hitchhike across Bronx Park to get the subway to go to a college in Harlem brimming with the excitement that this college is our first choice. A few of my classmates had gone off on scholarships to some Ivy League school, but this was a time before there were many scholarships for kids from the Bronx, particularly Jewish kids. It didn't matter. CCNY was the secular yeshiva and anything the *goyim* had was presumed intellectually, if not socially, inferior—and intellectual was what we cared about.

CCNY, the flagship of the municipal colleges, founded in 1847, has graduated more Nobel Prize winners than any other undergraduate public institution in the country. And it was free, which made us free. Books were once even provided without charge, to be returned. But more important, you could live at home, work at a part-time job, take the subway, and learn without draining the family resources. Arriving at City for the first time and seeing those beautiful buildings built from the black granite of Manhattan island, I felt that I had entered the grandest palace of learning. The feeling has never left me or hardly anyone else that I have ever met who went there. People remember the Great Hall, where Clarence Darrow, Felix Frankfurter, Bertrand Russell, and Norman Thomas had held forth. They remember the City College cafeteria with its dozen or so alcoves, each one populated by a different ideological or artistic tendency from Trotskyist to Ayn Rand libertarians, to Charlie Mingus jazz fanatics. And the debates in class: Marxist student Larry Gorkin standing in Stanley Page's Russian history class armed with three feet of citations to refute the previous day's lecture, while Herb Rommerstein of the Young Americans for Freedom waited his turn to refute Gorkin.

It's not quite like that now. Some blame open enrollment, which they claim lowered the once high standards for admission. Others note the deterioration of Harlem, which they claim frightened whites away. This time, when I was returning to City after a stopover at Columbus, the school's music teacher, also an alumnus, warned me not to drive there because my car would be stolen. She ruled out the train as a place of random but inevitable violence. Cabdrivers won't go there. And of course hitchhiking is suicidal. I took a chance on parking my Hertz rental and lost not a hubcap. But I was shocked at what time and urban blight had wrought. Before City went, Harlem went. Harlem was once a center of culture that enveloped City, and now it is a dangerous ruin. The capital of Negro America—filled with institutes, churches, bookstores, ideologies, orators, musicians, and historians—had become a fringe outpost of black America filled with drug addicts. Yes, there are churches and families and dreamers left in Harlem, but they are most often reduced to flotsam in a rollicking tide of druggie despair and stupidity that wells up at each street corner in brief euphoric highs that are then slept off in urine-filled hallways.

Into this came the "specter" of open enrollment. Anyone could go to the City University who had graduated in the top half of a New York high-school class or maintained an 80 percent average. Open enrollment, as an educational experiment, remains interesting and controversial, but it hardly proved the disaster claimed by its detractors. Quality education goes on at City and in some ways better than ever if the standard is one of serving the desperate need of the community for learning.

To begin with, the assumption by some critics that blacks seized City and destroyed its standards in order to grant worthless degrees is wrong on all counts. Statistics show that the initial benefit from open enrollment didn't go primarily to blacks or Puerto Ricans but, rather, to ethnic whites and newer immigrants who previously had not been able to measure up to the entrance requirements. Nor are the degrees phony. Proof of serious standards is offered by the unusually high attrition rate at City and the fact that those who do graduate take an average of six years to accomplish that feat. Not normal for a private clubby school elsewhere, but just about what one would expect from a working-class subway college whose students tend to be older and self-supporting.

What was wrong with open enrollment at first, most observers agree, is that inadequate preparation and resources were made available for screening, redirecting, remedial educating, and orienting of a vastly expanded and differentiated student body. The experiment was interesting but the experimenters, those politicians who voted for such a monumental change, were not seriously committed. As with so much of the "social engineering" of the sixties, open enrollment was a ploy rather than a plan.

To judge City, one has to first establish the standard, and I happen to cherish the one set out by Horace Webster, the college's first president, who in 1849 said: "The experiment is to be tried, whether the children of the people—the children of the whole people—can be educated; and whether an institution of learning of the highest grade can be successfully controlled by the popular will, not by the privileged few." Judged by that standard, CCNY today is an enormous success. Most of the "people" in New York City are black, Puerto Rican, and immigrants, and those are the people now educated by this college. Three out of four of City's students are nonwhite, which breaks down into 33 percent black, 25 percent Latino, and 17 percent Asian. City can also stand as the people's UN, with half its students having been born in more than eighty different countries. And, like most people, they work. Seventy percent have a job, and 30 percent work more than twenty hours a week. Despite this commitment to the work ethic, 85 percent of the student body still requires financial aid of some kind.

One positive result of open enrollment, which began in 1970, is that City is now fifth in the country in producing black engineers, coming right after schools that had been historically black colleges. The engineering program at City is highly respected and is one of the largest suppliers of engineers to AT&T, which has reciprocated by making some grants to the college. City is also among the dozen leading schools in the country for placing minority students in medical school.

City is different from when I attended it, as it should be. With each new wave of immigrants the college changed dramatically, and that was its strength, although few alumni seem to thrill to it. The children of German and Irish immigrants were the first to benefit and apparently enjoyed the stuffy atmosphere imposed by the West Point graduates who were the school's first two presidents. Many of the first graduates bemoaned the opening to the new wave of Jewish immigrants, who soon overwhelmed the school with their numbers and culture. Anti-Semitic resistance saw to it that Jews had a hard time getting on the faculty, as illustrated by the fact that no Jew was hired in the City College mathematics department until the mid-1930s. Now there are as few Jews among the students as there were blacks when I was there, and blacks complain about racial discrimination in faculty hiring. The tension is inevitable. This is a municipal college paid for by the sweat of taxpayers who want the place to work for them. If it can do that and keep high standards, then it succeeds. If it only does one, it fails. It's too early to tell.

But there is a spirit at City that makes me optimistic. The same spirit I found at Unterberger's P.S. 96 and, for all its problems, at Mrs. Rosa's Columbus High School. The spirit is not about athletics or social life, which are barely present. It is about the secular American dream. There is this naïve insistence that being touched by learning leads to salvation in this world. Naïve, because obviously there are many reasons to think that learning will not lift one out of the morass of the Bronx or Harlem. Naïve, because who believes in book learning anymore or that ideas matter?

Yet there it is. Up at City, people still read and argue. They may do this often in languages and accents that I find impenetrable, but what does that matter? Before departing I went up to pay my respects to the Great Hall in Shepard Hall that I had entered so reverently more than three decades ago. A bit worn, but still beautiful, and I thought now as then how wonderful it was that somehow such a fantastic place had been made available to people who are not of privilege. Albert Einstein lectured in Shepard Hall, giving his first series of lectures in the United States at City College in 1921. Einstein, who was judged not very smart as a youngster, who always looked and talked funny, a grateful immigrant who nonetheless remained a rebel and a critic even of those who took him in.

On my last visit one of the old-timers who is still on the staff was taking me around while bemoaning that "it's just not the same as when we went here." She had been in a sorority. I didn't know they had them. We went into a Quonset hut of temporary offices plunked down insultingly next to the grand Gothic Shepard Hall, home of the Great Hall and the famous alcoves of the cafeteria. True, the alcoves of dissent that I lived in are no more. True, there are guards all over the place, passes are required, thefts occur, and violence, too. But there in the Quonset hut we encountered the nests of thinkers and agitators from the Chess Club to the Anti-Apartheid Coalition, from the Black Engineering Society to the Caribbean Students Association. On the wall there was a sign that read FREE NELSON MANDELA. My old alum guide asked, "Who is Nelson Mandela?" Suddenly it was clear. We had not gone to the same college back in the good old days, and we were not looking at the same one now.

I politely excused myself from the tour and picked a Quonset office at random to flop down in. The next thing I knew, I was being organized to do good, just as I might have been some thirty years before. Seated in front of me was one Diana Kilos, a pretty, energetic, supersmart, Nisei senior who heads up the Ralph Nader-spawned public-interest group on campus. I had signed up for four projects ranging from lower subway fares and tuition to ending apartheid in South Africa before I remembered that my student activist days are over. City lives.

(*Los Angeles Times*, July 10, 1986)

The Jews of Los Angeles

1

*We are Jews. We are a minority and a lot of people don't like us. We don't
have to kowtow to anybody. We don't have to be weak . . . but we must also
use our heads. We are a very, very tiny minority in a tremendous majority.
. . . Such a people must know how to get along with people . . . let's also use
some diplomacy, some tact.*

—Rabbi Edgar F. Magnin, Wilshire Boulevard Temple

*You want diplomatic? . . . Greatest diplomats the world ever saw were the
German Jews. Where did diplomacy get them? A ticket to Auschwitz.*

—Rabbi Shlomo Cunin, Chabad House

Now comes the tendentious, sweaty, biblical Rabbi Cunin, a relic of the
time when to be a Jew meant to live by strict adherence to all 613 of God's
commandments, including the ones prohibiting contraception, homosexuality, extramarital sex, and even, as the old rabbis had it, men and women
shaking hands outside of wedlock. The rabbi, although only thirty-seven and
from the Bronx, is of the Hasidic Jews—a throwback to tiny Eastern European
villages, *shtetlach*, praying and studying the Talmud incessantly despite the
hostilities of czars and commissars—of pogroms, of tales of recurring holocaust,
of God's will and God's wrath, and, most of all, of Jewish observance and
Jewish survival. Now he is proprietor of Chabad House, a $2 million storefront
operation on the West Side for the rehabilitation of drug addicts along with
college organizations to counter the missionary activities of the Jesus freaks
and Hare Krishnas, who, in his eyes, all too effectively prey upon the Jewish
young. Black-frocked, with long, unkempt beard and funny black hat, he
trundles off into the vacant night of Wilshire Boulevard to save the souls,
but first the lives, of the children of Beverly Hills who have had too much
of the secular good life and now turn up overdosed in small hospitals of the
private Jewish type.

Across Wilshire Boulevard sits Rabbi Magnin, hearty, optimistic, American. His memories are not of *shtetl* pogroms but rather of the San Francisco
earthquake, when, as a fifteen-year-old boy, he could witness tough Jewish
roustabouts from mining camps—indistinguishable in speech or other man-

nerisms from their Gentile counterparts—come to the aid of the quake victims. San Francisco—the original sophisticated, ecumenical city, where religious rivalry was more a source of good jokes than of darker passions.

This Jew came to Los Angeles in 1915 to tend a flock of 15,000 brethren who had come as far and as fast from Europe as was then humanly possible and who found even San Francisco a bit too European and old-fashioned. They wanted desperately to be Americans—and they made it. The Los Angeles Jew is the truly American Jew, and he came here in pursuit of normalcy—gold, a cure for asthma and tuberculosis, and to escape the stench of East Coast cities. He came here originally in the Gold Rush days, without Jewish women, which, for the observant Jew, is the ultimate assimilation, for as one rabbi chided, "Jewish sperm without a Jewish egg produces at best an Episcopalian." In general, the very earliest Los Angeles Jews were a nonreligious, pistol-toting, hustling crowd like their Gentile neighbors in this forlorn village, for if they had any class, they would have been able to make it to 'Frisco, where the real Jewish (and Gentile) Establishment lived. To be sure, they soon developed a tonier upper crust—the Hellmans and Newmarks—good, solid, German-Jewish burghers who built their successful stores and counting houses. They kept a proper distance from the riffraff, but they did go in for philanthropy.

We know much about this class because its members commissioned various monuments in their own memory, including Hillcrest Country Club, Wilshire Boulevard Temple, and Kaspare Cohn Hospital—later to become Cedars of Lebanon. Unfortunately, we do not have the collected letters of Maude Silverstein, a prostitute so reckless in her abandon that the district attorney called her one of the "most notorious thieves in the city." Or the published memoirs of Louis Silverstein, her opium-addict brother, or the murderer Louis Lopez, whom the *Los Angeles Times* described in 1889 as a "half-breed Mexican-Jew." The vast majority of Jews were, of course, law-abiding and, as is typically the case, sported a much lower crime rate than was judged normal at the time. But they also were frontier people who knew how to survive.

Music teachers and occasional rabbis also made the journey west, and Jews, as is their wont, tried to establish some culture. In 1905 an anarchist saloonkeeper named Cohen started the first Jewish educational club. A network of socialist welfare organizations emerged under the sponsorship of the Workmen's Circle, a cooperative association of Jewish workers which began in 1909 and which produced, among other institutions, a sanatorium for tubercular patients which later became the City of Hope. According to the twentieth-anniversary publication of the sanatorium, its establishment was made necessary because "the wealthy local Jews refused to . . . render aid to those whom they termed 'transients.' " Chaim Shapiro, one of the City of Hope's founders, also started a radical secular school under the slogan "Jewish Intelligentsia for the Jewish Masses." Shapiro, California state chairman of the Socialist Party, was one of the first Jewish graduates of USC's law school and later went on to run for lieutenant governor on a ticket headed by Upton Sinclair. Mt. Sinai Hospital and Clinic and the Jewish Home for the Aged in Reseda were other achievements of Jewish workers in Los Angeles. Later Yiddishists and Labor-Zionists, the progenitors of Israel's Labor Party, were to expand the cultural offerings.

But it never was quite like New York City, with its massive educational alliances, shuls, radical intelligentsia, and social life centered around the Forty-second Street Public Library. Typically, the Western Jew was a Westerner and, therefore, unlike his Eastern counterpart, determinedly anti-intellectual and bored with the big religious and political issues. Some of them wanted to keep up Jewish ties, and all wanted protection from the occasional outcroppings of anti-Semitism. Outside of that, they wanted to make movies, build houses, design clothes, and, like everyone else in Los Angeles, make pots of money by any means necessary, but still keep right with God, in case there was one.

So to this Jewish flotsam came Rabbi Magnin, who, for decades, built the Wilshire Boulevard Temple into the center of some decency and order for the Jewish kin and who negotiated on their behalf with the *goyim*. In their useful history of the community, Max Vorspan and Lloyd Gartner note that "Judaism as expounded by Rabbi Magnin did not have much theological cutting edge." Magnin was gentle in his religious admonitions, but more important, he was terrific at working with Catholic and Protestant leaders in getting some of their more deranged followers to remember that it was the Romans who killed their Lord. It worked, and the Jewish people lived happily in this town, with minor reversals. They have rewarded Magnin by calling him "the Cardinal," more for his skillful civic diplomacy than for his efforts to save souls. Jews do not like men who play at God's work, but they tend, particularly in Los Angeles, to respect efficiency in this life's business.

But who remembers now? Magnin is eighty-seven and, although he is still sharp as a tack, his world has slipped away. In the thirties there were maybe 80,000 Jews in this outpost who were, or at least so it now seems, in the main eager to follow Magnin's ultra-Americanism—eager to use English, to look, dress, and think like everybody else, to be hardworking, useful citizens determined to make Los Angeles the best place on God's earth. Indeed, in 1939, at the great Hollywood Bowl rally for God, flag, and Martin Dies, chairman of the House Un-American Activities Committee, it was Magnin who represented the Jewish community, along with Irving Berlin. In a duet with Rudy Vallee, Berlin sang his "God Bless America" in what was to be the song's first public presentation. At the time, it was big stuff, although Magnin recently had difficulty recalling the event. But he is firm in his knowledge that the Jewish community of the time "belonged." Despite the coming of the movie industry and the attacks of native Fascists directed at it, the Jewish community remained a tightly contained and nondemanding sub-culture safely tucked away in a corner of Los Angeles society.

But even then there was another Los Angeles Jewry, the Jewish proletariat that was trickling in as an extension of the New York garment industry, which could not afford membership in the Wilshire Boulevard Temple. Not that they wanted to, being secular, mostly socialists, and tending to view Magnin and his congregation as class enemies—the bosses for whom they worked. These new arrivals swelled the ranks of existing socialist organizations, like the Workmen's Circle and International Workers Order, which were bitterly divided over their view of the Soviet Union and Communism. They formed schools, sold Yiddish newspapers and books, and organized political rallies. Historians Vorspan and Gartner note that in the thirties, the creative activity among Jews in Los Angeles was not in the religious sector, where learning was feeble, "but in Yiddish, where politics and culture were inextricably intertwined." There was also a burgeoning left-labor Zionist movement, which produced a network of cultural organizations. For example, David and Minna Yaroslavsky, the parents of City Councilman Zev Yaroslavsky, founded the important City Terrace Folk Shul in the late thirties.

There were actually two Los Angeles Jewish communities composed, on the one hand, of the older German Jews and, on the other, of the newer East European immigrants. Each group had its own organizations, and it wasn't until 1959 that they were brought together as the Jewish Federation-Council of Greater Los Angeles, which has run the affairs of the community ever since.

After World War II, the trickle from the East became a torrent, with hundreds of thousands of Jews stuffing their belongings into '47 Nash sedans for the drive west. They came after the Nazis, the Holocaust, and the creation of Israel, and from then on, the secure Jewish world that Magnin had helped construct would never be quite so simple. They came in huge numbers from the Midwest—Cleveland and Chicago—during the war and immediately thereafter. Then came the migrants from the Bronx and Brooklyn. Now what? Today there are Moroccans, Israelis, new Russians, a hopeless babble of languages, colors, confusion, and issues.

Rabbi Magnin is not a condescending man. It is not the new people he dislikes, or their Old World languages and dietary habits. It is the confusion that they have brought to his Los Angeles that he detests. His is a temple of simple Protestant order, of consistency, of *shrei nit* (don't shout), of authoritative leadership. Now there are noises, challenges, doubts, and the thing which to him is most reprehensible in Old World Jewishness—contentiousness. But it's happening, events have compelled change. The secure, provincial Jewish world of Rabbi Magnin is gone, and what will come in its place is very much in doubt. What does it mean now, in 1978—so many years after Moses, Christ, the Spanish Inquisition, the Eastern European *shtetlach* ghetto poverty, already a third of a century after Hitler, with Israel perhaps entering a new era of military prowess, with Russia perhaps being pushed to be less barbaric, when 80 percent of Jews don't belong to a synagogue and 40 percent intermarry and when Jews make up 25 percent of the graduates of Ivy League colleges and are no longer garment workers but are fighting for their right to be banking executives—what does it mean now, here in Los Angeles, to be a Jew?

Jew. The word has for so long been an epithet, a point of loyalty, a source of inspiration and mystification that it may never come to be used neutrally. The word itself performs as a social glue when all others seem to fail. Judaism is a religion, but only one out of five Jews in Los Angeles belongs to a synagogue, and only one in twenty is Orthodox. Jewish is an ethnic category, but the Los Angeles Jewish population includes 30,000 Sephardic Jews from Morocco, Spain, Tunisia, etc. . . . whose social bearing, mores, and even diet can be as different from those of the 2,000 recent Russian Jewish immigrants as that of any two ethnic groups in this country. Some insist that Jews are a race, but the bloodlines are by now so intermixed as to make the Jews as close as we have to a universal people. Jews are thought by some to be held together as a commonly oppressed people, and indeed, one-third of Los Angeles Jewry lost a relative in the Holocaust, according to one poll. But few Jews in Los Angeles have personally experienced oppression in this city deeper than verbal slurs and exclusion from social clubs, which most Jews would find hopelessly boring. Being Jewish is largely a state of mind, and any more formal definition would exclude most of the people in Los Angeles who consider themselves Jews. In the last comprehensive poll, conducted in 1970 by Dr. Fred Massarik of UCLA, 60 percent of the Jews of Los Angeles County agreed with the statement that "being a good Jew is the same as being a good human being—no more and no less." And an equally high 58 percent also agreed with the statement that "all religions are basically alike."

Most Jews in Los Angeles belong to what two sociologists, experts on the Jewish community, recently described as the "remnant." They, the silent majority, are not members of the Jewish organizations which would speak in their name politically, nor do they belong to the synagogues which would guide them spiritually. Surveys indicate that they are united in their commitment to the continuance of the Jewish people as a distinct group, but they are divided over whether that group should be primarily religious, ethnic, or philanthropic.

But the tenuous cohesion of the Jewish community is now beset by a host of problems which can no longer easily be managed by a small elite of professional fund-raisers and leading rabbis. The problems are real, the solutions elusive:

—The Jewish community is developing the "normal" problems of American family life. The divorce rate is going up notably, particularly in the San Fernando Valley; desertion by fathers is considered alarming; drug abuse is a major problem with 30 percent of Jewish youth considered to have used hard drugs; and drug-related crime is on the increase.

—Missionary movements such as the Jesus freaks, Moonies, Hare Krishnas, and the various gurus have high percentages of Jewish converts, with estimates ranging from 30 percent to 60 percent.

—Recent Russian and Israeli immigrants are having new problems adapting to community life, and they are a source of tension within the more established Jewish community.

—The traditional liberal political alliances are in disarray, with Jew pitted against Jew in emotionally charged debates over the Bakke and busing issues.

—The Jewish Federation-Council, the umbrella organization for virtually all Los Angeles Jewish groups, is faced with increasing criticism from dissidents within the community and is sharply at odds with the county's three feisty Jewish weekly newspapers, featuring tough columnists like Yehuda Lev (*Israel Today*) and Herb Brin (*Heritage*).

—A serious question Jews face is what to do if peace breaks out in the Middle East or is there life after Bonds for Israel? The profoundly felt and pervasive commitment to Israel has provided the American Jewish community with much of its identity and unity in the postwar period.

—The Jewish population is declining markedly. According to the Jewish population studies of UCLA professor Massarik, there were 511,000 Jews in Los Angeles County in 1968 and there are 450,000 today. This is due to a low birthrate and the fact that the Jewish population is weighted toward elderly people. The intermarriage rate is thought to be about 40 percent, while ten years ago it was an insignificant 5 percent. Most of these marriages are between Jewish males and Gentile females, who do not convert to Judaism. By Jewish law, children are not Jewish unless their mothers are Jewish or convert.

While the leadership of the Los Angeles Jewish community worries endlessly about Jewish disappearance through intermarriage, low birthrate, and assimilation into the dominant Gentile culture, the silent majority seems headed in just that direction. A similar national trend was noted with alarm by Harvard population expert Elihu Bergman, writing recently in the Jewish publication *Midstream*: "If present trends are not arrested or reversed, the American Jewish community faces extinction as a significant entity, by its own hand, during the first half of the twenty-first century." Orthodox Rabbi Maurice Lamm, head of the Los Angeles Board of Rabbis and one of the most respected Jewish leaders in the country, termed birth control "a self-imposed Holocaust . . . We're helping to destroy the Jewish people with birth control."

The American Jewish Congress warned of the process of assimilation in a recent pamphlet headlined: "The greatest exterminator of the Jewish people may turn out to be the Jewish people themselves." The rate of assimilation in Los Angeles is considerably higher than nationally. According to the National Jewish Population Study, conducted by Massarik and quoted by Bergman, Los Angeles Jews are even less inclined to attend a synagogue (20 percent as opposed to 40 percent) or to belong to a Jewish organization (25 percent versus 40 percent) than their counterparts nationally. Yet along with this specter of attrition of the Jewish community in Los Angeles, the activist Jewish minority here seems ever more energetic and outspoken. Activist Jews in Los Angeles are getting rambunctious, publicly hassling the President, the Russians, the Jesus freaks, the school system, and, of course, each other.

This fall there was the noisy attempt to boycott the President's Los Angeles fund-raising dinner, and there was a militant demonstration outside of the Century Plaza Hotel. Soon after, there was a full calendar of "street events" at the Russian trade exhibition at the Los Angeles Convention Center in protest of Soviet anti-Semitism. "Isfros" (natural hairdos), unbuttoned shirts revealing Stars of David as well as hairy chests, a smattering of Hebrew words and names, *We Never Lost It* bumper stickers are to a small activist group an antidote to an assimilationist culture—of nose jobs and Jewish princesses and commercially guaranteed straight blond hair.

It may now even be fashionable to look and sound Jewish. There are extroverted Jewish politicians like City Councilman Zev Yaroslavsky, an activist product of the militant movement in support of Soviet Jewry, and publicly Orthodox ones like Representative Henry Waxman, who was active in opposing the Vietnam War. Whereas Jews previously worked behind the scenes or, when they ran for office, did so as pale imitations of Gentile pols.

And again, among a minority of Jews, there are signs of a religious revival. Young rabbis like Hillel's Richard Levy are attracting larger audiences by experimenting with the traditional forms of the religion. At the opposite extreme, Orthodoxy, according to its leader, Rabbi Lamm, is the fastest-growing Jewish religious tendency in the city. This mainstream of the Orthodox religion is unlike Cunin's religious sect in matters of style. Its members dress and conduct themselves in the fashion of the American majority. But they share the same view of the religion as being based on God's revelations and claim to be equally observant of the religious laws.

On the economic side, Jews are no longer content to run the entertainment and garment industries, with side excursions into real estate, while systematically being excluded from the power centers of the top banks and corporations. Nor do they continue to graze contentedly at the Hillcrest and Brentwood country clubs, where Danny Thomas, a Lebanese, is one of the few *goys* they ever meet, but now demand entry into the upper-crust Jonathan and California clubs.

Some of the old-time Jewish leaders like Rabbi Magnin are wary of these developments. Some of the newer, tougher, and generally younger voices think it's just great. And the Jewish organization bureaucracy—as it is paid to be—is caught in the middle, yet determined to manage the tumult.

As Rabbi Magnin summed up the changes recently: "This is a different ball game today—you've got another Brooklyn here. When I came here, it was Los Angeles. Now it's a Brooklyn." To Rabbi Magnin, of the affluent, cathedral-like Wilshire Boulevard Temple, Brooklyn is roots—it's painful history, dirt, crowds, no cars to get around, the subway, beards, funny hats. It's not American. It's the ghetto. And Rabbi Magnin, whose family made it big with the department stores of the same name, has, for most of his eighty-seven years, celebrated his distance from the teeming culture of the Jewish garment workers who were at the center of Jewish ghetto life.

"I have no reason to go into the ghetto," Magnin explained. "One of my grandparents came out of it. I don't want to go back into it. I see these guys with their yarmulkes eating bacon on their salads at the club. They want to become more Jewish, whatever that means. It's not religious—it's an ethnic thing. What virtue is there in ethnic emphasis? Black isn't more beautiful than white, white isn't more beautiful than black, and we have beautiful Jews and we have stinkers, and so does everybody else. Who's kidding whom with all this nonsense? You know, it's insecurity, the whole thing is insecurity. Roots, roots, roots—baloney!"

The startling thing about this eighty-seven-year-old man is that, despite his odyssey in respectable Gentile society, he remains—in what should be his dotage but is probably his prime—a joyful, argumentative, nonconforming, intellectualizing ghetto Jew. The lifeblood of irony, issues, morality, jokes still pumps furiously through his aging frame. He's never laid back, spaced out, indifferent. When he kibitzes at Hillcrest with George Burns, his junior at eighty-one, about the causes of sexual impotency, the true meaning of life, the usefulness of a god concept—though neither seems to accept the Hebraic one—and their mutual need for thirty more years on this earth "to have fun— life's a ball—to do things," it is as if they never left Second Avenue in New York. Their voices grow louder, interruptions more frequent—a scene out of the old *Can You Top This?* radio comedy show. They break it off only when Magnin's wife (eighty-three) calls to tell him he forgot to do the shopping.

Anyway, at his age, he no longer has to play the cardinal role.

Those vestments seem to have been passed on to Rabbi Hillel Silverman and his Sinai Temple, the "in" temple on the West Side. But even at this fashionable temple, some of the members are restless.

Recently one group of couples met in a comfortable Tudor-style home to consider the state of Judaism and of their temple. Their leader, Rabbi Silverman, was described as "a great theatrical type," "the best fund-raiser in town," and "he plays golf at Hillcrest a lot, and one thing, you'll never see him without a tan." These remarks were made in the spirit of neither endearment nor contempt. They gave Silverman his due. Handsome, with a gifted tongue, he packs them in every Friday night and raises enormous sums of money for the United Jewish Appeal.

But the group has formed because they felt that for all the "functions" of Sinai Temple—the services, children's school, young adults, singles—the "Jewish part," the thing that presumably united them, was *shvakh* (weak— six cups of tea from one bag). But they were openly at a loss as to what was missing. They were not particularly critical of this temple's rabbi. They had tried other temples and this was no better or worse—some said it was conveniently located and others said it was prestigious. The fact that it was Conservative as opposed to Reform hadn't mattered in the selection. That night they had gathered, deadly serious and involved, over nine delicious desserts, to listen to the missing link, which appeared in the form of Rabbi Cunin, the Central Casting Old World rabbi. The rabbi had passed the afternoon officiating at a wedding, and he was still exuding the effects of what he gleefully identified as vodka. This detail is necessary here because, as it transpired, it was his condition—his enthusiasm and abandon—more than any of the 613 commandments that inspired the audience. The commandments they had trouble with. Homosexuality, unnecessary abortion, premarital sex, nonkosher kitchens are all serious transgressions not in any way to be condoned. A Los Angeles gay temple was described in horrific terms.

It was also difficult to get excited about the slogan that men and women are separate but different, when the rabbi acknowledged that his rabbinical peers must be men, and then lent some urgency to the question by refusing to shake hands with the women present. Such contact with women would be a sexual temptation. One doctor present blurted out, "You have to be kidding—in Beverly Hills, hands are not a big turn-on." But the rabbi stuck with it—he knows his religion. His consistency was appealing to the audience, which nodded vigorously when Cunin criticized their own Rabbi Silverman for bringing a Christian missionary—Pat Boone—before his congregation. But what they really loved was Cunin's commitment, his fire. He exhorted, he sang of the resistance of other Hasidic rabbis in Russia, and he spilled water, had crumbs in his beard, and belched, roared, and laughed with a spirit not often seen this side of the Bronx, which is where this young rabbi got his moxie.

Amazingly enough, it turned out that a good portion of the Beverly Hills couples group was from the Bronx, somewhere back before the Valley and Cleveland and Forest Hills . . . Now in Beverly Hills they have come to the end of their rainbow. Having done all the things America seemed to want of them, they spoke of being left empty and disconnected. They had tried psychology and self-realization, and now they wanted back into Judaism. But they confessed sadly to the rabbi that they had tried the religious rituals, and that magic didn't work either. One fellow seemed to sum up the mood by telling the rabbi that he wanted something called the "old *yiddishkeit*," to be Jewish in the way Irving Howe describes in *World of Our Fathers*. But that was a world of labor agitation, socialist politics, enthusiasm for social causes, all of which have become increasingly ludicrous in the modern world of Beverly Hills.

As the discussion progressed, the real source of anguish emerged—they had nothing to pass on to the young. The rabbi pounded away at the image of fallen Jewish youth, mangled by television and child psychologists, spoiled by a godless, materialistic existence, self-centered, alienated from their traditions, products of the banality of TV rather than the rich history of their people. Off to the side, chatting with the hostess, one heard television noises, explained by the sudden appearance of a thirteen-year-old in a too tight T-shirt with BEVERLY HILLS and a telephone number emblazoned across her front. Pointing at the disciple of the Seventh Lubavitcher rebbe of Eastern Parkway in Brooklyn, the child demanded to know: "Who is that nut and why is he shouting?"

2

How many Jews are there in big corporations in this community? How many Jews are there in big banks in this community? These are the people that run things when it gets down to push vs. shove. How many Jews are there in the Chamber of Commerce? Very few, very few . . . People have this mistaken notion about Jews and their power. I think it's a lot of —— myself.

—Irwin Goldenberg, President
Los Angeles Jewish Federation-Council

Lunching on cracked crab at Hillcrest—the Jewish country club—surrounded by the owners of the San Diego Chargers, the Portland Trailblazers, and City National Bank, as well as some of President Carter's top campaign advisers and many of Century City's most prominent attorneys, all of whom paid $25,000 each to belong—it was difficult to fully absorb Irwin Goldenberg's apprehension over the relative powerlessness of those Los Angeles Jews who are wealthy. Yet the feeling is there. Despite the fact that almost half the non-Jews queried in a *Los Angeles Times* poll agreed with the statement that "Jews have too much economic power," the leaders of the Jewish business community argue that exactly the opposite is true. They point out correctly that there are three times as many Jews who live below the poverty line than there are Jews who earn more than $50,000 a year. The vast majority of Los Angeles Jews are clearly middle-class. While some Jews have much money and control large businesses, they are judged by Jewish leaders to be marginal to mainstream economic power in this town, which is thought to be held tightly in Gentile hands.

It had once been quite the opposite. Jewish merchants dominated the economic life of Los Angeles in the second half of the nineteenth century. Beginning most frequently as itinerant peddlers hauling carts of dry goods out to nearby haciendas, they seemed to be the only group around who understood business. These early Jewish merchants were accepted easily as prestigious citizens of the Los Angeles community, and they had no difficulty rising to prominence in civic affairs. But they were seriously hurt by a national wave of anti-Semitism that began in the 1890s. And from that time on, Jews came to be excluded from the inner circles of power, including the elite business clubs they had helped found. When the California Club was formed in 1888, at least twelve of the 125 founding members were Jews. But succeeding generations were banned, and as the original Jewish members died off, this power center became off limits to Jews. Indeed, Hillcrest Country Club was formed in 1920 because Jews had been excluded from the nearby Los Angeles Country Club, as well as from the downtown clubs. But despite this exclusion, there continued to be some powerfully rich Jews in Los Angeles, particularly in the entertainment industry. When the late Louis B. Mayer of Metro-Goldwyn-Mayer fame held court in the Hillcrest Grill Room, he did so as the highest paid man in the country, with a salary reported to be larger than the combined wages of the entire U.S. Congress.

Ironically, anti-Semitic attacks through the years on "Jewish power" never took into account the fact that the most powerful Jews tended to be the least committed to their ethnicity. This certainly has been the case in the entertainment industry. Back in the old days, Jewish moguls dominated the movie business. To be sure, there were the Wasp enclaves like the Disney operation. But the most influential figures—the Warners, Goldwyn, Selznick—were European Jewish immigrants with accents who had been peddlers and who became moguls. But they did not impose any Jewish sensibility on the industry's product. On the contrary, their fear of anti-Semitic attacks led them to exclude Jewish actors—with rare exceptions—from heroic parts, to shun serious Jewish themes, and to be consistently hostile to Zionist aspirations.

In a survey of that era, Tom Tugend, an insightful writer for the Los Angeles Jewish press, observed that Jews probably would have gotten better treatment in films if they had not owned the industry. He quotes from veteran screenwriter Michael Blankfort, who worked with most of the moguls: "They were accidental Jews, terribly frightened Jews who rejected their immigrant background to become super-Americans. They were interested in power and profit. They would hardly ever touch a story with a Jewish character, and if they did, they cast a Gentile for the part." Tugend quotes Columbia Pictures boss Harry Cohn as saying: "Around this studio, the only Jews we put into pictures play Indians." There were Jewish stars, but the public did not know that, since names like Emanuel Goldenberg, Melvyn Hesselberg, Theodosia Goodman, and Betty Perske had been translated into Edward G. Robinson, Melvyn Douglas, Theda Bara, and Lauren Bacall, as with other ethnics.

The fear of anti-Semitic attack reached its height in the thirties, and Tugend reports a meeting of the moguls to deal with it that produced a three-point program: "(1) keep Jewish names off the screen, (2) all Jewish executives to sell their Cadillacs and Rolls-Royces, and (3) get rid of their *shiksa* mistresses." In the postwar period, these same moguls justified their support of the attacks on Hollywood leftists as being necessary to thwart a revival of anti-Semitism, since so many of the leftist (and non-leftist) screenwriters and producers were Jewish. The fact that eight of the famed Hollywood 10 were Jewish produced a show of anti-Communist fervor throughout the leadership of the Jewish community.

The moguls were not alone in their problems with the Gentiles. Just as the last century had been a time of open tolerance in Los Angeles, the twentieth century was marked by a definite if invisible separation of the Jewish and Gentile worlds. Many Jews who rose to prominence during those years have bitter memories of a widespread pattern of anti-Semitic exclusion. Take the case of Sidney Levine, a native of Los Angeles, son of a man who came here before 95 percent of the population, an alumnus of Franklin High and USC.

Levine, already rich by virtue of his father's cooperage business, became very rich by virtue of the law. He also became a Republican and a director of City National Bank. He sent his first-born and only son off to Harvard Law School—but it didn't help. He insists, even today: "The Wasp doesn't have me to his home. He'll have me to his club for lunch when he wants something. That's the only time . . . Sure, someone in the banking fraternity or a lawyer who belongs to the L.A. Country Club will invite me to have lunch with him. I've even played golf there, and it might be because I've already invited him to Hillcrest. It's a reciprocal thing. But not to his home." Levine has never tried to stick out, offend, or appear special in any way, and his son Mel, who has come back from Harvard to be an assemblyman, looks just like any other upper-middle-class boy who is being groomed for the Presidency. But despite all the outward appearances of assimilation, Sidney Levine, at the end of a long lifetime on the frontier of contact with the Gentiles, summarizes the place of the Jews in Los Angeles in terms of a story that his mother-in-law passed on, a folktale that one would have expected to hear in some forlorn settlement in the Eastern European Yiddish pale: "The peacocks were in cages in a zoo and the people were staring there, admiring their beauty and their color and their carriage and so on. A flock of sparrows was flying over; and one of the little sparrows looked and said, 'Hey, those are birds, and look how people are admiring them. Nobody looks at us at all. I'm going to go down and see why.' So he flew down; the flock kept flying, but he flew down to take a look. He saw the plumes and so on of the beautiful birds. And as the peacocks were strutting, one of the plumes fell out. So this little sparrow picked up the plume and stuck it in his tail and started to strut with the peacocks. Now people started to laugh. They thought it was hilarious. He realized that they knew he wasn't a peacock . . . and now he flew and flew and tried to catch up with his flock that had continued to fly. And the poor little sparrow died of a broken heart.

"And I think," said Levine when he finished the story, "that sometimes some of us [Jews] think that we are peacocks in the eyes of other people. But still they [Gentiles] think we're sparrows."

Levine's perceptions were typical of many of the older, wealthier Jews interviewed for this story. For example, Bram Goldsmith, past president of Hillcrest and also of the Jewish Federation-Council, and chairman of City

National Bank of Beverly Hills, feels that there is a line between the Jewish and Gentile worlds. It is a phenomenon which he and other Jews refer to as the "five o'clock shadow"—a willingness to do business with Jews during the day but an insistence on excluding them from one's social life afterward. As Goldsmith put it: "I am involved with a lot of non-Jews in business, involved with a lot of them in all kinds of philanthropic activities. But it is a rarity for me to be invited into their homes."

There are other Jews who disagree with this assessment, but it would be incorrect to underestimate the bitterness that is deeply felt by many prominent Jews. No one wants to be told that he is not good enough to be invited to dinner. That is bad enough, but to be told that you never will be good enough to invite, that there are no standards you can meet, no accomplishments that will matter, that you will never be civilized enough to be a decent dining companion because, and only because, you are a Jew—that's a death rattle. You never forget.

Goldsmith hasn't. While he is a wealthy man, he insists that he will never be accepted into the elite social and economic circles of Los Angeles. He was president of Hillcrest, but he cannot even be a member of the California Club. He heads up a large bank, the eleventh largest in the state and the largest Jewish-owned bank in California, but it is not on the level of the major banking and corporate interests which he feels have discriminated against Jews. He argues that his is one of the few token Jewish presences in the banking or corporate world: "How many major corporations are there where there's major holdings of Jewish interest? Take the top 500 corporations. You know darned well there's virtually none." Then he added, reflecting on the relative power of his own bank, "If you want to relate to the Bank of America, I'll tell you this, and this keeps my head firmly screwed on: the Bank of America grows about the size of our bank every six weeks."

Goldsmith and other Jews are particularly irritated by their being barred from the watering holes of the Gentile rich. Being rich, they are aware, appearances to the contrary, that these luncheon clubs and dinner parties are the sites of important decision-making. After all, Hillcrest plays that role in the Jewish community. Exclusion from the Gentile clubs carries an economic and political as well as a gastronomical price. For a while it didn't, and no one cared very much. As long as Jewish economic activity was concentrated in the entertainment, garment, and real-estate businesses, it was not terribly important to get to eat lunch with a bunch of Wasps—even powerful ones. One could withstand the cultural deprivation, and the people you needed to get to for aid in your line of work were at the Jewish clubs. As long as the Gentile Establishment opposed overt anti-Semitism and supported Israel, a reasonable and wealthy Jew could live within the "gentlemen's agreement."

But the Jewish population is changing from the world of the second-generation entrepreneur to that of the successful and assimilated American one. Attorney Sidney Levine, for example, represents the older generation which managed to thrive in what he termed the "gilded ghetto of the West Side," in a life that did not require much social or economic contact with Gentiles. But he is being replaced by the new Jewish business type—an executive rising patiently through the ranks of a top corporation or law firm along with his Gentile classmates from the better schools. Richard Volpert—Amherst, Columbia Law—the second Jewish partner accepted in the prestigious O'Melveny & Myers law firm—is an example of the new breed. He works downtown and is a stranger to the life of the West Side, but he is the new chairman of the Community Relations Committee of the Jewish Federation-Council, which is the most important contact point between the Jewish and Gentile communities.

It is this committee that is attempting to end discrimination in the downtown clubs because, as Volpert states most emphatically, that is where the power is: "In terms of the center of power, you've got the court system downtown, all of the county government, city government, federal government . . . you've got almost all of the big law firms . . . all the main brokerage houses, the center of all banking. Mid-Wilshire is weak at this point and really going down. Century City has a lot of bustle. But if you look at the statistics and dollars, the rentable space, what it costs, or the businesses headquartered (there), downtown is still the dominant one." Volpert then presented his list of downtown businesses in which there is virtually no Jewish presence: ". . . banking, oil, steel, insurance, automobile, aluminum . . . the newspaper industry in this city. I mean, they're major industries, major centers of power like the defense industry where at the executive level there is a noticeable lack of Jews. That couldn't possibly happen by accident. Not when you look at the statistics of Jewish graduates of colleges, particularly Ivy League colleges, professional schools, business schools, law schools—you couldn't have this result by accident."

According to Neil Sandberg, director of the American Jewish Committee in Los Angeles, fully one-fourth of the current graduates of Ivy League colleges are Jewish, and he argues they make up a logical pool for recruitment in the big corporations, banks, and Establishment law firms. Jewish organizations like the American Jewish Committee have launched a major "affirmative action" program to gain entrance for Jews at the highest corporate level. Because of this, they are also challenging the anti-Semitism of the downtown eating clubs, on the grounds that the new Jewish executive requires such membership for advancement up the corporate ladder.

But not all the prominent Jews in Los Angeles have felt excluded from

Gentile society. An example is Paul Ziffren, an attorney and former Democratic national committeeman. When told that some consider him an influential Jewish leader, Ziffren responded by listing his credits on both sides of the Jewish/Gentile *macher*/mover line: "I would suppose they would say that because I happen to be on the board of directors of the Music Center Foundation. I'm on the board of directors of the Otis Art Institute. I'm on the board of directors of Cedars-Sinai Hospital. I'm on the board of directors of Citizens Research Foundation. I'm a fellow of Brandeis University . . . I'm vice president of the Northwestern Law School Alumni Association . . . I'm also chairman of the Committee on Arab Influence in the American Jewish Committee."

But when Ziffren has a business lunch, it's not at the downtown Jonathan Club or California Club, which at the time of this interview had yet to admit a Jewish member who does not happen to be Secretary of Defense. Ziffren lunches, like most others in the Los Angeles Jewish elite, at the Hillcrest Country Club in Beverly Hills. But he is especially proud of the non-Jewish guests whom he has introduced to Hillcrest. "Well, Otis Chandler's had lunch with me at Hillcrest many times . . . Let's see, I had lunch with Tom Bradley out there. I had lunch with Ev Younger out there . . . I had lunch with [*Los Angeles Times* editor] Bill Thomas Thursday . . . the day before I had lunch with [City Councilman] Bob Ronka. The day before that I had to be downtown for a Music Center meeting. There was an American Jewish Committee executive board, I had lunch with Steve Gavin . . . Steve is [wealthy businessman] Asa Call's right-hand man. He used to be the executive assistant to Mayor Poulson. I had lunch with [producer] Jerry Weintraub the day before that . . . Well, you know, I could just go on."

One is impressed.

As the example of Paul Ziffren will attest, there has been progress in movement of powerful Jews into the ranks of powerful Gentiles. There have been other "victories." After a fifty-year battle waged by the American Jewish Committee, Heshy Brown of the Bronx High School of Science and Jerome Avenue was admitted to the California Club. Which would have been pretty stunning, except that he got in as Harold Brown, former president of Caltech and current Secretary of Defense.

There are a number of other powerful persons of Jewish origin in Los Angeles who have become totally assimilated into the dominant culture. They are in turn held somewhat in contempt by more self-conscious Jewish leaders. A high official of one Jewish organization said with considerable bitterness that he thought of Harold Brown as an "ice-cold Jew" because he appears to shun Jewish identification. He judged Paul Ziffren a "lukewarm Jew," for what he called his preoccupation with the Gentile world, while Jewish Federation-Council President Irwin Goldenberg was described as a "hot Jew."

Mark Taper, head of the American Savings & Loan Association, and Armand Hammer, chairman of Occidental Petroleum Corporation, were said to be two major examples of "ice-cold Jews." It is a cause of considerable chagrin in the Jewish community that these two most powerful and rich gentlemen of Jewish birth are not actively associated with the Jewish community. Hammer's father was a convert to the socialist currents strong in the Bronx of his day, and to Unitarianism, which seemed more compatible with those ideals than did Hebraic law. Hammer as a millionaire dropped the socialism but retained the Unitarianism. He is an infuriating figure to the Jewish leadership because he has been close to Russian leaders from Lenin through Brezhnev and does oil business in Libya. And yet, according to two highly placed fund-raisers, he has made donations to Israel.

Taper, an English Jew who emigrated and made it big, first in real estate and then in savings and loans, once was chairman of the Jewish Welfare Fund drive. He still gives token amounts. But his major philanthropic contribution has been to the Music Center, where one of the three theaters bears his name. Which, in the words of one Federation-Council staffer, "is nice, but why can't the *goyim* pay for it?"

The campaign for funds for the Music Center, conducted by Mrs. Norman (Buffy) Chandler, played a major role in bringing the Jewish and Gentile elites closer together. As the noted historian of the Jewish community, Max Vorspan, observed in a recent interview: ". . . The chief person who's bringing the Jewish community into the mainstream of philanthropy is Buffy Chandler . . . She's offered them [Jews] in essence social acceptance in return for their money. And I think until her time very few of the non-Jews would have been ready to make that offer."

There is concern in the Jewish community over the siphoning off of funds to non-Jewish causes. It is suggested that the entertainment industry, which is involved with the arts and which has generously supported the Music Center, has not been as responsive to appeals of the Jewish Federation-Council. Federation-Council president Irwin Goldenberg was not reluctant to show his outrage over the entertainment industry's poor showing: "Less than 4 percent of the total sums raised for the United Jewish Welfare Fund were raised by the entertainment industry. You can quote that." Goldenberg added that "the last time the entertainment industry contributed any substantial amount of money to the United Jewish Welfare Fund was in 1967 [during the Six-Day War]. See, they come to life when there's blood flowing, when there's a war on. But it takes somebody's blood before they start to give their money."

The entertainment industry has always been a "problem" for the organized

Jewish community. It comprises culturally and economically the most important but also the most independent group of Los Angeles Jews. The world of the moguls has now given way to impersonal bureaucracies. One of the only personalities—Jewish or otherwise—of note these days is Lew Wasserman, chairman of the board of MCA (Universal). Wasserman was identified in scores of interviews with prominent Jewish leaders as the most powerful Jew in Los Angeles, as well as the most powerful leader of the entertainment industry. Yet he is quite clear that his company is in business simply to make a profit and that it is not in any way a "Jewish company." He pointed out somewhat gleefully that MCA produced *Jesus Christ Superstar*, bringing down the wrath of the American Jewish Committee, which claimed that the movie resurrected the idea that the Jews killed Christ. Asked about his relation to the AJC, Wasserman said, "They're not in my life. Period."

Beginning in 1939 as a talent agent new to Hollywood from the super-tough nightclub circuit of the Midwest, Wasserman came to negotiate million-dollar deals with the entrenched movie moguls, and because he gave better than he got, he is now head of the twenty-sixth largest industrial company in California. But having conquered the old, he quickly mastered the new, and as glowing accounts in the business press attest, he is a paragon of modern business efficiency. There isn't much that a new Jewish graduate of Harvard Business School can teach him, although Wasserman never made it to college. But he made it, and therefore he believes in the essential justice, decency, and magic of the American system with a fervor that few religious experiences can rival. Certainly not his parents' Orthodox Jewish ones, which he abandoned immediately upon undergoing the obligatory bar mitzvah. When Wasserman rises at 5 a.m., as is his custom, it is to check box-office returns from throughout the world rather than to perform the rites of prayer.

Wasserman is an unabashed assimilationist who loves the notion of the melting pot as the natural order of things and has barely concealed contempt for those who make too much of their Jewish specialness. In his near forty years' residence in Los Angeles, he cannot recall experiencing one single act of anti-Semitism directed at him. He dines frequently with Gentiles, has never experienced a "five o'clock shadow," and doesn't know what those who use the phrase are talking about. He objects to the discrimination of the downtown clubs but points out that Hillcrest has consistently discriminated against non-Jewish members and that he would be, for that reason, no more inclined to join Hillcrest than the Jonathan Club.

Anyway, it's hard to convince Lew Wasserman that his business success has been curtailed by his lack of membership in an exclusive club. Being Jewish is in his view "no different than being Irish or Italian as far as I'm concerned. I feel first I'm an American." He even denies that there is a Jewish community as such. Coming from Los Angeles's most "powerful Jew," the following assessment is not without interest: "I must tell you in all candor, in my judgment, under oath, Pentothal—whatever you like—I would testify with my last breath that I don't know of a Jewish community if you're talking about a structured community. It is nonexistent. Are there many Jews who share the same concerns? Yes. There are also many Irish . . . And this bugaboo about the American Jewish Committee speaking for all the Jews in America, well, I know one Jew they don't speak for—they don't speak for Lew Wasserman. And I think it's unfortunate that the bureaucracy—and I'm not taking away the great work they have done and continue to do—I think it's unfortunate that bureaucrats believe they have to speak for everyone."

Wasserman may still be smarting from a recent tiff with the Jewish Federation-Council. It was Wasserman who chaired the $1,000-a-plate Century Plaza fund-raiser for President Carter this past fall, and it was the Federation-Council that sponsored a demonstration outside. This was after the joint U.S.-Soviet declaration on the Mideast and Carter's pronouncements about the necessity for a Palestinian homeland. According to Wasserman, a threatened Jewish boycott was not effective, and he has the figures to show that this was the most successful fund-raiser in California history. While the demonstration was sponsored by the federation, about half of those inside were Jewish.

All of which goes to illustrate the difficulty with any simple assumptions about the nature of Jewish influence in the Democratic Party. Wasserman is by all accounts the most powerful Democratic Party fund-raiser in Southern California and the local person with the best ties to the Carter Administration. If there is any "Jewish lobby" to Washington, then Lew Wasserman must be an important part of it. But he has supported Carter completely in his Mideast initiatives and feels it necessary to include the Palestinians, although "definitely not the PLO," in the negotiation process. "How you gonna convince anyone without talking to them? I never made a deal with an empty chair. I made deals with Harry Cohn and Jack Warner, Louis B. Mayer; I could give you thousands of people. Billions of dollars worth of contracts I made. Never made one with an empty chair . . . Well, there are a million Palestinian people, aren't there? You gonna pretend they're not there?" Interestingly, the rival center of Jewish fund-raising power within the Democratic Party of Max Palevsky, Harold Willens, and Stanley Sheinbaum—sometimes referred to as the Malibu Mafia—shares this flexibility on the Mideast. Many others, like Victor Carter and Hershy Gold, remain strongly suspicious of the President.

This divergence of opinion among the Jewish wealthy underscores the difficulty of attempting to perceive the makeup of the Jewish population through the activities of its most affluent and therefore most visible members. The unique importance of fund-raising in the Jewish community both to charity and politics has permitted the sloppy assumption that Jews who are prominent because of their wealth also are representative of other Jews. But most Jews live lives as dissimilar from that of the Lew Wassermans and Bram Goldsmiths as do most Gentiles from Gentile power brokers.

Most Jews are not wealthy. Almost one-fifth, mostly the elderly, live in poverty. Another 70 percent fall within the broad middle class and experience the accompanying economic strains. They are depositors in Goldsmith's bank, not its main stockholders. They buy plywood from manufacturers like Irwin Goldenberg to repair their homes. When they can afford it, they are clients of big tax lawyers like Paul Ziffren. And they stand in line, like almost everyone else, to see the movies that Lew Wasserman produces. And, like almost everyone else, the big issues of their lives are more likely to be muggings, busing, and the size of their take-home pay rather than their inclusion in a particular dinner party in Beverly Hills or San Marino.

In any event, the barriers between upper-crust Jews and Gentiles seem to be breaking down in Los Angeles, and every day brings reports of Jews being considered for the California or Jonathan Club and even one startling case of a Jew in the Los Angeles Country Club, which still maintains its ban on actors and, as with these other clubs, a total ban on blacks.

Jews are getting in, but is it good for the Jews?

Should a retired garment worker cooking her dinner on a hot plate in Venice, eking out an existence on her $100-a-month union pension, plus Social Security, rejoice over Harold Brown's election to the California Club?

It's a question.

3

Outside the Breed Street Synagogue in Boyle Heights, glass shattered on the sidewalk, producing a moment of fear. A retired Jewish garment worker in her late seventies, shaking somewhat from the diseases of the old and worn, sought to explain to her elderly companion why a group of young Chicano kids had just busted up some bottles in the street: "Perhaps it is because they don't own cars. Maybe if they could afford cars, they wouldn't want to put glass in the street." The fear was gone; it had been put in what the socialist garment worker lady called "social perspective."

Inside the Breed Street Synagogue, seven old men prayed without a rabbi. Two old women hunched behind curtains safely out of sight of the men. Being women, they did not count toward the sacred ten, the *minyan*, the quorum required for God to bother to hear their prayers in honor of the dead. They often miss the *minyan* now, though once Breed Street Synagogue was packed on the Sabbath. But the fifty-five-year-old synagogue has been virtually deserted since the Jews emptied out of Boyle Heights, which had been their ghetto in Los Angeles until after the Second World War.

Outside, the retired garment worker didn't care about the problems of the synagogue, for she had left Russia more than half a century ago, a rebel against the strict patriarchal orthodoxy that had the men studying and the women tending to everything else. The czar had not been the only oppressor. She didn't miss the synagogues of Boyle Heights, but she missed the Yiddish, the lectures, the meetings in the bustling Cooperative Center on Brooklyn and Mott, speakers brought in from outside, socialist leaders smuggled into Los Angeles and thereby avoiding the wrath of Police Captain William F. Hynes's "Red Squad." She missed the young Jewish girls in leather jackets, organizers in the fledgling garment district, transplants from the East Side of New York, trying to have their fiery idealistic commitment, and sunshine and oranges, too.

For many, the mix didn't jell, and they returned to the East, thinking that if a Jew has it too easy, maybe she stops being Jewish. Others stayed with the sunshine, worked, got little houses, and supported with their last breath any cause that came along with the barest hint or hope of being "progressive." They passed this secular religion of the Jews—this special moral concern that would not quit—on to their young, who then flooded the ranks of the civil rights and antiwar movements.

Now the old people wander the beaches of Venice and Santa Monica, poke around the stores of Fairfax Avenue, and too often for the good of their souls must talk about locks on the door, muggings, or rudeness on the bus. But their minds often are still occupied with social ideas, with what, for generations of Jews, had been the substance of life itself—with issues, with ideas, with what the contemporary Jewish writer Vivian Gornick captures best in her recent book:

> It was characteristic of that world that during those hours at the kitchen table with my father and his socialist friends I didn't know we were poor. I didn't know that in those places beyond the streets of my neighborhood we were without power, position, material or social exis-tence. I only knew that the tea and black bread were the most delicious food and drink in the world, that political talk filled the room with a terrible excitement and a richness of expectation, that here in the kitchen I felt the same electric thrill I felt when Rouben, my Yiddish teacher, pressed my upper arm between two bony fingers, and his eyes shining

behind thick glasses, said to me: "Ideas, dolly, ideas. Without them, life is nothing. With them, life is *everything.*"

Survivors of that world still gather in ritual meetings that are as sacred in their design and as serious of purpose as that of any church or academy of higher learning. They meet at the Yabon Cultural Center on Beverly Boulevard or, if they are more critical of Russia, at the Workmen's Circle Cultural Center, or at a synagogue session of the American Jewish Congress. They meet and debate the big issues of the day—Israel, Bakke, busing—as if they were not without power or position. And no matter where they meet, no matter how small the circle or how sectarian its agenda, they disagree, they cajole, they contend, they cite facts, they argue, and they dream their utopian dreams.

In the San Fernando Valley, where the new generation of Jews is found, the dreams are different. In the noisy dusk of Encino . . . music, horns, frozen yogurt, stores . . . cars jam up against the freeway and spill over into the lot of the synagogue school as parents pick up their teenagers, who dream of cars, girls, alcohol, and money, and who also happen to be Jewish. The Valley Jews, 150,000 strong. Also, the important Jews, because they are the ones with family, with young. They are the "normal" Jews, not the organization honcho, the college radical, the bohemian writer, the feisty labor organizer, the religious nut, the gangster millionaire—all of whom were full-throttle Jews of the past. These are the new Jews who want a drink, who worry about divorce, who lost their jobs when the B-1 was scuttled, whose children may be bused. They are the point men of the rightward turn of the Jews, the same Jews who once helped found the National Association for the Advancement of Colored People, who produced Andrew Goodman and Michael Schwerner—two civil-rights kids gunned down in Mississippi—who now give us Bobbi Fiedler and Bustop.

And sure enough, up the hill off Ventura Boulevard sits schoolboard member Bobbi Fiedler, a modest matron in a neighborhood of homes that used to cost $60,000 but now move for three times as much. They are often dotted with Pinkerton security signs instead of the *mezuzoth* called for in Jewish law. One night Mrs. Fiedler returned from the friendly school down the hill which had been her children's second home, shocked by the information that the security of Encino might not be: busing is coming. Sometimes in the Valley at late-night kaffeeklatsches that's all one hears—busing is coming—a crackling message from home to home, the end of the Valley, the end of a dream.

Mrs. Fiedler this evening sits alone, staring at her paneled living-room wall. The light of a streetlamp throws a strange pattern on the wall, and the image of Bustop is born. "I was sitting in my living room. My walls are paneled and the light was dim and there were shadows from the fluttering of the leaves outside, and it just seemed to begin to move, almost, in my mind. And I began to see what I viewed as the cattle cars that hauled off so many Jews during the course of the Holocaust. I could never understand as a child how they could go down without a fight. And I made a commitment at that time that I would not go down without a fight."

Mrs. Fiedler, who grew up among the non-Jews of Santa Monica, who rarely attends services, and who is consciously an Americanized Jew, nevertheless reaches for an image of the Holocaust to explain her purposes. She chuckles at the plight of the liberal rabbis who have backed integration and who are now up against its reality. She carries the air of *realpolitik*—a regular Henry Kissinger of the Valley—trumpeting pessimistic certainties about the human condition.

Down the hill and up Ventura Boulevard a few blocks from Bobbi Fiedler, one finds Rabbi Harold Schulweis, who must contend with the changes that Mrs. Fiedler and America have wrought in his flock. Schulweis has an impressive national reputation and is given high marks by his rabbinical peers. Which is nice to know. But on any given day he must deal with the reality of life in the Valley, not a small feature of which is the parents lined up outside his office wanting to know about the opening of a synagogue school so their kids won't be bused. The school will open soon, and although Schulweis believes in integration, he believes in Jewish education, and he will make the best of the school no matter what the motives of the parents. He does not resent the parents. He respects their concern for youngsters removed from their sights and sent on long, dangerous treks on the freeway. What he deeply resents is the closure of debate by those who, like Bobbi Fiedler, appeal to the deepest emotional fears of the Jewish people for vindication of their own particular solution.

"Busing is not Auschwitz," Schulweis says. "The yellow school vehicles are not death trains to crematoria. Such rhetoric only serves to cheapen the tragic martyrdom suffered by our people. To cry 'Auschwitz' for any cause only paralyzes the will and intelligence of people to solve a serious problem in our midst."

But exaggerated rhetoric notwithstanding, Mrs. Fiedler is, as Schulweis sadly concedes, typical of a new Jewish sensibility, a frontline soldier in what is fast becoming a national conservative campaign. It is a new mood that spells the end of the era of Jewish liberalism and extends from the coffee shops of Encino and the bistros of Beverly Hills to the Jewish intellectual crowd at *Commentary* magazine in New York, most of whom began political life as socialists and have now ended up more comfortable with the ideology of Phyllis Schlafly than with that of Rosa Luxemburg. What is at issue is a turning away from Jewish universalism—Jewish preoccupation with the problems of others—to a new Jewish privatism—a placement of the Jewish political self at the top of the agenda. As Schulweis critically described it: "The traditional enthusiasms of liberalism are disavowed. The ideals of civil libertarianism, the concern for freedom of speech, for the protection of minorities, the separation of church and state, the general belief that somehow it is necessary for the public sector of society to intervene on behalf of the disadvantaged, the sick, and the poor, and the minorities—all these are seen no longer, if they ever were, in the interest of Jews."

The position of the Los Angeles Jewish Establishment on these issues is not altogether clear. In Los Angeles, the Jewish community leadership as represented by the major organizations supported court-ordered school integration. Back in 1972 the major Jewish organizations filed *amicus curiae*—"friend of the court"—briefs in the Crawford case, which was the beginning of the long process which finally will result in kids being sent around town in yellow buses. Mrs. Fiedler claims that the Jewish leadership ignored the desires of most Jews in supporting Crawford, for they must have known that court-ordered integration would involve mandatory busing. The leadership refuses to be drawn into this debate and will only say that it favors integration and that busing may or may not be a useful tool toward that end.

There is some evidence that most Jewish parents oppose busing. In 1970, Jewish organizations conducted a poll of the community which showed that 61 percent disagreed with the statement "Busing Jewish children to racially mixed schools is a good idea," and only 26 percent agreed with the statement. This is the first time this information has been made public. Mrs. Fiedler suggests that the Federation-Council leadership is made up of people whose kids will not be bused and are therefore indifferent to the problem. Her words imply a class dispute between the people who run organized Jewish life and the majority of the Jewish community. The view of the Federation-Council is the view of the big financial contributor. Fund-raising is the organizing activity of Jewish life, and half the $26 million contributions in 1977 came from fewer than 1,000 contributors. These givers most often fall into the category of the 8 percent of Jews who made more than $50,000 a year in 1970. They tend to live in communities, such as Beverly Hills, which are outside city limits and are therefore unaffected by busing, and in any event, they could easily afford expensive private schools.

Mrs. Fiedler's husband is a pharmacist, while 1977's Federation-Council president, Barbie Weinberg, is married to Larry Weinberg, a major real-estate dealer and owner of the Portland Trailblazers. Both women are Jewish, but it would be pushing things considerably to suggest that they live in the same world. And the busing issue has forced a conflict between those two worlds.

It is easier for Mrs. Weinberg to be liberal on this one than it is for Mrs. Fiedler. On the question of affirmative action at U.C. Davis, their positions come together. Most of the Jews represented by Bustop and those in the Federation-Council leadership support the position of Allan Bakke that he is a victim of reverse discrimination. Both are alarmed at the possible loss of a system of meritocracy that has been the one avenue of upward Jewish mobility.

There are other Jews, many in organizations like the American Civil Liberties Union, who oppose the Bakke decision and strongly support busing. ACLU lawyers Mark Rosenbaum and Leonard Weinglass argue that their ethics are consistent with what they perceive as the historic concerns of Jews for the underdog. ACLU Foundation chairman and U.C. regent Stanley Sheinbaum, who is also on the board of the American Jewish Committee, argues that "the Jewish Federation-Council has turned too conservative. It's startling that they support Bakke, and while they say they're for school desegregation, they always back off in the crunch. The Jewish Establishment doesn't represent me—my kind of Jew is progressive."

But Sheinbaum's "kind of Jew" is no longer in the mainstream. As Rabbi Schulweis noted with concern: "Liberalism is no longer, as most surely it was, the American Jew's lay religion." Many Jews do remain deeply committed to the old left-of-center values, including many of those working for the federation. The problem is that outside of supporting the position of the Israeli government, which is a widely held sentiment, it would be difficult to define a consensus within the Jewish community on any other issue or to specify an organization that can articulate it.

What's wrong? There's something boring, dead, "non-Jewish" about life at the center of Jewish power in Los Angeles. It is a mood widely acknowledged in Jewish circles but blamed on this being, after all, Los Angeles. But it's not just the freeways spreading life so thin, forcing frustrating battles over the best surface route to get somewhere to keep a conversation going. Don't minimize it. A good chunk of the Jewish experience, of the religion itself, was based on being able to walk with and to friends, always absorbed in conversation, overwhelmed by conversation, conversations that are just not possible in a car, even in a Mercedes.

The Jewish leaders put a high premium on a public show of unity and order. It is thought that open displays of doubt, debate, and serious differences would somehow weaken the Jewish community in the eyes of others. The Jewish Federation, which was started originally in New York City by German Jews eager to contain the intellectual tumult and other disorders of Jewish life, has ended by being the official voice of the Jews—sonorous, uniform, bland.

At the center of organized Jewish life there is business, intricate bureau-cracy, fund-raising, agendas, political gossip, all necessary to the task of raising money for Israel's survival and holding the community together, but it is more like the incessant chatter found at a rummage sale than the heartfelt and often profound debate of the issues that was once the mark of the Jew. That spirit still exists among the old and some of the malcontent Jewish journalists, campus types, Soviet Jewry enthusiasts, liberal left-wing Jews, more militant Zionists and their dovish opponents in organizations like Breira. For example, there is more serious and diverse debate of the issues affecting the Mideast among Jews—albeit among a minority—than there is in the rest of the population.

But in the mainstream it doesn't surface, and partly so by design. For the Jewish Establishment is fervently the keeper of the party line, the correct line. Which is understandable, given the responsibilities of fund-raising and the requirements of partisanship, but it still leaves one with a sense of something awry. It is all so responsible and Establishment. A vacuum has been left by the evaporation of the Jewish social ferment of the past. Rabbi Sanford Ragins of Leo Baeck Temple in West Los Angeles summarizes the passing of that spirit. Referring to the themes raised in Irving Howe's book, *World of Our Fathers*, he suggests:

> The rich culture of *yiddishkeit* has indeed reached its final hour, and all that vitality, that raucous emotionalism and lively intellectuality— all that surging human energy generated by hundreds of peddlers and seamstresses and gangsters and rabbis and whores, by radical visionaries who crafted socialist manifestos in ringing Yiddish, and delicate artists who drew poetry out of the horrors of the sweatshops and the grinding poverty of the streets; all that pathos and suffering and vulgarity and dignity and glory which was Jewish life in the teeming ghettos of this land half a century ago has arrived at the moment of final, irreversible extinction.
>
> And though some may wish to read the signs differently, everything around us—including the current surge of fascination with the immi-grant generation—everything testifies that the world of the fathers is dead. It has been abandoned by the sons and is beyond the grasp of the grandchildren.

In the first half of this century, when most American Jews were poor, their liberalism and personal interest were not in conflict. While there was still anti-Semitism to deal with as a unique problem, the social concerns of Jews— better working conditions, trade unionism, racial, ethnic, and religious equal-ity and freedom, support for extensive social welfare programs—all directly benefited the bulk of Jews as well as non-Jews. Jewish idealism was substantial, and Jews of all classes tended to support such programs more so than most other groups. For the majority of Jews there was a harmony between their class interests and their social idealism.

There are still disenfranchised Jews. There is still substantial Jewish poverty—19 percent of Los Angeles Jews fall below the poverty level. But most of these people are old, retired workers. Now the garment workers are Mexican-American rather than Jewish, although to the chagrin of many old Jewish trade unionists, the employers remain largely Jewish. The other group of Jewish disenfranchised is made up of recent immigrants, most of whom are Israelis. These people, who are thought to number about 50,000—although estimates range from 20,000 to 100,000—are the nonpersons of the community.

The Jewish Establishment is given to the view that Israelis should not leave Israel, a position which annoys most Israelis here, who argue back that these same leaders should then be consistent and themselves embrace the harsher life found in Israel. But in any event, this group is substantial and growing, experiencing some of the travails of the earlier waves of immigrants. They tend to be better educated than earlier immigrants but still have difficulty finding jobs, and there are a minority of Israelis who are given to crime and other activities no longer associated with Jewish life. They are, in the main, perceived as an embarrassment to be papered over.

The Jewish Federation-Council, which allocates $1 million to the needs of 1,500 Russian immigrants, has no similar budget line for these Israelis. And the Israelis themselves do not seem to have developed any social organizations to deal with their problems, as did other Jewish greenhorns. But that seems to be a result of the fact that in the main they possess the skills and habits required for entry into the middle class. These Israelis have come here to "make it," and as a group they give every sign of eventually blending into the Jewish middle-class experience as exemplified by the Valley.

The new middle-class Jews of the San Fernando Valley do not, as did their forebears, necessarily work for other Jews. They work, as do most Americans, as cogs in corporate organizations that couldn't care less about their religion or any other values the workers might possess, be they ethnic or cultural. And as cogs, they experience the same problems of alienation as do the rest of the American middle class. The signs of the disarray of middle-class Jewish life are widespread. Alcoholism, once unheard of among Jews, is now a problem of alarming dimensions. In some urban communities, Alcoholics Anonymous claims that its membership is 40 percent Jewish, which is shattering to a culture that used to accept the identification of the word for drunk—

shikker—with that for a non-Jew—*goy*—and hence the popular Jewish ditty "*Shikker* is a *goy.*"

No more. So too with drugs, divorce, runaway children, runaway fathers, and the attraction of anti-intellectual and authoritarian religious and life-style sects. There is a saying that Jews are like everybody else, only more so, and many Jews do seem to have abandoned themselves to middle-class freedom with a vengeance.

In his recent keynote address to the national Council of Jewish Federations and Welfare Funds, Rabbi Schulweis decried what he termed the "perversion" of Jewish values by the new middle-class experience. Drawing on his own work in the San Fernando Valley, he reported:

> It is not simply, please understand this, that Jewish values have been supplanted by the values of middle-classism. It is worse. It is that middle-classism is considered to be identical with Judaism . . . To be Jewish is to be an achiever, to perform, to be oppressive, to be acquisitive, to be materialistic, to be this—worldly . . . Listen to Johnny Carson interviewing Buddy Hackett, listen to Merv Griffin interviewing Joan Rivers, and you will see the subversion of Jewish character and its acceptance as authentic.
>
> . . . Middle-classism has perverted in a remarkably subtle and perhaps even unconscious way Judaic values . . . When you take individualism and the pride of self to change the world, and you convert it into selfishness, into acquisitiveness, into aggressiveness; when you take this-worldliness and you convert it into hedonism, and when you take intellectuality and you convert it into shrewdness, you have severed the goal from the means and you are left with Duddy Kravitz. A drivenness with no purpose. And from this there is no solution except something much more radical.

Schulweis is no carping, uncaring critic standing apart from his people. He is in there on a daily basis stanching what he witnesses as the "hemorrhaging" of the Jewish home. In his world, the threat to Jewish youth comes not from governments with the power to frighten but from movements such as the Moonies or Jews for Jesus, which claim they can heal the walking wounded. The extreme Jewish drive has produced the extreme Jewish victim, the alienated, unhappy product of middle-class mobility.

But Schulweis is not given to a fatalistic despair. He will turn suddenly in the midst of a moral tirade to clutch at some source of optimism, and these days it is most frequently the new Havurot experience of his and other synagogues. These are groups of ten families which meet on a regular basis to restore a sense of communality to their Judaism. As the Havurot pamphlet says: "Try to be open, warm, accepting. Risk yourself. Trust more than you usually do. Remember that the people in your group need you as much as you need them. In this crazy mixed-up world, we all need to huddle together. That's the purpose of Havurot." But Schulweis, who got into trouble with his congregation in Oakland for attacking Jewish slumlords, is not content to view Havurot as merely an alternative to its therapeutic rivals in est or psychoanalysis. His emphasis is on the reinforcement of a sense of communal responsibility that includes responsibility to other Jews and non-Jews. He agrees with Rabbi Ragins over at Leo Baeck, who calls for a return to the great code of *mentschlichkeit,* which Irving Howe defines as a "readiness to live for ideals beyond the clamor of self."

Ragins is the voice of the Jewish moral nudge that just will not be still. Neither he nor anyone else I interviewed doubted seriously the continued existence of reservoirs of Jewish altruism or failed to connect that quality with Jewish identity. It was offered as the reason for Jews being astonishingly more generous in their charitable contributions than others. One recent survey indicated that Jews contribute as much to non-Jewish causes as to Jewish causes. It is also true that support for Soviet Jews and Israel on the part of the Los Angeles Jewish community has entailed considerable sacrifice and commitment when it would be easier to simply enjoy the pleasures of American prosperity. Jews continue to be active in disproportionate numbers in civil-rights and civil-liberties organizations, and they maintain an independent think-for-themselves attitude as individuals.

One obvious failure of any examination of the Jews of Los Angeles is that it is not possible to accurately survey the thinking of the Jewish community without interviewing all 450,000 Jews, for as the old jokes have it, everyone is a chief. But finally, there is the poll that in 1970 discovered that 60 percent of Los Angeles Jews agree with the statement that "being a good Jew means being a good human being—no more and no less." But how to attain *mentschlichkeit,* how to be a good human being, is a difficult matter. And as the modern rabbis will tell you, no people has a lock on that one. What the Jews do have is a historical fascination with and a commitment to the question. As the bony-fingered Yiddish teacher with his eyes shining behind thick glasses beseeched back in the Bronx:

"Ideas dolly, ideas. Without them, life is nothing. With them, life is *everything.*"

(*Los Angeles Times,* January 29–31, 1978)

The Making of Joan Lunden

MISS LUNDEN: *I was not an avid newspaper reader and I was very bad at keeping up with current events. That is why I said, "What in the world would I do in the news business?" I was not the kind that always watched the news.*

SCHEER: *How often would you say you read the newspaper?*

MISS LUNDEN: *Rarely. I was the kind that the newspaper would be out in the living room in the morning when I came in, and I would kind of thumb through it. Just look at the headlines and maybe the first two lines of a story. But I never really got into the news. I was always involved in whatever I was doing. Like when I had my modeling school, my whole mind was filled with nothing else.*

SCHEER: *Well, did you watch TV?*

MISS LUNDEN: *A little.*

SCHEER: *So when the news director offered you the job, you said, "I don't read the newspapers"?*

MISS LUNDEN: *Yeah. I said, "What would I do in the news?"*

SCHEER: *You said you didn't know anything about it?*

MISS LUNDEN: *Yeah. And he said, "Well, for one thing, you could be an anchorwoman."*

Joan Lunden didn't exist. She was invented by the people who run the local television news business to serve their needs. The real person behind the pretty blonde reading off the TelePrompTer for New York's ABC Eyewitness News was Joan Blunden, a Sacramento model who couldn't have cared less about news but was open to the idea of a career in show business. She was picked by a Sacramento television station's news director and was subsequently nurtured by TV consultants, agents, and network executives who must have thought her face would help boost the ratings, for Miss Lunden had no other apparent qualifications for the job.

Now, at the age of twenty-seven, she is a fast-rising television news reporter and weekend anchorwoman in the biggest market in the country and appears regularly on ABC's *Good Morning America*. She was considered a hot enough property to have been preferred for the position of co-hosting *Good Morning America*, by ABC top executives, and when she turned that down ("My agent thought it was too much on the entertainment side of the business and would hurt my serious news image"), the job was given to Sandy Hill. Miss Lunden is a leading figure in the ranks of those who know next to nothing about news but can expect to make a quarter of a million dollars annually dispensing it.

But the Joan Lunden story is typical of the state of local television news. Perhaps the only thing that differentiates Joanie Lunden from many of her contemporaries in current television journalism is the honesty with which she tells her story. There isn't much to tell about Joan Lunden's early preparation for a career in journalism. She went to Sacramento High, and although bright enough to skip twice and graduate at sixteen, she doesn't recall learning much about current events, history, or anything else, for that matter, that could help in her work. But yes, there was something. "A lot of people pooh-pooh this, but I was in a lot of beauty contests where I had to get up and perform in front of people and answer questions in front of an audience. I was in a lot of dance recitals. I danced all my life, from the time I was two years old, doing little ballet things and acrobatics. I marched in parades all my life as majorette. I ran for junior prom queen and senior princess and everything else.

"I mean, I went through the whole shebang. And I think every one of those things helped put me at ease in front of a group of people . . . You also have to keep up with current events and know what is going on—but they both go together—and if you don't have the other one, you can't be in the media. I mean, you can be a journalist, you know, I mean the other kind."

After high school, Joan went to Mexico, where she did odd modeling jobs and dated the most desirable of the Mexican upper class, including the son of a governor. But current events continued to elude her. "I missed the whole Vietnam period. I missed the whole college campus rebellion period . . . the whole rock period. I missed it all. We didn't get that down in Mexico; we just didn't get it. I was totally sheltered from it . . . When I came back things were just settling down again." The 1968 Mexican student demonstrations took place during this period, in which more than twenty-five were killed and hundreds arrested, and Mexico City was thrown into a state of civil war. But sheltered is sheltered.

Having avoided the sixties, Joan Lunden returned to Sacramento, enrolled in junior college, and founded her own charm and modeling school. It was in this capacity that she had dealings with the sales executives at station KCRA (the NBC affiliate), and on one fortuitous visit to the station, she was to get her chance. She was chatting in the hallway when the news director happened to walk by and the sales guy suggested that they all go to lunch. During lunch she discussed the financial failure of her charm and modeling school and her plans to leave Sacramento for Los Angeles, at which point:

"The salesman suggested, 'You shouldn't leave Sacramento. Why don't you work in the news?' " And with that non sequitur, a star was born.

But it wasn't all that easy. First there were weeks of apprenticeship with the weatherman, Harry Geiss, "very early in the morning, coming in, learning how to read the weather machines and everything." One day, after only three weeks: "All the people in the weather department were sick and Harry called me and said, 'You are going to do the show today.' And I mean I had been following him around, but I didn't know anything, as far as what cues meant, nothing. So I went and did weather that day and, as a matter of fact, did it for the next four days, because they all had the flu. And that's really how it started on television."

After this debut, Joan had a successful stint delivering the consumer report, although she was a bit nervous about the assignments. "I mean, now, I had never bought my own groceries hardly at this point; I mean, I knew zilch about consumerism. And I said, 'Anything you want me to do. I am a good student. Give me a month to get all this research and I will learn it.' "

A month must have proved sufficient for the education of a good consumer reporter, for Joan was soon promoted to the promised anchor position. Only now there were some problems. A local TV critic disapproved of her tendency to mispronounce words. "I remember one time, for instance—the first time I read a story about Russia and the Russian newspaper—I read *Pravda*, 'Pravada,' because it was typed Pravada. I didn't know, I had never heard of the paper before." This problem was solved by the show's producer sitting down next to her before she went on the air to go over the pronunciation of each difficult word. What is interesting about this incident is that while the station came up with a mechanism for correcting mispronunciation, it never seems to have occurred to the management that Miss Lunden needed some basic schooling in current events.

Instead, the news director sent her, as they did most of their talent, to the Marion, Iowa, headquarters of TV consultant Frank Magid to improve not her knowledge of current history but, rather, her "presentation." And it was at Magid's that she was "turned out." "I had never gone to any school, so when I got there I said, Hopefully they are going to teach me something. I really want them to help me. You know, I really think that was a kind of turning point in my television career, because when I left there I had a feeling of confidence that I had not had before." That this three-day crash course could inspire confidence in one so deficient in an elementary knowledge of the news suggests something of the glow of a Moonie conversion. Indeed, there was a bit of that sensory deprivation involved, as they forgot to feed Miss Lunden and instead had her watch tapes far into the night of other female anchorwomen and performances by herself.

Joan's day at Magid's training center began with singing about the Vietnam War: "So he [the Magid trainer] sits you down in this little room. All it has is this little table and a chair and this little mini home unit with a monitor, and he tells you to read the copy. Then he plays it back. Then he says, 'Okay, this time read it fast. Read it slow. Read it loud. This time I want you to sing the copy.' So I mean, you think, Jesus, I am not a good singer, but he says, 'Just sing the copy, you will understand later why I want you to sing the copy.' So you are singing, you know: 'Three hundred people died in Vietnam today' . . . so you are singing all these headline stories, except you are singing them like an absolute idiot." After that they went to hand exercises, because "Magid likes a little use of the hands, just to make you look a little more human." After these exercises, Lunden was treated to a review of the competition. By then it was evening and she had not been offered lunch or dinner, probably as a result of the enthusiasm she shared with her trainer.

"I was really hungry, but I stayed because they wanted to show me all these tapes. And they sat me down and showed me tapes of every other female in the country they had a tape of. I mean, I saw Sandy Hill, Christine Lund, everyone, including Kelly Lange. I mean, you name them and I saw them. And the guy just sat there and said, 'You see what she does? That is really good; that is really terrific; that is what we want you to do.' "

Well, all good things come to an end, and Joan returned to Sacramento. But the Magid people began to circulate tapes of her around the country, as they do with all the talent in their bank. Meanwhile, the ratings for Lunden's show kept going up back home. Magid's agent reviewed the program and showed that Joan was important to the station's success.

A reading of that report indicates just what is important to these consultants and the stations which hire them to sell the news. All the comments about Joan Lunden (as with the other talent on the show) dealt only with appearance. "The hairstyle she used in this segment was not as coiffed as ones we've seen on her in the past and therefore seemed to be more in keeping with the image of a professional. In the same vein, her clothing was much less 'showy' and contributed to a well-groomed, professional demeanor." Here, as elsewhere in the making of Joan Lunden, none of her advisers seemed to feel that an in-depth knowledge of the news was important to the image of a "professional" anchorwoman. What mattered was that appearances were getting the ratings.

Joan was doing so well in this local market that, according to her, the rival station sent copies of her tapes around the country to get her hired away, which seems to be a common practice in this industry. The best offer came from the important NBC affiliate in Detroit, which on the strength of the tape, and knowing nothing else of her news background (or lack thereof), offered her a job co-anchoring the news in that major market.

Not knowing whether to accept, she followed the advice of a salesman who told her to call Phil Boyer at ABC in New York. Boyer, then vice president of ABC-owned-and-operated stations, looked at her tape and got excited. He showed it to Al Ittleson, another ABC vice president, and they decided to top Detroit's offer and bring Joan to report and anchor on the ABC affiliate in New York, the number one market.

So Joan Lunden, who didn't know how to pronounce *Pravda,* and to this day does not know what James Reston, Tom Wicker, David Halberstam, Jules Feiffer, Mary McCarthy, and Gary Trudeau do for a living, and who thinks that Lillian Hellman is possibly a TV reporter for a rival station, was on her way to New York City to anchor the news for several million viewers. She prepared herself for this ordeal on the plane East by reading Sally Quinn's book, *We're Going to Make You a Star,* in which Joan discovered that Miss Quinn had been represented by Joan's new agent, Richard Leibner. Asked if she had ever confided in Leibner her concerns about her lack of news knowledge, Joan Lunden quotes Leibner as saying: "You get your chance at the big time, sweetie pie. You do it . . . don't worry about it. Just do exactly as they tell you. Read like they tell you. And if you don't make it, we will put you in another market."

Al Ittleson, the ABC vice president who along with Phil Nye, the local news director, made the decision to hire Joan Lunden, recalls the qualities that appealed to him: "I thought she was professional, attractive, believable . . . We hired her as somebody whom we could develop into a meaningful personality." Is Joan Lunden a potential Walter Cronkite? Ittleson says, "Yes, I think she could be one. She is at a point where perhaps Walter Cronkite was at her age."

Before she was signed up, Joan Lunden met with Boyer, Ittleson, and Nye and expressed her doubts about working as a reporter while waiting for the evening anchor spot to open up. "I had never gone out on a story at that point. I had never done one regular story. And they said, 'Don't worry, we are going to have field producers and writers, you will get a training program. And you will anchor on the weekends. We want you here because we are going to eventually use you as an anchor on the station.' "

The writers and producers didn't materialize, and Joan ended up being trained by the camera and sound men in her crew. It indicated something of the limits of television journalism that she was quite literally thrown into news stories and acquitted herself in ways that were consistent with the work of her colleagues. "They sent me to the U.S. mission of the UN, and they said, 'Kissinger is going to be arriving.' I went to the U.S. mission, which I had never heard of before, where he was speaking to all the leaders of the OPEC nations. They told me these few names—'We want you to get this guy and this guy'—they all looked the same, I didn't know who was who. I just said, 'Shoot a little of all of them, they will figure it out back at the station.' And I was thinking, How do I know when Kissinger arrives? I walked over and I said, 'Excuse me, Mr. Secretary,' and he turned around—this is one of the slight advantages of being a female in the business—Kissinger turned around and said, 'I will talk to the young lady.' He stopped and I thought, Oh, Jesus, now what am I going to say to him?" She recalls mumbling something, "and he gave me a non-answer, but they used it that morning on *Good Morning America* and the next night on the nightly news." It was on the nightly news because Joan Lunden had been the only reporter to obtain a "visual" with Kissinger. And it was this fact, and not whether Kissinger had actually said anything of importance, that turned out to be the operative principle.

Joan Lunden is bright, alert, aggressive, and has the presence and other qualities detected by the men who hired her. If she did not possess such qualities, she would no doubt have failed in the tough New York market, as her bosses suggest. They never once suggested that she had the capacity to ask Kissinger a significant question about the foreign policy he was then conducting. And perhaps if she had, the Secretary would have found her somewhat less cute and simply walked away, and goodbye visual for the evening news.

Joan feels that her experience in breaking into the business was typical of the other women she's worked with. As an example, "Roseanne Scamerdella did the same thing. They took her off the street and said, 'Do you want to be a reporter? We need a nice little Italian girl.' And they hired her and put her on the air, and she didn't know anything about what she was doing. She's at Eyewitness News. She has one of the highest Q ratings [indicating public recognition] in New York. She is really popular." There are many personalities in the Eyewitness News format and they are chosen pursuant to an ethnic balance formula. The station already had a black, a Puerto Rican, and that nice Italian girl, but they were lacking in Wasp representation. So Joan Lunden was hired to fill what in New York City is perceived as a minority quota. "They didn't have a white female, and they hired me and Peter Bann at the same time. And the office joke was that we were Ken and Barbie."

But Joan is not a Barbie, and she clearly could be trained to be a competent as well as an appealing reporter. It's just that the people for whom she's worked, who have consulted, trained, agented, packaged, and in every other way molded this woman into a marketable commodity, place a low priority on developing a serious understanding of the issues of the day. When they were asked about this missing ingredient in the making of Joanie Lunden, they replied there was a possible need for knowledge of the news, but not a compelling or even a very likely one.

The justification is that the public gets the news it pays for. Joan's boss, Ittleson, says: "The old idea was that the people were there to accept whatever a news organization presented—take it or leave it. I think the new idea is that the people have a real vote and a real say in what you put on the air." To complete the argument: Joan gives news, Joan gets ratings, ergo the people get the news they want.

The difference between Joan Lunden's perceptions of the business and that of her employers is that she is still sufficiently and naïvely honest enough to be willing to state just what her station's business is all about. "WABC, Eyewitness News specifically, tends to make all their reporters more than just reporters. They tend to make them personalities. They heave promotions on them, radio, newspapers, magazines—they build them up as being a specific type of personality. And essentially what we find is that people watch Eyewitness News just as much to find out what Roseanne did today and what J.J. did today and what So-and-so is wearing and what their feelings are that day, as they are tuning in to get the news. It is almost like a continuing soap opera, a serial . . . People feel they do not want to miss it, because if they miss it, they feel like they have missed one of the episodes. And I think that has a lot to do with why we are more successful."

Which about sums it up, except for a footnote as to how Joan Blunden became Joan Lunden. The news executives at ABC did not find her name sufficiently chic for the New York market, but they could not readily come up with a creative alternative. "I had been here a few days and I was going out to do a story and I had to do a stand-up close. I had to have a name, right? I had to say, 'Someone, Eyewitness News.' I said, 'If you guys wouldn't mind, I need a name so I can go out and do this story. Would you get your executive minds together and find a name for me?' And one of the men had a sudden idea: 'Just drop the B, call her Lunden. You are looking for a catchy name, easy to remember—Joan Lunden is like the city, it is like Julie London. I mean, it is something they will remember.' They said, 'We love it. Call yourself Joan Lunden.' And since then, I have been Joan Lunden."

And that's it for Eyewitness News.

(*Los Angeles Times*, May 29, 1977)

Ed Meese's Dirty Pictures

Down in Arlington County, Virginia, the lady dancers at what the locals call "tittie bars" had best be wearing pasties or prosecutor Henry Hudson will bust them. He once was quoted as saying, "I live to put people in jail."

For the past six years, Hudson has also been going after video stores and threatening to shut them down for renting movies depicting nonsimulated intercourse. "Our vice squad has a reputation," he has told me, "for checking periodically in the stores, and the people are careful about what they sell in the county; yes sir, they are. I don't apologize for that; I'm proud of that. We have a good family community here."

That stand-up-to-porn spirit caught the attention of the President of the United States, who commended Hudson for his actions and vowed to keep his eye on the young prosecutor.

One day in the spring of 1986, I find myself in Hudson's bailiwick in the Arlington civic center, in a cubbyhole at the end of a corridor decorated with WANTED posters. I am there because Hudson has now become a national figure as the chairman of Attorney General Edwin Meese's Commission on Pornography, whose activities I am tracking for my newspaper, the *Los Angeles Times*. We are sitting in his cluttered office, discussing more variations on a single theme—sexual conduct—than I have ever discussed with anyone. The topics range from the limits of anal sex to the many varieties of sodomy. Hudson talks about the proliferation of pornography and how he sees it as his obligation to return this country to the clean good old days.

I ask him, "By good old days, do you mean when they banned James Joyce's *Ulysses* or the novels of Kurt Vonnegut, Jr., and D. H. Lawrence, all of which have been censored?"

"I can't say I've read or seen the items in question," says Hudson. "I don't have time to read books or go to the movies."

"What is this thing called pornography you're now investigating?" I ask.

"Pornography, to a degree, is like the word 'love'; it means different things in different contexts."

"Great," I observe, "but you're head of a commission that wants to get rid of it, so what is the *it*?" Hudson then riffles through the search warrants and *Miranda* confessions in his briefcase but can't find the working definition with which his commission has been playing for a year (and on which it never manages to agree).

"Let me take a stab at it," he offers gamely. "It's any portrayal that is designed to be sexually arousing, that depicts sodomy, sexual degradation, humiliation, domination, or violence."

Why sodomy? Hudson launches into a stern, finger-wagging lecture on the menace of sodomy and how I obviously misunderstand the sodomy laws as they affect what the pornography commission calls "rubber goods" and oral sex.

A career of reporting, from Saigon to presidential primaries, has not adequately prepared me for this moment.

It seems that, as Hudson views the law in Virginia and quite a few other states, it is a felony to have oral sex with your spouse, even in the privacy of your own bedroom. That's sodomy. And apparently there isn't anything you can do with a dildo, including sticking it in your ear, that Hudson and his law will tolerate.

Depictions of violence, by the way, are okay, as long as they're not connected with explicit sex. The video stores in Arlington that are now forbidden to rent the unedited version of *Debbie Does Dallas* are doing a brisk business in *I Spit on Your Grave, Tool Box Murders*, and other splatter flicks uncensored by prosecutor Hudson.

As the manager of one of Arlington's more popular video stores said, "I can rent movies that dismember and mutilate but not those that show sex." He held up one cassette and said, "In this cute one, a woman is sunbathing by a river and this killer comes along and chops her head off with a shovel, and you see the blood spurting out. And then it gets worse. But it's legal; it's not considered obscene. There's no explicit sex."

When I ask Hudson how he could possibly find films that show decapitation of sexy women less objectionable than portrayals of sexual intercourse, he responds, "I just enforce the law, and the law refers to sex, not violence."

Now, why am I, an investigative reporter of some experience, telling you all this as if it mattered to anyone not planning a trip to northern Virginia? Why, indeed. Because the Attorney General's Commission on Pornography, which Hudson heads and of which, if you're like most people I know, you've probably never heard, has attempted to extend the legal mores of Arlington County to the rest of the country.

It has been a weird odyssey for Hudson and his fellow commissioners, hand-picked by the Attorney General and charged with slogging through smut, the better to know it, the better to regulate it. These pilgrims, or "sewer astronauts," as Vonnegut has called them, have trekked through tons—I'm pretty sure that's literally true, by the way—of photographs, videotapes, transcripts, and paraphernalia. But it was necessary. Witch-hunts need witches, and that meant hearings in six American cities, a parade of witnesses and "experts," and born-again porn stars and vice cops and all manner of people testifying as to the evils (mostly) of porn.

The goal of the commission was politically charged from the start. As announced by Meese in the charter of the commission, its purpose was "to make specific recommendations to the Attorney General concerning more effective ways in which the spread of pornography could be contained, consistent with constitutional guarantees." Note the wording: to "contain the spread," not to dispassionately examine the possible harm, if any.

Meese was taking up the rallying cry of an extremely odd alliance of New Right religious fundamentalists (such as Jerry Falwell) and a small but vociferous band of antipornography militants (such as ultraradical feminist Andrea Dworkin) who held that the increased availability of pornography was responsible for a rise in all kinds of crime, particularly against women.

Unfortunately for their cause, a federal commission reporting in 1970 to President Nixon had "found no evidence to date that exposure to explicit sexual materials plays a significant role in the causation of delinquent or criminal behavior." This did not deter them from their new campaign. Meese claimed that research conducted after 1970 would show evidence of harmful social effects and that, besides, pornography had become more violent. To overturn that earlier finding and recommend new laws dealing more harshly with the purveyors of pornography, the Attorney General chose eleven men and women, a majority of whom had already sided with the antiporn crusaders.

Chief among them were Hudson and his sidekick, another prosecutor and porn buster, executive director Alan Sears. From Kentucky, he, too, had made a name for himself by finding smut peddlers to prosecute. He was to figure prominently in the drama that enfolded the commission in its final days.

The other members included Father Bruce Ritter, a Catholic priest committed to banishing porn from Times Square. Father Ritter was always forth-right when, during breaks in the hearings, I questioned him on his views on sex outside marriage (it's a sin) and within marriage (it "wastes the seed" if the sex is not strictly for procreation). At one meeting, Ritter said, "I would say pornography is immoral, and the source of my statement is God, not social science." I must have missed the day God gave testimony to the com-mission. In any case, Ritter was an earnest commissioner, never batting an eye as the armada of law-enforcement officers (68 out of a total of 208 witnesses) testified as to how rough it was out there in the land of dildos and plastic-wrapped fetishist magazines.

James Dobson, a fundamentalist radio counselor, was considerably more emotional, though perhaps more practiced. He regularly broadcasts tales of sexual depravity on his radio program, *Focus on the Family*. Nevertheless, during the hearings, he exhibited an unnerving propensity to half pop out of his chair, with a "Gosh, no!" look on his face, at every new tale of a por-nography victim's woe. Although Dobson is undoubtedly sincere, there appear to be other forces driving him. He announced in a speech that since joining the commission he had become the victim of "satanic" attacks. He claimed that a mysterious black Porsche had been the demonic agent of accidents to his son and daughters.

Commissioner Diane Cusack, a councilwoman from Scottsdale, Arizona, had attempted to get re-elected by crusading against local adult-book stores. Among other things, she suggested that antiporn activists photograph the license-plate numbers of people attending an adult-movie theater. To boost her fortunes, some said, the commission even met in her hometown. She lost her election.

Commissioner Harold "Tex" Lezar had been an editorial assistant at Wil-liam F. Buckley, Jr.'s, *National Review* and a Nixon speechwriter before serving as an adviser in the Reagan Administration's Justice Department, where he helped formulate the idea for the porn commission. A solid antiporn vote, he was instrumental in choosing the commission's members.

This conservative majority was rounded out by Reagan-appointed federal judge Edward Garcia of Sacramento, who had been a municipal-court judge with a reputation for being hard on defendants in obscenity cases. Garcia, to his credit, did appear capable of boredom and often seemed to doze off during those sessions he managed to attend.

Commissioner Park Dietz is a psychiatrist and criminologist specializing in violent crime and sexual disorders. Thought at first to be a hard-liner, Dietz occasionally showed that he marched to his own drummer, though it was not always clear what the music was. He has written that he believes that all pornography is in some sense tainted with "sadism and masochism" and that masturbation can lead to "sexual disorders"; but during the hearings, he frequently expressed the view that violence, not sex, was the key problem.

(It was Dietz and Cusack who provided one of the high points of the year. Wrestling with some testimony about odd sexual practices, Dietz said for the record, "I think more people would agree that it's bad to encourage rape than would agree it's bad to encourage ejaculation in the face." (Another member of the commission noted, "One's a felony," at which Cusack, ever the eager teacher's pet, piped up with "Maybe both should be.")

Frederick Schauer was another one who was capable of surprise. A professor of law at the University of Michigan, he believed that the First Amendment did not apply to pornography. Nevertheless, as time went on and staff director Sears attempted to pressure the commissioners into accepting a sweeping, jail-all-pornographers draft, Schauer protested that it was "so one-sided and oversimplified that I cannot imagine signing anything that looks even remotely like this." He later said that *he* would write the report, an offer that was to prove a mixed blessing for all concerned.

The rest of the commissioners turned out to be more difficult to classify. But it is worth noting that, on a panel whose male members would often discuss the best ways to protect women from the dangers of pornography, three of the four female members on the commission formed the core of the loyal opposition.

Judith Becker, a Columbia University psychologist and head of an institute specializing in sex offenders, had the most professional experience of any of the commissioners in dealing with people who commit sex crimes. Through the months, she became increasingly dismayed by the misuse of available scientific data. "There simply is no serious body of evidence of a causal connection between pornography and crime," she would say. But the commission wasn't listening.

Deanne Tilton, the head of the California Consortium of Child Abuse Councils and an appointee of Republican governor George Deukmejian, had been counted on by Hudson as a solid antiporn vote. Instead, she emerged as a sharp internal critic.

Ellen Levine, the editor of *Woman's Day*, was the strongest dissenting voice on the commission. As she said to me at one point, "What I like is erotica and what you like is pornography." A strong defender of both constitutional and women's rights, Levine became a thorn in Sears's side.

Although Hudson, Sears, and the other conservatives loved the fact that they could drape themselves in women's liberation to combat porn, they deflected the criticisms from the three women by referring condescendingly to them as "the ladies" and by taking shots at their professional affiliations. (Levine's employer, the owner of *Woman's Day*, is CBS, whose interests in cable and records made a tempting target for Sears.) As a leader of the Southern Baptist Convention, Sears often made it clear that he could not abide Levine's more cosmopolitan ways, which included what he clearly perceived as an unseemly propensity, for a female, to independent thought. Toward the end of the commission's life, the two were barely speaking to each other and communicated by exchanging bitter notes.

The bitterness came not just from the clash of philosophies but from the fact that within weeks of the commission's creation, several of the commissioners had begun to feel as if they were on a runaway train.

For nearly a year, the commission and I wandered this country, seeking out the sickest, most pathetic examples of human sexual fantasy; the search went on for so long that it almost seemed as if all that was typical of American eroticism. But what we watched, in large part, was shit. And, again, I mean that literally.

For reasons best known to the staff (Sears and his aides), the commission exhibited an uncommon fascination with the scatological fringe of the porn world. No simple tits and ass for this crowd. Forget garter belts and even whips. This federal commission spent much of its time—and your money—on fist fucking, golden showers, child porn, asphyxiation, anilingus, with side trips into such rarely considered fetishes as toenail-clipping collections, being squirted with real mother's milk, and the private, carefully contoured world of sweat sniffing.

If all of this seems removed from your experience, join the crowd. The commission shunned the kind of mainstream erotica most of us might encounter—though carefully culled slides of *Playboy* and *Penthouse* photos were shown—in favor of the extremely bizarre. As attorney Barry Lynn of the ACLU would write: "It is as if finding the most despicable scene of sexual conduct ever photographed, the commission would be justified in urging suppression of all sexually oriented material."

Lynn, a United Church of Christ minister as well as a lawyer, a thirty-seven-year-old family man with a wife and two children and a station wagon, played an unusual role in this trek. Often staying at cheap hotels, he operated as a one-man truth squad, attending every hearing and preparing summaries for the press explaining the implications of some of the wilder proposals.

Was this hunt for the despicable, as Lynn charged, a campaign to smear erotica with the brush of the grotesque? Or did it reflect the sexual fascinations of the staff and the army of vice-squad officers who led them through descriptions of various dens of iniquity? Being there, I found it hard to tell. The commissioners mostly played hard to get to. A studied indifference permeated their responses to talk of sexual stimuli, as if they were biologically as well as ethically beyond the reach of their effects.

But because I was there, I can also tell you that the commissioners' public air of detachment was at odds with their more private comments. At one point, in New York, I happened to drive a carload of them, including a couple considered to be conservatives, up Broadway from lower to mid-Manhattan, in slow-moving traffic. The conversation about the often offbeat passing sidewalk scene was urbane. "Nice-looking hooker," said one, and there were approving grunts. They had been around a bit themselves and did not seem to be overly disapproving.

On another occasion, a woman commissioner was talking with one of the men, who had loudly declared his belief that masturbation could lead to sexual disorders. He remarked offhandedly, "Of course, none of this would happen if women learned how to give a really good blow job." When the woman objected, he said, "That's a lot of feminist crap."

Traveling with that crowd, I frequently became overwhelmed by the mountains of material, all of it unrelentingly squalid, all of it fodder for this evangelical soap opera. Lynn later estimated that 160 of the 208 witnesses before the commission—or 77 percent—had favored tighter controls on sexually explicit material. The intent of the men running the hearings was so transparent that it was almost embarrassing: transportation provided free of charge for those testifying to the evils of porn; tough, unrelenting questioning of those few who said otherwise.

In brief, it was surreal to be in an audience in which high heels and uplift brassieres were the norm even among women sporting antiporn buttons. Among the men, there was an obvious excitement in the air, much like that of a Rotarian stag show of old, when a disgruntled Playmate or an aging but feisty *Penthouse* Pet showed up, or when the lights were dimmed for a screening of the "hot parts" of X-rated movies confiscated by Sears's Kentucky State Police.

The pattern of what was to follow in each city was established at the opening session in June 1985 in the Great Hall of the U.S. Department of Justice in Washington, with Dr. C. Everett Koop, Surgeon General of the U.S., as lead witness that day.

Perhaps it was the early hour, 8:45 a.m., but Dr. Koop came through as a bumbler. The title is impressive; the man's mind is not. He spoke of caring deeply about the subject of pornography and wanted to assure his audience "that we are not operating in the dark on this matter, as may have been the case a decade or two ago," when the 1970 commission entered its report that porn had not been proved harmful. Koop stated that the earlier report "was based upon a very limited universe of scientific literature," and you would have thought that he was leading up to the presentation of some new findings.

Well, the Surgeon General had no new findings to present and seemed to regret it. He spoke emotionally about the new technologies of videotapes and cable, through which pornographers "have expanded their markets of sleaze and trash."

When Hudson asked, "Do you, based upon your experience and the evidence that you have seen over the years, find a direct connection between pornography and public health?" Koop replied, "Well, the simple answer to that question is yes, I definitely think there is a connection. But . . . sir, that is basically, at the moment, an intuitive reaction, rather than one based upon lots of science." Immediately after the Surgeon General had spoken, the commission presented the first of a long parade of porn "victims."

Bill sat in protective anonymity behind a screen, presumably because he and the commission did not want the world to connect him with his crime. Bill, who said he was forty, told how he had been convicted of molesting two fourteen-year-old girls while they were visiting in his home.

"I would like to tell you," he stated, as if on cue, "briefly what happened and what role pornography had to play in these events. In both cases, the girls were sleeping over with my daughter, and I had been drinking very heavily for several hours. After going to sleep, I awoke very abruptly, almost like someone had kicked me. With compulsion, I was driven to go into the room where the girls were sleeping. It was like an inner voice giving me instruction and direction."

For the benefit of the stilled audience, Bill provided further detail. "The first time this happened, I removed the sheet from the sleeping girl, fondled her breasts and vaginal area. After a brief moment, I committed oral sodomy on her. . . .

"In looking back on my life," Bill continued, "I would like to tell you a few things that happened that I feel led to these crimes that I just alluded to. I was raised in a Christian home, the third child of a police officer." He faltered, sensing quicksand—Christian cops causing crime? Bill recovered: "There was, and still is, a great deal of love between us. I would not ever say or think that my family had anything to do with causing me to commit these crimes."

No, it was pornography. According to Bill, it started with the kid next door, who showed him bodybuilding books; and from there, it was a predictable journey to nudist magazines and, finally, through exposure to men's magazines in the armed forces. "*Hustler* became my bible, and I had maybe the largest collection in the country," he noted with what seemed to me a faint trace of the pride of an art collector. "In closing, I suggest to you, distinguished panel members, pornography did not make me commit my crimes. No, I am held accountable for my actions. What I would like to suggest is the pornography industry is guilty of journalistic malpractice hiding behind the First Amendment. It is much like the person yelling 'Fire!' in a crowded theater." Or yelling "Sex!" in a crowded church. Just how Bill had come to be familiar with Justice Oliver Wendell Holmes's argument on the First Amendment was not made clear in his testimony. Nor did the commissioners ask.

There was, however, some cross-questioning.

LEVINE: Can you tell me whether or not drinking was also a problem of yours and whether or not it continues to be?

BILL: Drinking was a problem in my life. I was drinking approximately two to three six-packs of beer daily.

LEVINE: Was drinking in any way one of the triggers that allowed you to do things that otherwise you wouldn't have done?

BILL: Yes, it certainly was.

What Levine was driving at was the body of evidence connecting such deviant behavior with alcoholism. As in countless times to come, the link between deviant behavior and alcoholism was touched on but never followed up. Instead, Ritter came to Bill's rescue: "Bill, do you think that you could describe pornography as the match that lighted the fuse to the explosive?"

BILL: Yes, sir, it certainly did.

RITTER: Do you think that your use of pornography actually helped shorten the fuse to the explosive that ultimately injured these children?

BILL: Yes, it did.

RITTER: Do you think that your continued use and exposure to pornography actually increased the explosive fuse and abuse of those children?

BILL: Yes, it did.

RITTER: Thank you.

HUDSON: Thank you very much, Bill. We appreciate your testimony this morning.

Just to complete the circle, Bill, who had started life in a good Christian home, reported, "Right after I was arrested, I met the Lord, Jesus Christ, and I turned my life completely around."

Levine said that later, in private session, she had told Hudson that the witness seemed to have been coached, but Hudson had evaded the issue.

The commission's questioning of Bill was typical of what would happen for the rest of the year—pandering to the antiporn witnesses to buttress the case and attempting to discredit those with a different position.

A particularly clear comparison was to be the sympathetic treatment of a *Playboy* Playmate whose wild charges, including murder, went unchallenged, while former *Penthouse* Pet Dottie Meyer, who still works for the magazine and claims to love it, was grilled by the commission. Dietz all but snarled back at Meyer lines from the text that appeared in *Penthouse* and asked sarcastically, "You like your men rough-and-tumble, living on the edge of danger?"

She zapped him back with "Yes, I married a policeman."

I could go on with other highlights, but those snippets should convey the flavor. Well, just one more. We've had a medical expert and a criminal, so let's try a cop. That would have to be Dennis DeBord, investigator for Virginia's Fairfax County Police Department, who testified at some length about his specialty—the busting of adult-book stores. He put on the usual slide show, featuring such highlights as "another section of magazines appealing to different interests, magazines with deviant behavior, such as *Mother's Milk* or *Poppin' Mamas*. The 'poppin' mamas' are pregnant women engaged in various sexual acts, while the other is of women with milk in their breasts. Also, a magazine commonly known in this culture is *Fist Fucking.*"

Investigator DeBord went on to relate his own sad tale of victimization by porn—in this case, in the hallways outside peep booths in adult-book stores.

"This investigator has also been solicited outside the booths in the hallway. Individuals have solicited me in various ways, such as asking me straight out to commit oral sodomy, anal sodomy, etc. I have also had my buttocks fondled in the hallway."

It's rough out there.

Enough of anecdotes. What, after all this effort, did the commission uncover that might have been overlooked by the 1970 commission?

That earlier panel, much better funded—a two-year effort costing $2,000,000—and more serious about its work, commissioned more than fifty independent studies on the effects of pornography. The Meese commission made none. Meese would pony up only a miserly $500,000 for a year of commission hearings, including staff salaries and travel expenses. By Washington standards, that's lunch money.

It's also $250,000 less than this same Justice Department had previously given one antiporn crusader, Judith Reisman, a former songwriter for *Captain Kangaroo*, to do a survey of three magazines, including *Playboy*, to determine their pornographic content. Her study, among other travesties, counted each panel in the cartoon strip *Little Annie Fanny* in a running total of instances of pornographic child imagery (the original Orphan Annie was a kid—get it?). It came in for much congressional ridicule, and *The New York Times* included the Reisman study in an article about government-funded projects "with an ideological tilt bordering on fanaticism." Lawmakers were appalled at the lack of objectivity of the "research." For starters, she likened Hugh Hefner to Adolf Hitler.

To the evident frustration of the zealots on the commission, however, Reisman proved a bust as a witness when she testified at the Miami hearings, raising a shrill warning against "shaved genitalia," which she charged has "emerged as a new key phenomenon." She denounced Gahan Wilson's cartoons and Helmut Newton's photographs—to the discomfiture of at least one commissioner whose living room features Newton prints.

At hearing after hearing, the commission would gear up with high anticipation, bold claims about revelations to come, and long witness lists, only to founder, as it did in Reisman's case, on the paucity of any reliable social-science evidence to make its case that the 1970 commission had been wrong and that pornography caused antisocial behavior. The key researchers in this field refused to be drawn into Hudson and Sears's political agenda.

The star witness in Houston, for instance, was to have been Edward Donnerstein, a psychologist whose studies of college-student response to erotic and violent material is considered pioneering in the field. If there had been new evidence since the 1970 commission on the harmful effects of porn, it was expected to be found in Donnerstein's work. In one laboratory study, it had been shown that men exposed to a rape scenario—not common in most porn—showed some increase in "negative attitudes" toward women. The crusaders had seized on that finding to claim that porn in general led to violence toward women. But Donnerstein emphasized repeatedly to the commission that the crucial variable was not sex but violence and that nonaggressive sexual material produced no such effect. Commissioner Schauer asked Donnerstein if there were any "laboratory studies showing increase in aggressive behavior after exposure to nonviolent, sexually explicit material."

There it was, the $64 question, upon which the future of the sex-censorship roundup was riding. It was as open a question as you could get. Were there any lab studies, any at all? Give the wrong answer and you give away the ranch. And with a rare hush in the audience, Donnerstein responded, as cool as a killer of dreams in a Western, "Not that I am aware of."

"The problem," Donnerstein and his associate Daniel Linz later said, "centers on what we mean by pornography. Are we talking about sexually explicit materials? If we are, then one would have to conclude that there is no evidence for any harm-related effects. Are we talking about aggressive materials? In this case, the research might be more supportive of a potential harm-effect conclusion. The problem, however, is that the aggressive images are the issue, not the sexual, in this type of material."

Bam! The commission was up against a stone wall. This is what it was all about, right? Evidence that depictions of sex cause harmful effects. But here, the only witness so far to present cold, detached, nonanecdotal evidence tells the commissioners that it's not sex but violence. The same violence implicit on children's television and in toy stores in the forms of Rambo and Masters of the Universe? So if there's any serious intent, wouldn't the commissioners have stopped dead in their tracks at that testimony? Not bloody likely. That would mean redirecting the New Right's pop cause of pornography to that of violence, which seems to be built into the very red-white-and-blue muscle of American culture.

The Meese commission, of course, did nothing of the sort. Hudson's immediate response, since he was discombobulated by Donnerstein's testimony, was to cut short the discussion of scientific findings and turn the meeting over to the next slide show. Enter Sergeant W. D. Brown of the Houston vice squad. If the sergeant ran true to form, he would do what vice cops in the other cities had done: provide a juicily horrifying tour of his terrain—the now-familiar landscape of sleazy bookstores and scatologically oriented publications.

But Brown didn't deliver all the commission might have hoped for. "Presently," he said, "there is no child pornography that is being sold readily over the counter, nor is there any bestiality or defecation or those types of films."

Child pornography is, of course, that most toxic of terms, the great rallying cry of the antiporn witch-hunt. But society clearly recognizes its obligation to protect minors, and no serious person disputes it. As Lynn suggests, "It's a convenient way of getting everyone excited, but the fact is that the laws are very severe on child pornography and it exists only as an illegal cottage industry."

What does exist, as Brown went on to document with a slide show, are sad watering holes for primarily poor consumers of adult fetishist material. To underscore this fact, obvious to any visitor to the neighborhood of a downtown bus station, Brown intoned along with his slide:

"This is another typical bookstore that we have in Houston. You will notice that they also advertise giant booths. The booths that you will see in a moment are places where individuals go to have anonymous sex relations with other individuals in the bookstore. This is a typical counter which you will find in a bookstore. The shelves are stocked with different rubber goods and devices to stimulate sexual activity."

For some reason, dildos fascinate police forces more than any other item of erotica, as Brown's testimony indicated; and in Texas, as he noted, "possession of six or more of these items is a class-A misdemeanor. They are listed under Texas law as contraband and can be confiscated. Presently, Houston, I guess I would have to say, has the largest inventory of rubber goods. At last count, we had 27,000 of these things located in our property room."

Consider, if you will, the presence of 27,000 arrested dildos stacked neatly in the property room of the Houston jail. The commissioners sat in respectful and intent silence, apparently unaffected by the absurdity of the moment, as Brown marched bravely forward to the matter of rubber dolls that "are primarily used for sexual relations with individuals." Grotesque though some of the paraphernalia may be, no one broke the silence with the questions that begged to be asked: Is it harmful? Might it even be calming to some people and, therefore, to society's benefit?

So that the commission might fully examine the question of whether or not the public display of porn had harmful effects, it was determined that slides of these dingy sex stores would not suffice; the commissioners had to see for themselves. Research. So Sears hired transportation and marched them as a group, accompanied by Houston cops, into one of these establishments. In fact, it had been cased in advance by the police. As everyone watched, a bullet-headed vice cop yanked open the door and announced in a loud voice, "And here we have two men engaged in an act of oral copulation!" The two men looked up in astonishment at the eleven commissioners.

One commissioner said she couldn't tell the cops from the customers— except for the cops' white socks. And Lynn said it was all he could do to prevent the edgy police from arresting everybody there.

One might understand if this had been a meeting of the local board of health. But what business was it of a U.S. commission on pornography to get down and dirty into the pathetic attempts of some of this world's most forlorn, desperate, and lonely inhabitants to find a few moments of whatever brings them as close to joy as they will get? These were two human beings!

And what did this field trip yield?

HUDSON: Sergeant Brown, have you or any other member of your department developed any statistical correlations between the increasing number of adult-book stores and the incidence of sex-related crime in those districts?

BROWN: No, sir, we haven't. We haven't done any kind of studies in that regard. It would be impossible for me to give you a definitive answer.

The lack of reliable studies was to dog the conservative commissioners throughout the hearings. Sears and Hudson had made the mistake of hiring their own expert—an honest social scientist. Unfortunately for them, Canadian sociologist Edna F. Einsiedel is a scholar of integrity and issued a disquieting report to the commission summarizing existing studies.

After reviewing studies done on televised soap operas, men's magazines such as *Playboy* and *Penthouse,* and other magazines such as *Time* and *Reader's Digest,* Einsiedel reported, "No evidence currently exists that actually links fantasies with specific sexual offenses; the relationship at this point remains an inference."

Her report also risked the heresy that erotica could be good for you. Therapists, she noted, have used erotic material "to help patients with sexual dysfunctions overcome their fears and inhibitions." Also available was a 1982 report by Donnerstein and his colleague Neil Malamuth concluding that "exposure to certain types of pornography can actually reduce aggressive responses."

As a result of Einsiedel's study, when the commission convened in Scottsdale in February 1986 to summarize its findings, for one moment it came dangerously close to passing a logical resolution: that, according to the evidence, "nonviolent" and "nondegrading" pornography caused no harm.

Hudson quickly called a recess. The commission had to be brought to its senses. The commissioners met in private and Sears announced that any working papers including the Einsiedel report were to be secret—in effect, classifying them. Einsiedel herself, as if privy to the secrets of the Stealth Bomber, was placed under a gag order not to talk to the press.

That was when Lynn stepped in on behalf of the ACLU. Suing under the sunshine laws, which require government proceedings to be open to the public, he forced Meese's Justice Department to back down. Papers were released, the report was made public, and all hell broke loose.

It seemed that among the papers that had come to light in the ACLU action was a letter that had been dashed off by Sears. Among the commission's witnesses had been a Reverend Donald Wildmon of Tupelo, Mississippi, a man driven for the past several years to monitor all manner of publications and broadcasts for signs of dirt. He puts out a newsletter keeping a running count of corporations that sponsor offensive TV shows and advertisers who buy pages in *Playboy* or *Penthouse.* The newsletter informs its readers that "SARA LEE IS LEADING PORN PUSHER" and "*COSMOPOLITAN* FULFILLS DEFINITION OF PORNOGRAPHIC." Wildmon testified to the commission that such major U.S. companies as CBS, Time Inc., Coca-Cola, and others were "distributors of porn" because of various direct and indirect connections to material he deemed offensive, and that adult magazines had been linked to all manner of crime and social ills.

As usual, the commission did not cross-examine Wildmon, who made unsubstantiated charges that *Playboy* and *Penthouse* had been linked to "violence, crime and child abuse." When it was suggested to Sears that the corporations named by Wildmon deserved an opportunity to answer the charges, his response was to clip together ten pages from the testimony, without attribution, and send them to corporate officers with a letter on Justice Department stationery telling them that their failure to respond to the unattributed allegations would "necessarily be accepted as an indication of no objection."

It was an outrageously effective job of smearing. Most of the corporations answered the charges defensively and hastily, and one of them, the Southland Corporation, under constant attack by Wildmon and his pickets and mailing lists for more than three years for carrying *Playboy, Penthouse,* and *Forum* in its 7-Eleven chain stores, capitulated. Between the letter and the drafts that had come to light proposing that an offending store's assets might be seized, someone at the Dallas-based company said, "Whoa. Child porn? Forfeiture? The Justice Department? Bail us *out!*" All three magazines were promptly dropped in what a spokesman admitted was a response to the Meese hearings.

If the commission now proves to be a menace, I was not among the first to recognize it. Like those of a presidential primary, the antics of the commission had seemed little more than harmless fun and games, a lot of holier-than-thou rhetoric accompanied by winks of acknowledgment from the real world. The air of flirtation in the hearing rooms, the female witnesses in see-through blouses denouncing porn, the constant references to sex all had a carnival-like effect. This can't be serious, right?

So, charged with this sense of the inevitability of the sex drive and convinced that no one was truly intent on putting the sexual-freedom genie back into the bottle, I spent too many hours sitting at the hearings with Lynn, reassuring him that the republic was not about to fall.

In part, I was informed in my optimism by my conversations with Levine, Becker, and Tilton, all of whom were alarmed at the prospect of being party to an assault on the First Amendment and being cast as the arbiters of individual taste.

All three had been opposed to the frenetic pace at which the commission was being rushed to its conclusions. Levine told me that she had refused to join in voting on positions by mail, because she thought debate was needed. When Tilton was about to leave her Los Angeles home for the final stretch of meetings in April, she was startled to receive yet another two-foot stack of commission staff reports, memos, and proposals for legal changes. As she said, "We have a 1,200-page staff report to go through and a rival report prepared by Fred Schauer. My sense is we're not going to be able to get through more than one-third of this material in the allotted time. We have asked for an extension and it's not been granted. I feel like I'm in fantasyland."

That morning, Tilton was inclined to look back on her year with the porn commission as time "largely wasted." Her only consolation was the fact that she had pushed through some strong language and new concepts on child pornography, but she felt that her concerns in this area were being used to support far-reaching measures for control of adult erotica on which she was not prepared to act.

In the end, she and the other moderates won a few battles but lost the war.

The last meeting of the commission took place in a dreary corner of the old granite-and-marble Federal Home Loan Bank Board building in northwest Washington. The moment of truth was at hand. The commissioners had seventy-two hours to write and approve a report that would set out in detail what American society should do about the "pervasiveness" of pornography, according to Meese's mandate.

They were eleven men and women, some hardly speaking to each other, bored to tears with this material that was supposed to be more addictive than heroin, looking at their watches, thinking of the planes they had to catch. The only problem was, they didn't have a report.

What they had was a disjointed, Draconian and moralizing staff summary prepared by Sears, which a number of them felt was an acute embarrassment— the same shrill, hysterical document that had already had an effect, calling for vigilante groups, for the naming of corporate "porn" distributors, etc. Schauer had said that to sign it would be a travesty, and offered to write his own version, which he hoped the full panel would endorse. Schauer, it will be remembered, is the lawyer who believes that most sexually oriented material does not deserve First Amendment protection and did not have major policy differences with Sears's version; he simply didn't want to be laughed out of court.

And so, in the space of a couple of weeks before the legal deadline, Schauer wrote a 192-page draft. In its pristine form, it is a discursive but highly opinionated march through the history of constitutional law and censorship, a lifetime's worth of lecture notes by a professor who suddenly had a nation for a class. Sears did not want it on the agenda he had drawn up. The session opened with Ritter's moving successfully that the commission use the Schauer draft as the basic document into which it would meld Sears's proposals. Since it is highly probable that few of the commissioners actually read all 192 pages, what followed was a kind of insanity.

During those final days, the commissioners would gather around the table, which was usually piled high with documents, as Hudson read aloud from the Schauer draft. It made sweeping statements about pornography and the role of sexuality in America—all of it one professor's opinion. Hudson would finish one ten-page section and ask, "Everyone agree with the wording?"

The commissioners would then toss new phrases and wording at each other and, depending on whether or not they had been heard amid muttered remarks about betrayal, proceed to get lost in a thicket of proposals and counterproposals. No two commissioners with whom I spoke at the end could agree on what was definitively decided during those sessions. One member would offer a horse trade on a proposed jail sentence in return for a softer line on a constitutional question; another would make a sarcastic amendment to a hardline declaration. Entire topics would be left to be called up for a vote later on—though some would never be.

"We were told we had to have a product," said Becker. "We couldn't even see galleys, because Sears insisted that time didn't permit. When my colleagues ask me about this report, I've suggested they stop reading when they get to this commission's recommendations."

As voting on sections of the draft continued under deadline pressure, members would later admit that they were unsure of which sections were being passed and which tabled, which votes were binding and which not. At one point, when it seemed as if an important vote—nothing less than the exemption of print and cable from censorship—had been taken, I interviewed Dietz and mentioned the votes that I'd already reported in the *Los Angeles Times*, as had other reporters.

"We didn't pass them," insisted Dietz.

I said we should check with Sears. So we trooped over to his office and, after fifteen minutes of conversation, established that the commission had, indeed, voted 6–5 on just those points—but it was now agreed that the vote would be recorded as a divided one, not as a recommendation of the commission. You figure it out; I couldn't.

One thing on which the commissioners did agree was that there was no agreement on the definition of pornography. As an alternative to a single definition, they came up with a three-tiered one.

The first part, category one, was to include sexual violence, and there were no demurs, even when Dietz said *Miami Vice* was an example in this category. No one quarreled with judging this material offensive, if not necessarily legally obscene.

Category three—defined as nonviolent pornography that is nondegrading and nonhumiliating—was also easier to deal with. That was the category that had come close to being judged not harmful in Scottsdale but had instead been recorded as a split vote at Sears's insistence.

But it was category two—pornography defined as nonviolent but "humiliating and degrading"—that gave the commissioners their real trouble. Until the very end, they were not clear as to what kinds of materials fell into this class. Did *Lady Chatterley's Lover?* Did *Playboy?* The debate wore on. Sears passed around ads and photo spreads from *Vogue* and *Cosmopolitan* and suggested that they, too, might fit the category. Levine responded with what one wag called the "Bloomingdale's exemption," asking, "Do you want to take on the entire fashion industry? The ads for Bloomingdale's are just as sexy."

In frustration, an angry Dobson said, "Wouldn't you say a photograph of a woman masturbating, with a look of ecstasy on her face, is degrading and humiliating? I would!"

Other members said they would not, as long as the woman appeared to be enjoying herself. One commissioner said later she could not believe that these conversations were taking place in the final week of the meetings. The concept of degradation of women had been introduced to the panel when Andrea Dworkin testified before it. She had denounced the "humiliation" of women in mainstream publications, and her comments had obviously caught Dobson's ear. What the Christian broadcaster of traditional family values had perhaps overlooked was who his new ally was, for Dworkin had written, in an attack on the very idea of traditional heterosexuality, "I think that men will have to give up their precious erections and begin to make love as women do together."

In the middle of the voting, when the wrangling and confusion were at their height, Dietz dropped a bombshell. He announced to the panel that he had prepared a paper summarizing the "sentiments of the commission," though no one had been asked for one. Reading his newly minted manifesto aloud, Dietz tried to cut through Schauer's verbiage and get to what he saw as the heart of the matter—that pornography was just no good. "A world in which pornography was neither desired nor produced would be a better world," Dietz proclaimed. He called most pornography an "offense against human dignity," asking all Americans to shun it because "conscience demands it"!

There it was, as if handed down from the mountain. Ritter, the Catholic priest who had been so adamant about condemning any form of sex outside marriage, dramatically removed his white clerical collar and presented it to Dietz. The dissenters, Levine and Becker, were astonished. The moralists were obviously thrilled: the commission—for a moment, at least—had been reborn in their eyes. Hudson asked for a show of hands. No one is clear on what the vote was, but it was agreed that Dietz's declaration of morality would be included in the report as a personal statement and that the commissioners who agreed with it could affix their names to it.

As can best be reconstructed, what *was* voted on and would be recommended as this article went to press was a series of battle orders in a sweeping war against sexual explicitness. The report calls for the elevation of pornography to a level matching that of drug trafficking or organized crime: a national emergency. As the final draft was being prepared by Sears, these were the major recommendations to the Attorney General:

- The creation of a national commissioner—a porn czar—to push for and coordinate more vigorous prosecution of federal obscenity cases.
- The forfeiture of assets by any business found to be dealing in obscene materials, as is now done with drug traffickers.
- Banning the use of performers under twenty-one in "certain sexually explicit depictions."
- A vast computer-bank system, involving state and federal cooperation, to prosecute producers of porn more effectively.
- The elimination of the requirement, to trigger federal intervention, of proof that obscene materials have crossed a state line.
- The establishment of an automatic, mandatory felony conviction—with twenty-year sentences—for second offenses in the selling of obscene materials.
- The enlistment of the Internal Revenue Service to use its auditing power to go after porn producers.
- Endorsement of citizens' action groups to boycott, picket, and "socially condemn" local sellers of offensive materials, whether obscene or not.

As noted, the commission agreed to exempt printed words and cable television. These categories were strongly defended by such big guns as Time Inc.'s cable executives and by top book publishers, while magazine publishers and film makers did not show up in strength. (Historians may wish to note that vibrators, which were nearly criminalized by Hudson and Sears—to be left to languish like those 27,000 dildos in the Houston jail—were allowed to hum on.)

What would come of these recommendations? As far as the law is concerned, the answers will come from the government bodies that must enact the recommendations. But just as the earlier drafts have already had an effect on the marketplace, so will the final recommendations have their effect, with or without enactment.

What all the commissioners were concerned about, however, was the report that would precede the recommendations—the revised Schauer draft. This was what was supposed to make sense of the year and summarize the members' conclusions. It had been left to Schauer to return to his university office and assimilate the votes of the preceding week into his original draft report.

It was a daunting task, but the problem was that he had only five days in which to perform it. Why? Because, despite the national implications and the complexity of what he was to write, he wanted to make a previously scheduled trip to China.

Schauer delivered. The manuscript is a testament to the ability of word processors to merge disparate ideas and contradictory facts into a seemingly consistent whole. But upon reading it—and not many will—one realizes that the attempt to summarize eleven views on hundreds of points of law and morality and philosophy is, like the attempt to define pornography itself, futile.

Schauer accompanied the draft with a letter to his fellow commissioners informing them that he would not accept any changes that weren't agreed to by the ten others, including those in "wording and style and anything other than blatant grammatical errors." He wrote that the report was a "house of cards, as to which what in itself [sic] appears to be a small change might ultimately destroy everything." Then he left for China.

The report does not define pornography. In fact, it begins by saying that it cannot define pornography; nevertheless, it claims that "degrading" pornography—whatever that is—was found "likely to increase the extent to which those exposed will view rape or other forms of sexual violence as less serious than they otherwise would have." Schauer adds that as to violent sexual material, the commissioners are "unanimous and confident" that exposure leads to antisocial acts and sexual crime.

The wording in the Schauer draft led *The New York Times* to report that the Meese commission had concluded that "most pornography . . . is potentially harmful and can lead to violence." But the fact is that studies do not suggest anything like that. Becker, whose institute in New York has treated more than 700 sex offenders and who was originally recruited as the commission's expert in this field, had just finished reading the report when I contacted her on the day the *Times* story appeared. "It is wrong and it is ludicrous," she said flatly. "Not only did we not define what 'degrading' pornography is, but no social science or data has shown any causal connection between even violent pornography and crime." As to the conclusions' being "unanimous and confident," Becker and Levine were preparing their own dissent as the *Times* story hit the newsstands.

Schauer gave the right wing what it wanted—the words, if not the data, to repudiate the 1970 commission findings that porn is not a social menace. Virtually the only erotica given a clean bill of health were nude statues. "Michelangelo will not be banned," Sears said to me soothingly when I asked him for his score card.

Lynn, winding up his watchdog role from the audience, went back to his office to prepare a thick briefing book on his own. In a long discussion after the final tally, he summed up his perspective.

"It's just as bad as I feared from the onset," he said. "It calls for a Mc-Carthyite witch-hunt against material about which there is no evidence, whatsoever, of harmful social effects. The report has hysterical statements that presuppose that pornography plays a major role in causing a variety of social ills, even though after a year of work, the commissioners have not made the case. Our country would never allow the regulation of a food additive or a prescription drug on the basis of evidence as flimsy and tangential as the evidence the commission has heard to regulate pornography. The FDA would laugh these studies out of the agency.

"In my view, they have morally condemned virtually every kind of sexually explicit material, even that which depicts consensual, equal, loving, monogamous sexual activity."

Dietz conceded that point during a post-hearing interview. "Pornography is not a productive substitute for a relationship," he said, so why should any of it—except for a few "art" pictures—be protected? Did he mean there could not be any redeeming feature to pictures that were simply erotic? "As a steady diet," said Dietz, "they are the source of mischief."

Mischief? At last, it seems clear that the real issue is that would-be censors are elitists, convinced that while they can wallow in smut for a year and be unaffected, most people cannot and must be protected, and that they alone know best how Americans should conduct their sex lives.

When Meese announced the commission to study pornography, he chose his language carefully. "The formation of the commission," he announced, "reflects the concern a healthy society must have regarding the ways in which its people publicly entertain themselves."

Meese didn't attend the hearings, but all of this happened under his name, under the authority of the office of the Attorney General of the United States. I know Meese. I even like him. But talk about how one entertains oneself publicly: I was with him at the Mayflower Hotel in Washington, during the 1980 campaign, when he was a bit tipsy and was eying the scantily clad cocktail waitresses, as any Rotarian from Oakland would do when away from home in the big city. As I might do. This was the same guy left hanging in public by the Senate for more than a year while the boys deliberated over whether or not his financial dealings were too sleazy for him to become the nation's chief law-enforcement officer.

We all have standards, tastes, as well as personal centers of hypocrisy, and we all know it. Maybe we should lead different lives; maybe some do. But, one might ask, what have the Feds to do with it? And what are the all-American, God-fearing right-wingers doing leading the pack? Isn't it the most profoundly conservative, profoundly American impulse to keep the Feds' noses out of our private business?

In my opinion, much of what is lumped under the label of pornography is vicious and disgusting—no question. Sitting at the hearings, even a purist on the First Amendment is moved by the truly sad tales of victims of malicious, pimplike producers of seedy porn movies. In my view, all child pornography is foul, and society has an overriding obligation to protect minors. The celebration of violence, sexual or not, the cheapening of life, male or female, cannot but have a bad effect on a society. And that includes *Rambo*, celebrated by Reagan, as well as your low-budget, X-rated mutilation flick.

But more disturbing than the excesses of pornography is the denigration of all erotica, making it the scapegoat for the larger ills of society. I came away convinced that for all their rhetoric, the majority of the commissioners were not serious about decreasing violence or sexual exploitation in our culture. They were serious about stopping sex that they didn't approve of.

They turned their backs on proposals to go after the much greater amount of violence found in most R-rated movies in favor of a crusade against sexual explicitness. They consistently went after erotica instead of violence despite irrefutable evidence from virtually every witness, friend or foe, that it's violence, not sex, that's the problem. Becker said bitterly that she had tried in the final days to raise the topic of marital rape—which is still legal in some states—but Sears refused to consider it. In its zeal to make the nation march together in a lock step to paradise, the commission also rejected programs for sex education—proposals made by commissioner Deanne Tilton, its own expert on child abuse—because those programs ran against its notion of the proper Christian family.

In a piece on Reagan during the 1980 presidential campaign, I predicted—erroneously, it may turn out—that he would not be a hard-liner on this type of issue. I cited the freer life-styles chosen by Reagan's children, with his apparent approval, as evidence of his essential tolerance, his apparent faith in the ability of the next generation to make personal-life-style decisions free from the heavy hand of government-sanctioned conformity. This is a President who seems, by all accounts, to be untroubled and even pleased that his son Ron has found gainful employment as a contributing editor of *Playboy*.

In any case, until the formation of the Meese commission, I figured that the regular denunciations of porn I would hear from Reagan, Bush, Meese, and points right were just rhetoric to please the fundamentalist fringes who vote. After all, as Reagan said during a 1980 interview with me for the *Los Angeles Times*, he wasn't born yesterday. When we discussed the pervasiveness of loose morals, he pointed out that he'd been a Hollywood actor and even quoted from the trial of Oscar Wilde: "I have no objection to anyone's sex life, so long as they don't practice it in the street and frighten the horses."

Something disturbing has come out of these hearings. Never mind frightening the horses. In their zeal to make the nation conform to their tastes, the more zealous members of the Meese commission have, as McCarthy did, twisted the very ideals of freedom they claim to cherish. It's not what we may do in the streets that these people fear. It's what we do in our heads.

(Playboy, August 1986)

Zombies of the Left

Sitting in the anteroom of the People's Temple in San Francisco three days after the Guyana massacre, I could hear attorney Charles Garry arguing with the Temple's survivors in the next room. He was insisting that they end their isolation and talk to the press, which at that precise moment was me.

Suddenly I didn't want to be the press. I no longer cared about the explanations that would be offered by these puppets whose strings had been cut. Questions about a movement that had managed to take both Christ's and Marx's names in vain no longer seemed to matter now.

A day earlier I had conducted a telephone interview with one of the true believers, whose husband had died in Guyana. She still insisted that Reverend Jim Jones was "the greatest humanitarian the world had ever seen." What startled me was that these words came from an obviously intelligent person who had been sucked into this madness and was still lost. These people were trained by Jones never to say "enough." Like the Moonies, and Hare Krishnas who haunt the airports, they had surrendered their common sense and their humor—qualities that in recent history are turning out to be more important than one's ideology. Maybe they were always more important.

When San Francisco's mayor and supervisor were gunned down in City Hall several days later, one friend of theirs said, "Thank God it's a right-wing nut this time." Not very funny. But Mayor Moscone and Supervisor Milk might have chuckled anyway. They were both to the left of the political spectrum and were often held accountable for the antics of crazies posing as social idealists. Moscone was subjected to particularly vicious attack after the massacre at Jonestown for having accepted the support of the People's Temple and appointing Jones head of the San Francisco Housing Authority. The Reverend Jones threw his shock troops into a myriad of liberal causes and, in return, received approval from prominent Democrats including Joseph Califano and Rosalynn Carter.

The People's Temple had power because the death of the civil-rights and peace movements had left a vacuum on the grassroots level. Jones realized this early and sought to cop the left franchise. With a melange of Christian do-gooderism, faith healing, racial integration, and socialist rhetoric, he recruited successfully among the wounded veterans of the sixties youth culture and even more successfully among the black poor, who made up more than 80 percent of his followers.

It all seemed so reasonable, except for one horribly unreasonable fact: the man was a totalitarian.

It is not a new story for the left. The birthright of progressive idealism has been thrown away time after time to the spirit of totalitarianism because the exigencies of the moment seemed to demand that. This was the sad, horrific saga of the pro-Communist left, which ended in apologizing for the most ghastly acts of Stalin—the same Old Left that had termed concern for individual freedoms and the desire to limit bureaucratic power "bourgeois democracy." First Amendment restraints were deemed necessary to preserve freedom under capitalism, but never in the promised land of the socialist utopia.

Well, there is only one kind of democracy, and either you have it or you don't. Democracy means that people are not to have their essential wit and insights mangled by state, church, or corporation. And that manipulation can occur under any economic system and in the name of any god or cause. Eternal vigilance against the SOBs is the only safeguard (and anyone who presumes to have power over other people is potentially an SOB, be he Jim Jones, Nixon, you, or me). My own serious mistakes as an activist leave me all too aware of how easy it is to rationalize error. Such experiences should be sufficient to make one a born-again believer in the spirit of the First Amendment.

The First Amendment of the U.S. Constitution is not a manifestation of bourgeois society but rather the fundamental insight into making the human condition tolerable. The New Left of the sixties, as it first appeared in the civil-rights and antiwar movements, made this perception its unifying cry, along with a strong belief in social justice. It was this profoundly felt democratic, anti-elitist spirit that guided the early SDS, the Free Speech Movement, Women for Peace, and every other large left grouping of the sixties. In retrospect it will seem the healthiest period of American political life.

Many of that era are still loyal to the New Left democratic tradition. They are anonymous organizers in factories, protesters against unbridled nuclear power, active proponents of women's rights, people attempting to make the dreams of the civil-rights movement a reality. But their work is overshadowed by crazies who make better copy.

The New Left was born as a movement against alienation. Its memory is now mocked by a scattering of groups that foster the alienation of the individual, not only from institutions, but from themselves. People's Temple is just the latest in a series of movements that aim to create zombies in the name of establishing some social utopia.

It can never make any sense. It is like fancying the fruit of a diseased tree. The process perverts that which is most healthy about the human spirit— our individual capacity for growth, development, mystery, and passion—and would turn us into uniform mush.

If reading Marx and Mao can give rise to that, then it is necessary to temper them by reading John Stuart Mill, Bertrand Russell, and Martin Luther King, Jr. But perhaps that is too simple. Jones read more of Christ than he did of Marx, and it is Martin Luther King's picture that dominates the hallway of People's Temple. Indeed, we now know that Jones never permitted his disciples to actually read Marx or any other author. It was all interpreted for them in Jones's endless, rambling tirades.

What the crazies do have in common is their distortion of ideas, and indeed history, in order to leave themselves at the center of our attention. They have a contempt for ordinary life, for the right and the ability of individuals to make rational decisions. They become humorless, fanatical "saviors" of our souls. It finally doesn't matter if they claim to be of the left or the right, for Christ or against Him—they are inevitably the destroyers of life.

(*New Times*, January 8, 1979)

THE LANGUAGE OF TORTURERS

A Warning from Phnom Penh

The missionary spirit requires for its sustenance a stereotyped view of those who are to be saved and a horrific view of the devil who tempts them. Otherwise complex and individual personalities are reduced to so many "souls." So it is with great national powers bent on saving smaller ones from the forces that would bedevil them.

It is for this reason that we have been given the "domino theory," which is the basis of United States policy in Southeast Asia. This theory quite simply reduces a hodgepodge of peoples, each possessing its own lengthy, confused, and emotionally charged history and cultural patterns, into so many abstract names—neat black dominoes all ready to fall. The thesis is a simple one. The devil is China, obsessed with a desire to conquer the free and independent nations of Southeast Asia. The Chinese have created a pattern of successful subversion first in North Vietnam and now in South Vietnam. If they are allowed to attain victory there, it will create a momentum that will cause all of Southeast Asia to fall.

In the United States or in Western circles abroad this seems a plausible thesis. But outside of that rarified atmosphere, it soon becomes obvious that the theory doesn't hold. The simple priorities and concerns of the Cold War are not those of Asian leaders or of the masses. And our pictures of Asian reality are quite frequently ludicrous. There are hates and fears and desires among these people that are quite removed from ours—and which we have not begun to understand.

For example, Sukarno's "go-to-hell-with-your-aid" Indonesia, while moving closer to China's foreign policy, is at the same time determined to reduce the hold that Indonesia's 3 percent Chinese minority has on the country's economy. As in all Southeast Asian countries, the Chinese are the power elite of Indonesian business and commerce. Sukarno, for all his militant pan-Asian sentiments, wants to keep the Chinese in line. One of Indonesia's fears about Malaysia is that the 42 percent of Malaysians who are Chinese eventually will control Indonesian commerce.

We have helped create such immense barriers to understanding our "enemy" that it is often impossible for even the well-intentioned and dedicated observer to increase his understanding. We have come to accept the fact that Americans are not allowed to travel to the Communist countries of Asia, but there is now a growing list of non-Communist countries that choose to deny us access. It is impossible for any American to obtain a visa to Burma. American newspaper reporters are now generally denied access to Cambodia and Indonesia. There is a whole world in Asia that affects us more and more decisively as we know less and less about it. This ignorance of this other world allows Americans to hold to the most fantastic notions concerning it. There is, in fact, no proposition that one can utter about the Communists of Asia, no matter how absurd—e.g., they use babies for fertilizer—that does not seem plausible. For there are no observers to challenge it; there is no traffic of ideas.

During February and March of this year [1965], Western observers were offered a rare opportunity to enter this other world. The Cambodian government sponsored the first Conference of Indochinese People in the capital city of Phnom Penh, and some American reporters (at first I was alone, then we grew to five) were granted visas to visit Cambodia. The conference included a wide spectrum of political, social, and ethnic groups. Delegates from North Vietnam and the National Liberation Front (Vietcong) had to contend with Vietnamese neutralists who were as haunted by the specter of Communism as they were by American imperialism. Everyone listened politely as the dozens of ethnic groups explained their own very special problems, the religious sects going into the most detailed description of the harassment they have experienced over the centuries. The conference even broadened its concept of Indochina to include all those peoples found between India and China, and received President Sukarno of Indonesia for a four-day visit. And on the last day, a mass rally, presided over by the vice president of the NLF and Prince Sihanouk of Cambodia, seemed agreed that Ho Chi Minh, Charles de Gaulle, and Fidel Castro were the three great men of this era.

While all this was in progress, everyone, delegates and observers alike, was conscious of the distant and repetitive sound of American bombs falling on North Vietnam. (We couldn't really hear the sound of bombs, but it seemed that way as one listened to the speeches and read the dispatches in the local press.) Some people showed hatred for the few of us among the correspondents who were American. The vice president of the NLF banned us from his press conference, a rather fat French ex-colonial snarled over cocktails at me, "Vous êtes un assassin," and Sukarno, during his speeches, would pick out the American types in the audience to roil with fiery and derogatory phrases. Finally, after some frigid conversation with Chinese newsmen and a few trips to their embassy, I realized that we are each of us held responsible for America, regardless of our personal politics. It is difficult to exaggerate the gap between our worlds.

Sitting at the conference, often half bored and noncomprehending amid robed Buddhists, dark Austriennes, northern Catholics, Chams, Islamic Khmers, Cao Daiste Vietnamese, neutralist Laotians, and royalist Cambodians, it seemed that there has never been an arrogance quite as great as that of Americans. We not only presume to control events in this part of the world but must also impose a political ideology—a concept of freedom no less— on its peoples. It is cruel enough to push people around for their gold and ivory, but it is perverse and emasculating to dictate their history and believe that it is done in their interest. The best description of this is still provided by Graham Greene's Quiet American in Vietnam, who is busily making plastic bicycle-pump bombs to help the Cao Dai generals vanquish the Hoa Hao chieftains so that Democracy will reign supreme.

During a lull in the conference, I went to Angkor, the site of the high point of the magnificent Khmer civilization some eleven centuries ago. There I met an American foreign-service officer up from our embassy in Saigon. He was a genial and interesting fellow, and as we wandered through the ruins of Angkor for several hours, inspecting the intricate architecture and sensitive sculpture, he calmly explained to me that we might soon have to bomb Hanoi as part of our effort not to escalate the war. He wanted to be sure to "take in" the ruins before the war spread to Cambodia. He explained to me just how the Chinese Communists would sweep down through Cambodia the minute the United States withdrew from South Vietnam. If not the Chinese, then the Vietcong would take it over within three months. It was necessary to protect the Cambodians from this fate, despite their feelings to the contrary, because they were a simple people who did not understand the nature of modern Communism. He particularly understood this menace because he had read a book on Communism by a man named Brzezinski, which he strongly recommended to me. His favorite line was that it would be "irresponsible" of us to abandon these people to their naïveté. At first I thought he was putting me on—saying all this in the midst of the ruins of an empire that had to be moved every few centuries because of successive invasions of neighboring peoples, and about the modern Cambodians, who are perhaps the most sensitive observers of the intricacies of Asian politics. But after hours of this conversation, spun out in the dullest and most sincere fashion, I began to understand with horror that Jules Feiffer's cartoons do make up our most accurate history.

After this encounter, I returned to Phnom Penh with great sympathy for the position of Prince Sihanouk of Cambodia, who is potentially the most tragic figure here. For it is he who is caught in the midst of this nightmare and not the leaders of the Vietcong. After twenty years of fighting, the Vietcong no longer have illusions about the nature of the enemy. They seem almost to accept the conditions of war as the only coherent view of life. There is probably no other way to survive when one has spent his infancy, adolescence, and now his adulthood fighting for what he believed all along was his birth-right. These are the "just men"—noble, proud, defiant, idealistic, spiteful, and extremely petty and jealous of their prerogatives. One cannot help but hope they win; few have so earned their chance at history. But one can hardly expect that such a victory will produce a lovely or generous society. The soil has been too hard too long.

But the Cambodians have escaped all this, and they do have another vision of life. Their fortune is due not only to the suffering of the Vietminh and Vietcong but also to the skill and diligence of their leader Prince Sihanouk. It was the Vietminh victory over the French that forced the dissolution of the French hold on Indochina and gave Cambodia its independence, and it is Prince Sihanouk who has kept that independence from being mangled by America's obsessions during the Cold War.

To understand the current international position of Cambodia, one must first realize the enormity of the United States failure during the past ten years. Back in the winter of 1954 and '55, when the first phase of the Indochina war was drawing to a close, the Cambodian government of Prince Sihanouk was solidly allied on the side of the "free world" and Cambodian troops had fought under French command against the Vietminh. During the Geneva conference, the Vietminh wanted the rebels who had fought against Sihanouk to represent Cambodia. The United States helped the Cambodians to gain independence, but it did so because of the requirements of Cold War politics. As the Prince recalls his conversation with John Foster Dulles in 1953, the latter said, "I promise you to force the French to give you independence in order for us together to vanquish the Vietminh, that is to say, Communism." Dulles insisted that the French Army remain, or "you will be instantly de-voured by the Communists." But at that point Cambodian nationalism re-quired French withdrawal. It is now twelve years since then and Cambodia still has not been devoured. This United States obsession with Communist expansion and Cold War politics troubled the Cambodians even then, but it was only during the next ten years that they realized how totally divorced the United States perspective was from Asian reality.

In the simplest sense, it went contrary to the known facts. As the Prince has written: "At the Geneva conference we were opposed to the Communist powers because they, with the Vietminh, wanted to divide our country. . . . Since the Geneva conference, all the Communist countries, including the Democratic Republic of Vietnam, have respected our sovereignty and our frontiers. The allies of the free world, on the contrary, have attacked and menaced our independence and territorial integrity." This last is a reference to the border incursions of the Thai and Vietnamese armies, which the United States has built up to several hundred thousand strong—as compared with 29,000 Cambodian troops. Both these countries have traditionally represented a much greater threat to Cambodia than China. Units of the Vietnamese Army, accompanied by American advisers, have frequently crossed over into Cambodia and fought on Cambodian soil in their pursuit of the Vietcong. United States planes have "accidentally" sprayed Cambodian fields with insecticides as they sought to deny food and shelter to the Communists. It is this sort of blundering incomprehension on the part of the United States that alarms the Cambodians. But most frightening of all is the United States view of China.

In one of his writings the Prince recalls another conversation with Dulles in which the latter expounded on the "unpopularity" of the Chinese regime and his expectancy that the Chinese people would soon rise up against Mao. In recounting this anecdote the Prince added: "The aides of the American Minister agreed with respect and conviction. My friend Ambassador Nong Kimny looked at them with visible bewilderment. I was able, however, to manage a polite smile."

The Cambodians know the Chinese as well as do any outsiders, for there has been a good deal of contact in recent years. But their concerns are not ours and their comprehension of modern China is vastly different.

In an important statement in 1963, Prince Sihanouk systematically took apart the argument that the Chinese Communists have been an aggressive military power in Asia. He further presented the rather novel idea that the viability of Chinese institutions be judged in terms of the needs and history of China.

In order to realize that a comparison between the life of a Chinese peasant on his people's commune and that of a Khmer [Cambodian] peasant on his vast lands is nonsense, it is necessary to know that, prior to the institution of the new regime by Mao, the people of China were without any doubt the most miserable of the world.

The Westerners have always had the weakness—or the vanity—to believe that "their" democracy is the only means of answering the aspirations of the people. This is not a criticism; on the contrary, I sincerely admire the British or American democracy . . . in Great Britain or in the U.S.A.

The Prince does have his own fears of Communism. Cambodia is an underpopulated and lush country that neither needs nor wants the sort of militant commitment to rapid development and national order that has come to be associated with Communism. It is, amazingly enough, a rather happy kingdom, very effectively and undramatically modernizing itself. The Prince is aware of the currents running through Asia which have given the Communists great appeal as the champions of anti-imperialism—an appeal which extends to Cambodia—but his view of Communist expansion is totally different from that of the State Department.

The United States government bases its view of Communism (its containment policy) on the case of Soviet Russia's expansion through Eastern Europe following World War II. This was accomplished through either direct military occupation or quite obvious infiltration and civil war. It was above all Communism opposed to existing nationalist sentiments. Now, whether the State Department wants to believe it or not, Communism in Asia has been a very different phenomenon. The Chinese Communists have worked very effectively with existing Asian nationalist movements. That is why they now enjoy excellent relations with the most virulent and independent nationalists. The exception often thought of, Tibet, is seen, rightly or wrongly, by Chinese everywhere as an internal affair affecting one of the traditional provinces of China. As to the dispute with India, it is by now clear that the Chinese were in at least as "correct" a position as the Indians. It is simply wrong to take the war in Vietnam as another instance of Chinese aggression. The Vietnamese Communists have been at it as long as the Chinese and actually managed to attain power (1945) before their Chinese counterparts.

Many nationalists in Asia, including those in Cambodia, are worried about Communist expansion, not through military power or subversion, but rather as an ideal that has greater attractiveness than the charisma or program of the individual national leaders. The irony is that this ideal has become infinitely more attractive as a result of a United States policy which has made of the Communists the central fighters against imperialism and for nationalism. There seems little doubt that Sukarno was brought to the conference in Cambodia to demonstrate that one could be a strong nationalist even if not a Communist. But it is this tendency that Prince Sihanouk fears. In his opening speech to the conference he stated it in the most candid terms:

The American armaments have not restrained, much less driven back by one millimeter, the progress of Communism from which the U.S.

pretends to preserve the people of South Vietnam and Laos. On the contrary, the Americans have succeeded in attaining what the socialist powers themselves would have difficulty in doing: to know how in a few years to cast most of the population of South Vietnam and Laos into the arms of Communism, whereas the normal conditions of life of the inhabitants of the prosperous Conchinche and the religious and monarchistic convictions of the Laotians were scarcely predisposed to Marxism.

It is out of this concern with Communism as an ideal made more attractive by the American "presence" that the Prince so desperately desires peace and the withdrawal of the Americans. But he knows that American cooperation is necessary to the establishment of peace. He also has a sufficient enough understanding of American irrationality not to permit himself that hysterical anti-Americanism so common in Asia. His concern is that the United States will cause an extension of the war that will spell the end of Cambodia, and perhaps non-Communist nationalism in Asia as well.

In his address to the conference he stated that it was true that if America was foolish enough to attack China with her 700 million people she would prove indeed to be a paper tiger—*for China*. But for the small countries of Indochina, *"l'impérialisme U.S. est un tigre très réel."*

Sihanouk planned this conference with the hope of producing agreement among the participants on a solution to the war that would ultimately be acceptable to the Americans. In his scheduled opening remarks he tried to introduce this "constructive spirit." He pointed out that the most important thing was to convince the unconvinced—the people of the West—"beginning with the people of the U.S.A." He explained just how difficult this would be, because the United States, "profoundly wounded in its self-respect and its pride," was capable of pursuing the most dangerous course. To the Americans so concerned with "saving face" he offered the example of France. As a result of de Gaulle's policy of withdrawal from the colonies and subsequent support of their independence, the prestige and popularity of France in the underdeveloped world "has never been so great." De Gaulle himself was presented to the delegates as "the greatest chief of state of the 'free' world and the only Western leader worthy of the name." The Prince asked for a reasonable style in the wording of resolutions, "calm and moderate, without hatred or passion."

His program for peace involved a reconvening of the Geneva conference, which would work out the means of foreign withdrawal and the reunification of Vietnam by popular and democratic consultation. The most controversial point was his suggestion "for authentic neutralization of South Vietnam, at least until the time of popular consultation toward unification of the country."

Over the past years, proposals very much like these have been offered by the National Liberation Front, and the main obstacle was the refusal of the United States and England to permit a reconvening of the Geneva conference. But now there was a new difficulty: the NLF had changed its position and it, too, was opposed to any negotiations at this time.

It was clear from the beginning of the conference that Prince Sihanouk's proposals would not be adopted into the final resolutions. When the conference formally opened, Sihanouk merely made some welcoming remarks and contented himself with distributing among the delegates and the press printed copies of his scheduled remarks, rather than delivering them orally. He said that he wanted his address distributed "for history," so that the record would show that a peace proposal did exist. In another time it might have been accepted and ultimately will have to be if peace is to return to Indochina.

The NLF and the North Vietnamese delegations had become intransigent. They maintained throughout the conference that total United States withdrawal from South Vietnam was a prior condition for any negotiations. The Pathet Lao, on the other hand, did accept the Prince's proposals for a reconvened Geneva conference on Laos.

But why the NLF obstinacy and change in position? The answer has to be the United States bombing of North Vietnam. Prior to the start of the bombing, the NLF had continuously called for a new Geneva conference. Immediately following the bombing in January, their leaders in an interview in the French Communist paper *L'Humanité* withdrew the offer. In private conversations the North Vietnamese delegates and those from the NLF expressed the view that to go publicly on record at this time for a negotiated peace would be—to use two old American expressions—"talking with a gun at your head" and "appeasement." The NLF states publicly now that it is quite willing to go on fighting for another twenty years if that is what is necessary to force the Americans out. Perhaps this is partly a bluff, although the Prince thinks otherwise. But what is certain is that neither the NLF nor the North Vietnamese will ever give in to the bombing. To do so would violate not only the essentially obstinate, idealistic, and perverse spirit of the Vietnamese themselves but also the heart of Asian nationalism. American planes and their bombs and rockets are the symbols of "neo-colonialism," just as the sun helmet and rifle were symbols of the older variety. No one in Asia doubts that the white man has superior firepower, but to expect Asians to kowtow to that superiority seriously misreads the times. It is the almost unanimous opinion among those knowledgeable about this part of the world that the Vietnamese and Chinese are quite prepared to take up guerrilla fighting once again rather than give in to the American planes.

It is quite certain that before there can be any possibility of negotiations, the United States will have to desist from such raids for at least several months. But getting the NLF to a peace conference is going to be difficult under any circumstances. They can be expected to dig their heels in at the merest threat of negotiation because of their past experience with such techniques and the history of their movement.

The people in the NLF have been waging a long, hard war for ten years now—despite American insistence to the contrary—with very little support from anyone. They had to fight this war largely because of (as they see it) the treachery of the Geneva conference of 1954 and the subsequent role of the United States. It is important to recall that these people, including the "hard core" Communists among them, were left behind in the South to fend for themselves after the division of the country in 1954. They were told by their leaders in the North that the elections scheduled in the Accords for 1956 would actually be held and that they should prepare for that day. The day never came, since the United States had discovered in Diem a new hope for "democracy" and used its military and financial power to support him in blocking the elections.

The years that followed were very hard on these ex-resistance fighters, who were left to the caprices of the Diem regime. They were rounded up, forced to give public confessions, imprisoned, and tortured. In this period (1954–59) they received no support from the North, which was preoccupied with its own problems and contented itself with periodic calls for the United States to live up to the Geneva agreement.

The second stage of fighting started in the South when these same cadres had had enough of Diem's repression, enough of hoping for a peaceful solution, and took up arms. By all indications, this was done without the approval of the government in Hanoi. They have since fought almost entirely on their own, painstakingly securing arms and building up combat units with little more than moral support from Hanoi and Peking. They are, therefore, not particularly eager to give all this up at the moment of their greatest military successes—with the Saigon regime tottering—simply because the North is now suffering bombardment and Cambodia fears an extension of the war. Neither are they terribly concerned with world peace for the world has not shown itself to be very concerned with their tranquillity. They would, perhaps, under certain circumstances go to the conference table, but they would be skeptical and suspicious bargainers.

It would be nearly impossible (as much for psychological as for political reasons) for them to deal directly with the United States. More importantly, the United States would have to give strong indications prior to the holding of a conference that it accepted the fact that its role in Indochina was at an end. This is what the French did prior to the '54 conference. At the moment, it does not seem likely that the United States will accept any such arrangement, but one must then ask, What is it that the United States wants?

A reading of the American press produces the confidence that there is a great Johnsonian design behind the apparent chaos of our policy in Vietnam. The deliberate sowing of confusion and the contradictory stances have come to be known as the President's manipulative stock-in-trade. One almost expects, as a matter of faith, that he will come up with some grand compromise which will be accepted as a victory by all parties concerned. But traveling in Southeast Asia, one realizes how great a distance separates this world from the one President Johnson inhabits. The idea that Southeast Asian politics may be treated as those of a convention of Democrats or of the United States Congress is perhaps the most dangerous of the Cold War years.

The central problem is that the United States has come to rely on attaining a military position of strength as a prior condition for negotiations. This is particularly dangerous when one realizes that the military position of the South Vietnam–United States Army has never been weaker. Our own officials accept the fact that 80 percent of the countryside is in Vietcong hands, that the South Vietnamese Army will not fight, and that we may not be able to hold out much longer. The prospects for a position of military superiority have never been so dim. This in turn has produced a feeling of desperate frustration among our officials and advisers, many of whom have developed a personal obsession with a "win" policy.

A particularly committed group is the military, which has placed so much of its prestige on victory here. They are convinced that this is the new type of war they must learn to win—a view held in isolation from the political history of Vietnam. Then, too, Vietnam is the only war they have at the moment, and that is why there are seventeen American generals and innumerable colonels in Saigon. A mere major has no status at all. It is the place for quick promotions and the establishment of a combat record. An instance of this is offered by the experience of the Special Forces. Originally sent to Vietnam in '61 as actual combat units, they were granted higher pay, more status, and quicker promotion than other "advisers" in Vietnam. As a result, many of the military careerists occupying desk jobs in Saigon infiltrated the Special Forces, and it soon had no taste for fighting and enough influence to avoid it.

For various reasons, this obsession of a relatively small group of Americans with victory in Vietnam grows. But given the refusal of the South Vietnamese Army to fight (many of the officers have already made their deal with the Vietcong), the United States reliance on a military posture must find another outlet. And thus we have the business of bombing, which if it accomplishes nothing else does allow our personnel in Saigon to feel that they are doing something "dramatic."

We are then at a very dangerous impasse in Vietnam, with neither side willing to make the first moves toward negotiations and with the United States moving toward an irreversible extension of the war. In this impasse it would seem that the proposals put forth by Prince Sihanouk offer the only hope of establishing peace. Time is running out for those who do care about world peace, of those using their influence toward the end of allowing countries like Cambodia, France, and the Soviet Union to take the initiative in Vietnam. If the United States would drop its insistence on a strong military posture, which is hopeless in any case, and support the idea of a Geneva conference, it would have a good chance of success. A reconvened conference would allow the Soviet Union, France, and Cambodia to work out a proposal that could enlist the support of China and England. To date, the English have shown no independence at all from the American position, but perhaps once they are pushed onto center stage they will act more responsibly.

In order for a solution to be acceptable to the NLF it must involve a complete end to the American "presence" in Vietnam. But some Western influence could be retained if the United States passes leadership of the Western position to the French. In return, the NLF would probably accept a period of continued division of the country, some appearances of neutralism, and participation in a coalition government with some mechanism for elections. It must be expected that the NLF will very likely be the dominant force in South Vietnam. For it to be otherwise would require rewriting the history of the past twenty years. But it would be a serious mistake to think of the NLF as a mere pawn of the North, which can ignore the power that various groups in the South, such as the Buddhists and students, have amassed. And to cite Prince Sihanouk again, the longer the United States holds on, the more likely it is that the government of the South will be a replica of the one in the North.

The main problem now is to convince American policymakers that they are not going to obtain a military position of strength, that if they continue using their air power over the North it will make negotiations impossible and will ultimately involve them in a ground war in Asia that nobody wants. They must be convinced that the United States has had its day in Southeast Asia, that the program didn't work and it is now time to retire gracefully. The alternative is to forget what it was that the United States was originally after and simply pursue an adventuristic policy of military victory. This would very much heighten the danger of Communism in Asia rather than lessen it, for the non-Communist nationalists would be squeezed out and the Asians forced to choose between the United States and Asian Communism. There is no question but that they would choose the latter.

It is significant that Sukarno decided to come to the conference, for he is one who knows something about the political winds of Asia. He came, he said, because "I believe that it may be one of the most significant events in the history of Asia." He said that he wanted to show the world that the "nationalists" of the "new emerging nations" were aligned solidly alongside the NLF, the North Vietnamese, and China in "our common resistance to American imperialism."

The French are much more at home in this part of the world than we are and they know that the time of Western leadership is over. As a result, they have been invited back in as a guest, and the impact of French culture and politics will continue to be important. This can be the role of the United States as well. But if it insists on playing out its hand to the end out of a spirit of obstinacy or whatever nightmarish vision of China it might have, it will leave a legacy of hate in Asia that will make the English and French experience seem a love feast. As one old British colonial officer told me: "The timber's here; all that's needed is for you damn fools to go ahead and light it."

(*Ramparts*, July 1965)

The Winner's War

The Pentagon Building, whether by choice or design, seems always to be at war. The lights in its endless corridors are dim and flickering, as if powered by some temporary generator. The offices are in "bays" connected by "rings," and the dull pigment of the walls renders the effect of a bomb shelter. It is only in the past six months that the architecture seems to match the reality of the Pentagon's activity. The military now has, at last, a real war of its own in Vietnam. The time of counter-insurgency, of American advisers helping the Vietnamese "fight for their freedom" is over, and has been ever since the United States escalated the war with the bombing of North Vietnam. The war in the South is now being fought primarily by American troops and American air power against the Vietcong. The Vietnamese who are not with the Vietcong are outside history, unless, as is frequently the case, they happen to get accidentally bombed or shot. The United States has made the decision to use whatever firepower it takes to win in Vietnam, and the men who staff the higher circles in the military carry the air of winners.

All signs indicate that this is the mood of official Washington in the fall of 1965. I was given added confirmation of this as I took my turn around the Pentagon briefing course. The admiral, who is Assistant Secretary of Defense in charge of the Far East, was waiting for me on the fourth floor, Ring D, Corridor 7, Bay 61. He had been, as his secretary said, "alerted" to my arrival, and he was, as is the custom, cheerily optimistic about the war. But this time you can tell he meant it. Vietnam was, he felt, at last defined as basically a military problem of using sufficient American firepower to destroy the enemy. The admiral suggested that if civilians chose to live in areas controlled by the Vietcong, then they became the enemy. Such areas make up about 70 percent of the countryside. He was not overly concerned about Vietnamese civilian reaction to the bombing. He seemed convinced that they would place the blame for their destroyed villages on the Vietcong, that elusive target and "cause" of the bombing, rather than on the Americans, who actually dropped the bombs.

It takes a trip down to the Pentagon public-affairs office to really comprehend the dimensions of the new war. A harried sergeant was munching a tuna-fish sandwich while in animated telephone conversation. It concerned a killed-in-action pilot who had shown up on the Air Force press release but had somehow been left off the joint services weekly total. This department also handles the more important statistics of American air sorties over North and South Vietnam. Most occur in the South, and they average over three hundred a day. The grisly new element is, of course, the B-52 raids (each plane carrying fifteen tons of bombs) which began on June 18, 1965, and have continued as an almost daily occurrence. It might be added that while a very large variety of statistical compilations are maintained in the Pentagon, there are none for Vietnamese civilian dead.

In one of the Pentagon corridors I nodded at a Rand Corporation scholar with whom I had sparred during a teach-in. As I watched the disappearance of this man with his little cluster of officers, I was tempted by a spirit of sportsmanship to run after him and offer my congratulations on his victory in the real world. And it has been a victory of no mean proportions, for it embarked America on a very different course than it had been traveling during the Cold War years. The New War in Vietnam of the Johnson Administration represents a sharp departure from the theory of counter-insurgency developed by the Kennedys. It is, in fact, an attack on the basic assumptions of Kennedy's foreign policy.

Upon coming to power, the Kennedy Administration very quickly implemented the theories of counter-insurgency which up until that point had occupied a vague and minority status within the military Establishment. The basic concept, as applied to Vietnam, held that the Vietnamese would fight against the "Communist" guerrillas if we could convince them of the presumed ultimately disastrous consequences of Communism for their lives. At the same time, it was held essential that we provide them with the military know-how to withstand guerrilla warfare and the technical economic knowledge to implement reforms which would make life in the areas controlled by the government more attractive than under the rule of the guerrillas.

Toward this end, the United States sent its first shipment of 13,000 American advisers—the Special Forces troops that would live with and fight alongside the Diem government's troops. It was also toward this end that we designed the strategic hamlet program, which was intended to give the peasant population security by placing it behind barbed-wire fortifications. While an element of force was at first necessary to get the people into the hamlets, it was expected that they would soon see the advantages to them and that, eventually, the Saigon troops could be replaced with local guards. There were also loans to farmers, community well digging, and other devices which had worked so well on the American frontier.

There is in all this theory of counter-insurgency a basic premise shared with the Communist theory of guerrilla warfare which it opposes. That premise holds that the inhabitants of the country *are* important to the outcome of the struggle being waged there. Both sides take winning the peasantry to be the first and basic step toward victory. Both sides hold that the peasant must be made to care about the war's outcome, since he must do the ultimate fighting. In a strange way, both theories tend to enhance, if not the dignity, then certainly the significance of the individual native of the area. He is, to use an old-fashioned expression, the agent of history.

Unfortunately from the State Department point of view, the Vietnamese didn't turn out to be very useful agents of history. After six years of our designing, financing, and building an economy and government for them, and four years of our advising, equipping, bitching, and fighting with their Army, the situation, by 1964, was far worse than it had been in any of the preceding ten years of United States involvement in Vietnam. By the end of last year [1964], the desertion rate among South Vietnamese troops was said to be up around 30 percent per month, and it was clear that those who remained had no taste at all for fighting. The Vietcong guerrillas were growing ever stronger. Despite everything that we had done to win them over, the Vietnamese peasantry was supporting a guerrilla army that was larger, more elusive, better armed, and more effective than ever—the only difference being that much of the special new anti-guerrilla hardware that we had thrown into the fight was now in their hands.

The theory of counter-insurgency was a highly political one which had never been really believed by the military pros. The only parts of it they bought were the 700,000 helicopter sorties (with repressive fire) that were flown and the snappy new plastic-butt rifles that fired bullets capable of really breaking a man up. But the theory didn't hold water: the peasants didn't buy it and the military pros tired of it. The Kennedy Administration had kept them in line, but President Johnson hardly shares the Kennedy enthusiasm for counter-insurgency.

It was the Air Force which felt most neglected during the counter-insurgency fad, and in the new President they had an ally of long standing. As early as March 15, 1948, in the House of Representatives, Johnson rose to proclaim: "No matter what else we have of offensive or defensive weapons, without superior air power America is a bound and throttled giant; impotent and easy prey to any yellow dwarf with a pocket knife."

Johnson throughout his Senate years remained a strong Air Force lobbyist, and when he assumed the Presidency, one can only guess at the relief felt by Air Force officers who had been forced by the Kennedys to listen to interminable lectures at the Army war college on the political nature of anti-guerrilla war. Now a no-nonsense President would take off the gloves. The first step was the air retaliation against North Vietnam in August 1964 as a result of fighting in the Gulf of Tonkin.

The resistance by the counter-insurgency people to the new Johnson doctrine that was evolving found its most public expression in an article by General Edward G. Lansdale in the October 1964 issue of *Foreign Affairs*. Lansdale, it should be remembered, was the one man most responsible for the theory of counter-insurgency, as well as for our involvement in Vietnam. Lansdale felt that the answer lay in placing even greater emphasis on civic action, and he rejected the course of negotiated peace. But in that issue of *Foreign Affairs* he most pointedly disagreed with what was then clearly shaping up as the Johnson Administration's new policy:

> Some people believe we should plainly identify that struggle as a war and make use of our military proficiency to force the Communist regime in Hanoi to cease its adventure in the South. Some believe we should continue along the present course but greatly increasing the quantity and effectiveness of what is done so that it eventually smothers and kills the Communist insurgency. The anomaly in these reactions is that each falls short of understanding that the Communists have let loose a revolutionary idea in Vietnam and that it will not die by being ignored, bombed or smothered by us. Ideas do not die in such ways.

Perhaps it is true that ideas do not die in such ways, but people do, and as the American military had long perceived, it is the people who must bear the brunt of the ideas. If one could make it very costly to hold such ideas, they would lose their currency.

This is the new program of the all-out American war. Lansdale and others of the counter-insurgency school held theories that were devoid of racism. They thought the peasants were capable of forming and holding political judgments. The Special Forces soldiers had been taught to trust the ultimate wisdom of the peasants—to be willing to go out and live among them. The new "Winner's War" is racist not only in that it is contemptuous of the ability of the Vietnamese people to define and build their own society but more significantly in that it places absolutely no political significance on their hopes, prejudices, and aspirations. It holds that the only significant variables are fear and hunger. Restricting the Vietnamese people to this lower level of animal life not only takes care of any moral concern over systematically bombing them but allows belief that such bombing as a demonstration of American power will induce respect. Similarly, the large-scale deployment of American troops will not rouse nationalist support for the Vietcong (as it would, say, in a European country), but, primarily again, only fear and awe for the Americans. The new program involves a demonstration of military power with local political consideration presumed to be of slight importance.

The significant point here is that the Americans are now doing the main fighting in the South as independent units under their own command and from military bases which they alone protect. High-ranking Vietnamese are not even trusted with advance notice of the battle plans of American troops. The basic tactic of the war has shifted from that of small units fighting small guerrilla forces to massive air attacks, which soften up the enemy, followed by equally massive mopping-up operations. The battle plan is set by the Air Force and involves very simply a demonstration of the capacity of the American war machine for vast destruction in the Vietnamese countryside. The tactic is one of devastation, demoralization, and mopping up.

The new policy, as any follower of evening TV newscasts can perceive, is one of all-out war against the countryside. Its aim is to make the rural areas in which the Vietcong operate unlivable. It is assumed that the populace, for one reason or another, supports the Vietcong, and that the United States, with its saturation bombing, is going to make the price of that support too high. The result will be increasingly large numbers of refugees from the bombed areas. There are already a million refugees, and the policy makes good military sense, since a refugee is by definition so completely disoriented and demoralized that he is incapable of any course of action other than desperately searching for food and shelter. The side which can give him rice and protect him from bombing becomes his master. We now consider it essential to preserve the freedom of the Vietnamese by destroying their ability to choose. "Better dead than Red." This is the clearly established political purpose of the crop spraying, napalm, fragmentation bombing, and B-52 raids.

While it seems obvious that the United States can score a military victory in Vietnam, our planners have not been completely candid on the political implications of such a victory. A nation of the power of the United States can destroy all life in a country as small and weak as Vietnam, and there is little that anyone else can do about it. Neither the North Vietnamese nor the Chinese have the air- or firepower to seriously interfere with the destructive power of the U.S. Air Force and Navy. The Soviet Union, despite all that used to be said about its aggressiveness, seems altogether too defensive and conservative to challenge our military power in Vietnam. The United States can maintain a string of bases along the coast of Vietnam and, by using the

Seventh Fleet and Air Force, protect them with an impenetrable wall of fire. If the United States is willing to commit upward of a million troops (Hanson Baldwin's figure in *The New York Times*), then it should be able to mop up after the air havoc is complete. But to presume that a stable, independent, or free Vietnam will emerge from the ashes, or that American institutions will be admired in that country for anything other than creating and wantonly using military power, is insane.

(*Ramparts*, December 1965)

Lord Russell and the B-52s

I was ambivalent about taking the train that cold February day in 1967 up past the surly coastal towns and trailer camps of North Wales to Penrhyndeudraeth, where I was to interview Bertrand Russell. The prospect of meeting Russell was exciting enough, but as I respect his work, I didn't relish the possibility of having to send back an interview with a man I fully thought could be mad. Perhaps "mad" is too harsh a word, but it is in the spirit of most journalistic accounts of Russell's activities.

The American press works continuously away at its captive audience, and I had come, despite myself, to accept the plausibility of our media's recent and massive denigration of Russell. The object of the attack was his call for an International War Crimes Tribunal on America's actions in Vietnam. The bleaker accounts had it that Lord Russell was all but stuffed and under the control of a wicked puppeteer—the American Ralph Schoenman, whose only passion was a hatred of the country which had raised him. The more responsible *New York Times* merely inquired editorially if "this unsavory business [is] the work of Bertrand Russell, or, in reality, that of Ralph Schoenman? Some will say it makes no difference whether the aged philosopher has become a mere stooge of a bitter propagandist; but it adds a poignant touch to this episode that the answer cannot be known."

I was intrigued by the harshness of the *Times*'s language and the mystery it implied. Since I had come to think of Lord Russell as a sort of international ombudsman concerned with the dangerous global games played by the more recognized heads of state, I was disturbed by the charges. And then, too, why didn't one ever hear any answers to the questions posed by the *Times*?

It was teatime when I arrived at the old Welsh home with its magnificent view of an agriculturally useless valley, rocky but beautifully green. Chris

Farley, one of Russell's aides, ushered me into the lord's sitting room, the one with the flower-print chair. Farley functions as Russell's personal secretary and spends more time with him than does Ralph Schoenman, who is usually trotting around the world somewhere, as he was that day. Russell had not yet descended from the upstairs room where he does most of his work, and I began to scan the bookcases lining the walls, one-third of which were entirely filled with his own contributions.

One of the volumes, *The Practice and Theory of Bolshevism*, had established Russell as a staunch anti-Communist. He persisted in this view during the years that followed its publication, which allowed *Life* magazine on Russell's eightieth birthday in 1952 to excuse his occasional transgressions. In a flattering editorial entitled "A Great Mind Is Still Annoying and Adorning Our Age," *Life* held: "No intellectual in the world has a better anti-Communist record; he went to Russia in 1920 and called the turn in *The Practice and Theory of Bolshevism* so accurately that the book could be reissued unchanged and unchallengeable twenty-nine years later."

But that was fifteen years ago, and I was reflecting on the ups and downs of the lord's relations with the Luce empire when he shuffled into the sitting room to shake hands and offer me China tea and the sandwiches which had been set out on a little table near the fireplace. He was older and weaker-looking than I had expected from those fiery pictures of him that one sees. There is some initial shock in recognizing that the man is, after all, to be ninety-five years old this May. His body is marked by the fragility of age, his walk is more shuffle than stride, and as he goes up and down the staircase, it seems a point of pride for him to rely on the bannister and shun all assistance. It is also clear that he tires easily. But once one is over the impact of Russell's age, it seems a remarkable thing that he has held up so well. There is none of the nervous shaking or doubled-up posture that is associated with the old. The famous Russell head juts out aggressively, just as it does on the bust in his hallway, and when he speaks, his voice dominates the listener and is uncomfortably lucid.

Russell dictates most of his books, and his logic is quite clear, as I discovered when we talked. But he is terribly shy, and that quality combined with his age causes him to speak in a low, distant tone. I was told that his interviews frequently remain on this level, which may account for some of the negative press reports.

After adjusting my little Japanese tape recorder, I began by asking Russell the inevitable question: Why was he no longer as hostile to Communism as he was in *The Practice and Theory of Bolshevism*? He answered: "Well, I think that Communism now is a very much better thing than it was in 1920. It was in 1920 that I condemned it, and in 1920 it was already the embodiment of whatshisname—Stalin. I visited the Soviet Union in 1920 and they all seemed to have a kind of personal bitterness and, well, a punitive psychology, which is not the right one."

Russell's attitude toward the Soviet Union began to shift with the death of Stalin and the liberalization under Khrushchev. He told me, "It is the effect of Bolshevism that it entirely depends on the individual leader. You think it doesn't, but in fact it does. The Soviet government under Khrushchev was a very different thing from the Soviet government under Stalin." I interjected that Khrushchev had suppressed the Hungarian uprising and that Russell had condemned him rather severely for that. He replied, "Yes. Well, I thought it deserved condemnation." And as the old man went on, one was drawn into his world of terribly simple logic and moral consistency.

Professor Sidney Hook and others who now attack Russell had been pleased with his earlier indictment of the Russians. Those Cold War intellectuals had loved Russell on Hungary, but when he came to turn the same moral and logical guns on U.S. involvement in Cuba and Vietnam, they pronounced him a "non-person."

This was the main issue in Bernard Levin's article on Russell, which appeared in *The New York Times Magazine*, on February 19, 1967. Levin, a hawkish English intellectual, was outraged at Russell's refusal to use a double standard in his judgments of the Cold War. The article bore none of the usual marks of obvious restraint which has been the *Times*'s most salable commodity:

What, then, has happened to Russell, grandson of one of Queen Victoria's most distinguished Prime Ministers . . . relentless critic of Communism in theory and practice, friend and associate through three-quarters of a century of many—perhaps most—of the world's greatest statesmen, writers, thinkers? . . .

How has it come about that a man possessed of one of the finest, most acute minds of our time—of *any* time—has fallen into a state of such gullibility, lack of discrimination, twisted logic and rancorous hatred of the United States that he has turned into a full-time purveyor of political garbage indistinguishable from the routine products of the Soviet machine?

Could Levin have been serious in accusing Russell of "rancorous hatred" in the same sentence in which he himself uses the words "full-time purveyor of political garbage"? But Levin is serious, as are *The New York Times*, *The*

(London) *Times*, *Newsweek*, *Look*, and *Time*, which have scorned Russell and held him in contempt.

What the critics cannot accept, psychologically or politically, is Russell's bent for defining the U.S. role in Vietnam as analogous to the German occupation of Czechoslovakia, the French colonialists in Algeria, and the Russians in Hungary.

Levin could hardly be expected to accept this analogy, since he had co-signed a letter to *The* (London) *Times* some weeks before his *New York Times* article was printed which offered "unequivocal support" for the U.S. position in Vietnam. It is certainly his prerogative to offer himself up in that way, but it strikes me as dishonest for him to pretend that his support for the war has nothing at all to do with his criticism of Russell. It is worth noting here as typical of a favorite ploy of Russell's critics who prefer to dwell on the "unreasonableness of Russell's style" rather than confront the issues which he has raised.

Some of the criticism has been humorously beside the point. A recent article in *Look* magazine developed a psychological critique of Russell, centering on his personal relations. The magazine wrote of Russell's ties with his wife: "In her youth Russell had preferred her sister. She was fifty-two, he was eighty, when at last her dream came true." Which is a significant detail, no doubt, but a spokesman for Russell's office pointed out that Lady Russell had no sister.

Russell remains unperturbed by his critics and responds only when it serves to extend his forum, as is the case with his innumerable letters to the press. He is deadly serious about the Vietnam War and keeping the peace, and regrets that he does not have as much time as he used to for indulging the more obvious apologists. I reported on Sidney Hook's most recent criticisms of Russell, and he answered, "Well, I never . . . I can't be bothered with Sidney Hook." And when I asked why there are so many attacks on him, Russell responded, "I suppose they think I'm effective. I cannot see any other reason, but it is the only thing that encourages me."

Since Russell has been accused of being myopic about the government of North Vietnam and simplistic in his support for its position vis-à-vis the United States, I found the following exchange with his assistant, Chris Farley, interesting:

FARLEY: In underdeveloped countries—for example, Ho Chi Minh in North Vietnam has power in a small country, but he has devoted nearly all that state power to development programs, to education, housing, agriculture, that sort of thing. That's not a very dangerous form of state power, do you think, sir?

RUSSELL: No, except for the Vietnamese.

Russell then went on to argue that although the North Vietnamese had been beleaguered by the West and "I support them because of that," their rigorous development programs and discipline had nonetheless been over-emphasized. It was the same mistake the Russians had made earlier: "You see, the Russians in 1920 and following years developed their military entirely, and the result was that when they finished they were all militarists."

Russell has been attacked by many in the English peace movement for allegedly having abandoned his earlier concern with the dangers to the peace of nuclear war, great power rivalry, and chauvinism. He was quite clear in refuting this assertion: "I think that nuclear war is the greatest peril facing the world. I think that it is a greater peril than Communist dictation or conservative dictation, and I should certainly oppose anything that would involve a difficult nuclear war . . . On the whole I think people make too much of the differences between nations. I think the Americans are bad. I think the Russians are bad. I think the Chinese are bad. I think everybody has some badness in them, and I think as they get more power it will get worse. I can't be too enthusiastic about any scheme that involves one power to be given greater power than another."

But, for all his generalizations, in Russell's view the United States is currently the excessive power in the world. Russell was shaken by the lengths to which the United States was willing to go during the Cuban missile crisis to express that power. He was, of course, rather centrally involved in that dispute, becoming at one point a middleman in the exchange between Kennedy and Khrushchev. The behavior then of the Americans—coming as it did after the Bay of Pigs and the increased involvement in Vietnam—convinced him that the United States had assumed primary responsibility for the continuance of the Cold War.

Russell's political categories all deal with power and the personalities who have misused it. In viewing the America of the fifties, he recalls that he disliked John Foster Dulles most of all: "He was a plain prosecutor. It was quite simple. You could have put him in the place of Robespierre, or you could have put him in the place of Bloody Mary. As long as there was someone to prosecute, he was very happy." And his counterpart in the sixties is Lyndon Johnson: "I think he is just an ordinary murderer."

When asked if the United States currently bears the major blame for the continuance of the Cold War, he replied, "Yes, I do . . . but that's just talk. I think the Cold War is essential to the success of the American people on top, and they have to keep it up into a hot war if necessary. They can't live without it, because nothing else will keep them in power. They are in power because they are able to fight those wicked Communists, and then the wicked Communists have a purpose. Otherwise America would go liberal."

While he holds the Americans responsible for the current impasse and condemns them vociferously for the Vietnam War, Russell retains his libertarian suspicions of any governmental power: "I don't really feel inclined to favor any party or nation, or anybody at present—they all seem to be ruffians." Assuming my best college debater stance, I challenged him as to whether he would include the National Liberation Front (Vietcong) with those he placed in the category of ruffians. He replied, "No, not including them, but they haven't been in power. The big nations, the ones that have power, all seem to engage in betraying one another."

Toward the end of our session Russell apologized. "I'm afraid I've given you a very inconclusive interview, but I can't help that because my views are inconclusive. We've come out of one crisis into another." Which, I think, adequately sums up the problem of the two Russells. There have always been two: Russell in contemplation and Russell in combat. Events of the past ten years have forced him to be in sustained combat while the world reality has changed so rapidly that neither he nor his peers have had time to work out a systematic overview or grand theory. Russell has been forced to rely heavily on the political liberalism of the last century. And it is difficult to readily encompass the problems of revolution, underdevelopment, and nuclear violence within that framework. The one principle which does clearly apply is that of self-determination, and Russell clings to it with ferocity. He supports the NLF against the Americans because the NLF is fighting for self-determination in Vietnam, whereas the American are neo-colonialists.

Strangely enough, Russell has turned out to possess a great deal of intellectual humility. This, perhaps, is one of the reasons he surrounds himself with youthful aides in the twilight of his life. Contrary to reports in the press, Russell was not "captured" by these young men. It is quite clear he chose *them*, and primarily for their intellectual as well as physical vitality. They include David Horowitz, author of *Free World Colossus* and *Shakespeare: An Existential View*. He is energetic and humorous and has a great deal of difficulty keeping his creative and prolific outpouring within any specific intellectual or political boundaries. They also include Chris Farley, a solid, hardworking Englishman who was assistant editor of the respectable English publication *Peace News* before joining Russell's staff.

Though Russell's aides are certainly more inclined toward Marxism than their chief, and more radical left than liberal, they are not as entirely predictable as American press reports would have it.

The aides commute between the house in Wales and the London office of the Bertrand Russell Peace Foundation. The entire organization is terribly amateurish and amazingly poorly financed for what is supposed to be a worldwide operation. For all the talk of puppeteers, the fact is that very often Russell does not have any assistants on hand at all. Often they are needed in the London office because the staff there is so thin.

The Bertrand Russell Peace Foundation is run out of two dilapidated rooms on Shavers Place, and one could boost the efficiency of the operation a good deal by donating a decent Xerox machine. It is sad to think that people throughout the world expect this one-woman office to save the peace, and ironical that it has actually done a better job of it than the more highly endowed peace operations throughout the world.

In addition, the Peace Foundation has become a sort of world ACLU, but one which relies on tough letters from Russell to various heads of state in place of legal briefs. A casual visitor to the foundation office gets the impression that every time an Iranian peasant, a Russian poet, or a Chicago Negro is harassed a call is placed to the Peace Foundation.

Any discussion of the Russell operation would be incomplete without the political attitudes of Ralph Schoenman, who is the most influential of Russell's aides-de-camp, and has figured so prominently in the American press's criticism of Russell.

Schoenman's politics began with his undergraduate years at Princeton, where he was beaten up by his fellow classmates for attempting to integrate the eating clubs. He had been drawn to Princeton because H. H. Wilson, who taught there, had developed a reputation for independent radicalism. Schoenman recalls that Wilson later told him, "You have an innate capacity for erecting brick walls and using your head as a battering ram." This remains as good a capsule description of Schoenman's politics and personality as one can provide.

The young Schoenman read Russell voraciously and, as he records in an autobiographical sketch, "was determined to acquire the Russell touch—to become deft and light and devastating." But whereas Russell's iconoclasm was developed within the bosom of the English Establishment, his writings were used by an alienated Schoenman "to do battle with America's cruelty, crassness and impenetrable, superior manner of the chosen Princetonian." It is a phrase which captures his shrillness. Both men are intensely active and involved—but Russell's activity seems part of a natural flow, whereas Schoenman's has a forced intensity which breaks all rhythm.

Schoenman has met many heads of state, and is even rumored to have run a country or two for brief periods, yet he seems a perpetual intruder. It is Russell's letters of recommendation, Russell's intercession, and Russell's correspondence which pave Schoenman's way. Without the majesty of Russell, Schoenman would have the appearance of a hustler. But the appearance would not be accurate.

Schoenman may be thoroughly obnoxious and insolent, as most people who meet him seem to conclude, but he is committed. Russell is one of the few people who can actually stand him, and it is a source of wonder in the British peace movement that Russell is able to spend so many hours in his presence. Perhaps Russell recognizes that much of Schoenman's insolence is warranted. Most people "sell out" their convictions short of risking all. Schoenman seems to risk all several times a month, every month of the year.

He pops up continuously in the most obscure countries with barely legal papers (the United States government has called for his passport several times), an easy target as he plunges determinedly into the hottest sectors of local political life. He slips in and out of countries where he could easily be detained, and has probably demonstrated more courage in the James Bond sense than the most covert operator in the CIA. He is well-informed about the specifics of the political scene in various countries, and in particular about the United States role there. Knowing too much of this sort of thing can make one terribly hardbitten, and Schoenman is that. But he hangs tough, and perhaps that's what Russell was looking for in April of 1960, when Schoenman first approached him for a job. The British peace movement was mushy at that point, and Russell was working toward firmer ground from which to resist the compromisers.

Schoenman came to play an important role because he pushes himself hard (literally eighteen to twenty hours a day), is a totally committed radical, has enormous respect for Russell's work, is bright and easily informed, and in general has the sort of activist's energy which a ninety-five-year-old man must find complementary.

Russell and his chief aide hardly share a common philosophical base, but they do share a sense of immediacy about the world crisis, alarm about the enormous power of the United States, and a disgust at the uses to which it is being put throughout the world—particularly in Vietnam. Schoenman and the other Russell aides hold to a variant of Lenin's theory of imperialism— the United States is the most advanced capitalist nation and controls and exploits the world, Vietnam being a striking example of this.

Russell's own view is closer to Lord Acton than to Lenin. He holds that every national power is a danger to world peace and that the United States and the Soviet Union have switched roles in the Cold War. In the first years following World War II, Stalin's Russia was the most aggressive nation and therefore rightfully had to be contained even, as Russell once suggested, with the threat of nuclear weapons. But with de-Stalinization, the Russians ceased to be so threatening and the ensuing years brought McCarthyism, Dulles, the Bay of Pigs, and finally Vietnam, with Johnson replacing Stalin as the major threat to world peace.

There are real differences, however, in the basis of their positions, and certainly in matters of rhetoric. Those close to the operation claim that Russell gets to see or hear every statement issued in his name. But the pace is at times frantic, and one can imagine hurried calls from the London office to Wales that do not receive the consideration they deserve. The most glaring example of this was Russell's message to the Tri-Continental Conference in Cuba which took a pro-Chinese line in the Sino-Soviet dispute. Russell agrees with Schoenman's position that the Russians are eager to compromise with the West, but he is not as disapproving of this as his aide, for his own fear of accidental nuclear war is more conducive to compromises of this sort.

However, Russell did personally chew out the Russian ambassador for his country's failure to "adequately support" the Vietnamese. His position on this question is not consistent. The problem is that the enormous nuclear power of the United States can be used to blackmail the rest of the world into accepting the political status quo, involving a moratorium on revolution in exchange for one on nuclear war. But for most of the underdeveloped countries, the political status quo assures an economy of desperate poverty and hopelessness. Russell refuses to barter the right of revolutions for "peace," but he remains enormously concerned with the threat of nuclear destruction.

The documents issued over Russell's signature are consistent as to content; but there are clearly two styles. The statements drafted and worked over by Russell have elegance, logic, and restraint, while Schoenman's are terribly crude. It would be better if Lord Russell issued fewer statements.

Schoenman has also done Russell a serious disservice in his handling of the mass media. He is petty, overprotective, and embittered, the qualities least fortunate in a PR man. And his judgment is bad. For all his protection, some of the worst reporters slip through, while more objective ones are kept at arm's length. There was even a very fat man from Chicago who arrived at the Russell home unannounced and managed somehow to fall, literally, on Lord Russell, who was walking in the garden. Because of Russell's age it was a serious incident, but the fat man from Chicago slipped away unquestioned.

There can be no doubt that in their relationship Schoenman has had an impact on Russell's thinking and that Russell has, during this period, moved toward a more radical and more anti-American stance. But it is terribly parochial for Americans to assume that this is because Russell has been manipulated rather than because of what has happened to America during these past six years. The fifties are remembered by most of us, correctly or not, for Korea, Hungary, and Berlin—for Stalin and the vestiges of Stalin. But the sixties are Cuba and Vietnam, and it is during the sixties that Russell has become increasingly anti-American. Russell is a voracious reader of the press and has a steady stream of visitors of all political persuasions. It is impossible that Schoenman could have made up or denied Russell relevant facts. Nor would it have been necessary. If Russell had selected an assistant who attempted to soften the implications of the United States position on Vietnam, he would have verbally cut him up and sent him packing. In the *New York Times* article criticizing Russell, Levin stated the relevant question: "Russell is not *senile* . . . What Russell puts his hand to, he believes. What we have to decide is why he believes it."

Throughout this century and a good portion of the last, Russell's thin, reedy voice has called the powerful to task for their excesses, and his War Crimes Tribunal is in that spirit. It is the fight he loves best, and one can imagine him up at eight with his first morning tea, shuffling about in slippers, dictating at a furious pace his calls to conscience and letters to heads of state and *The* (London) *Times*, urging that the logic of the matter be considered. It is a pace that is maintained with the aid of four Red Hackle Scotches, Metrecal, and innumerable cups of tea (he is no longer permitted solids) until after ten at night, when the lord often arises from his bed to add a particularly incisive point before the day's mail is sent out.

The irony is that for all the vaunted Marxism of some of the leaders of the War Crimes Tribunal—Ralph Schoenman, Jean-Paul Sartre, Vladimir Dedijer, Isaac Deutscher, and others—it is nevertheless an event which falls squarely within the English liberal political tradition. The standards to be used are those of the Western "democracies"—the Geneva conventions, the Nuremberg trials, and the Kellogg-Briand Pact. The very act of lone intellectuals, devoid of the power of party, movement, or state "judging" the real powers-that-be should appear somewhat ludicrous to an old European Marxist. But the official call to the War Crimes Tribunal is in a language more reminiscent of the great documents of Western democracy:

> We command no state power; we do not represent the strong; we control no armies or treasuries. We act out of the deepest moral concern and depend upon the conscience of ordinary people throughout the world for the real support—the material help, which will determine whether people in Vietnam are to be abandoned in silence or allowed the elementary right of having their plight presented to the conscience of Mankind.

Russell himself supplied the basic "material" help for the tribunal by lending it the $200,000 advance which he received from American publishers Atlantic–Little, Brown for the rights to his autobiography. In his initial statement about Vietnam to the tribunal he said:

As I reflect on this work, I cannot help thinking of the events of my life, because of the crimes I have seen and the hopes I have nurtured. I have lived through the Dreyfus case and been party to the investigation of the crimes committed by King Leopold in the Congo. I can recall many wars. Much injustice has been recorded quietly during these decades . . . I do not know any other conflict in which the disparity in physical power was so vast. I have no memory of any people so enduring, or of any nation with a spirit of resistance so unquenchable.

Lord Russell is joined on the tribunal by Jean-Paul Sartre, who is its executive president. These two great philosophers respect each other for mutual integrity and courage, but not for their philosophies. Sartre is noticeably absent from Russell's A *History of Western Philosophy*. Russell is, of course, totally unappreciative of Sartre's Marxism, or of any other variety. When interviewed by NBC on his eightieth birthday, he remarked: "Marx pretended that he wanted the happiness of the proletariat. What he really wanted was the unhappiness of the bourgeois and it was because of . . . that hate element that his philosophy produced disaster."

Sartre, for his part, considers Russell to be one of the best of the bourgeois thinkers and lets it go at that.

The attitude of the various members of the tribunal toward their colleagues is a mixture of wariness and admiration. When Russell appeared at the first meeting of the tribunal with most of its members present, he turned to one of his aides and asked, "Which one do you suppose will abandon us first?" Sartre accepts the work of the tribunal as useful but not revolutionary. In an interview which appeared in the English *New Left Review* he stated, "We have been reproached with petit bourgeois legalism. It is true, and I accept that objection."

Sartre's defense of the tribunal involves a notion of "limits." "The whole problem is to know if, today, the imperialists are exceeding the limits. . . . Our tribunal today merely proposes to apply to capitalist imperialism its own laws."

In the process Sartre then accepts, as do the other members of the tribunal, what he defines as "an international jurisprudence which has slowly been built up." In this sense, it is Russell who has influenced the Marxists and not the other way around, for the notion of international jurisprudence would seem to conflict with that of class struggle and revolutionary ethics.

The tribunal is not concerned with pronouncing on the wisdom of the war in Vietnam, which is more properly the subject of political analysis and polemic; it is concerned with whether specific acts of the United States have violated the international law which American society itself has accepted and applied freely to others.

One of the major charges leveled against the tribunal by the Western press centers on its refusal to judge the NLF as well as the Americans. The response of the tribunal has been that a resistance movement, almost as a matter of definition, cannot commit war crimes. Sartre has stated:

> I refuse to place in the same category the actions of an organization of poor peasants, hunted, obliged to maintain an iron discipline in their ranks, and those of an immense army backed up by a highly industrialized country of 200 million inhabitants. And then, it is not the Vietnamese who have invaded America nor who have rained down a deluge of fire upon a foreign people. In the Algerian war, I always refused to place on an equal footing the terrorism by means of bombs which was the only weapon available to the Algerians, and the actions and exactions of a rich army of half a million men occupying the entire country. The same is true in Vietnam.

It seems to me that the critics of the tribunal have difficulty accepting not the logic of this argument but the analogy. For surely they would not have had the Nuremberg commission investigate the Resistance fighters of the Warsaw Ghetto, or the Dewey commission the behavior of the victims of Stalin's purge. Obviously, Levin and others who support the war in Vietnam cannot accept this analogy, but they would be more honest to argue about that than the lack of "neutrality" on the part of the tribunal members.

The tribunal has done important work, particularly by sending teams to North Vietnam to investigate the effect of American bombing. It was through the work of one such team that the world learned of the extensive use of "pineapple" and "guava" fragmentation bombs against the civilian population of North Vietnam. At the time, the Defense Department denied it was using such weapons, but it has recently owned up.

But the tribunal has to date failed in its potential for confronting America with the enormity of its actions in Vietnam. The responsibility for this failure must be traced to the poor organization of the tribunal, which has fallen into the nightmarish world of little left sects, and in the center of all the confusion—apparently enjoying every minute—is Ralph Schoenman.

The tribunal offices in London and Paris are in very bad condition. The four members of the London staff spent the better part of the afternoon of my visit in a room of cracked green paint fixing the inevitable mimeograph machine on which so many hopes rested. Given the poverty and limited manpower of this operation, I hesitate to make any criticisms, particularly of

Ralph Schoenman, who has struggled to hold the whole thing together. But he has also been its worst enemy. He is the sort of political organizer who determines the purity of his organization by its ability to resist members.

The whole operation of the Peace Foundation and the War Crimes Tribunal has been devoid of cadres. One member of the foundation defined it as a political party of four. The Paris and London offices of the tribunal until recently had no more than twenty-five volunteers between them. These were drawn almost exclusively from one of the Trotskyist groups and from a splinter of the Paris Maoists, who, as is the nature of such people, tended to fight inordinately and were constantly walking out. At one point in March, when I was in Paris, there simply was no working staff in the office. It would seem that Schoenman's whole method of operation is geared to driving out anyone who will not be subjected to his discipline.

The tension between Schoenman's sectarianism and the broader purposes of the tribunal as publicly defined by Russell and Sartre broke out into the open last March, when Paris members of the tribunal asserted their prerogatives. The members of the tribunal, outside of Russell, are generally critical of Schoenman, and the main work of the tribunal is now in Paris. Schoenman has been barred from entering France by the de Gaulle government.

This is probably the only organization of its kind in which the "big names" do the bulk of the work. Isaac Deutscher, the biographer of Stalin and Trotsky; Vladimir Dedijer, who is Tito's biographer; Giselle Halimi, the beautiful French woman who is Sartre's lawyer; and Simone de Beauvoir meet every second or third weekend for work sessions which set the policy of the tribunal. Sartre himself has been more intimately involved than in any political activity since the Algerian war.

It is strange company for Lord Russell, who began his century of life on the knees of men like Gladstone and ends it by writing letters to Vladimir Dedijer, the Yugoslav Communist partisan, concerning the failure of the leaders of the West to retain their reason. The journalists who came to query Russell at the tribunal's press conferences were irritated that he did not accept questions and shuffled off after reading his text. They indicted him in their articles the next day for rudeness. Why were they not irritated with the other famous democrats of Russell's time who had left him to stand alone before the kleig lights burning his old eyes, to once again confront madness with logic? Perhaps it is the century that has been rude to Lord Russell by failing his hopes so completely that in the weariness of ninety-four years he was forced to travel once again the five bone-shattering hours from Wales to London to "prevent the crime of silence."

On the rare occasions when the mass media in America have been inclined to criticize the war in Vietnam, their critique has been marginal. Vietnam has always been referred to as that "dirty little war," something we were "dragged into," an "aberration," the result of a series of "mistakes." We can't take Russell, for he tells us that this is arrant nonsense, that we in fact bear total responsibility for Vietnam. And, as he reminds us in almost daily incantations, it was United States financing which made possible the return of French colonialism between 1948 and 1954 when we put Diem in power, which instituted the strategic hamlet program of putting the Vietnamese peasants in "camps," and which has systematically obliterated the countryside of North and South Vietnam.

It is a war nurtured within the Cold War bureaucracy which, like any other bureaucracy, must justify its activities in a perfectly "reasonable" and matter-of-fact tone. Even company critics Arthur Schlesinger and James Reston talk of the anguish of the President and the loneliness of his decision-making, and newspaper editors universally shore up the image of American innocence by depicting the plight of a President who has been forced to wage war because the enemy will not let him wage peace. And this is actually believed.

Well, Lord Russell has cut through all that with his War Crimes Tribunal, and like it or not, there now exists an alternative frame of reference in which to place the specific incidents of the war. We are a people who with complete equanimity judged Khrushchev the Butcher of Budapest, but must now seek to destroy the reputation of a man who passes similar judgment upon us. We charge Lord Russell with having "betrayed" the values of Western civilization, with having been "captured," because we cannot accept the concept that it is we who are the "betrayers" and the "captured."

Lord Russell, the godson of John Stuart Mill, will die the quintessence of the democratic citizen—the *Citoyen Terrible*. If in his last years he is "anti-American" and must now judge our President a murderer, then it is not his actions that ought to be scrutinized but our own. We have lost face with Lord Russell, and all the bombs of the B-52s will not change that.

(*Ramparts*, May 1967)

The Language of Torturers

Daniel Ellsberg twisted his tanned athletic body out of the poolside lounge and dropped the telephone receiver back into its cradle. "Well, so much for Bob McNamara; he can't testify—the World Bank won't let him. You know, he said that he still hasn't gotten around to reading the Pentagon Papers!"

Ellsberg's look of disappointment indicated that Robert McNamara had finally broken some special ethical code which the two of them had once shared.

In a former life, Professor Daniel Ellsberg had been one of McNamara's bagmen. It had been his job to take details of planned sabotage ventures against North Vietnam over to the White House to Professor McGeorge Bundy for presidential review. Once Ellsberg got back to the Pentagon with the shopping list approved, the plans were put into action: fisherman were kidnapped, fishing junks booby-trapped, bridges demolished, villages bombarded, and anti-personnel mines planted in populous areas.

This all had to be a top-secret, high-level affair, for it contradicted international law, the Geneva Accords, and the speeches of the American President to the American people. Then, as now, the President was babbling about "aggression from North Vietnam." But as the Pentagon Papers so clearly illustrate, quite the opposite was true. As Ellsberg recalls, "The situation that I entered in mid-1964, as it looks to me now, amounted to a conspiracy. The officials who became my colleagues were concerting, in secrecy, to plan and ultimately to wage aggressive war against North Vietnam."

Ellsberg came to realize that he, McNamara, and the other higher officials were co-conspirators to commit war crimes, and in an act of confession he turned over the Pentagon Papers to the public. He now faces 115 years in jail for his troubles.

McNamara has confessed to nothing and has as a result been given the very trusted position of head of the World Bank, where he can continue his work with the "underdeveloped countries."

This, then, is the great irony of the Pentagon Papers: that for all the detailed minutiae of criminal activity recorded in their pages, and although their veracity is unchallenged, the only indictments to occur are of the men who made it all public.

It is a stunning tribute to the resiliency of the American system that the man responsible for those indictments should be Richard Nixon, who as much as anyone is associated with the crimes recorded in the papers. Nor has the publication of the papers, which clearly define the United States as the aggressor in Vietnam, in any apparent way inhibited the ability of this President to raise the war to its most atrocious level.

But Nixon is an old hand at playing the games of American and Vietnamese democracy. As Vice President he had helped devise the idea that the French were the real saviors of Vietnamese freedom and that we should risk general war with nuclear weapons to support them. Later, in 1964, when his ex-running mate Lodge was rigging elections in Vietnam, he bounced into Saigon, where he met with Ellsberg and others at the house of CIA agent Edward Lansdale, who was then Ellsberg's boss. When Lansdale, ever the "Quiet American," naïvely informed Nixon that he was trying over Ambassador Lodge's objections to get a fairly "honest" election, Ellsberg recalls Nixon saying:

" 'Oh sure, honest, yes, honest, that's right—so long as you win!' With the last words he winked, drove his elbow hard into Lansdale's arm, and, in a return motion, slapped his own knee."

Well, the old knee-slapper knows how to deal with the "crisis of the Pentagon Papers." The best defense is a good offense—call them traitors and hit 'em with espionage charges. Which is what Ellsberg and his co-defendant Tony Russo are charged with. Russo's fingerprints did not appear on all the documents, so he faces only thirty-five years. The first indictment charged them with "theft." But once the publicity died down the heavier counts were added on.

This escalation of the charges aims at preventing a domino effect throughout the federal bureaucracy, the Pentagon Papers being merely a peek into one corner of one agency. If the information available to the Defense Department bureaucrats is so shattering to public perceptions about the war, it is still only a mere fraction of what a Kennedy, a Johnson, or a Nixon has known all along. With the proliferation of Xerox machines throughout the government there is now the technological base for similar leaks in all governmental agencies.

Petty theft would not justify the heavy sentences needed to frighten off future Ellsbergs. The espionage charge provides just the right note of dastardliness to the "crime." But espionage for what enemy? The defense will center on the fact that it is the American Congress, press, and public who are defined as the "enemy" to whom Ellsberg and Russo turned over these secrets. The espionage count may also permit the defense to introduce evidence about the illegality of the war because it relates to the defendants' intent. It may also allow for an examination of the connection between Vietnam and national security.

The government took this risk because it needs the aura of espionage. The government requires "criminals" of a high order outside its own loyal ranks to conceal the real indictment of the Pentagon Papers. For no matter how restrained, balanced, and gentle a temper of mind one brings to a reading of the Pentagon Papers they remain an irreducible record of the activities of restrained, balanced, and gentle mad-dog killers. Even those who authored the Pentagon history shared the mental set of its death prose. Ellsberg and Russo shared it. They only began to break it by "theft"; by conspiring in Chinese restaurants to Xerox in advertising agencies—two Cold War Whiz Kids freaking out over a whole other way of using their energy and brilliance.

If it had only been for some future book on America's policy options or private gossip, hell, that could be understood. It's traditional in such circles, which thrive on "top-secret" cocktail chatter and prudent government leaks. But Ellsberg and Russo broke the rules. They became obsessed with the idea that the *public* had a need and a right to know this stuff. Bad form. It is one thing to let your mistress or colleagues at Harvard in on some choice tidbits, but quite another for an untrained public, unaware of the complexities of data gathering and evaluation, or the subtleties of foreign policy decision-making, to just be presented with an official certified record of the whole mess.

Ellsberg at first attempted vainly to give the documents to "responsible" members of Congress. But the Fulbrights, McGoverns, and McCloskeys all balked at being a party to "theft." At which point, according to the accepted script for such matters, these concerned scholars should have shelved the papers and signed another petition or two. In pushing past that point Ellsberg and Russo have brought themselves to the brink of a fairly radical view of the illegitimacy of current American governmental power. Ellsberg now says that the government is so morally compromised that it has basically lost its right to have secrets, and that the people should grab back what scraps of information they can as the only possible check on its perfidy. Russo goes further and argues that it is not just a question of knowing what this government is up to and challenging it, but also of going on to dismantle it.

Secret Documents & Beer Cans

The political and stylistic differences between the two are obvious and have caused serious tensions. Ellsberg worked at a higher rank, was an intimate of important Washington officials, and a consultant at a fairly high level in sensitive matters such as the Cuban missile crisis. He is intensely cerebral and still enamored with the trappings of upper-class power. He attends his Harvard class reunions and is never publicly gross. Even minor imperfections do not sit well with him. One person working on the trial told me that talking to him is like going to see your high-school principal. He can be aloof and stiff, but he is also, I think, very decent, well-intentioned, humorous, and even warm. Unfortunately he is one of those people who associates such qualities with weakness and chaos. Daniel Ellsberg hates chaos and loves Harvard, and it is a serious measure of the disarray of American society that he should now have to turn even in this limited way to the company of radicals for sanity and support.

Tony Russo loves every moment of it, including the chaos. His one-bedroom apartment near the Rand Corporation and the beach bars of Santa Monica is a litter of clothing, articles, secret documents, unwashed dishes, and beer cans, with Tony plunked down in the middle of it, oblivious to the clutter, furiously scratching his stomach and laughing about the stupidities of some article he's reading. He is easily distracted by just about anyone who drops by, which happens frequently. Where Ellsberg is very jealous of his time and will put people off unless they are pursuing an intense and logical train of thought that interests him, Tony seems to really love to get down with people—any people, and on any level.

These differences showed up early in working styles during the trial. The Ellsberg team keeps its distance off in plush Bunker Hill Towers, a high-rise security complex which, with its intricate system of passes and locks, is more inaccessible than the Pentagon. There is some bitterness among younger people working on the trial toward the "towers"; one reason being that it's famous as an example of people removal—urban renewal. The Ellsberg setup has the feel of the McGovern operation—professional, liberal, and run by middle-aged men who talk about the "kids." The kids work out of the funkier 4th Street office, which houses Russo's lawyers and the Pentagon Papers Peace Project. There is no discernible distance between Tony and the Movement-type younger people working on the trial. Along with his wife, Katherine Barkeley, and the lawyers, including Leonard Weinglass of the Chicago Conspiracy trial, this part of the trial is the typical Movement mélange—sleeping bags on the floor, midnight forays for pizza and other amenities, a continuous babble of controversy about what it all means, hard work, disarray with a nice communal feel to it.

Katherine is the opposite of the "wife," and is therefore an irritant in the male environment of the trial. She has been the main person pushing the political aspects over the legal, which is the goal of the Pentagon Papers Peace Project she organized. Lenny Weinglass is disciplined, determinedly working on the legal stuff, but for a well-known lawyer he is unique in not pulling rank on political questions. He was even hesitant to assert his need for some peace and quiet and at one point picked his head out of a massive legal volume to state plaintively over the ringing phones and the heated discussions about who should drive the truck to the launderette, that "they want me to live in a dome in the back yard in Echo Park. A dome!"

Both the defendants are in agreement that the trial should expose the government's deceptions on the war as revealed in the Pentagon Papers. The government prosecutor will fight this to the end. He will claim that the only criminals are Ellsberg and Russo, "nor is the government or any other person on trial for anything . . . it does *not* involve policies concerning United States military involvement in the defense of South Vietnam . . . it does *not* involve the question of whether or not the Congress or the public was entitled to know what the 'Pentagon Papers' contained."

Which, if true, is eloquent testimony to the irrelevance of the American judicial system to serious questions of public issues or justice. Here is a government which, according to its own biased account, the Pentagon Papers, has for almost one-quarter of a century, in violation of its own statutes as well as international law, contributed to the maiming and death of hundreds of thousands of people. Yet one which claims the absolute and inviolable right to keep a record of such infamy from its people, to automatically punish those who attempt to make it public, and which asserts that such guilt "does not involve the questions of the defendants' motives . . . does not involve the nature, motivation, or conduct of the government."

In requesting that the judge so instruct the jury, the government, which had managed to so effectively deceive the public about its record in Vietnam, presented itself as a helpless victim of a mass media that seemed to be controlled by the two defendants: "They and their counsel have been objects of adoration in many articles . . . these create, among others, the false impression that the case involves or relates to . . . the morality, course and conduct of the U.S. military involvement in Vietnam . . . the government is characterized as secretive, abridging freedom of the press, concealing information from the public, opposing Congress' right to know, corrupt and inept in bringing the case; conducting abusive, harassing and illegal investigations; and committed to pressing false charges." Well?

The judge is then asked by the government to instruct the jury that none of that is true. In the pretrial motions, the judge seemed to follow the prosecutor's wishes. It is difficult to see how men can be judged criminal for turning over papers necessary to the national security without discussing the content of the papers, or how one can discuss the content of the papers without dealing with the "morality, course and conduct of U.S. military involvement in Vietnam." But then again, most of us are not legally trained, and that is why we pay prosecutors Nissen, Reese, and Barry to do it for us. They are the attorneys for the plaintiff, which is us—the People of the United States of America. We as a people, then, have a complaint against these two men—we complain that they gave us information about what was really going on in Vietnam. Terrific.

Why Vietnam?

In any event, no matter what happens inside the courtroom, some working on the trial hope that public interest in the case will provide an opportunity for extensive educational work outside of it. The Pentagon Papers Peace Project was formed with the express aim of distributing video, radio, and printed material about the papers, including a new condensed version.

The sad fact is that for all the furor over their publication, few people have bothered to read the papers themselves, even in the Bantam–*New York Times* abridged version. The papers are formidable in detail, repetitive, and, in the absence of a larger context, dull. They are interoffice memos in the death house—cold, impersonal, bureaucratic. As Ellsberg noted on CBS just after releasing them: "The fact is that in the seven to ten thousand pages of this study, I don't think there is a line in them that contains an estimate of the likely impact of our policy on the overall casualties among the Vietnamese, or the refugees to be caused, the effects of defoliation in an ecological sense . . . That says nothing, more or less, than our officials never did concern themselves, certainly in any formal way or in writing, and I think in no informal way either, with the effect of our policies on the Vietnamese."

United States aims were broken down statistically by Assistant Secretary of Defense John T. McNaughton as "70 percent—to avoid a humiliating U.S. defeat; 20 percent to keep South Vietnam [and the adjacent] territory from Chinese hands; 10 percent to permit the people of South Vietnam to enjoy a better, freer way of life. Not to 'help a friend'—although it would be hard to stay in if asked out."

But this begs the great unanswered question of the Pentagon Papers: "Why Vietnam?" If the United States hadn't gone into Vietnam to support the

French and the puppets who came later, then the question of defeat—humiliating or otherwise—would never have come up. If we were there not because of the Vietnamese but rather because of China or Russia, then why is the war at its most intense point after Nixon's "friendly" visits to those two countries? What was the "threat" of Ho Chi Minh when the papers show beyond any doubt that he was a nationalist Communist concerned, above all, with the independence of his country, and that his actions were as often opposed as supported by the Soviet Union? Whom did he threaten? Certainly not the vast majority of the Vietnamese people, who the papers tell us supported him enthusiastically. What has it all been about?

It is perhaps the single most important revelation of the Pentagon Papers that their authors—as brilliant and well-trained a group of intellectuals as the government could assemble from within its ranks—never got around to dealing with the one question which any untrained citizen, brilliant or not, who was not working for the government, would have asked from the outset: Why did we do this? Not why did we exercise option A rather than B, or why was this agency's estimate more accurate than that one's. But rather, why did the U.S. government for the past twenty-five years, under four different Presidents, systematically and fanatically subvert, obstruct, coopt, pervert, decimate, maim, butcher, and kill the Vietnamese people every time they moved to make their own history? Why did the United States of America do this?

It is rather strange. Imagine a seven-thousand-page study of Rome-Carthage relations which never once examined the causes of the war in terms of the social structure of either society, class tensions, racial animosities, foreign and domestic needs, the role of ideology, or the power structure, but instead concentrated on such questions as whether it was correct to use chariots.

The training which these Cold War intellectuals received was aimed precisely at such brilliant irrelevance—what C. Wright Mills called "crackpot realism." Such training was essential to their utility to the government because anyone with half a brain intact who had access to the Pentagon files would have come up with an analysis so radical and far-reaching in its implications as to make him or her unemployable in the government. For it would have had to deal with the specter that was haunting the United States in the Cold War—not Russian or Chinese aggression, but rather the thing that comes up continuously throughout the papers but is never brought together—the specter of a popular revolutionary struggle. The deeper the United States got in, the more ominous this specter. It is one thing for a revolution to defeat a dying French colonialism, and another to thwart the United States in the finest hour of its burgeoning empire. Particularly after it has committed a half million of its troops to the effort. That is the "humiliating defeat" John McNaughton was talking about. Humiliating, not primarily in some Maileresque psychological sense of the familiar abstractions of "pride" or "face." Humiliating as an example to the world that, with all its power massed, Uncle Sam could be taken. And if thirty million Vietnamese with their primitive technology could do it, what people in the world, with similar organization and politics, couldn't? That was the specter. What exactly was being threatened? Imperialism?

Early Intentions

Despite the Cold War bias of its authors and the selectivity with which they quoted from the original documents, the evidence is still quite clear. The history of Vietnam since World War II, as recorded in the Pentagon Papers, is a history of revolution and neo-colonialism—it is never a matter of repelling Soviet or Chinese Communist aggression.

First there was French colonialism. "France has had the country—thirty million inhabitants—for nearly one hundred years, and the people are worse off than they were at the beginning," stated President Roosevelt. "France has milked it for one hundred years." But, as the Pentagon study observes, "despite his lip service to trusteeship and anti-colonialism, F.D.R. in fact assigned to Indochina a status of free territory to be reconquered and returned to its former owners."

The policy was not to change. "Shortly following Truman's entry into office, the United States assured France that it had never questioned, 'even by implication, French sovereignty over Indochina.' "

The American public has been continuously misled by five Presidents into thinking that the Vietminh, led by Ho Chi Minh, were some kind of foreign agents sent there by Moscow as a move in the Cold War to upset the balance of power and test our resolve. But the Pentagon Papers state "the Vietminh was the main repository of Vietnamese nationalism and anti-French colonialism. . . ." Yet, Secretary of State Dean Acheson told the American public that Ho Chi Minh was "the mortal enemy of native independence in Indochina."

The United States projected first Emperor Bao Dai and then Diem as the true champions of independence. This was the non-Communist alternative of what the Pentagon study calls the "reform parties. . . . Narrowly based among the small educated Vietnamese elite, these parties made little pretense at representing the masses of the peasantry—except in the ancient mandarinal sense of paternal leadership . . . The reformist parties were further discredited by collaboration with the Japanese during World War II. These parties formed the basis for the Bao Dai solution to which France and the U.S. gravitated in the late 1940's."

By contrast, "the Viet Minh was irrefutably nationalist, popular, and patriotic. It was also the most prominent and successful vehicle of Viet nationalism in the 1940's. To a degree it was always non-Communist." Pity we didn't have that admission when the Pentagon was sending its intellectuals around to campuses during the teach-ins. And pity we didn't have the 1948 State Department report that "evidence of Kremlin-directed conspiracy was found in virtually all countries except Vietnam . . . If there is a Moscow-directed conspiracy in Southeast Asia, Indochina is an anomaly so far."

A State Department appraisal of Ho Chi Minh in July 1948 noted that the "Department has no evidence of direct link between Ho and Moscow but assumes it exists, nor is it able to evaluate amount pressure or guidance Moscow exerting. We have impression Ho must be given or is retaining large degree latitude . . . Furthermore, Ho seems quite capable of retaining and even strengthening his grip on Indochina with no outside assistance other than continuing procession of French puppet governments."

The specter was not "international Communism" led by Moscow but revolutionary Communism led by "native" nationalist figures. In fact, the Pentagon Papers show that Moscow and the French Communist Party under its influence hesitated to even support the Vietnamese politically.

During the last years when the French public was tired of the war, the United States under Dulles tried frantically to rev it up, even at the risk of nuclear "general war." Nuclear weapons were frequently mentioned as the necessary response to an anticipated Chinese intervention. The language of the memos is chillingly matter-of-fact on this: "Nuclear weapons will be available for use as required by the tactical situation and as approved by the President."

The United States wanted "nothing short of a military victory in Indochina . . . the United States actively opposed any negotiated settlement in Indochina at Geneva." Why this willingness to risk "general war" involving nuclear weapons? Because the "free world strategic position, not only in Southeast Asia but in Europe and the Middle East as well, is such as to require the most extraordinary efforts to prevent Communist domination of Southeast Asia." This says a great deal about the needs of an American empire challenged by forces of revolution and nothing at all about the self-determination of the Indochinese. They are referred to throughout the memos as "natives," presumed to be on the other side.

Dulles stated in a cable two months before the Geneva agreement that "cease-fire generally would involve serious risks of native people's rising with resultant massacre of French." The United States opposed a negotiated settlement because it would mean Ho's coming to power in Vietnam by popular mandate. Eisenhower had said as much in his memoirs and we all noted it in endless teach-ins, but it remained for the Pentagon Papers to "prove" it. For example, the Joint Chiefs of Staff reported on March 12, 1954, that "current intelligence leads the Joint Chiefs of Staff to believe that a settlement based upon free elections would be attended by almost certain loss of the Associated States to Communist control."

The documents of the last months up to the Geneva truce are a macabre dialectic of assertions of the popular base of the insurrection in Vietnam and the need for the United States to risk general nuclear war to suppress it.

Major General Thomas Trapnall, Jr., Chief of MAAG (Military Assistance and Advisory Group), stated on May 3, 1954: "The battle of Indochina is an armed revolution which is now in its eighth year . . . where the leader of the Rebels [Ho] is more popular than the Vietnamese Chief of State [Bao Dai]."

Two days later, Dulles asked, "Is the United States prepared to acquiesce in the clearly engineered Communist aggression . . . even though we evaluate the loss as very serious to the free world and even though we have the military means to redeem the situation (the A-bomb)?" (Dulles's parentheses.)

The documents show top generals foaming at the chance to use those nuclear weapons against China. Arthur Radford, Chairman of the Joint Chiefs of Staff, couldn't contain himself: "Employing atomic weapons, whenever advantageous, as well as other weapons . . . against those military targets in China . . . such action requires an enlarged but highly selective atomic offensive." Against these maniacs the other side did well, for the sake of all of us, to pursue the negotiations at Geneva. Fortunately, French public opinion did not allow the French government to go along with the United States schemes to intensify the war. So the Geneva Accords happened—but Dulles was already on the move.

The new face of Ngo Dinh Diem was brought in to replace Bao Dai as the symbol of "independent Vietnam," and United States neo-colonialism replaced old-fashioned French colonialism. Document 95 of the Pentagon Papers is a partial summary of CIA agent Edward Lansdale's exploits in helping to set up and maintain the Diem regime.

Lansdale created the Saigon Military Mission, which was "born in a Washington policy meeting early in 1954" before the fall of Dien Bien Phu. It was a covert operation with the highest governmental support, run through CIA channels and operated in blatant violation of the Geneva Accords.

The United States role was characterized by a racism more subtle but no less vicious than that of the French. By racism I mean not merely the slurs about "loyal natives" but rather the basic notion that the Vietnamese are incapable of making fundamental decisions about their lives that are correct for them, even if incompatible with American goals. Lansdale and the U.S. mission then as now had one central aim—to prevent the coming to power of a Vietnamese revolution which had an ideological basis the United States found repugnant.

The "Elections"

Even if a revolution were to be voted into power through the free elections called for in the Geneva Accords, that would only mean that people had voted "wrong." The United States sought to cover its opposition to elections by having Diem propose conditions for an election so stringent that the other side could not accept them. Diem refused, knowing that no matter how stiff the conditions, the Communists would agree and go on to win.

As the papers state:

> Although the U.S. opposed elections in 1954 because Ho Chi Minh would have won them handily . . . the U.S. communicated to Diem its conviction that proposing such conditions to the DRV (North Vietnam) during pre-plebiscite consultations would lead promptly to a flat rejection to Diem's marked advantage in world opinion. Diem found it preferable to refuse outright to talk to the North, and the U.S. endorsed his policy . . . The DRV communicated directly with the GVN (South Vietnam) in July 1955, and again in May and June of 1956, proposing not only consultative conference to negotiate "free general elections by secret ballot" but to liberalize North-South relations in general. Each time, the GVN replied with disdain, or with silence. The 17th parallel, with its demilitarized zone on either side, became de facto an international boundary, and—since Ngo Dinh Diem's rigid refusal to traffic with the North excluded all economic exchanges, even an interstate postal agreement—one of the most restricted boundaries in the world.

All of which destroys the fundamental assertion of every pro-government speaker in the last ten years, as well as Nixon's recent nonsense about an invasion from North Vietnam. If it was Diem and the United States who blocked the peaceful and political means to the reunification of Vietnam, then it is Diem and the United States (which selected, financed, and ran his government) who are responsible when revolutionaries resort to military means. This is the irreducible point upon which all four Vietnam War Presidents have begun their trails of lies.

When incoming President Kennedy met outgoing President Eisenhower in the White House Cabinet room for a chat about Indochina two days before the inauguration, President Eisenhower "wondered aloud why, in interventions of this kind, we always seem to find that the morale of the Communist forces was better than that of the democratic forces. His explanation was that the Communist philosophy appeared to produce a sense of dedication on the part of its adherents, while there was not the same sense of dedication on the part of those supporting the free forces." (This incident appears in the original papers but was censored out of the official version printed by the Government Printing Office.)

It is not recorded anywhere in the Pentagon Papers that anyone at any rank in the government paused to consider that perhaps the Communists were the "free forces." It is recorded that the young and liberal Kennedy followed directly in the footsteps of the old and conservative Ike in sending CIA agent Lansdale right back to Vietnam to win their hearts and minds for freedom.

The clear verdict of the papers is that for all the difference in style of the various Presidents they were as one in not being willing to let the Vietnamese make their revolution if it involved Communism. But at least Kennedy could have used some hindsight gained from Ike's experiences. After all, as President he could read the documents used for the Pentagon Papers before we could . . . Perhaps he did. What then was it about Communism which so troubled him? Kennedy and his advisers made up the most sophisticated administration of the Cold War. Yet they did what Eisenhower was unwilling to do—send American combat troops to Indochina. It was not an "accident" or a "quagmire." It was simply a matter of exporting counterrevolution.

Kennedy's Obsession

The Pentagon Papers are quite clear about the narrow class base of Diem's rule. It turns out that the Communists were correct all along. The war in Vietnam is a matter of class struggle: "When the Vietminh 'liberated' an area, they distributed these lands free to the farmers. . . . One of Diem's primary failures lay in his inability to similarly capture loyalties among his 90 percent agricultural people. The core of rural discontent was the large landholdings. . . . Government officials, beginning with the Minister for Agrarian Reform, had divided loyalties, being themselves landholders."

Recently Nixon claimed, as had his predecessors, that the Communists got public support not from their land reform but rather because they have killed so many village officials and thereby terrorized the village populations into submission. This was the main theme of the State Department White Paper first issued under the Kennedy Administration. These village officials were pictured as innocent idealists trying to better the lot of the people until rubbed out by the vicious NLF.

The Pentagon Papers tell a very different story about these village officials and how they came to power:

> A further example of Diem's maladroitness was his abolishing elections for village councils, a step he took in June 1956, apparently out of concern that large numbers of former Vietminh might win office at the village level. The Vietnamese village had traditionally, even under the French, enjoyed administrative autonomy. . . . Under the national regulation of 1956, members of council and the village chief became appointive officials, and their office subject to scrutiny by the Diemist apparatus.

As the Pentagon Papers conclude, "Ngo Dinh Diem presided over a state which, for all the lip service it paid to individual freedom and American-style government, remained a one party, highly centralized, familial oligarchy in which neither operating democracy nor the prerequisites for such existed."

The papers estimate that by the time Kennedy became President in 1961 there were at most 12,000 hard-core Vietcong as compared to 150,000 ARVN troops. The NLF program was consistent with the aspirations of the Vietnamese who had clearly had it with Diem. Yet Kennedy plunged in.

Kennedy was obsessed with a global strategy for stopping wars of national liberation from Cuba to Vietnam. It was a political view of guerrilla warfare concentrating on logistics. General Giap was to be answered with an updating of the Boy Scout manual. The Communists fought small-scale guerrilla warfare, our special forces would fight small-scale; the Communists had ideas for social reform, we would get some ideas. The fact that the Communists happened to be Vietnamese and we happened to be Americans was not allowed to obscure the vision of this most enlightened and diffident of the modern imperialists. Kennedy's cynicism toward the Vietnamese is revealed by the Pentagon Papers to have been much greater than Ike's.

The crack-up of Diem's government was obvious. But Kennedy would take neo-colonialism to yet a higher level, bypassing the Diem regime with advisers, strategic hamlets, special forces, gadgets—no end of gadgets. By God, we'd show them how to make a revolution. The American way, like the frontier, cowboys, stockades, the works. How to start—how to get our boys "in country" without the American public getting wise? Lansdale had sent a memo that Diem did not want U.S. combat units—"Afraid of losing control"—smart man, given what was to happen to him later. How to fool both Diem and the American public? The Kennedy team was in a quandary.

But wait, fantastic news out of Saigon: "Serious flood in Mekong Delta area . . . (worst since 1937) raises the possibility that flood relief could be justification for moving in U.S. military personnel for humanitarian purposes."

General Taylor sounded it out in Saigon and sent a cable: WHITE HOUSE EYES ONLY FOR THE PRESIDENT STATE EYES ONLY FOR RUSK AND UNDER SECRETARY JOHNSON DEFENSE EYES ONLY FOR SECRETARY MC NAMARA. "To relate the introduction of these troops to the needs of flood relief . . . gives a specific humanitarian task as the prime reason for the coming of our troops and avoids any suggestion that we are taking over responsibility for the security of the country." But the Kennedy program of sending advisers and special forces to Vietnam meant *taking over*. "A joint effort . . . to improve the military-political intelligence system beginning at the provincial level and extending upward through the government and armed forces to the Central Intelligence Organization."

That was October 13, 1961—two years later no more Diem. Which illustrates the importance of intelligence organizations.

In any event, Taylor was eager to get on with the "clean up." He noted that "SVN (South Vietnam) is not an excessively difficult or unpleasant place to operate." But time was running out for humanitarianism; "the possibility of emphasizing the humanitarian mission will wane if we wait long in moving our forces or in linking our stated purpose with the emergency conditions created by the flood."

What was the larger moral purpose which justified such chicanery? What was John Kennedy's in accepting Taylor's view? It was not fear of either the Soviet Union or China. This was 1961, after the Soviet-American thaw. At that time, China was pictured as weak and on the verge of internal collapse as Taylor claimed ". . .the starvation conditions in China should discourage Communist leaders there from being militarily venturesome for some time to come." Then why the need for "victory" in Vietnam? Taylor's answer: "What will be lost is not merely a crucial piece of real estate.

". . . the United States must decide how it will cope with Khrushchev's 'wars of liberation' . . . it is clear to me that the time may come in our relations to Southeast Asia when we must declare our intentions to attack the source of guerrilla aggression in North Vietnam and impose on the Hanoi government a price for participating in the current war."

This shows that the Kennedy Administration realized that it was committing the United States to the path of escalation. The "Rostow Plan" of bombing the North and Johnson's later use of large-scale American troops were both foreseen. But why? Intelligence reports of the time not only are devoid of any evidence of Soviet or Chinese support for the insurgency in the South but also de-emphasize Hanoi's involvement. A State Department report on October 1, 1961, conceded that the "vast majority of Vietcong troops are of local origin" and that "there is little evidence of major supplies from outside sources, most arms apparently being captured or stolen from GVN or from the French during the Indochina war." Although McNamara appeared on TV waving "captured Chinese arms" and prattling about the Ho Chi Minh Trail, the President was being told by his assistants as late as February 1963, two years after the Special Forces were sent to Vietnam: "No weapons have yet been captured which could be proved to have been brought in *after* 1954. Thus, the conclusion seems inescapable that the Vietcong could continue the war effort at the present level, or perhaps increase it, even if the infiltration routes were completely closed." (Author's italics.)

So what's this about Khrushchev and Hanoi? It hangs on the word "Communism." Throughout the memos there is one overriding ideological supposition—that a revolution which is Communist-influenced is by definition illegitimate. It is the *idea* and not the weapons or the outside troops which is threatening—the idea of profound revolutionary struggle against United States domination. It is this "Communist offensive" which is challenging the status quo of American power in the Third World. The domino effect has always been primarily a political effect rather than a military one.

The perceived threat was that of popular insurgency—as in Cuba and Vietnam. The Kennedy Administration could not care less about the established Communism of Eastern Europe precisely because of its unpopularity. That "Communism" was incapable of inspiring people elsewhere to take up arms against United States power. Eastern Europe could be accommodated, but Ho Chi Minh or Fidel Castro could not be. The fear was pervasive. As New Frontiersman John Kenneth Galbraith noted in a memo, "Washington is currently having an intellectual orgasm on the unbeatability of guerrilla war."

The response was a fanatic commitment to counterrevolution as an alternative to Communist revolution. The reactionary regimes would not only be propped up, they would be redesigned. The era of counter-insurgency exhibited an even more pernicious meddling than traditional colonialism. The French asked Bao Dai only to be a front for them—not that he stop being a playboy. But the Kennedys wanted Diem to become a Kennedy, and when he failed to, they had him killed.

Galbraith warned of the contradictions: "Diem will not reform either administratively or politically in any effective way. That is because he cannot. It is politically naïve to expect it. He senses that he cannot let power go because he would be thrown out." A counterrevolution must be repressive, for by definition it is an attempt to hold power for a small group. But it took the Kennedy Administration two fruitless years of trying to remold Diem to learn this.

Diem was supposed to be "our" Ho Chi Minh, but there can be no such person. A nationalist revolutionary who is created by the leading Western capitalist country is a contradiction in terms. Diem's repressive and elitist regime was necessary for the task the United States wanted him to carry out— to turn back the revolution that had been under way in Vietnam for some forty years.

By 1963 Diem had become an enormous embarrassment, and instead of dealing with the source of the problem, which was U.S. neo-colonialism, the Kennedy Administration turned to public relations. They decided to change the faces—to have a palace coup.

To Kill a Mockingbird

The United States government has attempted to hide its role in the coup against Diem, but the Pentagon Papers expose that involvement in detail. In what has to be one of the more cynical chapters of American history, it is revealing that the very dignified patrician figure of Ambassador Henry Cabot Lodge should emerge as the central character in this shady operation.

On the day of the coup Lodge paid Diem a ceremonial call. Diem "called Lodge aside and they talked privately for twenty minutes. Diem . . . indicated that he wanted to talk to Lodge about what it was the U.S. wanted him to do. The atmosphere of this meeting must have been strained in the extreme in view of Lodge's awareness of the imminence of the coup."

At that very moment, as Lodge knew, a high-ranking United States CIA agent, Lieutenant Colonel Conein, was with the Vietnamese generals who were plotting the coup. For months he had worked out the intricate details, which were cleared through Lodge and Washington for approval.

CIA agent Conein stayed at the generals' command post, leading the coup through the rest of that day and night and maintaining constant phone contact with Lodge in the U.S. embassy. The palace was under attack when Diem telephoned the ambassador at 4:30 in the afternoon, but Lodge played dumb. Diem was pathetic and Lodge was cold.

DIEM: Some units have made a rebellion and I want to know what is the attitude of the United States.

LODGE: I do not feel well enough informed to tell you. I have heard the shooting but am not acquainted with all the facts. Also it is 4:30 a.m. in Washington and the U.S. government cannot possibly have a view.

Washington, of course, not only had a view but had prior knowledge of the coup's details and had given the go-ahead. Diem must have known this, but he plodded on.

DIEM: But you must have some general ideas. After all, I am a chief of state. I have tried to do my duty. I want to do now what duty and good sense require. I believe in duty above all.

LODGE: You have certainly done your duty. As I told you this morning, I admire your courage and your great contributions to your country. No one can take away from you the credit for all you have done.

A few hours later the hunted Diem and his brother Nhu escaped through a secret palace exit into the Saigon sewer system. After a night of hiding they surrendered early in the morning on a promise of safe exit from the country backed by Lodge and were promptly shot. So ended the career of this former French colonial official, who had been plucked out of the obscurity of a life in the Maryknoll Catholic Seminary in New Jersey to become, at the U.S. government's command, "the George Washington of his country." While George Washington was scurrying through the sewers of Saigon, Henry Cabot Lodge, untroubled by any sense of crisis, retired early at 9:30 and slept well past the hour of the execution.

The State Department was concerned by the image problem of killing off someone you have billed as the leading patriot of Vietnam. But Lodge was true to form. "Lodge closed the cable by taking exception to State's excessive preoccupation with the negative public-relations problems of the coup and decrying its failure to note the brilliance with which the coup was planned and executed."

But State was still worried about image. "Rusk felt that a delay [in recognition] would be useful to the generals in not appearing to be United States agents or stooges and would assist us in our public stance of noncomplicity. He further discouraged any large delegation of the generals from calling on Lodge as if they were 'reporting in.' "

For eight years the United States had kept up the image of an independent government of South Vietnam headed by its founding father, Ngo Dinh Diem, and threatened by foreign aggression. And then the United States overthrew him. It was bald. As General Harkins, the top military man in Saigon, argued in a secret memo opposing the Lodge–White House plans before the coup: "After all, rightly or wrongly, we have backed Diem for eight long, hard years. To me it seems incongruous now to get him down, kick him around, and get rid of him. The U.S. has been his mother superior and father confessor since he's been in office and he leaned on us heavily. Leaders of other underdeveloped countries will take a dim view of our assistance if they too were led to believe the same fate lies in store for them."

It was not merely "incongruous," but more than any other single episode of the Vietnam War, it denied the stated rationale of American policy. There never was an independent South Vietnam government—the United States constructed it, a CIA agent wrote its "democratic constitution," and the United States paid all its bills. But there was an illusion of independence under Diem; he at least had a small independent base of power among the northern Catholic refugees, a cantankerous style, and some sort of peculiar ideology. When this "independence" got in the way of United States plans, he was killed. Diem had some minimal machinery and a few followers; the "leaders" who came after had literally nothing other than their tie to the U.S. embassy. Diem was a ruler/killer who tried to do things his own way, but he wasn't efficient enough, so they brought in a long procession of better company men leading up to Thieu. But after Diem the illusion was gone and the United States simply took over.

The Air War

The American air war and troops followed inevitably, and the decision was as much Kennedy's as Johnson's. L.B.J. was for the antiwar movement a relatively easy and grotesque target. But let's not forget the Lodges, Kennedys, McGeorge Bundys, and McNamaras, for they represented the genteel arrogance of the empire. As Henry Cabot Lodge observed: "My general view is that the United States is trying to bring this medieval country into the twentieth century and that we have made considerable progress in military and economic ways but to gain victory we must also bring them into the twentieth century politically."

It was inconceivable to Lodge or Kennedy that the Vietnamese, through the morality and social commitment of decades of struggle, had developed politics on a level at least equal to, let alone higher than, that of, say, Boston. Cultural arrogance is an essential ingredient in the makeup of modern imperialism. It permits the unqualified participation of "reasonable" and "civilized" men. It allows just the necessary degree of self-righteousness for a Kennedy, after months of plotting coups to overthrow Diem, to cable Lodge instructing him "to make it clear that the United States government is not open to Oriental divisive tactics."

Whatever the errors of the Kennedy Administration, the new President, Lyndon Johnson, moved quickly and decisively to compound them.

In December 1963, two months after the overthrow of Diem, McNamara visited Vietnam and filed the first of a series of dismal reports to the President. These reports all focused on the fact that the post-Diem Saigon government barely existed. "The new government is the greatest source of concern. It is indecisive and drifting." Bombing the North would answer the drift in the South.

The United States had been sending sabotage teams into North Vietnam since 1954. Now, as a prelude to the bombing, such operations were to be stepped up. In McNamara's prose: "Plans for covert action into North Vietnam were prepared as we had requested and were an excellent job. They present a wide variety of sabotage and psychological operations against North Vietnam."

The next month Maxwell Taylor, Chairman of the Joint Chiefs, called for the United States to "conduct aerial bombing of key North Vietnam targets, using U.S. resources under Vietnamese cover, and with the Vietnamese openly assuming responsibility for the actions." The United States was to "advise and support the government of Vietnam in its conduct of large-scale commando raids against critical targets in North Vietnam."

The motivation for this escalation was not the publicly claimed "aggression" from the North but rather the collapse of the Saigon government in the wake of the overthrow of Diem. The United States replaced General Minh with General Khanh, but McNamara's subsequent report was even more forlorn: "The greatest weakness in the present situation is the uncertain viability of the Khanh government . . . he does not yet have wide political appeal and his control of the army itself is uncertain." But "on the positive side . . . it is highly responsive to U.S. advice." The U.S. Secretary of Defense announced a plan for Vietnam: "to put the whole nation on a war footing . . . a new Mobilization Plan should be urgently developed by the Country Team in collaboration with the Khanh government." The Country Team was made up of U.S. officials in Saigon who ran the show. It never occurred to them that they did not have the right to put the "whole nation" of Vietnam on a "war footing."

The South Vietnam government represented no one except the United States, and instead of concluding from this that the United States "presence" had failed to rouse the people and it was time to withdraw, the Administration revived the old charge of an "invasion from North Vietnam."

In its Alice in Wonderland world, the following memo made sense to the Administration:

> U.S. policy had been to pacify South Vietnam by aid and advice and actions within the borders of South Vietnam. This policy will not work without a strong government in Saigon. It has become apparent that there is no likelihood that a government sufficiently strong to administer a successful pacification program will develop. It follows that our current U.S. policy, which is based on such a program, will not succeed.
>
> The odds are very great that if we do not inject some major new

elements—and perhaps even if we do—the situation will continue to deteriorate . . . ending in a demand for a negotiated settlement.

The United States was never to permit a negotiated settlement in this war of example which required victory at all costs. That meant that "major new elements"—the bombing of the North and the massive introduction of U.S. troops—were necessary. It was stated U.S. policy to create a viable government in South Vietnam by bombing North Vietnam.

But the U.S. leaders had to wait until after the election. Bombing the North before the election would have hurt Johnson's image as a dove who attacked Goldwater as an irresponsible extremist for advocating bombing the North. Meanwhile, they planned the publicity campaign to make it all believable. William Bundy wrote a paper justifying the policy. This paper "was drafted as a possible article to be issued with authoritative anonymity in some mass circulation medium, such as *The New York Times Magazine.*" A furious campaign about the "aggression from North Vietnam" against poor, independent South Vietnam was mounted. It was claimed that the South Vietnam government "asked for our assistance" at the very time when internal government dispatches expressed doubt that there even was a South Vietnam government.

"Independent South Vietnam has been attacked by North Vietnam," Lyndon Johnson thundered. "From Munich until today we have learned that to yield to aggression brings only greater threats."

The United States at that moment already had about 50,000 troops in South Vietnam. According to Document 243 of the Pentagon Papers, the CIA estimated that from 1959 to the start of the bombing by Johnson, the total number of infiltrators from the North was between 19,000 and 34,000, most of whom were already dead. This was the "aggression." Even Taylor was baffled:

The ability of the Vietcong continuously to rebuild their units and to make good their losses is one of the mysteries of this guerrilla war. We are aware of the recruiting methods by which local boys are induced or compelled to join the Vietcong ranks and have some general appreciation of the amount of infiltration of personnel from the outside. Yet taking both of these sources into account, we still find no plausible explanation of the continued strength of the Vietcong if our data on Vietcong losses are even approximately correct. Not only do Vietcong units have the recuperative powers of the phoenix, but they have an amazing ability to maintain morale.

Okay, Taylor, is it just the least bit possible that this "amazing ability to maintain morale" might have something to do with the justice of their cause? And if so, shouldn't the United States just get the hell out? No, because the larger considerations of empire were at stake. "Never let the DRV gain a victory in South Vietnam," Taylor warned, "without having paid a *disproportionate* price." (Author's italics.)

William Bundy, the other half of the wax museum brother team, thrilled a Dallas audience with "a fascinating story of the emergence of these new nationalistic forces in South Vietnam." But in his secret memo, which the Bundy brothers read, Taylor explained that there was no South Vietnam government: "It is hard to decide what is the minimum government which is necessary to permit reasonable hope for the success of our efforts. We would certainly like to have a government which is capable of maintaining law and order, of making and executing timely decisions, of carrying out approved programs, and generally of leading its people and gearing its efforts effectively with those of the United States. As indicated above, however, it is highly unlikely that we will see such a government of South Vietnam in the time frame available to us to reverse the downward trend of events . . . Anything less than this would hardly be a government at all, and under such circumstances, the United States government might do better to carry forward the war on a purely unilateral basis." Which is really what the half million troops and the air war over North Vietnam was all about. It was either genocide or withdrawal.

Death Prose

At about this time demonstrators at San Francisco's Fairmont Hotel called Taylor a murderer when he arrived there to speak. The city fathers and the mainstream press were shocked at their "extremist language." There is no extreme language in the memos of the Pentagon Papers. There are only thousands of pages of cool dispassionate discussion about whether to unleash the air war over North Vietnam. Such emotional categories as "death," "hurt," "burning," or even "people" are never introduced. It is a numbing experience to read these memos, for they derive from a bureaucratic language which excludes compassion, morality, and serious political choice.

White House Memo 328, authored by McGeorge Bundy, a professor of International Relations, states matter-of-factly: "We should continue to vary the types of target, stepping up attacks on lines of communication in the near future, and possibly moving in a few weeks to attacks on the trail lines north and northeast of Hanoi . . . Blockade or aerial mining of North Vietnamese ports need further study." McGeorge Bundy is said to pride himself these days on his restraint in not advocating the mining of Haiphong Harbor, as Nixon has finally done. But what about the hundreds of thousands of people that *his* bombing policy killed? Is there any way to rub his nose into the smell of that death?

I am weary of reading the Pentagon Papers over and over. As yet I have not found a single instance of an individual inside the U.S. government who reckoned the death of Vietnamese people as a "cost" of the bombing. For example, William Bundy: "Our actions against the South should be carried on at a maximum effective rate. This could include substantial use of B-52s against VC havens, recognizing that we look *silly* and arouse criticism if these do not show significant results." Does a B-52 payload have to fall on Cambridge before Bundy can perceive its effect in terms more serious than public relations? A B-52 raid tears skin, crushes skulls, draws blood from the mouths of human beings in their ancestral home. By what deranged calculus of power can it "look silly"? He did mention U.S. casualties in an earlier memo, but even so, "this program seems cheap."

The only reference I can find to Vietnamese casualties is in a memo prepared by McNamara and his aides after they had turned against the bombing in May 1967. He began by stating that "the primary costs, of course, are U.S. lives," each of which must then be worth ten thousand Vietnamese lives. Vietnamese deaths are brought into the discussion only insofar as they affect public relations. "An important but hard-to-measure cost is domestic and world opinion: There may be a limit beyond which many Americans and much of the world will not permit the United States to go. The picture of the world's greatest superpower killing or seriously injuring 1,000 non-combatants a week while trying to pound a tiny backward nation into submission over an issue whose merits are hotly disputed is not a pretty one." In addition, he cited a technical opinion that "we cannot, by bombing, reach the critical level of pain in North Vietnam" and that below that level, "pain only increases the will to fight."

Undoubtedly, McNamara brought this up at one of the Target Tuesday luncheons, which had become a regular event at the White House. In a conversation over lunch "punctured by the whirl of Mr. Johnson's battery-powered pepper grinder" and after the preliminary Scotch or Fresca, McNamara must have raised this point about "the critical level of pain." Professor Rostow, one may conjecture, probably frowned at the unscientific basis of such a category. Professor Rostow more than Rusk is a "pour-it-on man." McNamara would then pull out the new target list he had assembled, and the eating and discussion would continue on into the afternoon. After that week's bombing targets had been selected, President Johnson would retire for his nap.

The Unmaking of a Whiz Kid

I cannot go on anymore with the papers. They are so mechanical and amoral as to become grisly. The monotone prose drones on, a continuum of statistics and options, overpowering in its dullness, a paean to the death trip of reasonable men.

Who are these guys? Their brittle style makes all the questions I want to ask them seem corny. Do they have bad dreams, play with their children, enjoy eating out? Do they recycle their garbage? Will they be witnesses at the Ellsberg-Russo trial? Can one just interview them? Are Ellsberg and Russo like Rostow or Bundy?

They're not, but you could have fooled me back in Saigon in 1966. The hotels were all full up with American officials in town for the escalation, but Stanley Sheinbaum arranged for us to sleep at Len Maynard's house. Maynard was a deputy director of the aid program and had been hired by Sheinbaum back in the days of the Michigan State project. At Maynard's house, we met the liberals of the U.S. Country Team. Sheinbaum now opposed the war and they reacted to this as if his health were failing. Johnson's air war was on in deadly earnest, but they were still jubilant, buoyant of spirit, unmarred by the smallest doubt that they did not fully understand the needs and aspirations of the Vietnamese people. They were all excited about the revolution "we" were bringing to the people. Whenever Stan or I doubted them, Maynard would call over his maid for corroboration of the respect and feeling the average Vietnamese had for the United States presence.

Later in the evening some guys from Rand came over and talked about the interviews they were doing with captured members of the NLF. The work they were doing outraged me—what right did U.S. agents have to be in this country, let alone to harass the very people who were fighting for its liberation? One of them was Anthony Russo. He was to turn increasingly against the war in the course of that work. "I wanted desperately to believe that what my country was doing was right," Russo recalls. "The United States and J.F.K. and the Mother and the Flag got the benefit of every doubt as far as I was concerned, because I wanted it to be right. But it just wasn't right. It just wasn't and there was no way that I could make it that way. You know, without lying to myself.

"These people—the VC—were not automatons. They were not robots. They were not indoctrinated to go through the motions. The ideology was internalized. It became part of them. So therefore it was not cheap propaganda, it was principle. I guess what impressed me more than anything was the difference between these people and the Vietnamese working for the Americans, who had very little motivation except to make money, to maintain their bourgeois life-styles. The idealism, and the commitment of the VC— the staunch commitment is something that really impressed me."

It was a pretty grisly business trekking around Vietnam to the different prisons, the little interrogation rooms. Prisoners were brought in bound and blindfolded to be interviewed by American professors—the information was then put on IBM cards and run through the machine back in Santa Monica for Rand analysis.

"Many times those captured were summarily shot. Nixon bullshits about the captured U.S. pilots—he wants detailed information on their condition— shit, in South Vietnam the jailers didn't even know who was in the jail— the conditions were incredibly miserable."

One of the main interrogation centers was run by the CIA in Saigon, and that is where Tony spent two days interrogating the NLF prisoner who most "got to" him.

"He had been in the movement since before the French war was over in an agit-prop cadre traveling with actors and singers from village to village getting the word out—that was his job. He was intensely committed, and even in jail he recited poetry, sang songs, and spoke movingly about what the United States was doing to his country. There was this dude singing at the top of his voice in that interrogation room. One of the lines of the songs which really got to me was 'Our hatred for the American is as high as the sky.'

"But at the same time we clearly didn't hate each other. That kind of left a riddle in my mind which to this day I have tried to answer. When I reflected on it more of an answer came. The essence of it is that he and I were brothers and there's a lot about my country that I hate, too." And then only partially joking: "He recruited me. Even captured and stuck in that little CIA room, he had the spirit to do it."

That prisoner had been tortured a great deal before Tony met him. But others had been tortured worse—"One poor guy was just a basket case, he had been tortured very badly and he was incoherent, he could barely talk. All he did was sit there and ask if he was going to be killed the next day.

"I'd talk to the Rand people about the torture and they just didn't care, nor did anyone else. The brutality was an inherent part of the whole thing."

Life was pretty good at the Rand compound. The Rand Corporation was paying high salaries. Tony, a lower-level type, was making $17,000 over expenses and could bank the whole salary. Higher Rand scholars were making

$25,000 to $40,000 a year—hopping in and out of the country. The style at the compound was one of "low-keyed colonial elegance"—discreet Vietnamese maids and cooks. There would be a lot of talk over dinner about the wine and the French cooking, and details of the American war effort, but never of the "enemy" as a viable alternative.

"You could not penetrate the cynicism with which that Establishment view is encrusted," Russo says. "Any idea of a new socialist man, which Che wrote about, or of a different morality as a basis for explaining the Communists would be dismissed as naïve. I was constantly raising this and always I would hit a brick wall . . . I never had a discussion with any of those guys that was in any way stimulating. What it gets down to is acculturated cynicism. No other way is possible. No other human nature is possible." Communism is an alternative and Rand intellectuals could not deal with alternatives—only options.

As Russo describes the difference: "A rearview mirror on a car is an option; a bicycle is an alternative. Government intellectuals thought exclusively in terms of options—bombing versus special forces. Thoughts about alternatives—that Communism might be good for the Vietnamese, or at least that it was their business to decide—were not part of the game." Even at the highest level of the bureaucracy it would be merely a matter for musing, not practice. Some top people in the Pentagon have speculated about such alternatives but in practice they helped plan the bombings anyway.

As Ellsberg recalls: "McNaughton himself said to me that he thought that Communism was the best thing for them. He said it looked as if a Communist government was the best thing that could happen for those people, 'no two ways about it, we really have no business grinding those people to dust to prevent a Communist government from taking over, because they really ought to run their own country and it's really bad what we're doing.' So long as he kept those doubts or those accusations totally within the family and said to the public what supported the Administration line and carried out the policies of his superiors, there was no problem.

"That's another aspect of the system," Ellsberg continues. "It does not require true believers to run it. That's why I use the word corruption so often. The system consciously runs by men who—in order to stay in the game to be close to the center of power, to have the hope that someday the moment may come when their own true values will be served—will go on for years serving values that are the opposite of what they privately believe. That's understood. In fact, you expect such corrupt behavior on the part of your subordinates; it scarcely worries you. It's not a bad sign."

Ellsberg is extremely perceptive in dealing with this corruption. The last section of his book, *Papers on the War*, is devastating in its treatment of the "reasonable" style of men whom he has come to view as war criminals: "Neither had my year in the Pentagon taught me to read the 'contingency plans' and proposals that had passed through my own hands with the same eyes that my wife and children brought to them six years later. Here is some of the language they read in the Pentagon Papers about our bombing policy:

'Judging by experience during the last war, the resumption of bombing after a pause would be even more painful to the population of North Vietnam than a fairly steady rate of bombing.'

'. . . "water-drip technique" . . .'

'. . . the hot-cold treatment . . . the objective of persuading Hanoi would dictate a program of painful surgical strikes . . .'

'. . . our "salami-slice" bombing program . . .'

'. . . ratchet . . .'

'. . . one more turn of the screw . . .'

"These were phrases written by senior officials I worked with and respected [and] that I had read and discussed in offices in the Pentagon and State, often in disapproval of their contents yet without ever seeing or hearing them as my wife did when she characterized them, in horror, as 'the language of torturers.' "

I remember Pat Ellsberg as a radio reporter who was against the war when Dan still believed in counter-insurgency. She had none of his specialized knowledge, but she was right and he was totally wrong. The irrelevance of his own brilliance and training has shaken Ellsberg up as much as anything. In his book he quotes at length from Albert Speer, the Nazi war criminal known for his "intelligence," who observed: "There is unfortunately no necessary correlation between intelligence and decency; the genius and the moron are equally susceptible to corruption."

This is not quite accurate, for the geniuses of the defense Establishment were more susceptible—it required a certain deftness at game theory to so totally obliterate the requirements of common sense. It took a good deal of ingenuity to accept an environment which should have been unacceptable.

Basic to the environment which made Vietnam possible was acceptance of the ideology of modern capitalism—that American institutions were not exploitative and indeed were always the necessary mechanism for human progress throughout the world. There was a rejection out of hand of the possibility that the American system was imperialistic—that its interests were in conflict with those of the Third World. The corollary of this was the refusal to consider Communism as a positive force. Back in 1965 in my study, *How the U.S. Got Involved in Vietnam*, I wrote: "In my examination of the American mass media for this report I found no instance where a 'Communist' could be described as altruistic or genuinely committed to the well-being of his fellow man. If individual Communists appeared to be so, it was because they were being deceptive or were themselves deceived by higher-ups who better fitted our image of the Communist. The idea that Communist or Vietminh rule under Ho Chi Minh might be better for the Vietnamese than any alternative political system has never been really examined in the United States because it is unthinkable."

At that time it was definitely "unthinkable" for Ellsberg, who wrote of the Vietcong: "On the VC side, much of this 'platform' is cynical and expedient in the minds of the Communist elite, whose covert ideals call for 'modernization' on a fifty-year-old blueprint of forced-draft industrialization under totalitarian controls, capitalized by exploitation of the peasants and preceded by a bloodbath to destroy or terrorize potential opposition: a vision so stark and repelling it must be kept esoteric."

He was enamored with the counter-insurgency program of John Vann. Both Ellsberg and Vann were excited about beating the NLF at its own game— revolution. As Ellsberg now notes, " 'Good colonialists' was what we were all trying to be, and what Vann [was]. It was, and is, the wrong aspiration to have. . . . Two subsequent years taught me much, but not—I realized later—about the Vietcong . . . I had been shot at by Vietcong, but had never 'knowingly' met one." He first started to get an insight into the NLF by reading the interviews at Rand that people like Russo had done in Vietnam. But that insight is limited. Turning against anti-Communism means more than turning against the Cold War. Ellsberg has shown a remarkable clarity in stripping away the fabric of Washington's lies. But a large part of him resists making that emotional leap from the environment of Rand and the Pentagon to a deeper understanding of its opposite, say that of the NLF, or at least the American peace movement. His book, which contains many important ideas, still subscribes (except for its conclusion) to the prose style and rationality of the think tanks. He still cares what Arthur Schlesinger, Jr., thinks, or Ted Sorenson, or Arthur Goldberg or any of the other pompous fools of his past.

When John Vann was shot down by the NLF, Ellsberg raced off to his funeral. It is understandable that friendship should survive political differences. Nor is it unreasonable that Ellsberg should be socially more comfortable among Cambridge liberals than among the radicals in the Peace Project office with their NLF buttons. But there is the unmistakable impression that Ellsberg still takes the Vanns and Schlesingers to be the agents of social change. Perhaps now he adds a Chomsky, a Berrigan, or an I. F. Stone. But there is that persistent elitism which is a very real throwback to Kennedy counter-insurgency and Rand, and that same inability to comprehend revolution or the NLF. For all his analytical brilliance, he does not yet grasp, as Tony Russo does, that to understand the NLF he must first begin to understand the Movement "kids" working on his own defense. He must learn to struggle with them because it is necessary for a thrashing out of the real issues involved in the trial. These issues are not personal, technical, or legal; they are political and affect all of us.

For example, what are the witnesses to testify about? Is it that the papers are harmless and should therefore not have been secret? That's not true, and Ellsberg more than anyone knows the real power of the papers. If Arthur Goldberg is to be a witness, then he should begin his testimony by stating that the Pentagon Papers show that as Johnson's ambassador to the United Nations he was a mouthpiece for war criminals. Anything less is a con. Nor should Schlesinger testify that the war is a horrible "mistake," for as Ellsberg has written and the papers have shown, it flowed directly from the mainspring of American foreign policy. Most importantly, the papers refute the essential ideology of anti-Communists and clear the decks for an examination of American imperialism. It is up to Ellsberg to see to it that the trial does not do what the Establishment—in or out of office—wants it to do, which is trivialize the papers. The main goal of the trial should be to throw the indictments back at Nixon. To accomplish this the defense must develop a strategy in and out of the courtroom to show that the content of the Pentagon Papers refutes every single assertion of Nixon's Vietnam policy. Whether such a strategy emerges obviously depends on Ellsberg's own development during the course of the trial.

We should expect this to happen. For whatever criticism one may have of Ellsberg's style, it is important to understand the significance of his act in turning over the papers. It came from a man who was mired in the elitism and arrogance of American power and for all his intellectualism and aloofness, it turned out that Daniel Ellsberg really gave a shit about the public and the truth.

There are many historical examples of those outside of power denouncing its excesses, but frighteningly few defections from the inner circles. Ellsberg could have written his cautious articles against the war and stayed in the club, but by releasing the papers he turned not just against the war but also against the system behind it. This was most recently demonstrated by the radical implications of the last chapter of his book, which concludes with the lines:

> Speer was, after all, regarded as the most liberal, humane, and intelligent of the Nazis. What is disconcerting is to find that this means that he would not at all have been the least creditable member of recent National Security Councils. . . . In the end, after twenty years, the "one unforgettable experience" that dominates Speer's impressions of

the past remains . . . the Nuremberg trial itself, with its photographs and testimony presenting, inescapably, not "enemies" but individual human beings, victims, who had become, at last, real to the criminal defendants. In particular, Speer recalls ". . . there was one photograph of a Jewish family going to its death, a husband with his wife and children being led to the gas chamber. . . ."

When I began to read these passages aloud to an audience at the Community Church in Boston in late May 1971, my private mood as I began was, I thought, detached. I was, in fact, imagining that Robert McNamara, McGeorge Bundy, Dean Rusk, or the Presidents they served were listening—until I heard my own voice growing low and halting . . . I knew that it was myself who was the listener, my eyes, my voice responding to these indictments.

There is nothing else to add except perhaps Anthony Russo's remark that it is Nixon's B-52s which have become the gas chambers of the seventies. But don't look for the Pentagon Papers trial to be our Nuremberg. For, after all, the criminals are still in power.

(*SunDance*, August–September 1972)

The Hoax of Tonkin

Twenty years ago, on the blackest of nights in the Gulf of Tonkin, when the moon died and dense fog, angry seas, electrical storms, and luminescent ocean microorganisms conspired to play tricks with a sailor's mind, America went to war. A murky incident—a purported attack on U.S. vessels by North Vietnam—led President Lyndon B. Johnson to order the bombing of North Vietnam, to obtain a congressional resolution approving the Americanization of the war in Southeast Asia, and eventually to station half a million U.S. troops in Vietnam. However, a reconstruction of those events, based on once-secret government cables and formerly classified eyewitness accounts, indicates that the attack never occurred.

The confusion began the night of August 4, 1964, high on the bridge of the *Maddox*, an aging destroyer outfitted as a spy ship. Unable to see objects a few feet into the blustery dark, dependent on electronic information gleaned from radar, sonar, and intercepted enemy communications, Captain John J. Herrick—a forty-four-year-old veteran of two wars—concluded that the mysterious dots on his radar screen were North Vietnamese PT boats bent on attacking his two-ship flotilla.

Herrick, commodore of the Seventh Fleet's Destroyer Division 192, radioed an emergency call to Pacific naval headquarters in Honolulu that would soon be read to the President, who was eating breakfast in the White House twelve time zones away. Johnson was furious.

Two days before, the *Maddox* had fired first on three North Vietnamese PT boats that had closed to within ten miles of the *Maddox* in what Herrick believed was an imminent attack. Now there had apparently been a second incident, and for the next fourteen hours, the President's men would plan a retaliatory air strike.

Johnson—in the midst of an election campaign—insisted that decisive action be taken soon enough for him to announce it on television that night, even as his staff frantically tried to determine whether an attack had indeed occurred. In order to meet that deadline, Johnson would overrule the commander in chief of the Pacific Fleet and announce the bombing of North Vietnam before some of the U.S. pilots had even arrived over their targets.

In the daylight of Washington it was all very clear and simple—but not so clear back in the darkened Gulf. From its inception, the purpose of Herrick's mission—which had been conceived in the White House and directed by the President's National Security Adviser—was largely secret, even to him. It had begun a week earlier, when the *Maddox* was re-equipped as an intelligence-gathering ship and sent to obtain information on Hanoi's radar and communications, as well as to make a show of force close to the North Vietnamese coast.

Simultaneously, South Vietnamese Navy personnel, trained by the United States and using U.S.-supplied boats, had begun conducting secret raids on targets in North Vietnam. Unknown to Herrick, one such attack had begun the night of July 30, immediately before he began sailing along the North Vietnamese coast. The North Vietnamese PT boats that closed on the *Maddox* on August 2 were probably retaliating for that assault.

Then-Secretary of State Dean Rusk conceded as much in a classified cable to General Maxwell D. Taylor, U.S. ambassador to Vietnam, the following night. The "*Maddox* incident is directly related to [North Vietnam's] efforts to resist these activities," Rusk said.

On August 3, the day after that first Gulf of Tonkin episode, Herrick requested that his patrol be ended because he thought the mission made the *Maddox* vulnerable. He was turned down by Admiral Ulysses Grant Sharp, Jr., commander in chief of U.S. forces in the Pacific, who felt this might call into question the United States' "resolve to assert our legitimate rights in these international waters." Sharp recently said that he had obtained permission from the Joint Chiefs of Staff to strengthen Herrick's patrol by placing a second destroyer, the *Turner Joy*, under his command.

Radio monitoring—which was the purpose of Herrick's mission—was conducted by a communications box that had been placed between the *Maddox*'s smokestacks. Intelligence experts stood watch inside the box, intercepting and translating North Vietnamese communications. Occasionally the officer in charge of monitoring these communications would pop out with messages about what he thought the North Vietnamese were doing.

On the night of August 3, another U.S.-directed South Vietnamese commando raid was launched and, according to communications monitored by the *Maddox*, the North Vietnamese confused that mission with Herrick's patrol.

Early on the evening of August 4, the intelligence officer reported to Herrick that the radio communications indicated an imminent attack on the *Maddox* and her sister ship. Herrick passed the warning on to Washington. It was 9 a.m. Eastern Daylight Time when the message was handed to Secretary of Defense Robert S. McNamara. Twelve minutes later, McNamara called the President, who had been with Democratic congressional leaders.

"They have?" Johnson thundered when he heard about the supposed attack, according to then-House Majority Leader Carl Albert, who had stayed on after the congressional breakfast. "Now I'll tell you what I want," Johnson said to McNamara. "I not only want those patrol boats that attacked the *Maddox* destroyed, I want everything at that harbor destroyed; I want the whole works destroyed. I want to give them a real dose."

At this point, however, Herrick had not said that his ships were under attack, only that his radio intercepts pointed to the likelihood of an attack.

Immediately after breakfast, Johnson—who was preoccupied with his campaign against Republican presidential nominee Barry Goldwater—took a walk with adviser Kenneth O'Donnell. "The President was wondering aloud as to the political repercussions and questioned me rather closely as to my political reaction to his making a military retaliation," O'Donnell recalled four years later in a letter to Senator J. William Fulbright (D-Ark.), then chairman of the Foreign Relations Committee. "The attack upon Lyndon Johnson," O'Donnell wrote, "was going to come from the right and the hawks, and he must not allow them to accuse him of vacillating or being an indecisive leader. The emergence of the [Gulf of Tonkin] resolution itself was nothing but political coloration for a decision already taken."

After the Gulf incident and the U.S. retaliation, a Harris poll showed that public opinion on the U.S. role in Vietnam had reversed. Before the incident, 58 percent of those polled had a negative view of the Johnson Administration's handling of Vietnam policy; after, 72 percent approved.

While denying that Johnson wanted to expand the war, then National Security Adviser McGeorge Bundy said recently that the President was concerned about his image as a leader. Johnson wanted "to be seen to be capable of an adequately quick response, no doubt about that," Bundy recalled.

While Johnson's reaction may have been quick enough that morning, it was based on reports from the Gulf that became more uncertain as the day went on.

On the *Maddox*, the man in the communications box whose reports of an impending attack started the incident was known to some as "the hairball man"—after the character in Mark Twain's *Huckleberry Finn* who looked into a hairball and foresaw the future. "Every time the hairball man came out of that van, I got worried," said Dr. Samuel E. Halpern, who was the ship's physician and is now a professor of radiology at U.C. San Diego. "He'd go running onto the bridge, and then the order came over the intercom and said that these PT boats were approaching us and that they were going to try to torpedo us. And so we weren't going to wait, we were going to fire and we did, of course." Halpern added that, after the battle, "some of the chiefs were really upset about the hairball man and the box . . . And one of them said, 'We ought to throw the goddamned box overboard.' "

Later, investigations within the executive branch and Congress would cast doubts on whether the radio intercepts of an impending attack even applied to the action around Herrick's ships. In testimony four years later, before the Senate Foreign Relations Committee, McNamara revealed that the communications intercepted that morning of August 4 consisted simply of North Vietnamese orders to "make ready for military operations" sent to two boats that were incapable of carrying torpedoes.

That night, though, with the radio man's intercepts in hand, Herrick and his officers began to interpret oddly moving radar dots and sonar noises as torpedo attacks from enemy vessels they could not see. The *Maddox* increased speed to its maximum 30 knots and followed a zigzag course. At 9:52 p.m., Herrick reported that both his ships were under torpedo attack. Between twenty-two and thirty torpedoes were counted during the next two hours, during which the destroyers thrashed about in high-speed evasive action while frenetically firing their cannon at targets that simply were not visible.

The report of so many torpedoes aroused suspicion among the *Maddox*'s officers, because the North Vietnamese Navy was thought to have only twenty-four torpedoes on all its PT boats. Ultimately, the Americans began to suspect that whatever their instruments said, no attack was in progress.

As Halpern recalled: "Immediately after the attack, the officers came streaming into the wardroom and it was hysterical . . . just hysterical laughter. Everybody was laughing like mad, and then suddenly I realized I was laughing, too, the same way. And it was this tremendous release from pressure."

Fighter pilots from two nearby carriers that were providing cover for the destroyers swooped down dangerously close to the breaking waves to drop flares and fire volley after volley where the radar dots said the targets would be. However, they also could not confirm the presence of enemy boats or torpedoes. Retired Vice Admiral James B. Stockdale, a pilot who flew above the *Maddox* and *Turner Joy*, searching out their attackers, recently broke a silence his superiors had asked him to observe because, he said, "I thought twenty years was a decent interval." Stockdale now says categorically that the attack never occurred.

In his book, *In Love and War*, written with his wife, Sybil, Stockdale recalls returning to his ship and consulting with the other pilots. None had seen anything. He quotes one pilot as saying, "No boat wakes, no ricochets off boats, no boat gunfire, no torpedo wakes—nothing but black sea and American firepower."

At the end of the "battle," no destroyers had been hit and no torpedoes exploded. Back in Washington, however, the gears were moving inexorably and without the complications of doubt.

About 10 a.m. on August 4, McGeorge Bundy's brother, William, Assistant Secretary of State for East Asian and Pacific Affairs, who was vacationing on Martha's Vineyard, got an urgent call from Rusk asking him to return to Washington forthwith. "So I got down to Washington at 3:30 in the afternoon," William Bundy recalled, "and I went to the office and learned that [Undersecretary of State] George Ball and Abe [Abram] Chayes [who had recently resigned as the State Department's chief legal adviser] were drafting a congressional resolution. I was told the basic story that there . . . apparently had been a second attack and that the President was determined to retaliate and . . . to seek a congressional resolution."

Bundy said that he never heard anyone in the State Department that day, from the Secretary of State on down, express the slightest doubt about the facts of the attack. "My understanding was that the President was looking to McNamara, and he in turn was looking to Admiral Sharp and other intelligence people for what he, in the end, judged to be solid evidence that it had taken place."

In the Gulf, the evidence was collapsing. Several hours after the so-called attack, Herrick climbed to the bridge of the *Maddox*, his stomach tight with apprehension that a bizarre error might have occurred. As Herrick reached the top of the ladder, his worst fears were confirmed. He was met there by his second-in-command, Commander Herbert L. Ogier, skipper of the *Maddox*, who informed Herrick that the reports of the attack were wrong.

The destroyer had been going unusually fast and zigzagging, and some, if not all, of the sonar sightings had simply been the ship's electronic signals bouncing off its own rudder rather than enemy torpedoes, Ogier told Herrick. Then Herrick and his top officers huddled and agreed on the source of the error and the necessity of informing Washington.

Herrick cabled word of his discovery: "Review of action makes many reported contacts and torpedoes fired appear doubtful. Freak weather effects on radar and overeager sonar men may have accounted for many reports. No actual visual sightings by *Maddox*. Suggest complete evaluation before any further action taken."

Herrick's decision to reverse himself was not an easy one. "You know, we've led them on now for three or four hours and all of a sudden we're changing our tune," he recalled in a recent interview, "and you wonder how they're going to react to that . . . There's a sort of gung-ho spirit in any of the services, and not many people like to admit they're wrong or have been wrong, but the stakes were too great in this case. I couldn't stonewall this thing then and pretend—you know, yeah, damn it, it really happened, I just can't take that chance."

He did hesitate about sending the cable.

"I talked it over with Ogier and Jackson [Lieutenant Commander Dempster M. Jackson, executive officer of the *Maddox*] and my staff, and of course I had to make the decision. But pretty much all agreed that—you know—God, this could be serious if it goes all the way, and of course it did."

Herrick's report went up the chain of command to McNamara, but back in Washington a gung-ho spirit every bit as strong as the one Herrick had fought to overcome was driving events. "There were two factors at work," recalled Bill Moyers, the long-time presidential aide who was then working on Johnson's re-election campaign.

"The threat from the right of a Barry Goldwater and the threat within his own party from the hawks, from the Cold War wing of the Democratic Party— which a lot of people have forgotten was still very pronounced in the early sixties and chiefly had been carried into Democratic policy by the Kennedy wing of the party. Johnson would look at the Kennedy people around him, like Robert McNamara and McGeorge Bundy and Dean Rusk, and he would later muse out loud as to what they would think if he had taken a position which in their mind would have seemed softer."

McGeorge Bundy insisted in an interview, however, that it was Johnson himself who took the initiative: "This, I remember quite specifically. He called me up and said we're going to go for a resolution and I said something skeptical [because] of a general feeling that if you want a durable congressional resolution you don't go for it on the basis of some snap event and a surge of feeling around the snap event. And he makes it clear to me that the matter's decided and he's not calling for my advice—he's calling for my staff action in carrying out a decision, which I then do."

That telephone call between Bundy and the President took place in the morning. There was still no reason to doubt that an attack had occurred when, at 1 p.m., the President had lunch at the White House with Mc-Namara, Rusk, Bundy, CIA Director John A. McCone, and then-Deputy Secretary of Defense Cyrus R. Vance. Johnson was insistent that the North Vietnamese be punished.

The record shows that Herrick's cable expressing doubt about the attack arrived in Washington at 1:30 p.m., but there is no indication that the men at lunch were informed of its content. McNamara received the cable sometime after lunch and then called Admiral Sharp in Honolulu. The conversation between Sharp and McNamara, which was not declassified until 1982 under the Freedom of Information Act and which was omitted from previous Defense Department compilations of telephone conversations pertaining to the Gulf of Tonkin incidents, reveals the developing uncertainty that afternoon.

McNamara asked Sharp, "There isn't any possibility there was no attack, is there?" Sharp replied, "Yes, I would say there is a slight possibility." McNamara then said, "We obviously don't want to do it [attack North Vietnam] until we are damned sure what happened," and asked Sharp, "How do we reconcile all this?" When the admiral suggested that the order to retaliate be postponed "until we have a definite indication that this happened," McNamara instructed him to leave the "execute" order in force. McNamara informed Johnson and McGeorge Bundy about the doubts, but Bundy said he depended on McNamara's evaluation of the data.

"Look at the realities of how these decisions are made," said Ball, who participated in key meetings that day. "They sit around a Cabinet table with the President. The head of the CIA briefs you on what the events are, or maybe the Secretary of Defense briefs you on what the events are. You don't look at the cables, you don't look at the underlying documents. If he tells you that the evidence is that there was an attack, then that is the basis for the discussion, that's the underlying assumption, and you discuss on that basis. If you're Secretary of State or if you were in my position as a deputy secretary, you don't insist on looking at the intelligence yourself in a situation like that, because, presumably, it's been vetted with the experts, who are much better able to interpret it than you are."

At 4:34 p.m., Washington time, Herrick, in response to Sharp's insistence for clarification, cabled, "Details of action present a confusing picture although certain that original ambush [on August 4] was bona fide."

Herrick said there were also some sailors on the *Turner Joy* who reported seeing lights on the ocean as well as torpedo wakes. Some experts, including Herrick and Sharp, now discount those sightings as a common visual effect created by luminescent ocean microorganisms.

In his cable, Herrick was responding to what he had been told about intercepted North Vietnamese communications rather than to what he saw. As he recalled recently: "Who am I to doubt stuff that's coming to me in official messages from the intelligence people in the services, you know? And I think that's what McNamara used. I think that's how he made his decision."

Four years later, McNamara would tell the Senate Foreign Relations Committee that the second Herrick cable removed all doubt that an attack had occurred. However, Fulbright, who had not known of either cable until the 1968 Foreign Relations Committee hearings, said that he and the rest of Congress were misled in 1964. If he had known of the telegrams, he said, "I certainly don't believe I would have rushed into action" and introduced the Gulf of Tonkin Resolution for the Johnson Administration. "I think I did a great disservice to the Senate . . . The least I can do . . . is to alert . . . future Senates that these matters are not to be dealt with in this casual manner."

At the time of the Fulbright hearings, McNamara cited then-classified government cables to counter the committee's suspicions that no attack had occurred. Yet recently declassified documents show that throughout the evening of August 4, the Defense Secretary had his own doubts but was under mounting pressure to make sure the matter was resolved in time to get the President on the evening news. In a now-declassified phone conversation with Sharp at 8:39 p.m., Washington time, McNamara said: "Part of the problem here is just hanging on to this news, you see. The President has to make a statement to the people, and I am holding him back from making it, but we're forty minutes past the time I told him we would launch."

At 9:09 p.m., Sharp told McNamara that the planes could not finish arriving at their targets before midnight, Washington time. "How serious do you think a presidential statement about the time of launch would be?" McNamara asked. Sharp replied: "I don't think it would be good, sir, frankly, because it will alert them. No doubt about it . . . Wouldn't recommend it."

In the next hour, Sharp had to inform the Defense Secretary that the air launch had to be delayed further for technical reasons. But McNamara replied, "The President wants to go on the air at 11:15 p.m., that is the problem."

The pressure to make a televised announcement before the nation went to sleep went on to distort two interconnected and critical processes. One was the still-annoying detail of determining whether an attack had, in fact, occurred. After Herrick's cable, Sharp continued frantically to send messages out to ships demanding clarification on the attacks. The military's other concern was that all the planes sent to attack North Vietnam must hit their targets before a presidential announcement robbed them of the element of surprise.

There was to be failure on both counts. Planes were sent to bomb North Vietnam before definitive word was reached from the ships about the torpedo attack—and a number of those planes arrived at their destination after Johnson had informed the world of the raid.

To this day, Sharp remains bitter that the President's refusal to delay his televised address alerted the North Vietnamese and endangered the lives of American pilots. "That's a very bad thing to do," said Sharp, who lives in retirement in San Diego, in a recent interview. He said he argued the point with McNamara, who "decided to do it anyway. Just doing things like that for political reasons, without considering the lives of our pilots and the lives of our soldiers, you know," Sharp said. "The wrong thing to do, goddamn it, just as dumb as hell." The problem, Sharp said, was "you alerted the North Vietnamese that an attack was going to take place. So naturally, when they're alerted, they're better able to strike at you, and the pilots lose as a result of that. A surprise is extremely important in military operations."

Sharp added with some bitterness, "The President had to get on evening TV."

In the attack, two planes were shot down. One pilot was killed and the other captured.

Sharp still believes that there was a North Vietnamese attack on the two destroyers August 4. Vehemently tapping a coffee table in his living room, he said United States retaliation was necessary to "send a message, especially when you're dealing with a bunch of goddamned Communists, because they're ruthless bastards."

On the night of the Gulf incident, though, the record shows that Sharp was concerned up until the end about whether a PT boat attack had actually been made by the North Vietnamese. A couple of hours before the planes were launched, McNamara had a top aide contact Sharp at his Honolulu headquarters to check once again. Sharp sent a message to Captain Herrick asking him to confirm that his ships had been attacked. Herrick's reply was received in Washington at one minute before 11 p.m., sixteen minutes after the first U.S. planes had taken off to attack North Vietnam:

> *Maddox* scored no known hits and never positively identified a boat as such . . . Weather was overcast with limited visibility . . . Air support not successful in locating targets . . . There were no stars or moon resulting in almost total darkness throughout action . . . No known damage or personnel casualties to either ship . . . *Turner Joy* claims sinking one boat and damaging another . . . The first boat to close *Maddox* probably fired torpedo at *Maddox* which was heard but not seen. All subsequent *Maddox* torpedo reports were doubtful in that it is supposed that sonar man was hearing ship's own propeller beat.

Recently, Herrick told me that he confirmed the one torpedo firing because he assumed that the *Maddox* was moving at a slower speed, and the sonar equipment only picked up rudder noises as torpedoes when the ship was moving at more than 25 knots. But when shown for the first time that his notes and the ship's log indicated that the *Maddox* had been traveling at 30 knots when the first alleged attack occurred, Herrick conceded that in all probability no torpedo had been fired.

At 11:37 p.m., while Sharp was still searching out evidence to confirm an attack, thirty-eight minutes after Herrick's last cable listing the missing signs of a battle, Johnson went on television and denounced the North Vietnamese for their unprovoked attack. "Renewed hostile actions against United States ships on the high seas have today required me to order the military forces of the United States to take action in reply," Johnson said. He continued, saying that he would ask Congress for a resolution that authorized him "to take all necessary measures to repel any armed attack against the forces of the United States and to prevent further aggression."

What had begun as a murky skirmish against mysterious dots and slashes on a radar screen became the Gulf of Tonkin Resolution, a finely honed legal justification for America's participation in what would become its most divisive foreign war. The United States presence in Vietnam, limited at the time of the Gulf incident to 21,000 so-called military advisers, eventually reached 543,000 combat and support troops.

Despite Johnson's rhetorical certainty that night, doubts about the attack would continue to pour in. The skipper of the *Turner Joy*, Captain Robert C. Barnhart, answered Sharp's last request for information on witnesses with the plaintive query: "Who are witnesses, what is witness reliability? Most important that present evidence substantiating type and number of forces be gathered and disseminated."

But it was too late for gathering evidence, for that message was received at 1:15 a.m., Washington time—almost two hours after the President had spoken to the nation.

By then, it was daylight out in the Gulf, where a startled Herrick stood on the bridge of the *Maddox* watching planes fly overhead. At first he thought they might be Chinese. Then he realized they were U.S. planes on their way to bomb North Vietnam, and he recalls feeling despair and muttering "Good grief," or harsher words to that effect.

Then-Captain Stockdale led that air attack. In his book, he recalls that he had read Herrick's cable before going to sleep, thankful that "at least there's a commodore up there in the Gulf who has the guts to blow the whistle on a screw-up, and take the heat to set the record straight. As I lay down, and turned out the bed lamp, musing on the . . . absurdity of the goings-on up in the Gulf, I would never have guessed that commodores in charge on the scene of action are sometimes not allowed to blow the whistle on a screw-up or set records straight themselves."

At 4:45 a.m., Saigon time, Stockdale had been rudely awakened by a junior officer and told: "We just got a message from Washington telling us to prepare to launch strikes against the beach . . . The [skipper] wants you to start getting ready to lead the big one, sir . . . Your target is Washington's priority No. 1."

Stockdale asked the young officer: "What's the idea of the strikes?" He was told "Reprisals, sir." "Reprisal for what?" Stockdale asked. "For last night's attack on the destroyers, sir," came the answer.

Stockdale wrote: "I felt like I had been doused with ice water. How do I get in touch with the President? He's going off half-cocked." Stockdale went on that raid and others—until he was shot down and held prisoner for seven and a half years.

The Herricks now live in retirement in Santa Fe, New Mexico, in a modest home, with the CAPTAIN HERRICK shingle proudly displayed over the front door. A likable, no-nonsense type, Herrick was on his way to promotion to rear admiral's rank. He never made it. His dream died that night in the Gulf of Tonkin. He won't quite come out and say it, but his wife—whom he dated as a midshipman at Annapolis and who waited at one Navy base after another while rearing three children during three wars—will.

The President got his television appearance and won re-election. Goldwater suffered a crushing defeat that November, and in a recently published 1980 interview told the Congressional Research Service that he thought the whole Tonkin Gulf incident was politically motivated. "I'll be perfectly honest with you," Goldwater said. "I think it was a complete phony. I think Johnson plain lied to the Congress and got the Resolution."

Johnson aides like McGeorge Bundy say such accusations are false, but there are indications that even the President had his doubts. As Ball recalled in a recent interview, the President complained to him about "those goddamned slaphappy admirals shooting at flying fish." Ball added that Johnson "wasn't convinced at all after the thing . . . but they had been waiting for a provocation for a hell of a long time . . . I don't think he was sure, I think he had grave doubts that this attack had occurred . . . but from the point of view of the President and those who were around him who were eager for a stronger American line to be taken, this served the purpose."

Indeed it did. Three days after Johnson's televised speech, Congress, stunned by what it had been told was an unprovoked attack on American ships peacefully sailing the high seas, passed the Gulf of Tonkin Resolution. Johnson would carry a copy of it in his coat pocket until the day he left office. As Moyers, now a CBS News reporter and commentator, recalled recently: "Any time that anyone would raise the question of the grounding for his actions in Vietnam, he would pull that out and say, 'Look, I have the overwhelming support of Congress.' "

For the remainder of his Presidency, Johnson would claim that the Resolution legally authorized him to send a total of 3.7 million American servicemen to Indochina. By the time the war ended, eleven years later, 58,022 of them had died.

(*Los Angeles Times*, April 29, 1985)

SCRAMBLING
AFTER POWER

✦ ✦ ✦

Pepsi Takes Moscow

Once upon a time at the Stork Club, Joan Crawford spied Ernest Hemingway across the room. Interested in meeting him, she dispatched her escort, a young Pepsi-Cola executive, to inform the writer that he ought to join her table. Don Kendall, playing the eager protégé (Miss Crawford was then married to the Pepsi-Cola chairman of the board), dutifully went over and said, "Mr. Hemingway, Miss Crawford would like to talk to you." To which Hemingway roared out for the benefit of the attendant and gossipy patrons, "Tell her to bring her ass over here if she wants to meet me." Being untutored in the ways of New York society, there wasn't much that Kendall could do but assume the abject role of the typical male in a Crawford flick and retreat humbly to his boss's wife.

Nowadays if anyone tries to tell him that PepsiCo (of which he is chief executive officer and chairman of the board) is Joan Crawford's company, this exuberant and normally cheerful ex-tackle gets a little testy. Joan Crawford falls into a category, along with Richard Nixon (who played the piano at Kendall's second wedding), his first wife, and Coca-Cola sales, that Don Kendall does not want to talk about. What he does love to talk about are PepsiCo's conglomerate acquisitions, ranging from Wilson Sporting Goods to Frito-Lay snack foods, with North American Van Lines and Monsieur Henri Wines (Yago Sant'Gria) thrown in for good measure. Beyond that, the current favorites include "free trade" (particularly with the Soviet Union), corporate responsibility ("What Boy Scouting means to the corporations of America"), and the general virtues of multinational corporations.

Kendall has emerged as one of the more visible and articulate corporate spokesmen, is a friend of Presidents, and even knows David Rockefeller, who picked him to be chairman of the Emergency Committee for American Trade.

ECAT lists the heads of the top sixty-two corporations as members and is the chief lobbyist for multinational companies. Kendall also serves as U.S. chairman of the U.S.-U.S.S.R. Trade and Economic Council. He is a man to be reckoned with, and the day when he was Joan Crawford's schlepper must seem very far behind. (Crawford is still a board member of Pepsi-Cola, but that once proud company has been reduced to a mere division of PepsiCo, the big multinational conglomerate that Kendall built.)

It is with an uncharacteristic meanness that Kendall now has Miss Crawford playing bit parts for Pepsi-Cola. (She is still on retainer but her appearances are rare.) His is an expansive, almost jolly spirit that tends more to the bear hug or at least the bone-crunching handshake than toward a prissy spite. But as one close associate told me, "He made the jump from being a flunky around the place. He took an awful lot of crap from Joan Crawford."

It galls him that most people still think of it as her company—the expected result of massive PR campaigns back in the fifties when the Pepsi-Cola Company was being run by her husband, Alfred Steele.

Steele's what they used to call whirlwind courtship of the famed movie star and many others had established his reputation as a tough, flashy guy who got what he wanted; a syrup salesman's salesman. He thought he detected similar qualities in big Don Kendall, a young college football player turned naval hero, and Steele guided Kendall's rise in the company from route salesman to VP.

Steele's management/personnel philosophy was summarized for me as I was having my back rubbed at company headquarters by Gunnar Ohberg, the reflective and friendly Swede who has been director of Pepsi's physical health services for twenty-four years. "Al Steele once told me that the whole trick in hiring executives is to find a good man and turn him into a prick. He said that a good man would be able to stand the course, but if the guy was a prick to begin with he'd crumble along the way."

Gunnar said this in a spirit of admiration for both Steele and Kendall, whom he seems almost to worship. "Kendall is an earthy, regular kind of guy who just doesn't realize that a lot of the time he scares people—but he's a good guy under it all." Gunnar, who has a master's in phys. ed., was lent by Kendall to the Nixon regime on various occasions, and when he praises Kendall, one must not forget that he has had to work on the likes of Haldeman, Kissinger, Ehrlichman, and the ex-great man himself. He says that while Kissinger is not in as bad a shape as he looks, he's not in the same league with bulls like Steele and Kendall. He predicts that Kendall, who jogs three miles every morning and gets in some tennis every weekend, will live to be a hundred—a great test case for the expanded cardiovascular-system cult, in which Gunnar is a true believer.

Any exec who wants to get anywhere in PepsiCo works out in Gunnar's gym and jogs for lunch—there's a widespread sense that Kendall is watching from his office window to see who just rounded the Giacometti. The landscape of the 141-acre PepsiCo spa in Purchase, New York, is dotted with the objects of famous sculptors and it is estimated that the distance from the Henry Moores to the Lipchitzes (the beginner's track) is a good three-quarter-mile run. Before I could interview Kendall I was given whites and told to jog a mile, but I think that was for my own good.

I took it easy, though, because I'd just been reading the official company biography where I learned that Alfred Steele died of a "wholly unexpected and instantly fatal heart attack" at the age of fifty-eight.

After that, the widow Steele went bravely (and for substantial remuneration) up and down and across this and other free-world lands tirelessly cutting ribbons, opening new bottling plants, saying a few words to the boys at the regional sales conventions, and doing the hundreds of other things necessary to maintaining the memory and good works of her late husband, and, of course, the price of his company's stock. But waiting in the wings, like a Cash McCall ready to conglomerate on the faithful widow's family syrup firm, was Don Kendall, who already had secret ambitions to mix Pepsi with rent-a-trucks, tennis rackets, and potato chips.

He was not without sentiment for the old Pepsi-Cola, but the company just wasn't working . . . in fact it never had worked. Pepsi was always tailing behind the dreaded Cola-Cola, which, to this day, is rarely referred to by name but only as "the competition." Robert J. Abernathy, vice president for manufacturing, spoke the name to me once when he told me that "Pepsi is more to the spice and Coke more to the citrus." But Abernathy is in a select group, being one of the three men permitted to know the secret formula. The three can never travel in the same vehicle.

Kendall loved Pepsi-Cola even more than Joan Crawford did. He still drinks a lot of Pepsi in a day (and I've never seen a single potato chip in his office). He used to sell the stuff and, like an old wine maker, can tell the variations in years and even vending machines. On one visit to Japan, his PR man, Mike Moynihan, recalls that he tasted a Pepsi from the airport machine and rejected it as of inferior quality—it had turned.

In 1963, Kendall got the company president to move upstairs to become chairman of the board and give Kendall his day. In ten years' time Don Kendall was to kick, pull, and mash a bumbling, relatively small, one-product company into a modern multinational conglomerate giant. One of his first acts was to begin plans for the new world headquarters in Purchase, New York, ten minutes from his Greenwich, Connecticut, home. Another was to move to acquire the giant Frito-Lay Company, the nation's largest snack-food business, thereby increasing Pepsi's sales and establishing the company as a major conglomerate. He named the new conglomerate PepsiCo, and it has come out of things on top, or at least number 93 in the *Fortune* 500 ratings. It's finally breathing hard on "the competitor" (number 69).

The Purchase, New York, world headquarters of PepsiCo is on choice Westchester property, snuggled in between country clubs, sullied by not a single Pepsi-Cola sign. An "elegant modern" seven-building complex designed by Edward Durrell Stone is focused on an imported-cobblestone courtyard. A flock of Canadian geese, which have multiplied and now number in the thousands, was brought in to nestle in the man-made lake at the rear of the buildings, and six thousand daffodils "promised a profusion of colors" (to use Kendall's prose), which was delivered on time. Five thousand new trees (thirty-eight varieties), it is said, remind Kendall of his native Washington State, and as a somewhat personal touch, there is a *jet d'eau* in the lake which shoots up eighty feet whenever Kendall pushes a button on his desk.

Kendall presumably is rarely reminded of the Pepsi bottling plant in Long Island City, where he started out as a route salesman. That plant is still in operation and it's still hot, drafty, and disheveled. Bottles explode regularly on the assembly line, making for a debris of glass and cartons throughout the plant floor. In the concentrate section, black Pepsi essence leaks from overhead pipes into some pots placed randomly below, and 1940s-style occupational-safety posters are as profuse as the sculptures in Purchase. The workers in the bottling plant are not tracked, as was naval hero Kendall, to move up through the management ranks. And the dirty gray walls and puddles on the floor indicate that making it a "fun place to work"—the slogan at the Purchase executive headquarters—is not a provision of the Teamster contract. Kendall's brief stint there was a contrivance of an executive-trainee program for getting the "feel of the field," and he never had any fears of being stuck there. He was always a young man going places.

For all of the exercising, success has added a good-size paunch to Kendall's muscular frame. This he blames on the incessant travel and banquets that are a large part of his job, which is: *establishing the company's presence*—as much in a political as in a business sense. A stiffer, more efficient type, Andrall E. Pearson, the company's president by way of the Harvard Business School and a brilliant track record as a management consultant, tends to the daily functioning of the company. This mix is typical of the large multinational conglomerate, which essentially has two basic elements—the political and the accounting. These corporations are obsessed with attaining a growth rate in sales and profits that exceeds that of the rate of inflation, and with continuously improving shares of the markets which they have entered. To get all this, a company needs the political savvy and muscle of a Kendall and the organizational efficiency of a Pearson.

Kendall's responsibility is to open markets—for Pepsi in Russia, for Frito-Lay in Japan—to initiate mergers or conquests of other companies, and to gain the acquiescence of various governments for whatever business is at hand. It is Pearson's job to work out the details of prices, patents, franchise ownership, etc., in such a way as to make it all profitable. Their personalities, as well as those of their aides-de-camp, reflect these diverse but complementary roles. For all of their talk of a "fun place to work," it's a hard business, and from the top men on down, you either produce or you're out. When Kendall decided to go big and conglomerate he needed a Pearson, and with that worthy came the planning techniques which are essential to the survival of a multinational company. As a result, the company has its own monitoring system of reward and punishment built into the operation.

Since PepsiCo does not make public the details of its internal financial strategy and performance targets, I can only pass on what I managed to wheedle during my interviews. What emerges is a corporate and personal preoccupation with the accounting of growth. The PepsiCo pecking order has grade-level numbers attached to it, starting with Kendall at level 31, Pearson at 29 on down to an executive secretary at 4, and abject peons below. For those on levels 14 and up, there is a Management Incentive Compensation Plan, which provides a possible annual bonus for top executives of each company division. The compensation can be more than 50 percent of base salary, which in Kendall's case in 1973 was $201,176; the incentive compensation brought that to $326,176.

Kendall, being the boss, has no great difficulty getting his full measure as long as the overall growth and profit targets are met, but lesser lights are kept hopping. Each year the targets for sales, profits, and share of market growth are meticulously broken down for each company division. The bonus for each executive at level 14 or above is contingent upon three variables: (1) whether the executive's division achieves its target goal, (2) the executive's grade level, and (3) an evaluation by his superiors of the executive's individual performance for the year. If the division makes its goal the executive is in line for the bonus stipulated by his grade level, but this can be increased or decreased as a result of the personal evaluation. Similarly, an outstanding individual performance can secure a large bonus even if the division falls short. These compensations affect only about 190 top people in the company, but the anticipated bonus is considered to be the prod which sets them to pushing those below. One company honcho told me, "Most people here will learn how the system works for the first time when they read your article. We're not happy that you got this."

There is still another compensation program for those who occupy positions at 16 and above, and this is called the PepsiCo Performance Share Plan. It was started in 1972 to replace the traditional stock-option plan. At the beginning of a four-year period, each executive is "given" a Performance Share Award which, however, he can collect only at the end of the period. Its value is determined by the market price of PepsiCo stock at the end of the four years, and, most importantly, a full payout occurs only if the company has maintained a 10 percent compound growth rate of earnings annually. This stake in the future market price is calculated, in the words of one insider, to "stimulate overtime, to motivate the top executives, to help the corporation attain its growth targets, which will presumably show up in the market price of its stock." If the growth rate is only 9 percent, the executive will collect only 75 percent of his award; at 8 percent the award drops to half, at 7 percent, to one-fourth. The award is zero if the company achieves only a 6 percent growth rate.

PepsiCo is considering revising its target growth figures to take into account the inflationary spiral. Such upgrading, when accomplished by a number of larger companies, obviously increases the inflationary pressure and the figures will once again be upgraded, which provides some insight into why we have an inflationary spiral in the first place. But individual executives in a company, and indeed the profit planners up to the chairman and president, are not in a position to take national economic concerns into account. Their precision and planning is internally logical, but their response to the overall economy is to run a rat race to keep ahead of the game.

It was not inconsistent in his mind for Kendall, who supported his friend Nixon's appeals to hold back wages *in general*, to be given a fifty-thousand-dollar raise at the same time. He could justify this by raising other exec salaries proportionately to keep the company's rewards competitive with those being offered elsewhere. By the same token, if he personally arrived at the conclusion that zero growth was a better goal (he hasn't), he, like any other executive in the company, would end up being fired for working against the projected growth targets for that four-year period. These gentlemen have a great deal of power, control, and rewards as long as they move in the direction of growth; let them move the other way and it all evaporates.

I asked Kendall for his opinion of John Kenneth Galbraith's theory that corporations, being large planning units, could simply plan to have lower levels of growth. I might just as well have advocated bisexual love. "No growth! What?" It was the same disbelief that I found when I put the question to the other execs—like telling a missionary that the number of converts doesn't matter. "Well," said Kendall, "I know Galbraith and I like him, he's a very funny person, but he doesn't know anything about economics." What Kendall meant to say is that Galbraith doesn't know anything about survival in the modern corporate world. In that world, growth (in market shares, p.e. ratios, and sales) is chanted like a religious litany; in the hour I spent with Pearson he could talk of nothing else.

PepsiCo's growth is dependent on acquisitions and expanding markets that require political intervention or at least acquiescence at virtually every level, from the SEC to foreign governments. And it's those strings that Kendall knows how to play. As Pearson notes, in giving Kendall his due, "You couldn't *be* as political as Don." Pearson went to Russia with the Pepsi board and never met Brezhnev, while Kendall and the Soviet leader have had several four-hour private sessions. Kendall has been at ease with Johnson and Nixon and he knows Gerald Ford. Pearson, who comes from Southern California, met then-Senator Nixon (by accident) at Santa Barbara's San Ysidro ranch, but Pearson did not see him once during his years in office. Kendall was popping down to the Nixon White House regularly, and that pattern continues with the new President. "I've never met Ford—I'd say that Don is, by design, [political]—he likes to do that and he does it superbly. I don't covet that side of things and I'm very proud and impressed with the job he does, and I think it does have some of the benefits that you have cited for us."

The benefits which I cited ranged from Kendall's establishment of important domestic business and political contacts to opening up the potentially lucrative Soviet market to Pepsi. Of course, Kendall is above all a company man and understands that were his political activities to have a negative impact on sales, he would simply be out. Pearson noted that the board of directors would be informed of any digression from company targets: "A lot of guys' bonuses are at stake, and they sure as hell are not going to sit around and let somebody, even the chief executive, fuck up their business for them."

Pearson was quick to assure me that Kendall's impact has been quite the opposite. He brushed aside the effect of a boycott of Pepsi on the issue of Soviet Jewish emigration. He noted that Pepsi sales were up in New York City and that a Soviet trade deal had gotten Pepsi a lot of favorable publicity, particularly in the business press, as well as a huge potential market.

But it would be an error to think of Kendall as small-minded or exclusively preoccupied with the trade deals of his company. Along the way, while selling both Chiang Kai-shek and Khrushchev a Pepsi, he has picked up a broader perspective of what's good for America. And there's no reason to deny the sincerity of his espousal of a host of causes, from free trade to the corporate conscience, for they are consistent with the perspective and the needs of a multinational corporation, which, by the nature of its far-flung operations, is given to a certain cosmopolitanism. You get used to hiring dark people who speak funny languages (although the only black vice president at PepsiCo is VP for community affairs), and you get passionate about wanting to bring down tariffs. You also have few qualms about interfering in other people's (or nations') affairs; you need assistants who can act discreetly.

Cartha "Deke" DeLoach, a former FBI agent, is Kendall's right-hand man. Somebody should do a book about Deke. While an account of him might be short on life-style or color, DeLoach could probably tell you where 90 percent of the political bodies are buried in this country. (For instance, another ex-FBI agent has said that it was DeLoach who supervised bugging and wiretapping of the Reverend Martin Luther King, Jr., at the 1964 Democratic Convention.) He was hired by Kendall in 1970 to be PepsiCo's vice president of corporate affairs after a twenty-eight-and-a-half-year stint in the FBI. He began as a special agent in Norfolk, Virginia, and ended as Hoover's number-three man. No one is quite sure just what he does at PepsiCo, but it certainly includes protecting Kendall's time and image. Over several days of interviews, the only time he left us alone was when Kendall asked him to get me a Cuban cigar.

It is certain that whatever Kendall is into it includes DeLoach—he wanted to recruit him badly from the FBI. DeLoach now supervises the writing of many of his speeches and is an almost constant traveling companion.

While DeLoach's style does not always suggest humor or inspire warmth (he rather pointedly warned me that Kendall was an open guy until you crossed him), he does seem to have a genuine affection and loyalty for Kendall, and it seems to me that of the two he is the one in awe. He only has his years with Hoover to go on, so by contrast Don Kendall easily represents a vision of freedom and sanity. Or as he put it, "Don Kendall is a J. Edgar Hoover with heart."

There has been a discovery by multinational administrators like DeLoach and Kendall that their Soviet counterparts are, in a real sense, kindred souls with similar motivations and appetites. One wonders where that leaves the rest of us—the administratees. In any event there can be no doubt that they do end up liking each other, whatever the initial reasons for contact. Ex-G-man DeLoach, who once ordered his eight thousand agents, each working two hours overtime, to put domestic Reds under surveillance, now says, "I deal with the Soviets on a regular basis and I enjoy it tremendously, but I see that as a broadening of my own thinking and personality and I'm glad to have the opportunity. I have some good friends among the Russians today—we visit back and forth all the time—I admire them; I enjoy it tremendously—

I admire their stick-to-itiveness; I admire the loyalty they have to their country. In short I'm having a ball."

"Mr. Kendall, it's the White House, General Haig calling." Keeping a polite distance I overheard only grunts of agreement and the hearty ending, "Well, it's the only thing to do; we've just got to look ahead." With that done, Don Kendall offered me yet another Diet Pepsi and turned back to telling me about the bright prospects for Soviet-American trade. Although in those last hours only he, Rebozo, and Abplanalp remained among Nixon's close business friends, Kendall was not one to let sentiment interfere with schedule or ritual with power. Three hours after the President tendered his resignation to the nation on TV, Don Kendall had placed his full confidence and "excitement" in the prospects of the new Ford Administration, and was working once again on his tennis.

Kendall knew the track record of both men and was certain they (and he) shared a common perspective: "I do think that people will settle back down again. . . . I know Jerry Ford and have a high regard for him. He certainly knows where to go to get all the advice he needs, and there are a lot of people down there now who could give him very good advice."

Those people included the network of corporate lobbyists, known to Kendall, who had worked closely with Ford as a congressman; men such as Rodney W. Markley, Jr. (the Ford Motor Company's top lobbyist), and Bryce N. Harlow of Procter & Gamble, who, according to *The New York Times*, are among Ford's "closest and most trusted friends." Gerald Ford had long before established his reasonableness on the key issues in the eyes of the business internationalists and there was no cause for Kendall to be alarmed at his ascension to the Presidency.

But while Kendall trusted Ford's political judgment he would never again personally be as central to the functioning of the Presidency as he was under Nixon. For over a decade Kendall and Nixon had taught each other much while servicing their common needs.

Kendall was one of the business internationalists whose obsession with sales in the world market helped Richard Nixon transcend the hysterical anti-Communism of his earlier years. Nixon's serious apprenticeship for the Presidency began (after the 1962 defeat) when he joined the Wall Street firm of Mudge, Rose, bringing in PepsiCo as his main client. When Kendall first gave the PepsiCo business over to Nixon he was not simply extending a personal favor. Nixon possessed the sort of international connections that were useful to PepsiCo, and vice versa.

One of the people who traveled with Nixon in those days was Herman A.

Schaefer, the PepsiCo vice president for finance. He recalls, "Nixon was an unofficial guest of Nasser, and I arranged to be there then to resolve some problems we were having. I spent three days with him." Schaefer's recollection of his first session with Nixon on that trip provides a nice footnote on the past President's work habits: "When we first went into some room at the Nile Hilton he [Nixon] said, 'Now let's get off in a corner someplace and make sure we're not bugged because we're gonna talk about what you want me to do tomorrow when I see such and such and what I'm supposed to tell him.'" Schaefer now thinks that Nixon always had an obsession with tapes that was part of a pattern of self-destructiveness. When I interviewed him the day of Nixon's resignation, he was chortling somewhat happily, but perhaps out of deference to Kendall's sensibilities, he made me turn off the tape recorder first. He did *not* ask me to turn off the tape recorder when he recounted the purposes of his and Nixon's trip to Egypt: "At that time Coke had been blacklisted, boycotted [in the Arab countries], and we wanted to be able to really move that market—take it over."

Aside from the pragmatic business usefulness of his Soviet contacts, there is no doubt that Don Kendall has a genuine respect and indeed enthusiasm for the Soviet leadership dating back to Khrushchev's Pepsi-quaffing day. (Nikita's drinking Pepsi before the cameras of the world supposedly saved Kendall's job because, as head of the International Division, he had put money into an exhibit in Moscow after Coke had turned it down, and some guys at the home office had their knives out for him.)

For the then-president of Pepsi-Cola International it was the beginning of a gripping awareness that the Soviet leadership was made up of human beings. It is a perception that has been confirmed on his subsequent trips to the Soviet Union: "General Secretary Brezhnev is a very warm, very outgoing person, he's an extrovert, not an introvert. I've got some pictures taken in June and you can see it [emphatically]. He's a *warm* person. He's very outspoken. When you talk to General Secretary Brezhnev and he says something, you don't have to wonder what he meant by that, which I like because I'm a direct outspoken person myself. I don't want to think, What did he really mean?"

At one trade dinner after Kendall finished his speech, the head of Soviet exports came bounding around the dais and gave him an enthusiastic embrace that lifted him a good foot off the ground. Then Kendall, smiling broadly, picked the equally massive Russian up two feet. It is at least an interesting addendum to the history of the Cold War that a tackle from a Sequim, Washington, high school, who has always voted Republican and really believes in the virtues of Pepsi-Cola, Richard Nixon, and the rest of our system, should now come to us as a fifties pinko. When one considers the human and economic costs of those years spent "containing" the Russians, it is ironic that the most scathing denunciation of containment should now come from a man who once canceled his daughter's subscription to *Ramparts*, and only recently railed that McGovern would destroy our freedom and our way of life.

Do you recall the endless litany about broken treaties and the line about any agreement with them not being worth the paper it's written on? Well, here's Kendall on that: "I can't find anybody who's an authority on the Soviet Union who can show me or tell me that the Soviets have ever violated any agreement that they've ever written as long as it's spelled out. I don't know anyone who says they've ever violated a commercial agreement. I don't know anyone in real authority and experience that can say they've violated a political agreement where it was spelled out."

We have to assume that Kendall frequently found Richard Nixon, who was never reticent in telling the rest of us about how the Soviets had violated *every* agreement they had ever made. But Pepsi and the Chase Manhattan Bank and Nixon needed détente when the U.S. empire became unglued in the Vietnam debacle. Enter the good Russians, exit the godless devils. We can live with the Russians because they can live with us, by which is meant a common need to prevent the troubling skirmishes of the have-nots.

This is why Kendall most frequently refers to the successful overthrow of the Allende government in Chile as the most convincing illustration that détente works. Under Allende, Pepsi was expropriated in Chile much as it was twelve years earlier in Cuba, but the difference is that this time around Pepsi got Chile back. I heard Kendall address the Sales Executives Club of New York in the Grand Ballroom of the Waldorf-Astoria. This was the sanctuary of General MacArthur when Truman compelled his return from Korea, yet here was the head of old red, white, and blue PepsiCo flanked by four high Soviet officials and the heads of Coca-Cola and *Reader's Digest*. The Sales Executives Club was sponsoring yet another jaunt of drummers to Russia and Kendall was there to assure them of the permanency of the current peace: "In Chile you had an elected government that was elected Communist, and I think that anybody who knows the power of the Soviet Union knows that, if they wanted to maintain that government in Chile, that Allende would probably still be there today. But I think this is a sign of change in their policy that did not occur at the time of Cuba and you know the results of that."

Don Kendall does not want to tell the Russians how to treat their minority groups (Jews, Czechs, poets, etc.)—that's their internal affair—and he doesn't want them telling our companies what to do in Chile—that's our internal affair. We (meaning Kissinger, Nixon, Ford) do not intervene when the

Russians throw their weight around in Eastern Europe, and they pay similar respects to our prerogatives in Latin America, and as Kendall frequently points out, once you've got that understanding down, it will be kept, because it's in the interests of both sides.

That the Soviets share Kendall's perspective on all this was indicated by the response of their officials at the Sales Executives meeting. I expected that they would be at least embarrassed by Kendall's blunt references to Chile at the Waldorf gathering, when the subject was just then being discussed a few blocks away at the UN. But they were actually pleased with Don's performance. I had bounded around the dais, hot little tape recorder in hand, to catch some faint stirrings of outrage or at least guilt—after all, a lot of people were killed in Chile who still believed in the Soviets. But all they wanted (or were allowed) to talk about was the future Soviet-American market. The first guy I cornered wasn't allowed to talk at all:

SCHEER: Excuse me, I wonder if I could ask you a question. Do you have any reaction to Mr. Kendall's speech?

HIGH SOVIET TRADE OFFICIAL: I can't comment.

SCHEER: The comment on Chile was pretty provocative, do . . .

H.S.T.O.: I still can't make any comment, hah, hah.

SCHEER: Is there anybody who can talk?

H.S.T.O.: See Mr. Kolov.

SCHEER: Mr. Kolov, I was wondering if you'd comment on Mr. Kendall's speech. Did you feel it was a good summary of the situation?

MR. KOLOV: I enjoyed his speech. I think it was a really good representation of the view on Soviet-American trade from the point of view of a big American businessman who knows a lot about Soviet-American trade. He's the chairman of this trade council [the Committee on United States-Soviet Relations] and I think he knows what he's talking about.

SCHEER: Yes, but what about his remarks about Chile?

MR. KOLOV: What remarks?

SCHEER: You didn't find that interpretation of détente objectionable?

MR. KOLOV: No, I don't think there is any special objection to the substantial background of his speech. I think he is right in general.

The Soviets want or need trade, consumer goods, and a lower military budget, and they therefore need a Don Kendall more than an Allende. And the Kendalls, or rather the multinational corporations that Kendall speaks for, now need trade and normalization of relations with the Soviets more than the anti-Communism (and defense contracts) of the Cold War. For the Soviets, the Pepsi connection is a very good deal and it certainly has less to do with the desire for that magical syrup than with the formation of certain alliances with the United States.

Kendall may have dreams of a vast market with a "Boss" Pepsi bottle replacing vodka and kvass in every Russian home, and the Russians do seem interested in getting their people off alcohol (certainly our experience shows that people work harder when they're guzzling Pepsi rather than booze). As Kendall told the sales execs, "We're gonna sober them up with Pepsi and bring their vodka over here and get the Americans drunk." But it's this second part—increasing Soviet exports to the United States to earn hard currency as a basis for importing more sophisticated industrial equipment—that is at the heart of the trade deals. In the process the Soviets are rewarding and further enlisting the support of Kendall, who has been useful as a friend of Presidents and perhaps the most vociferous business lobbyist.

The specifics of the Pepsi deal are illustrative of what the Russians are really after. Pepsi will be sold at the high price of forty cents (local drinks sell for pennies), and plans at this stage call for its being marketed in areas frequented by foreign tourists who are hooked on the stuff. Further expansion of sales is tied to Pepsi's ability to market Soviet vodka and champagne within the United States. Over a five-year period Pepsi's sales within Russia have to be balanced out by equal sales of Soviet products here. Which means Pepsi is putting its marketing expertise into opening the American market to Soviet products.

That's why Kendall had a real stake in obtaining most-favored-nation status for the Soviets, for it would bring the price of Soviet goods into a competitive range.

Most favored nation is itself a misnomer, since most of the U.S. trading partners are "most favored," including horribly coercive regimes. (That the Soviets do not have it is a hangover from the Cold War.) Business writers now use the word "nondiscriminatory" to explain the MFN, because the concept basically involves cutting back or negotiating out the high protectionist tariffs erected with the Hawley-Smoot Act of 1930. These rates still stand on the books, but for the past forty years U.S. Presidents and Congress have been cutting them way back for most of our trading partners, with the payoff being that the other nations also reduce theirs.

Kendall's *bête noire* in all this has been Scoop Jackson, who moved to strike MFN from the U.S. government's trade bill unless the Soviets moved to change their policy on Jewish emigration. The Soviets resented this, termed it meddling in their internal affairs, and in January 1975 said *nyet* to the trade agreement. This leaves most favored nation for Russia still a goal to be achieved by Kendall and his colleagues, and it makes him even more annoyed with Scoop Jackson.

Jackson's motives are as difficult to discern as Kendall's, for personal ambition and gain are joined about equally with moral sloganeering in the rhetoric of both men. Jackson accuses Kendall of selling out the Russian and American people for a cheap shot at the Soviet soft-drink market and Kendall thinks Jackson is just hustling the Jewish and organized-labor vote for his future presidential campaign.

However, when Jackson made a speech specifically attacking détente by focusing in on the Pepsi connection, it was a voice from another time, certainly one prior to this era of multinational sell: "We are asked to believe that the prospects for peace are enhanced by the flow of Pepsi-Cola to the Soviet Union and the flow of vodka to the United States. In fact, we will move much further along the road to a stable peace when we see the free flow of people and ideas across the barriers that divide East from West."

Kendall is perplexed by this and with good reason. He knows the free world very well, and certainly the common denominator of "free world countries," where Pepsi has its five hundred bottling plants, is not a common emigration policy or the rights of free political expression. What the "free" countries do have in common is their willingness to permit Western sales personnel and products to cross their borders. Kendall gets no flack for importing Yago Sant'Gria (the country's largest-selling wine import) from Fascist Spain, or for Pepsi's past operations in South Africa. But bring in a little vodka and you've got trouble. And he doesn't really get it—he can't understand why the American Jewish Committee "indefinitely postponed" its plans to grant him a leadership award in the wake of the Pepsi/vodka deal. He thought he was "opening up the Soviet Union" to our influence.

It is not just that Kendall feels his company should not monitor or control the political life of all the countries in which Pepsi is sold; he has a more aggressive view that America is a consumer/capitalist society and that its important ideas are products that can be sold. The open society is defined by corporate internationalists like Kendall as one in which you can do business—period. The expectation is that before too long the Russians will permit the kind of advertising seen in Hungary, Poland, and Yugoslavia, that they will become consumer-oriented in their cultural life, and the whole science/art of retailing, packaging, and sales will come into its own in that barren wasteland.

Pepsi, being a modern corporation, takes its cultural contributions seriously and all the execs from Kendall on down are quite aware that they have never been in the business of simply selling a product but, rather, a way of life. Throughout the years of Pepsi-Coke rivalry the arena has always been in the packaging and sales effort and not the concentrate, which has stayed the same while the companies' fortunes have gone up and down. It was, therefore, not the taste that mattered but, rather, how the public was taught to perceive it. The same stuff could be "light," "sociable," a healthful tonic—it could make you "stay young and fair and debonair" and get you into the Pepsi Generation. This magic is worked for a concentrate that is basically the same for all of the colas and the much-guarded secrets can be obtained from a flavor chemist's handbook—a minuscule amount of extract from the kola nut, the oil of orange and lemon peels, spices, and lots of citric acid or phosphoric acid and caffeine. This forms the concentrate that, when mixed with sugar and carbonated water at bottling plants, makes up the drink. It's not even an American achievement, since the cola flavor was developed originally in Africa and was in wide use throughout the world (in Australia it was known as Hot Tom Kola) before its introduction here. What was American about it was the association of the drink with a desirable life-style.

For Pepsi that began with the famous jingle. For those who think that life started with the Pepsi Generation in the sixties, I'll refer them to the words that promised America plenty during the years of the Great Depression:

> *Pepsi-Cola hits the spot!*
> *Twelve full ounces that's a lot,*
> *Twice as much for a nickel, too—*
> *Pepsi-Cola is the drink for you!*

On October 7, 1940, as Hitler swept through France, *Life* termed Pepsi's jingle "immortal." Recently Kendall told the Boy Scouts of America, "Pepsi-Cola's most prized possession for two decades was its jingle, 'Pepsi-Cola Hits the Spot!' In 1942, a survey showed that this jingle was the best-known tune in the United States—even ahead of 'The Star-Spangled Banner.' "

After the war that jingle was followed by the tonier, "Be sociable, have a Pepsi," and then, for the sixties, the youth imagery of the Pepsi Generation, described in a company report:

"Now 'It's Pepsi—For Those Who Think Young' is designed to have the widest appeal and the most stirring impact. The new ads show up-to-date people enjoying Pepsi-Cola with a friendly, enthusiastic and lighthearted approach that characterizes the Pepsi personality."

Now that the competition for the "hearts and minds" has, in the world of Kendall and Brezhnev, somehow fizzled into a contentless blather, it is no doubt fitting that Pepsi, whose first jingle gave us our real national anthem, has produced a new "Internationale": "Feelin' Free," the jingle for '74. That phrase was selected over thousands of contenders because it proved through hundreds of scientific tests that it excelled in "memorability" and "aura," the two things sought in the competitive market when the products themselves are virtually indistinguishable. There is some anticipation in Purchase that "Feelin' Free" may be a biggie in the aura sweepstakes. Alan Pottash, Pepsi's senior vice president for creative services, is particularly taken with the universality of the phrase: "We were afraid in the beginning, and this is an interesting sidelight here, that some countries which don't have democracies would oppose the concept of 'Feelin' Free' on the possibility that they would take it very literally. This was quickly washed away when we analyzed for ourselves the double meaning of the word or the sense of feelin' free, because if you substitute the word 'carefree' for the word 'free' you're getting closer to what we're really saying—feeling carefree, not feeling free in the sense of breaking the chains that bind you, but feeling free in spirit, and feeling free in thinking and independent enjoyment. So feeling carefree was the best way to explain what we meant in foreign languages and that's what we've done."

The point is that if one can separate an aura of feeling free in spirit from the reality of whether one is "in chains," have it associated with Pepsi, and if Pepsi is free to be in that market, why then everyone will make out. Admittedly Pepsi by itself will not deliver the Promised Land, but if you throw in Gillette Trac II razor blades and quiet Fords and dog food with eggs, then you've got a winning package. Which is precisely what the vision of the multinational corporation comes down to. It is based on a denial of any other aspirations, or indeed history, outside the one that advertising makes. Nothing else that has ever gone on in a country really matters. For example, for Herman Schaefer, the PepsiCo VP for finance, all the complexity and scope of Chinese history is reduced down to a gullet that needs a Pepsi. Speaking on the prospect of that market "opening up," the Bamboo Curtain coming down after the Iron Curtain has fallen, he said, "There are eight hundred million gullets in China and I want to see a Pepsi in every one of them."

It is necessary to internalize such a view, for otherwise how can one totally dedicate one's life to pushing sugar water and chips on a world that undoubtedly needs powdered milk instead? Nobody wants to feel like a crumb. Pepsi execs are an intelligent group whose children tend to tell them that they are not exactly making the most useful contribution to the world's food problem, and that this preoccupation with the growth of company sales, while it may produce bonuses, will not lead to the most effective utilization of scarce resources.

As their house-organ article on "Feelin' Free" states: "Every human being likes to think that he functions individualistically—not as a cipher, a mere member of the herd." That goes for PepsiCo execs, too; they need the aura of feelin' free. Yet most of the executives I talked to, including Kendall, said that they had required their own children to drink milk and not spoil their appetites before dinner on Pepsi, while at the same time they were out in the world conning kids who didn't get milk to hustle up their quarters for a cola.

Whenever I pushed this contradiction in interviews, the obviously intelligent person I was talking to suddenly became one of those blank smiling faces in a sixty-second spot; they said silly things like "Well, you can't put meat and potatoes in a soft drink, Bob"—(Kendall); or, "It gives them a source of sterile water"—(Abernethy); or "It's a moment's refreshment"—(Pottash). They all reminded me that they loved their work, that Pepsi's a "fun" thing, that Purchase was an exciting place to work, and suddenly I could no longer maintain the effort to differentiate between the Pepsi execs and the caricatures that make up their ads. It was just not helping me feel free. Every time I had brought up those annoying questions like: "But does the world really need a 20 percent growth in snack-food sales?" or, "Why don't you put some vitamins and proteins in your chips like they do with dog biscuits?" or, "Doesn't sugar water rot teeth?" I would get zapped with the aura. Fun people do not ask questions like that, fun people just live a little and have another Pepsi. So I'm not a fun person.

(*Esquire*, April 1975)

Scoop: The Hawk That Haunts

[*The late Scoop Jackson was one of the key proponents of the ideology of Cold War liberalism, that unique meld of big military spending and generous support for the welfare state that has for so long dominated America's political culture. His ideas and his disciples are still very much with us.*]

Since the morning of April 16, 1975, Scoop Jackson has known, just *known*, that he would be the next President. Cambodia had finally fallen, détente was in disarray, and Scoop seemed at last to have turned the Vietnam War to his personal advantage. He rose at 6:30 and, as is his custom, soon began flicking between the network TV news programs, got CBS radio news going in the background, and simultaneously attempted to shave. But the news reports merely confirmed what Jackson had known for some time: that Henry Kissinger was crumbling. Kissinger was left holding the "Honor in Vietnam" bag, and Scoop, who had just recently dropped it, was having a field day, charging Kissinger—accurately—with making secret agreements with Saigon.

Now, the next President is a man whose happiness is nearly perfectly measured in inches of AP wire copy that mention his name. His pockets are stuffed with crumpled news clippings, and he fished one out for me while he got the coffee. It said Scoop was right about Kissinger, and maybe he is, but all the same I suddenly found myself in the unbelievable position of feeling sorry for the drowning, bubbling figure of Henry Kissinger. Such is the effect of six weeks with Scoop.

It's hard to focus a portrait of Henry Martin Jackson; he's so good, so gray, so earnest—and so wrong. If only he were simply the senator from Boeing, or the oldest, most faithful Cold Warrior, or the new energy populist, or even just a very ambitious congressman trying to be President before he dies. All of these things are easy to understand. But Jackson transcends such classifications and comes to us now as a far more complex, serious, and ominous personage than his dull public image would suggest.

Even Scoop's close aides and friends welcome a reporter with the disclaimer that they know of no anecdotes, color, personal idiosyncrasies, or jokes about the man. "The Scoop you see is the only Scoop there is," says Stanley Golub, the treasurer of his 1972 campaign and friend of forty years. The head of the Washington State Labor Council says Scoop "has changed less in twenty years than any man I know—he's a workaholic, going all the time."

Those who do not take Scoop very seriously chalk his colorlessness up to an ineffective speaking style born of a pedestrian intelligence and his Norwegian, Northwestern upbringing. On the day Jackson announced for President, the *Washington Star-News* said his campaign style was so dull that "if it gets any duller someone may pass a law against it." Scoop aides, however, think of that style as an asset—the non-charismatic unemotional pragmatism needed in these times. There is, however, nothing ethnically preordained about Scoop's style—it is, rather, a necessary contrivance for resolving the logically irreconcilable and it has worked well in bringing him the votes of Washington State Democrats and Republicans, labor and big business. If there is anything regionally inspired in Scoop's performance, it is that the head moves more than the hands—a Southern senator's filibuster without the flourishes, offered always in a deadly serious monotone. He stands there, this penguin of a man, clutching the microphone stand, lips pursed, droning out the words in a constant stream from some hidden crevice in that massive head, almost as if prerecorded.

But make no mistake—he's great at it. Pick any subject, and bits of ideas and facts pour forth from him as though from a paper shredder. The main thrust of what he says is that he has always been right on every question. It was he who anticipated every problem, warned about it in time; the Administration (all of the past five) chose to ignore his advice and that's why we're in whatever pickle we're in at the moment. If only they'd listened to Scoop.

But Scoop's eternal rightness is especially hard to believe in on an issue like Vietnam, about which he has probably been the wrongest man in the country, always chiding the Administration from Eisenhower on down for not going in fast enough. Yet now he says—or seems to say—he knew all along that there was no light at the end of the tunnel: "My position was very early that I oppose a war of attrition. I want that war to come to an early end or get out. I opposed moves to expand the conflict. . . . My objection was, 'Look, don't get into a protracted conflict.' Once our troops were committed we had to give them the support so they had a chance of coming out of there.

I didn't change any position. Now, you know consistency is . . . who was the English author, who's the genius, hobgoblins I believe was the comment. I'm trying to think of the author of that. Uh, I just do what I think is right, call 'em as I see 'em, you know."

Well, inconsistent hobgoblin or not, the point of that statement, once I replayed my tapes about twenty times, was that Jackson never really supported going into Vietnam but only wanted to give our boys enough support so they wouldn't be shot in the back while we tried to pull them out. Which is simply untrue. Jackson was for going into Vietnam when the French were still there, and he attacked Eisenhower because he was "unwilling to face up to the real threat that America and the free countries are up against in the event Indochina should fall."

Jackson was left almost alone in the Democratic Party as an outspoken defender of Johnson's policies after 1965. Indeed, he was to the right of L.B.J. just as he had been Eisenhower's most persistent hawk critic. While Jackson now claims, "I voted against adding a quarter of a million troops to Vietnam," the record shows that in 1965, after getting jacked up by Westmoreland in Saigon, he returned home and called for "a doubling of the American troops in Vietnam from 200,000 to 400,000. The sooner we get on with this business the sooner the major part of this conflict will be over and the sooner we will begin saving lives." When Bobby Kennedy delivered his famous Senate speech in 1967 breaking with Johnson on the war, Lyndon had Scoop jump up immediately with the Administration's rebuttal.

Although Jackson came to be Johnson's closet Senate confidant on Vietnam, and they were to meet frequently at Scoop's house for small dinners when L.B.J. needed to feel less isolated, the President was wise enough to reject Jackson's call for an invasion of North Vietnam. He did, however, go along with Scoop's public call for massive bombing of the North. In a fiery speech to the American Legion, Jackson addressed a question to the White House. "How long should we wait before making the shoe pinch in North Vietnam by destroying key economic installations there?" The bombing of Hanoi, he said, was embarrassing to the Soviets "from a psychological point of view. . . . This puts Moscow in a most humiliating position and you can be sure she is having to do a lot of explaining in the other Communist capitals." And there is nothing Scoop loves as much as embarrassing the Russians. Indeed, confrontation with the Soviets is the one all-consuming passion in his life.

A recurrent myth in the reporting on Scoop Jackson holds him to be politically formidable because he is the ultimate typical American; typical in tastes, habits, aspirations, culture, and needs. As a matter of fact, it is only necessary to observe him in his daily routine to see that there is nothing "typical" about him. His whole style of life, from what he eats to the hours he keeps, seems to be the necessary conditioning of a combatant in some war that the rest of us do not know about.

Hour after hour, from 8:30 in the morning until 7 at night, he chugs up and down the corridors of the Senate buildings from committee meeting to office. Since 1940, he has lived this rhythm of public life, punctuated by roll calls, press conferences, chats with visitors, his evening swim and sunlamp, embassy receptions, business breakfasts, and weekend speaking gigs. They all do it in the Senate, but the consensus is that Scoop does it a hell of a lot more and thrives on it. He flourishes on the endlessly droning Senate committee hearings, with their "expert witnesses," that make up such a large part of his life. He's extra conscientious about making all Senate roll-call votes, welcoming each bell as another indication of the intense order of his life; and then he's off, scampering like a kid through the narrow hallway shortcuts he's discovered.

He was only twenty-eight when he started in Congress and it has formed the total substance of his adult life. During World War II he underwent basic training while remaining a member of Congress. Without casting aspersions on his courage or patriotism it is safe to surmise that he did not fully share the travails of inductees who were not congressmen. After he left his home in Everett, Washington, for the U.S. Congress, he liked his new surroundings so much that he frequently admitted to feeling no need to get married, since his needs were simple and the House, and later the Senate, met them. During twenty years of bachelorhood he usually lived near Capitol Hill, poached an egg in his small apartment in the morning, and took his other meals in the Senate cafeteria. Now, hip to cholesterol and determined to thwart the aging process, he no longer eats eggs and for the past ten years has had All-Bran and prune juice each morning. Lunch, as his wife, Helen Jackson, observes, has always been the same: "At lunch he doesn't mind having the same thing day after day. He sits at the same chair and at the same table in the Senate dining room; the waitresses peek out and see him coming and put on a hamburger and that's it. He has cottage cheese and tossed salad and a little ground beef."

For dinner, Helen reports, they simply heat up a can of Campbell's tomato soup and throw some frozen crab in it. It is necessary to descend to such detail if one is at all interested in the private Scoop, for there isn't that much else to know. Scoop refuses to discuss his personal life other than to suggest that he is solid and substantial in a Norwegian sort of way. A Jackson press aide, Gene Tollefson, assured me that "Norwegians tend to be reserved people. That does not mean they are not warm, that does not mean they're not human, they just tend not to be overtly emotional." This explanation died when a Norwegian journalist, sent over to cover Jackson, asked me whether all American politicians are that boring.

His campaign aides are eager to suggest that Scoop shares the life-style, and therefore understands the needs, of the average American. One Jackson adviser, contrasting Scoop with his more elite Eastern opponents for the Democratic presidential nomination, called him the candidate of the Thursday-night bowlers. But Scoop Jackson does not bowl, or even golf. The statistically typical American does not wait until he is forty-nine to get married. Nor does he think eating is a waste of time and reading Senate documents is exhilarating. Jackson never shops, rarely drinks, never watches anything on TV except the news, is indifferent to spectator sports, never listens to music of any kind, and disdains most movies. He has virtually no self-doubts, the barest sense of humor, and all his friends will tell you that he seems never to be possessed of an erotic thought. It is therefore safe to suggest that he hasn't the foggiest notion what most Americans do during most of their days. It would in fact require an immense condescension bordering on treason to suggest that he is a typical citizen. He is, rather, the ultimate typical senator—the most unreal in a pretty unreal crowd.

How did Scoop Jackson get this way? He himself insists that a stern Lutheran mother and an even more forceful schoolteacher sister were the main forces in his early development. Jackson considered his sister, Gertrude, his mentor in virtually all matters of importance, from the morality of his personal life to the conduct of his early political campaigns. Jackson's press secretary, Brian Corcoran, a former sports editor of the Everett *Herald*, told me: "Gertrude was public-spirited and she instilled that in her brother. He was her voice in the nation's affairs—she wanted him to do things that helped people. She's the one who gave him his nickname." ("Scoop" was the name of a lazy comic-book character; Gertrude applied it as a continuing admonition to work harder.) Two biographers who researched Scoop's youth describe her: "Tall, with a large masculine face and build, she was awesome to many of the students." The same biographers offer the further insight that "Henry Jackson grew up in a matriarchy with his mother as the captain and Gertrude as the chief lieutenant." When Gertrude was dying of cancer, Scoop took her for a last vacation to a U.S. military R and R base in Hawaii, populated by G.I.s recuperating from Vietnam.

Scoop's father was a small construction contractor who never prospered greatly. The Jackson family, along with most people in Everett (a company mill town built by Eastern banking interests led by the Rockefellers), knew occasional hard times. Scoop delivered newspapers on Rockefeller Street and hoped to grow up a responsible provider. He was happy, a few years after marrying at the age of forty-nine, to move out of the old family frame house and into the mansion formerly owned by the town's richest banker—a move, if not from rags to riches, still in the tradition of the American dream. But it's the American dream as reinterpreted by F.D.R.'s New Deal government spending that kept Everett, and Scoop's career, from going down the tubes. Jackson's entire non-government work experience adds up to a few college summer jobs and two years of private law practice. His life left him a true believer in big government and full-employment stratagems of the New Deal–Fair Deal variety. He has a profound contempt for laissez-faire economics and considers it unworkable. The prosperity of his home state always depended upon government subsidization of large business—particularly the missile and bomber business of Boeing. He regards the Boeing Company as an ideal model whose success can and should be expanded and emulated everywhere. Like so many communities in America, Scoop's has been dependent on military spending, and its Cold War economic structure is the only one he really trusts.

Jackson's family's values—discipline and hard work—could not avert suffering during the Depression and bore fruit only with the manufacture of bombers. Scoop is uncomfortable with disarray, economic or otherwise; and within the confines of government service and the military program he has fulfilled his sense of order. He wants to lead a good solid hardworking life and he wants everyone else to do that, too, but they can't if the economy is not functioning right. He aims to defend the gains of the new middle class through continuous rapid economic growth by big business, underwritten by big government. That's all he's ever seen that worked. He's also seen the dire alternative. Not everyone back there in Everett was a disciplined, morally upright Lutheran trying to hold things together. Radical currents run deep in the state of Washington, and the parents of many of Scoop's school chums were Communists, Wobblies, socialists, anarchists, Henry Georgists. John Salter, his closest childhood friend and later administrative assistant, had an uncle who was the first socialist mayor of Everett—and that wasn't considered very far-out. Jackson's father fought the Communist militants in the labor movement when he was head of the local labor council and it was just in the nick of time that the New Deal and, some might say, the Big War arrived to save the day for decency.

Press secretary Brian Corcoran took me on a tour of Everett, calculated to interpret the candidate's early life to me and other voters. "We'll start out at the house where he was born. Then we'll go over to the Longfellow School, where he went through grade school, and then we'll look at his junior high school. And we can look through the area where he delivered papers as a youngster, where he won a national award—at Everett High School, where he went to high school. There's the Snohomish County Courthouse, where Jackson first served, at twenty-six, as prosecuting attorney. Then I can drive you down into lower Hewitt Avenue, where all the whorehouses were and that he raised hell with, all the gambling joints and so forth where he won his reputation as Soda-Pop Jackson [1938–40]. I think he delivered papers down in that area, too, and that's where he got his first impression of what was going on down there. You'll get a feel for the flavor of Everett."

Well, downtown Everett, all eight blocks of it, stayed clean after Soda-Pop Jackson's crusade against the madams and it no longer has a discernible flavor. But there's plenty of history around about wild old days down by the wharf section with the Wobblies and Bolsheviks and preachers and whores and gamblers all madly competing for the consciousness of a mill hand or long-shoreman. As prosecuting attorney, Scoop got his political start as the last man to tame that town.

Brian Corcoran's tour is aimed at establishing the ordinariness of Scoop and, of course, garnering the vote of anyone who ever went to junior high school, delivered a newspaper, or indeed was born. But even long ago, an ordinary newsboy's first impression of what was going on down there on lower Hewitt Avenue must have been more enthusiastic than Scoop's. Wasn't there a summer of '32 in Everett when kids walked around aroused and preoccupied? Maybe, but not Scoop.

In Seattle, I talked to John Salter, Jackson's roommate for his first twenty years in Congress and the best man at his wedding. Salter had been the one who put the campaigns together. He made the deals, twisted the arms, coddled the friends, and knifed the enemies while Jackson studied the issues.

At sixty-three, Salter remains a loyalist but is painfully aware that he has been moved to the fringe now, a once useful local crony but a potential embarrassment in the national politics that now preoccupy Jackson. It's not that Salter doesn't have things to do; he still represents Boeing and Weyer-haeuser just as he has for the past twelve years since he left Jackson's payroll, and he's still got to line up the Washington convention votes for Scoop against the onslaught of local "crazies," including the local McGovernites who control the county Democratic Party, as well as Muskie people who haven't yet swung over. But there really isn't a central place for him in the new liberal scheme of things required for a Jackson Democratic convention. The last thing Scoop wants to be remembered for is being the Senator from Boeing, and John Salter, who ran the SST campaign out of Jackson's Senate office, is in the unfortunate position of representing Scoop's closest link with that firm.

Salter and Jackson handpicked the state's congressional delegation and they line up pretty well, according to Salter: "Tom Foley was here last week and I made arrangements for him to have a briefing as to what Boeing is doing. He's the chairman of the Agriculture Committee, so it's terrifically important to Weyerhaeuser, since the forest service comes in that department. So we had lunch down there and had some of the top management people ask questions of him as to what he thought was going to happen in the committee and the new reforms of Congress. Floyd Hicks was out last week and he was briefed on the various programs that Boeing has up this year. He's on the Armed Services Committee, and I made those arrangements. Brock Adams was out here and he had a briefing and we went out on a hydrofoil boat. It's a new program."

Adams, chairman of the House Budget Committee, is now independent of Jackson, but Foley is one of Scoop's hatchet men within the national Democratic Party. The Boeing people have got to decide soon which one should replace Jackson as senator, now that he's moving up to the Presidency.

Jackson now seeks to obscure Boeing's (and his) connection with the military. He stresses the commercial production of the company. But Boeing's advanced-technology sales base originated with military contracts. Government-sponsored military research assisted the development of commercial planes like the 747, and much of the research has been possible because of Jackson. Indeed, there is a story that Eisenhower had Jackson and his role in promoting government contracts chiefly in mind when he spoke out against the "military-industrial complex." It's not that Jackson likes violence; he was even offended by the stabbing scenes in *Murder on the Orient Express*. He does not make martial noises when he thinks of B-52s. On the contrary, he pushes MIRVs and Polarises and atomic bombs with the detachment of a delicatessen owner summarizing his collection of cold cuts. He has never witnessed war except from a guided tour and thinks of it more in terms of points to be scored against the Russians, or even the Secretary of State, than of pain to be suffered by people. His concern is an abstraction called national security, a science that he feels he has mastered. He is therefore displeased by press descriptions of him as a missile maniac with no human qualities.

"The press runs the same thing—I'm the non-charismatic guy, bland, dull, and only have missiles around."

True enough, there is another side to Jackson's personality; he occasionally exhibits warmth and humor, and he's not a snob. He's a reporter's dream of accessibility; he's unpretentious, direct, and available. He disdains the palace-guard approach, makes his own phone calls, dresses himself, and can even park a car—all things that many other presidential candidates seem never to have learned.

He likes his kids and his wife, even though he sometimes forgets to introduce her at fund-raising dinners. But he's preoccupied with larger questions. What he is is hooked, and what he is hooked on is a Winston Churchill complex. Over some thirty-five years of Cold War, he has become obsessed with the notion that he, more than any man or woman in this country, understands the enemy that lies outside our shores and that it may be he alone who can act to save us. Scoop believes so strongly in the image of Western Civilization as the center of all that is decent in life, and in the unique role of American military power in preserving it, that he will act even when the rest of us are, in his eyes, afraid to. He will be a strong President as he is a strong senator, marshaling his forces toward ends whose morality is not open to serious question. Scoop is the most perfect child of the Cold War, and no matter what changes occur, he cannot now desert it, for it holds too many things together for him. It is too late to start over. This is why it took him so long to let go of the Vietnam War. More than any other event it challenged his vision of America's role in the world as pure and redemptive.

Scoop's refusal to learn from the war surfaced last spring in an episode generated by the issue of the Vietnamese orphans. Jackson was campaigning in San Francisco and was scheduled for a fund-raiser hosted by high-rise landlord Walter Shorenstein, when the orphans arrived. All of Jackson's worlds came suddenly together in a great moral release. World Airways president Ed Daly, a big Jackson campaign contributor and former gunrunner for the U.S. military in Cambodia, was now a John Wayne hero for flying the orphans out. The Presidio, formerly command headquarters for the Vietnam War, was now a humanitarian orphanage. And Scoop, who had so vehemently urged L.B.J. on to more bombing, was now Father Flanagan. After a few minutes with the kids, Scoop opened up a sidewalk press conference: "What's most heartwarming is to see the outpouring of assistance by volunteer groups in the Bay Area here—the way the Army has moved in and taken over and provided the necessary support facilities. I think it is a great tribute to our whole system of government, and I'm very very proud to be an American observing this kind of performance in the name of humanity. I want to congratulate everybody who has been involved in this, both civilian and military."

Brian Corcoran had meanwhile persuaded Ed Daly's daughter to bring out one of the kids to stand by the senator for the picture-taking, a four-year-old, one of the whiter ones, obviously the son of a foreigner. The child looked scared and cold. Corcoran tried to get the senator's attention and finally did:

CORCORAN: Senator, Senator, here's one of them.

JACKSON (*Doesn't hear*): Protect the innocent. I'm not going to pass judgment . . .

CORCORAN (*Turning him around*): Senator, here's one of them.

JACKSON: Oh, here, hi, how are you, what's your name? We'll call you Scoop.

A few reporters stood there in the midst of hundreds of brass while stiffened MPs sternly guarded the children against us. One reporter, Richard Saiz of educational television station KQED, finally started needling the senator:

SAIZ: Do you have any particular thoughts that the orphans that you've seen here today are in part the result of America's policy in Vietnam? That we might be responsible for some of these kids here today?

JACKSON: Well, we're not going to redo the Vietnamese conflict. I think this is our finest hour and money cannot measure alone what we've done.

SAIZ: At what point was it a mistake to have continued our intervention in Vietnam?

JACKSON (*Very agitated*): Look, we're not going to, the children come first, we're not going to discuss Vietnam.

SAIZ: Senator, fifty thousand Americans died in this war. Now I want to know if you think it was a mistake.

JACKSON: Well, I'm sorry, I'm not going to discuss it. I'm here on children now. We're here to help.

ANOTHER REPORTER: Senator, aren't you here on a campaign swing, sir?

JACKSON: *I'm here on children!*

REPORTER: You're campaigning for the Democratic nomination.

JACKSON: I'm here in a nonpolitical role.

WALTER SHORENSTEIN: Brian, let's go now. He's made all his points and it's only going to go downhill from here.

CORCORAN: Thank you. We've got to go right now. We're late for the next one.

SAIZ: That's all you're going to say about our involvement in Vietnam?

JACKSON (*Visibly angry, turns from Brian, who is trying to maneuver him into the car*): Look, you know I responded by no comment, so that's it. Period.

SAIZ: You were a superhawk for ten years and that's it? No comment?

The senator slammed the door and Shorenstein's Lincoln sped off behind two MPs on motorcycles with sirens on a dead run for Trader Vic's, where Mayor Alioto and Cyril Magnin, the department-store king, were waiting.

Now, Scoop Jackson is not a cynical man. He is simply so totally self-righteous that it could never occur to him that any of the policies he advocated over the past twenty years might in any way have led to the suffering of the Vietnamese. Try as he might (and try he must, now, given the doves in his party), he could never come to view that KQED questioner as anything more than a wise-ass kid who had not studied history and was naïve about the enemy. Kissinger may become naïve, Ford too, not to mention obvious bleeding hearts like Galbraith and McGovern. But he, Henry Martin "Scoop" Jackson, will always be there to keep the faith.

But Jackson is not a provincial like Wallace or Reagan. Facts contrary to his obsessions do come to his attention, but they are somehow absorbed in ways that keep the original vision intact. Take the Sino-Soviet dispute and the opening up of China policy during the Nixon years. Almost twenty years ago, Jackson, disgusted with the weakness of the Southeast Asia Treaty Organization, was crusading for a strong anti-Red organization on NATO lines in Asia. He added that the United States "should put up an effective NO TRESPASSING sign—and back it up." Ten years later he was still proclaiming that the main problem in Vietnam was the determination of an "expansionist-minded Red China" to take over Asia and the world.

Asked whether it had *ever* been realistic to think that a Red Chinese Army could have conquered Asia if we had not entered Vietnam, he conceded: "No, they didn't have that capability. But the unknown answer is if they had had that transport, logistic, and backup capability, would they have done so?"

SCHEER: Yes, but in your report to the Senate [after visiting China] you said that they are not going to have that sort of capability for at least fifteen more years.

JACKSON: Yeah, I'm saying that now but you're asking me back in . . .

SCHEER: Well, if they don't have that now and they won't have it for fifteen years more, they certainly didn't have it in 1950 or 1960. Couldn't an accommodation similar to the one we now have with the Chinese have been worked out back then?

JACKSON: Knowing what we know now and what the Chinese have told me, I think initiatives at that time might have avoided all the trouble in Southeast Asia and with China.

Jackson is not taken aback by such major errors in past calculations, for he prides himself on being firm no matter the shifting sands of reality. "I don't know myself very well, but I am determined. . . . I don't change under pressure and I like to stay put." And what he wants to stay put on is his total commitment to massive military spending based on the inevitable calculation of the Cold War. If the world Communist movement is now divided, and the old Cold War hypothesis of the international Communist conspiracy and its "timetable for world conquest" now appears outdated, to Jackson the Russians (the only bad Reds we still have) are only that much more ominous. "They're going to take greater risks, as I view the world of the 1980s, than they would if their position were equalized with or without the satellites."

Though Scoop sounds scary on the intensification of the Cold War into the eighties, he seems mild in comparison to his two top foreign-policy aides, Dorothy Fosdick, staff director of his Permanent Investigations Subcommittee, and Richard Perle, her thirty-three-year-old assistant. Fosdick is the daughter of minister Harry Emerson Fosdick and an old Acheson hard-liner in the State Department. In the mid-fifties she joined Jackson and has not let the Ruskies get away with a thing since. A spinster who has built her life around Jackson, she has become the sister Gertrude of his Senate days—always at his side. Perhaps to counter any mellowing tendencies in her old age she took on Richard Perle as an assistant, fresh out of Cold War think-tank seminars. Perle, who called Fulbright "one of the most superficial senators ever," now finds Fosdick and Jackson soft on Mao's China.

Fosdick, Perle, and author Ben Wattenberg are the hard edge of the Jackson camp, but they could frighten off liberal delegates to the next Democratic convention. To soften the hawk image, veteran Humphrey and Bayh campaigner Bob Keefe, a man given to considerable fat and other compromises, has been brought in as campaign director. Keefe's first ideological victory came over the President's request for additional Vietnam aid. Keefe and Brian Corcoran insisted that Jackson must break with his old Vietnam position or lose the Democratic nomination. They won over the senator and Fosdick, but Perle and Wattenberg would not give in. Months later, only one week before the fall of the Saigon Army, Perle was for giving Saigon "everything they need to resist the aggression." Perle still writes most of the senator's foreign-policy speeches, but he's watched by the others.

Jackson's hard line on Russia has led him to fight for Jewish emigration. This has earned him a base of support in the Jewish community. He does not hesitate to speak for that community, as when he told me Henry Kissinger is one of those "Jews who like to get away from their Jewishness." Secretary Kissinger has charged Jackson with being counterproductive and blocking progress by grandstanding on the emigration issue.

Jackson is not above making crude applications of his Jewish support for political muscle. In the Samuels-Carey gubernatorial race in New York in 1974, Samuels charged in private that Carey's brother, a big oil dealer, was tied into the Arab boycott. Carey forces in turn got Jackson people to let Samuels know he'd get hurt in the Jewish community if he pushed the charge in public. In April 1974, at the big Soviet emigration rally in New York City, Zmira Goodman, co-chairperson of the Jackson for President Committee, reminded Carey of the debt. In the car going out to the airport afterward, Scoop said to Zmira, "Carey owes us one big favor and we are going to get it."

The Jackson people are well aware that the Jewish community is anything but monolithic, and that the majority of Jews are concerned with a host of other questions on which they might have their differences with Scoop. For example, Jackson has not dealt with big-city issues and doesn't fully understand the concern or anger of ghetto minorities. He has maintained a good civil-rights voting record but is impatient with those who cannot drag themselves up by their bootstraps as his Norwegian ancestors did. His first real lapse into white majority arrogance occurred during and immediately after World War II, when he made internment speeches on the Japanese character. Though Jackson now says, "I never made any statement against the Japanese as a race or as an ethnic group or as a nationality," a *Seattle Post-Intelligencer* article (October 17, 1945) shows a different line: "The United States should be brought to the understanding that the utter bestiality of the Japanese Army in war is more nearly representative of Japan's true nature than is the present ingratiating conduct of the conquered population. . . . General MacArthur's inexorable program is immensely satisfying to the West Coast, where the Japanese and their true instincts are understood as nowhere else in this country."

Jackson's love affair with the military is not calculated to help him with minorities either, nor is his continuing attempt to outreach Wallace, beginning with his opposition to busing in the 1972 campaign. The following exchange indicates that his position will be the same in 1976.

SCHEER: Is your position on busing now the same as it was in the Florida primary?
JACKSON: My position is basically the same. I would support the constitutional amendment that would prohibit busing solely to achieve racial balance.
SCHEER: So this is a substantially different position from Senator Kennedy's?
JACKSON: I don't know Senator Kennedy's position.
SCHEER: Well, he's under attack in his state for supporting the court order.
JACKSON: I understand, but I don't think he favors the constitutional amendment.
SCHEER: You favor a constitutional amendment that would in effect overturn the court's decisions?
JACKSON: That's correct.

Jackson is less willing to discuss his position on abortion but it was summarized for me by Mrs. Jackson: "My husband thinks that abortion is immoral—that from a religious point of view it is just plain murder, and he's very much against the taking of all life no matter how young. He's a deeply moral person. He's very quiet about this, but he feels very strongly about certain issues and he thinks that abortion is just against God's ways. On the other hand, I do think that women should have a certain amount of control over their own bodies and their own lives."

Mrs. Jackson's influence is reserved for other issues:

HELEN: I've succeeded in getting him to begin to break away from the button-down collar.

SCHEER: That's a relief.

HELEN: It sure is. The button-down collars kind of bulge out and I just never liked them.

Which is not as minor as it sounds. The Jackson campaign committee is more concerned about the TV registration of the large pouch that hangs under their man's chin and his drooping left eyelid (which has been held up by surgery) than they are about any other single issue.

My talks with Jackson took place during a period in which the shenanigans of the CIA were very much in the news. The Rockefeller committee had been formed in the wake of Seymour Hersh's *New York Times* reporting on the Chilean intervention and domestic surveillance. Jackson, who was off and running for the Presidency, had been going after whatever Administration programs he could find to attack. But he showed absolutely no interest in taking on the CIA, even though he was for years a member of the CIA subcommittee of the Armed Services Committee, the only group in the Senate that is told how much the CIA spends and on what sorts of things. The CIA is security and Jackson has had a cozy and uncritical relationship to it.

SCHEER: In all the time you have been in the Senate have you ever initiated any investigation as to whether the CIA has overstepped its authority?

JACKSON: During the time I was on the CIA committee I was never aware of any presentations which on the face of it warranted the charge of the CIA exceeding their authority as I understood it. I was never privy to such information.

It was the CIA that gave him his big issue in the fifties—an attack on the Eisenhower Administration for underestimating the missile gap between us and the Russians. Jackson's concern was based on information supplied by CIA director Allen Dulles, which Scoop ran with, blasting Eisenhower for leaving the nation undefended: "I say we can't afford the risks the Administration is taking." In the presidential campaign he talked Kennedy into making the missile gap a key issue. As one press account had it: "Kennedy would come to Jackson for advice on campaign strategy involving defense issues. And Jackson's advice was pointedly repetitious: missile gap, missile gap, missile gap."

As it turned out, the CIA information was all wrong, and in fact the Soviet missile program was floundering. But Jackson was able to increase U.S. production of missiles, and, if the Soviets needed a spur, they, too, had Jackson's exhortations to go by. But this incident did not cause him to lose faith in the CIA any more than did its Bay of Pigs misinformation; wrong or not, it supported Jackson's belief that the Russians were an increasing, not a diminishing, menace.

Jackson has recently rediscovered the missile crisis. His current speeches deal with the failure of the Administration to protect our national security in the Vladivostok and SALT disarmament talks. He is in step with a rear guard of old Cold Warriors who have regrouped around George Meany, and who feel that Henry Kissinger is selling us out to the Russians. One central figure in this group is Jay Lovestone, whom Jackson and Perle consult with frequently.

Lovestone's name comes up in many exposés of the CIA. A typical description is one offered by Drew Pearson and Jack Anderson in February 1967, when they reported that the CIA was pumping around a hundred million dollars a year into labor operations under Meany, "probably the biggest fund dished out by Central Intelligence to anyone." They went on to note: "Jay Lovestone, sometimes called Meany's minister of foreign affairs, is a Lithuanian immigrant who became secretary general of the American Communist Party, then turned strongly anti-Communist. Lovestone takes orders from Cord Meyer of the CIA. No CIA money for labor is spent without Lovestone's approval, and few labor attachés are appointed to American embassies abroad without his okay."

I asked Jackson about Lovestone's activities.

SCHEER: Most of the books on the CIA mention Lovestone as an agent. Have you raised this with him?

JACKSON: I've never raised it with him because no one has ever indicated that he was involved with the CIA during the time I've been on the [Senate] committee.

SCHEER: You mean to say that until I brought it up this time you have never heard of his alleged CIA connections?

JACKSON: I recall references being made.

Since announcing his candidacy Jackson has been able to embarrass the Administration almost daily by having very recent and secret information about, for example, the Vinnell Company's deal to train the National Guard in Saudi Arabia and Kissinger's secret commitments to the Saigon government. It is clear that Jackson is being tipped off by some elements in the intelligence community. In both the Mideast negotiations and the disarmament talks with the Russians, Kissinger has implied that Jackson was running another State Department with his own intelligence branch. The Jackson people only chuckle confidently at the suggestion.

Jackson's silence about possible CIA misfeasance is repeated in the case of the Senate Interior Committee, of which he is chairman, and the Amerada Hess oil company. Back in the 1972 campaign Jackson expressed outrage at what he termed the grandstanding of Senators Muskie and McGovern in volunteering the sources of campaign funds and charged that voluntary disclosure was a "gimmick." Jackson held out until the Senate Watergate committee subpoenaed the records, and when that committee briefly opened its files to reporters it was revealed that fully one-fifth of his funds (or $225,000 out of approximately $1,100,000) had come in the form of a secret contribution from Leon Hess, the chairman, chief executive officer, and principal stockholder (18 percent) in the Amerada Hess oil corporation. Hess had given another secret contribution of $250,000 to Nixon. These gifts were suspect because both Nixon, as President, and Jackson, as chairman of the Senate Interior Committee, were at that very time involved in critical governmental decisions affecting the fortunes of the Amerada Hess company.

In 1967 the Johnson Administration had taken the unprecedented step of granting to the Hess Oil and Chemical Company (in 1969 that company merged with Amerada Oil to form Amerada Hess) the exclusive rights to build and operate one of the world's largest oil refineries in the Virgin Islands. It had also granted the Hess company an allocation to import that oil into the mainland United States. The ten-year agreement has been under attack since its inception, and in February 1970, the President's Cabinet Task Force on Oil Import Control of the Nixon government issued a report that covered the Hess case: "The beneficiary companies obtained these special privileges through bilateral contracts privately negotiated with the Interior Department. There was no public bidding procedure open to all. This highly discriminatory manner of conferring a substantial benefit on particular companies is indefensible and should not be repeated."

The Oil Import Administration inspected Hess's operation and then threatened to revoke the company's quota to import finished products from its refinery because Hess had not lived up to its agreement to aid the Virgin Islands economy—the justification for this special arrangement in the first place. This continuing investigation was threatening to the company because Hess had acquired the oil-rich Amerada company, with its access to Libyan and other foreign oil, as a source for its new refinery. The profitability of the arrangement would end with the loss of the refinery and in the next months the Hess people scurried to prevent that.

Jackson now claims that there was nothing he could do that Hess wanted. This is hard to believe, for Jackson, as chairman of the Interior Committee, was precisely the person responsible for overseeing the Department of the Interior and all events that occur on the Virgin Islands. For all of Jackson's investigation of the energy situation he never felt it necessary to call Hess as a witness or in any other way pursue an investigation of this case.

One of the nicer things that Jackson has done for the oil industry has been his crash program calling for rampant development of U.S. oil. This program culminated in his stewardship of the Alaska pipeline bill. Amerada Hess has a 3 percent interest in the Trans-Alaska Pipeline System, subject to receipt of permits from the Department of the Interior. In 1969 the company bought $83,700,000 worth of leases on Alaska's North Slope, most of which is in the Prudhoe Bay area (11,896 out of 12,394 net acres), and as *Moody's Industrial Manual* reported, "The commercial operation of the North Slope acreage will depend on the company's ability to develop its acreage and to transport the product to market."

Jackson believes on principle in big corporations, big military, big GNP, big unions, and big government to hold it all together. It is the vision of progress he has held all his adult life, and as President he is not likely to conceive of any other. After all, we have to be strong for that showdown with the Russians in the eighties.

There is much in common between Jackson and Richard Nixon. Besides the Cold War mentality there are big schemes, considerable paranoia, and above all that near-total inflexibility. He's smarter and tougher than Nixon and would probably have a more cooperative Democratic Congress. But as President, given a crisis similar to Nixon's, he would be likely to come unglued in much the same way. Unlike Nixon, however, he would never voluntarily resign. Scoop does not mind being isolated and he has never been known to retreat no matter how wrong.

The question used to be posed as to what the peace movement would do after the Vietnam War. But it is of greater moment now to inquire what will become of the military-industrial complex and its political spokesmen. Men like Scoop have possessed a great deal of power and purpose during the Cold War, and it is not likely that they will gracefully accept retirement. Not Scoop, anyway, who knows, just *knows*, that he will be the next President.

(*Esquire*, September 1975)

Nelson Rockefeller
Takes Care of Everybody

O_n our first pass over the tiny mountaintop airfield, it seemed like we were going to hit the side of the mountain, which would have meant the end of me, Nelson Rockefeller, and my story. But it would have been a bonanza for conspiracy buffs. What was the ex-editor of *Ramparts*, who had done so many CIA exposés, doing on a little prop plane with the Vice President, who was just then completing his committee's investigation of the CIA? Of course, there was no sinister connection; I was just a reporter conning his way onto a flight, hoping for one of those spontaneous interviews that had embarrassed Rockefeller so many times before. If it had been up to the Secret Service, I never would have made it. I tilted their computer so badly that I was never even allowed to go to the bathroom in the old Executive Office Building without an escort. But the Rockefeller people themselves were less uptight.

Indeed, Rockefeller's most striking quality is his total confidence in his ability to coopt anyone, even an aging New Leftist like me. Once it was clear that I was just another intellectual and not a potential assassin, I was able to hang around with him for over a month. He permitted it because of his deeply ingrained assumption that people with brains or pens who could possibly annoy him by what they write can simply be hired and made to forget "all that negative stuff"—by which he means a less-than-full understanding that Rockefeller is our most useful and disinterested "problem solver," as he puts it.

The man does not feel that he can be hurt by words. Rockefeller's aides cannot even get him to read major articles about himself, unlike Henry Kissinger, who begins his morning by reading clips of everything said about him on the previous day. We may have social mobility in America, but we also have an economic class structure and Rockefeller *knows* that this is his country and his government, while Kissinger has always believed that he is passing and living on borrowed time. When I tried to talk with Kissinger at press conferences, there was a nervous look in his eye that reminded me of my days of trying to hustle someone's girlfriend at a Loew's theater in the Bronx. By contrast, when I was introduced to Rockefeller, he looked me right in the eye, grabbed my arm, and said, "Hi ya, hear you're writing a book about me. What a great opportunity for a young man. This is going to be very interesting for you." Well, if a Rockefeller can't be confident, who the hell can?

So off we went each day: he in the first limousine, the Secret Service men in the station wagon behind, and I and press secretary Hugh Morrow or deputy press secretary John Mulliken, both friendly types, in the third vehicle. The Secret Service guys looked like either Charles Aznavour or Robert Redford. They wore sunglasses and sat in that station wagon with their fingers on the triggers of their Uzi submachine guns. Two of them stared out either side of the car and one looked through the back window at us. It was really quite dramatic: When the Vice President's car pulled to a stop, the doors of the station wagon would fly open and—the car still moving—the SS guys popped out and rushed ahead.

Once we stopped to have cocktails with the entire Supreme Court, another afternoon it was an hour with the Empress and Shah of Iran, and on a third occasion Rocky spent a relaxing evening at the Kennedy Center with Nancy and Henry Kissinger. In the process, I kept finding myself squeezed up against a lot of the people whom I had spent most of my adult life demonstrating against. They are not a bad bunch of people to have hors d'oeuvres with, if you can forget things like the Shah's secret police or Attica. But I came away from all this with no doubts at all that America has a ruling class and that it gets along quite smoothly with its counterparts abroad.

Ironically, I had just published a book (*America After Nixon*) on the power of the top multinational corporations and the ways they run this country. The day I was trying to get onto the Rockefeller plane, *Business Week* had come out with a long, serious review. Although the reviewer considered me a Marxist, he said my main thesis about the crisis of corporate power in America was valid. As I stood in Morrow's office, I looked down on his desk and saw my picture and the review staring up at me. My immediate thought was "Damn, it's all over and the Secret Service is going to hustle my ass out of here in two minutes."

But it was just the opposite. Rockefeller greeted me with "Hey, fellow, I see ya got a best-seller on your hands. Looks like a really interesting book." Since the main point of my book, which is hardly a best-seller, is that people like the Rockefellers pretty much run this country at the expense of the rest of us, I was perplexed. But after getting to know the man, I came to understand that Rockefeller implicitly believes in the Marxist analysis of economic classes and struggle—he's just on the other side. It's a refreshing contrast to all of those liberal academics who tell us that we live in a pluralistic society.

Nelson Rockefeller was born to rule. But he was not trained in the grabbing, hustling tradition of his grandfather—those days are over. You can no longer just take from people. You have to make them want to give it to you. Since earliest childhood, the Rockefeller boys were perfectly trained in the art of doing just that. Nelson Rockefeller is the Godfather; he takes care of his own, he envelops all who come his way. He charms and binds you to him and is probably better at it than any other man in this country. He is very clear about his class interests and the central role of his family in making capitalism work. He's so secure in his power that he cannot conceive of the possibility that there are people in this world with whom he cannot cut a deal. And no matter who they are, if they have a measure of power and have survived, then he will deal.

For decades, through his purchase of intellectuals, his various commissions, and his private dinners with the powerful of this world, he has been "solving our problems," and the less we know about it, the more effective he can be. Indeed, becoming vice president, just like becoming governor, was, in a sense, counterproductive, because the public began to be dimly aware that he and others like him, who share none of our daily travail about paying the bills and holding a job, have, in fact, determined that they are the neutral, and the best, arbiters of our fate. The Rockefellers are not powerful simply because of their immense wealth. Critics of Rockefeller at the Senate and House confirmation hearings missed this point. There are other rich people in this country. What makes some, like Nelson and his brother David (and Averell Harriman and C. Douglas Dillon), particularly important is that by adroit use of their wealth and training they have become the arbiters of our essential political consensus. They will not be grubby. They are trusted by other rich and powerful people precisely because they are expected to look out for the larger interests of their class and not just the bank or corporation they happen to own. If you believe in the survival of corporate capitalism, the Rockefellers are the "good people" who are above petty interest and conniving.

In the Godfather view of corporate capitalism, you have to give favors to hold the whole thing together, and holding it together is Rockefeller's main task in life. In his view, society is a web in which he is the chief spider. Rockefeller believes that *he* must plan for our future:

ROCKEFELLER: I'm a great believer in planning.
SCHEER: What kind of planning?
ROCKEFELLER: Economic, social, political, military, total world planning.

SCHEER: Does the question of class enter into this at all?
ROCKEFELLER: Not to me.

I asked him when we were on that plane ride about any possible conflicts between the needs of the multinational corporations and labor, and he said there were none: "My feeling is that that segment [labor] is terribly important, but they're going to be taken care of if our economic system works, which is what I was talking to these guys about—we're hobbling the economic system by accelerating social objectives."

The "guys" that he had been talking with were Arthur Burns, head of the Federal Reserve Board, and Alan Greenspan, the President's top economic adviser. Rockefeller had been huddled with them in one corner of the plane. I did not then understand the importance of our destination. Why were we flying to this Virginia mountaintop? The presidential photographer told me that the year before, Vice President Ford had made the same trip and almost crash-landed. When we disembarked, there were fifteen limousines waiting and a few helicopters circling overhead. In a scene reminiscent of James Bond, our caravan wound its way through the hills of Virginia guarded by those helicopters. I sat in the back of my limousine—the poor little rich boy—with a telephone next to me and no one to call. Finally, we arrived at the Homestead, a spa made famous in the thirties, when Mrs. Cornelius Vanderbilt threw her lavish parties there. It's an ornate affair of colonnades and high ceilings and I knew something important must be happening, because as I crossed the lobby with Morrow, he suddenly said, "Oh, there's David. Hi, David, this is Bob Scheer. Bob, this is David Rockefeller and his wife, Margaret."

David was in a golfing getup and was very relaxed and friendly, as was his wife, who wanted to know if Nelson's wife, Happy, had gotten in yet. Within the next half hour, I saw Thomas Murphy, chairman of General Motors, and Edgar Speer, head of U.S. Steel.

It turned out that we had flown down to one of the very important quarterly meetings of the Business Council, a group of the country's top two hundred industrialists and bankers. Rockefeller closeted himself with some of the leaders to go over his speech for that night. I wandered the lobby in a daze. After fifteen years of doubts, college debates with professors, and confusion about whether America really has a ruling class, I had suddenly found myself right smack in the middle of it.

Rockefeller, of course, was in his element, and that evening, once the crab cocktails and steak had been put away, he rose to tell the assembled corporate heads what they wanted to hear: "I enjoy this opportunity because, frankly, ladies and gentlemen, I feel that those of you in this room symbolize, really, the essence of what our country stands for. . . . Now we find ourselves in a situation in which many of these values are challenged as never before. . . . No group knows this better than you, because you men and women— so many of you representing much-maligned multinational corporations . . . we, as Americans, should be so grateful that your ingenuity and your imagination and your drive has seen the opportunities that existed in this world."

We tend to think of large multinational companies as independent and rival entities, but the opposite is actually the case. The top men of finance and industry meet frequently for hard talks and friendly social encounters. They speak the same language and generally like one another, or at least it seemed that way to me at the Business Council gathering. Waiting in line for dinner, Walter Wriston of First National City Bank and David Rockefeller of rival Chase Manhattan were almost backslapping. Coke and Pepsi were about five feet apart in the receiving line. Farther down the line was Dr. Frank Stanton, former president of CBS, David Packard of Hewlett-Packard, Arthur Wood of Sears, Roebuck, and on and on through the corporate elite. Douglas Dillon, who served on the CIA commission with Rockefeller, is also a member. It's a club of the people who actually run things in this country, and the unique value of Rockefeller to all this, believe it or not, is that he is the club member who is supposed to have his finger on the public pulse. He has taken it upon himself to be *their* contact with *us*. He has chosen to be the politician rather than the banker or the captain of industry, and that decision flows not merely from ego needs but also from an understanding of the division of responsibilities within the Rockefeller family. On the plane back that night, I asked Rockefeller about the difference between his role and David's. He said, "Well, David is concerned with the world, he's the banker, so he has to take care of the global problems, and I started with the domestic— how to build domestic consensus for what has to be done."

This building of domestic consensus—that is to say, agreement among all of us on what we should *not* agree upon—has been Rockefeller's outstanding contribution to the corporate world. It involves the selling of that peculiar and perverse notion—which would be ludicrous in any country not so hooked on notions of classlessness and social mobility—that Rockefeller is somehow best qualified to interpret our needs and aspirations. He grabs your arm, gets close to your face, and says, "You know, we've got a great country. I'm optimistic about the future and we're going to solve these problems."

Never, never in his entire life has Nelson Aldrich Rockefeller been permitted to think that his family and its holdings might have contributed to, let alone created, any of those problems. Since his youth, he has been surrounded by the "best" minds of the era, who have constantly reassured him that the Rockefellers were synonymous with virtue.

Rockefeller informed me that his mother had told him it was very important to associate with people smarter than yourself. That's why her husband, John D., always brought the most famous intellectuals in the world to the house. Take Nelson's favorite professor at Dartmouth, Stacy May. Nelson liked him so much that upon graduation *he hired him*. That gentleman has, in fact, been in and out of Rockefeller's employ for the past forty-odd years. "He was the chief economist for the War Production Board [World War II]. He worked for me for years afterward. . . . He made these studies for me in Latin America." Can you imagine hiring your favorite college professor? Kissinger worked for Rockefeller for fifteen years, and, as someone who comes from the neighborhood next to Henry's, I can assure you that this sort of relationship is pretty one-sided. Rockefeller says that Henry is smart the way men used to say a woman had a cute ass—it's a useful attribute, it even turns you on, but it's negotiable. He didn't buy Henry with his $50,000 gift (which, along with similar gifts to other Rocky intimates, was revealed during the vice-presidential confirmation hearings)—the purchase occurred long before and was hardly so crass. Kids like Henry are raised not to believe in their own legitimacy. They can make up for it in all kinds of ways: Be witty or head of the class or at least a ladies' man; but deep down there is the horrible perception that you are on this planet by the barest of accidents. Nothing you say or think, none of your angst and none of your term papers matter one iota unless you plug into the people who have real authority. You can go to New York's City College at night, read *The New York Times* on the subway, even get to study and teach at Harvard, but real authority and power come rarely and they come only through association with those who were born to rule.

And that's how Rockefeller buys you. Most of the people around him are upwardly mobile—they still have to worry about their checks bouncing. But the world is divided into those who worry about their checks bouncing and those who don't, and our reality is not Rockefeller's, no matter how many campaign blintzes he eats. Last year, Rockefeller stopped to make a phone call at the Washington National Airport, the first such effort at personal dialing in many years, and he turned to Morrow and asked him for a nickel for the phone.

On the flight back to Westchester, I wondered how I was going to get down to Manhattan, but you soon learn not to worry about things like that when you're around Rockefeller. A limousine, chauffeured, no less, with a phone in the back, was put at my disposal. Chauffeured limousines just suddenly appear if you're on the right side. And, of course, what's really scary is that all of a sudden an important part of you wants to be on the right side.

Rockefeller knows how to take care of people, but he also will frequently cut them off. Bill Ronan now works in the Rockefeller family offices in Rockefeller Center after getting $625,000, without which he could not have survived that "family crisis." Morrow, it appears, was able to deal with his personal problems for less—he got $135,000, plus a $30,000 loan. This is the big time and that's why people hang in there. Some get big gifts and then get cut out. Henry Diamond (who was the *Wunderkind* New York State Commissioner of Environmental Conservation when Rockefeller was governor and then executive director of the Commission on Critical Choices) has now been dropped from the inner circle. But he had previously received a gift of $100,000. Some say he's on the outs because he's Jewish; others that it's because he turned his air conditioner on at the wrong time. It seems that in the Fifty-fifth Street headquarters of Critical Choices, Rockefeller would not tolerate air conditioners above him leaking drops of water. That meant that those above him would sweat like crazy in the summer so that Rockefeller would not be disturbed by dripping water.

I honestly don't know if that's what turned him off about Diamond, but I do know that Diamond left Critical Choices and went off to join a law firm founded by William Ruckelshaus. Diamond is now on the list of people who don't get to see Rockefeller. I witnessed the depressing effect of his fall from grace when I last visited him. He was moody and had lost his sense of certainty and power. Kissinger is a brilliant intellectual opportunist and Diamond is only so-so. I guess that's why he couldn't cut the mustard.

On rare occasions, Rockefeller has come up against intellectuals who are not opportunists and it has confused him. Take Diego Rivera, the famous Mexican Marxist painter. Well, Rockefeller's mother had this terrific idea that Rivera should be commissioned to do the principal mural for Rockefeller Center. It was part of the radical chic of the thirties and young Nelson was then a director of Rockefeller Center—cutting his business teeth negotiating salaries with the Rockettes. So he said, Terrific, I'll go get Rivera, "who's one hell of a guy," to come here and do a mural.

Rivera painted a huge mural in the lobby of Rockefeller's father's building— and right there in the middle of the mural was Nikolai Lenin as the hero saving the people from the capitalists. Rockefeller and his mother told Rivera that it had to go. And you know what Rivera did? He said no. That is an error you can be sure Kissinger has never committed. But Rivera didn't know how to handle success and Rockefeller simply ordered the offending mural chipped away.

The real point of all this concerns the relevance, or rather the political relevance, of art and, in a larger sense, ideas. Rivera wanted to do the mural precisely because he felt that Rockefeller Center was the *symbol* of capitalism. The Rockefellers wanted the mural because Rivera was a well-known artist who should have had his price.

According to Joe Alex Morris, the approved family biographer, who had full access to all correspondence on such matters:

> As the painting progressed, the directors of Rockefeller Center became alarmed. Instead of following the sketch and synopsis that he had presented, Rivera was putting on the wall a picture with far-reaching political implications. On May 4, 1933, Rockefeller wrote to Rivera: "While I was in the . . . building at Rockefeller Center yesterday viewing the progress of your thrilling mural, I noticed that in the most recent portion of the painting you had included a portrait of Lenin. The piece is beautifully painted, but it seems to me that his portrait appearing in this mural might very seriously offend a great many people. If it were in a private house, it would be one thing, but this mural is in a public building and the situation is therefore quite different. As much as I dislike to do so, I am afraid we must ask you to substitute the face of some unknown man where Lenin's face now appears.

When Rivera refused, Rockefeller wanted the mural removed to the Museum of Modern Art, where he could charge 25 cents admission (it was the Depression). This proved impractical, however, and Rockefeller ordered that it be destroyed.

> One Saturday midnight in February 1934, workmen began chipping the painting from the plaster wall. . . . It was typical of Rockefeller that he held no resentment against Rivera, although the artist wouldn't speak to him for years.

Ponder that last sentence—Rockefeller held no resentment. Imagine! He has scraped off the goddamn mural—broken up the plaster—and it is thought to be wondrous that he does not harbor resentment. He doesn't even harbor resentment over the fact that we have not yet elected him President. These are viewed as mere details in the management of our affairs that can be taken care of in due course by the right assistants.

Rockefeller learns from his tactical mistakes, and years later he told an admiring crowd at New York's New School for Social Research (whose administration admires the financial contributions it has received from the Rockefeller Foundation) that the Rivera mural should have been put on exhibit at the Museum of Modern Art not for a quarter but for a dollar. We all know that MOMA is a tax-deductible club for the Rockefellers. They use it for celebrating birthdays and the like, as well as for boosting the works of artists whom they have patronized. A driving force at the museum since its inception, Rockefeller is a major collector who can buy up much of the output of an artist and then "make" his reputation by exhibiting the work at the museum. The value of the collection owned by Rocky goes up accordingly. So when Rockefeller talks about the museum, it's as someone might talk about finding the wherewithal for his tropical-fish collection; it's a hobby that can be made profitable, and even if it doesn't make money, it's a hell of a lot of fun and it's tax-deductible. In the New School speech on March 15, 1967, made long after American students had begun to think for themselves, Rockefeller had the nerve to talk about the destruction of the Rivera mural as a funny little anecdote:

> I could relate another incident that grew out of a partly cultural, partly commercial experience, and that was this: My mother and I tried to help my father in the decoration of Rockefeller Center. Some of you remember that, too. We had Diego Rivera there and he undertook a major mural. Frieda, his wife, who was very attractive, but whose political implications [*sic*] were even stronger than his, got him incorporating the most unbelievable subjects into this mural [*laughter*]. I know that birth control now has become more acceptable. In those days, it wasn't. Of course, we were right across from Saint Patrick's, as you know [*laughter*].
>
> And then he got into politics, and he had Stalin—or was it Lenin? I've forgotten—featured in the center. And then he started some social commentaries on American life, and there was a lady with a syphilitic ulcer on her face playing cards [*laughter*]. I finally said, "Look, Diego, we just can't have this. Art is free in its expression, but this is not something you are doing for yourself nor for us as collectors. This is a commercial undertaking. Therefore, we have to have something here that is not going to offend our customers but is going to give them pleasure and joy," and so forth. "And you've got this so you have about every sensitive subject incorporated into your mural."

Now, Rockefeller has trouble reading speeches, because he has dyslexia that perhaps dates back to the days when his old man tried to turn him from a left-hander into a righty by attaching a rubber band to his hand with a long string at the dinner table and pulling on it every time he tried to use the left one. As a result, Rockefeller is a joy to cover because much of what he says is extemporaneous, outrageous, and close to what he really thinks. In that little lecture on art and Rivera, he presented his entire view of ideas and intellectuals. That which can be collected and stored, no matter how weird or controversial, will produce no social change and might fetch a higher price someday—just as long as it can be placed in a museum or a scholarly book. It will be an entertainment for the elite and that, too, will not threaten real power. But ordinary people would be going into the lobby of Rockefeller Center, and for *them* to see that mural was threatening.

While I was following Rockefeller around he went to the Museum of Modern Art and spent an evening gloating. Elite guests of the museum were drinking champagne in the sculpture garden when Rockefeller came bounding through with Happy in tow, exuding all of that compulsive energy of his. I hung around while he greeted wealthy sponsors of the museum.

The first thing that hits you when you're standing next to Rockefeller is that he's shorter and fatter than you would have expected from his pictures. He is also older in appearance. There's a splotchiness to his skin that suggests the palsy and liver ailments of the old. There is one other thing. The face doesn't really hold together after the smile. When he can't hold that half-grimace, half-smile any longer, his face begins to decompose and reveal him for what he is—a fairly tired, very overextended older man. Still, that huge energy propels him through dozens of events each day, in and out of cars and planes, with the smile always back in place at the right moment. It's as if a new motor has been implanted in a body too old for the strain. There is a persistent sense that something has to give soon.

Even in his older years, Rocky continues to demonstrate a warmth and charm that are not totally contrived. He was educated to be warm and open in a fraternity-boy sort of way, and one senses that after these many years, it sits naturally with him. Rocky is as alive and sexy as he is rich and cunning, and it is just that package that has made him so formidable and dangerous. The charm works right up to the point that you remember something like Tom Wicker's book on Attica. But too often he gets to set the stage and then he can really milk an audience.

That night at the Museum of Modern Art, Rockefeller gave a speech about enthusiasm, and, in particular, enthusiasm for art and artists. His great observation, then as so often, was that ideas and art need not be threatening to the rich of this country if only the rich will learn to manage those ideas properly. To make that point, he went back to an incident involving Henry Luce, founder of Time Inc., who, along with Rockefeller, was one of the early trustees of the museum. But before he could get to that, it started to rain and the guests fled the garden. There were broken champagne glasses all around. Happy was wandering about, repeating what seems to be her one permitted line in public life: "So good to see you." She said it to me three times. I asked her in a moment of journalistic abandon if all of those ruined hairdos and broken champagne glasses and the other disarray symbolized the fall of the American ruling class, much like similar scenes in the czar's Winter Palace in St. Petersburg. But it was as if I had not spoken at all. She just said, "It's so good to see you."

Rockefeller was equally irrepressible. He was going on about the wonderful bed he'd bought Happy. "You read all about it in the papers, didn't you?" he asked. There was a "serious" woman art critic from *The New York Times* at the reception. She was one of five specialists covering the event—it involved the five *Times* reporters covering society, architecture, politics, art, and fashion; so there was a lot of news fit to print. Rockefeller enthusiastically told her about the Max Ernst bed he had bought for the new Vice President's residence in Admiral's House. Rockefeller always loves to talk about art, even in a crushed press conference in the rain:

CRITIC: I'm very interested in the Max Ernst bed you bought for your wife. [*Two schnooks from UP tried to ask about the CIA investigation he was heading, but Rockefeller was there for art.*]
ROCKEFELLER: You are? How about that? Have you seen it?
CRITIC: I have seen it. I'm writing it up for the *Times.* I was wondering why you would happen to buy it.
ROCKEFELLER: Well, I'll say it. I take all of the catalogues of all the exhibitions and all of the auctions and I saw this and I was crazy about it. Happy's furnishing the house, so I thought this would be my contribution—she's doing all the rest and I thought the bed was in the spirit that I believed in—
CRITIC: Thank you, thank you—
ROCKEFELLER: And I've always admired Max Ernst and I thought this was a very fitting entrance to Washington of Max Ernst.
CRITIC: What was the price?
ROCKEFELLER: *Don't ever ask about price.*

It was later reported that the bed cost $35,000.

After the interviews were over, William Paley, chairman of the board of the museum and of CBS, spoke of his forty-year association with Rockefeller in the running of the life of the museum.

The mood was chummy and Rockefeller was relaxed, so he told the Luce anecdote:

Let me end by telling you about a most interesting evening spent at the end of World War II following a little dinner here when Henry Luce [who] was a member of the board of trustees . . . had a concern as to whether really modern art, so called, quote, unquote, was or could be a subversive influence in this country, and this was, well, it's hard to think of it now that way, but I'm going back, this was '45 and we had a dinner, Bill Paley, Jock Whitney, Henry Luce, Alfred H. Barr, Jr. [a professor of art history and first director of the museum] and myself. After dinner, we went around the gallery. The museum was closed and Alfred gave one of the most fascinating, interesting, perceptive philosophical discussions which he and Henry carried on. The rest of us observed and supported Alfred, but at the end of that evening, Henry was totally reassured as to the vitality of a free society and that rather than being subversive, modern art in all of its forms was the only true area in which freedom still existed uninhibited and that it was the greatest force for the future of America that we could have.

It is an anecdote that defines the role of the artist as one of political impotence.

When I went upstairs after Rockefeller departed with his "Good to see yous" and "Isn't the museum getting just terrific and marvelous?" even Picasso's *Guernica* seemed literally the castrated bull put out to pasture. They had done it again. When you hang out with Rockefeller, you know that there is a *they* and it's not a radical's paranoid fantasy. This man who chipped off the Rivera mural can somehow emerge not as a Brezhnev bullying sensitive artists but as what he calls himself—an "avant-garde collector." And the utter gumption of the man is epitomized by the fact that he thinks he did Rivera a favor by instructing him about the taming of his "destructive" or "subversive" emotions. It is in this same spirit that Rockefeller discusses the youth rebellions of the sixties: "those times of emotion that we have to get behind us."

What Rockefeller wants from his art is what he wants from his politics. He doesn't want the rest of us to get "emotional," because to be emotional would mean to be pissed off at the Rockefellers. Get it? Anger, hate, emotion are expressed or contained in one corner of a museum. If you can accept that, baby, then make your funny-looking beds or weird constructions, or drip paint all over the fucking canvas; he couldn't care less.

It's only when the finger of the artist points at the sources of power in this country that he reacts. Do that and you're being rude, adolescent, simplistic, fanatical, and, worst of all, emotional. People of real power are never emotional; they don't have to be, because they can just administer. If you have power and can just administer, then emotion is wasteful.

Rockefeller's influence over the arts now extends into the worlds of symphonies, ballets, operas, and individual fellowships. This is done through the vehicle of a lifelong friend, Nancy Hanks, who has been in his employ virtually throughout her adult life. She is now on the government payroll as the chairman of the National Endowment for the Arts. Do you know what that means? It means that you are in your loft somewhere and there's no money for going out for *tacos* anymore and you're about to give up on the whole bit—and how do you know you can paint or write, anyway, and who says you're special and why don't you get a real job, like, in the post office and forget this art stuff? Right? And just at that moment, an old professor of yours hears that you're going nuts and says, "I'll tell you what. I'll write a letter and maybe, just maybe you'll get a grant from the National Endowment for the Arts." And do you know what that means? Why, to begin with, you get a cabin somewhere in the country so you can get your head together and create. Your kid goes to a private school and isn't beaten up for a while, and you take your love out to the best French restaurants. And you have a year to screw around and create, and you want to really know what? You don't have to produce a goddamn thing. They don't even want you to produce something, because then they have to edit it, print it, or hang it, and that causes problems for them. All they really want you to do is acquiesce (know the word: Adapt with grace and the world's your oyster).

And Nancy, by virtue of her association with Rockefeller, is *the* lady in this country who can give you so much money that you can hardly handle it. And you want to know what's even more terrific? It's called a fellowship, and therefore a good chunk of it is tax-free.

Art has its place, all right, and Nancy has worked out a scheme to make sure it doesn't become a public issue. For those interested in the subject, I would recommend a reading of *The Performing Arts*—the Rockefeller-panel reports on the future of theater, dance, and music in America, which Nancy told me contain ten-year plans already implemented to prevent the socialization of American art. What she means is keeping the power over ballet, opera, Lincoln Center, museums, etc., in the hands of the same people who form the boards of directors of the largest corporations—yet getting the public, you and me, through tax dollars, to pay for it. (In 1975, the National Endowment for the Arts received over $74,000,000 of the taxpayers' money and only $7,500,000 from private contributors.) Nancy told me that the Rockefeller art plan has already succeeded. It involves matching government funds to tax-deductible corporate gifts and leaves power over the distribution of those funds in private (read corporate) hands. If it had not already succeeded, we might now have things like the BBC or serious arguments about what ought to be shown on friend Paley's CBS.

The Hanks-Rockefeller relationship is typical of a whole series of such relationships that he has had with women. They all involve strong personal as well as political ties, with the emphasis, as always, on loyalty to him. The women generally start out as idealistic volunteers in some Rockefeller-related project and end up as lifelong functionaries, as well as members, of his inner clan. Joan Braden is the closest of such associates.

Joan Braden met Rockefeller in 1942, when she was blushing and beautiful and eager to help powerful men help the world. The idea that it might involve a contradiction has only recently entered her head. But back then, in the forties, when the Rockefellers owned a nice chunk of Latin America, Joan actually believed that her boss, who was the Assistant Secretary of State for Latin-American Affairs, was on the side of the peasants of Latin America.

Where do such ideas come from? Joan is a very intelligent and capable person. But who can believe that the Rockefellers, who hire people for a nickel an hour, also want to help them? The intriguing thing is that the Rockefellers themselves believe it. They were raised to believe it and an army of scholars was hired to provide them with the data saying it's true. So what's an impressionable young girl to do? Rockefeller mesmerized her with what are called facts, and he told her of his best intentions. And he does have the best intentions. You remember you can't just take, you have to make them want to give it to you. So Rockefeller learned Spanish. He can say "Hi ya, fella" in five languages. He'll do or say anything to make it look as if it really all does come together in the end.

Well, Joan—as often happens with unmarried women close to Rockefeller—found a husband who was also in Rocky's camp, and that was Tom Braden, who, two years after their marriage in 1948, became an official of the CIA. Now, let's not get paranoid—just conspiratorial or cynical. The CIA has never been a manifestation of right-wing hysteria—it has always been a Yale-Dartmouth-Harvard show. It is the old-boy network par excellence and Rockefeller has been as close to the CIA as any other man in America; and if that is not public knowledge, it only attests to the effectiveness of his press staff. Tom Braden has been one of the most significant public apologists for the evil (and I'm sorry, but trying to bump off Castro *is* evil) that the CIA has committed. Joan was the one who brought Rockefeller over to the CIA in 1954.

Last May, I was in the Rockefeller family archives in Rockefeller Center and I found a letter that said that Rockefeller was invited to CIA headquarters to give a talk. Guess who sent the invitation? Joan Braden.

Tom has described in some detail his work for the CIA. He was a division chief in charge of dealing with the cultural organizations and foundations that were fronts for the agency. When our exposure in *Ramparts* of some of these fronts caused a major flap, Braden wrote an article in *The Saturday Evening Post* titled "I'm Glad the CIA Is 'Immoral.' " He described funneling sums of money through the labor movement. As an illustration: "It was my idea to give the $15,000 to Irving Brown [of the American Federation of Labor]." Brown has worked directly under a fellow named Lane Kirkland, who is George Meany's number-two man at the AFL–CIO and also a close associate of Rockefeller's. Kirkland now serves on Rockefeller's Commission on Critical Choices. He told me that he had full knowledge of all CIA monies funneled through the AFL and that they were all spent under his supervision. And he told me this in an interview held during the very weeks last May when he was serving as a member of the commission that was supposed to be looking into abuses of the CIA's power. The farce of that investigation was obvious. All Rockefeller had to do was sit around with his buddies Kirkland and Braden and Richard Helms, former director of the CIA, and talk about what they knew. Or, more to the point, how much they were then forced to reveal.

Since the focus of their inquiry was supposed to be on the CIA's interference in domestic American life, the Rockefeller-Braden relationship has some interesting ramifications. For instance, we know that these gentlemen share a profound enthusiasm for cultural institutions.

Joan described how she and Rockefeller and Tom all got together. "[Nelson] actually got Tom to come down to the Museum of Modern Art, but Tom really worked less directly for him than I did. He worked for the board of trustees of the museum. He never worked, as I did, directly for Nelson. I met Tom through him."

There seems to be no limit to MOMA's uses, particularly when we refer to Braden's *Saturday Evening Post* description of what he was doing with other cultural institutions between 1950 and 1954 in his CIA role:

> I remember the enormous joy I got when the Boston Symphony Orchestra won more acclaim for the U.S. in Paris than John Foster Dulles or Dwight D. Eisenhower could have bought with a hundred speeches. And then there was *Encounter*, the magazine published in England. . . . Money for both the orchestra's tour and the magazine's publication came from the CIA and few outside the CIA knew about

it. We had placed one agent in a Europe-based organization of intellectuals called the Congress for Cultural Freedom. Another agent became an editor of *Encounter*. The agents could not only propose anti-Communist programs to the official leaders of the organizations but they could also suggest ways and means to solve the inevitable budgetary problems. Why not see if the needed money could be obtained from "American foundations"? As the agents knew, the CIA-financed foundations were quite generous when it came to the national interest.

Now, of course, Rockefeller also knows a great deal about foundations and solving budgetary problems, and one of the revelations about his generous gifts to friends concerned a loan he made to set Tom up with an Oceanside, California, newspaper. It would seem that the Rockefeller Commission should have begun its inquiry by investigating the Rockefeller-Braden relationship.

The connection gets so intricate that there are too many bodies in too many closets to keep up with. But let's focus on two. At the very time Tom was running those CIA programs, wife Joan was running quite a few things for Rockefeller—particularly the International Basic Economy Corporation (IBEC) programs in Venezuela and Brazil. It would be naïve to think that Joan would not want to coordinate such programs with the agency and that letter in the Rockefeller archives indicated a very informal working relationship between Joan and Rockefeller. At the meeting Joan set up, there were eight days of intensive analysis of the covert activities of the CIA throughout the world. All sessions took place in the auditorium of the U.S. Department of Agriculture.

The first were August 4–7, 1953, and for those who are sticklers for details of this sort, the secret manual said that they met from 0900 to 1200 hours each day. The second group of meetings that Rockefeller addressed took place November 3–6, 1953. The whole affair was treated with great cloak-and-dagger secrecy, as the following excerpt from the official instructions indicates:

> This training course as a whole is classified SECRET. You are cautioned to guard your conversation going to and from the auditorium. Since passes are not shown upon entering the chartered Capital Transit buses, anyone may be riding with you and overhearing your remarks. You are also cautioned not to drop any classified papers on the floor of the auditorium.

Well, somebody must have dropped one of those papers, and as a result, I know that Rockefeller held forth on the role of the CIA in a changing economic world. He was then Undersecretary of Health, Education and Welfare, as well as the chairman and president of the board of IBEC and president of the American International Association for Economic and Social Development. But it really doesn't matter which hat Rockefeller has on at any given moment. He wears so many and it is his firmest philosophical belief that there could never be any conflict of interest in anything he does or with which he is concerned.

If IBEC is in Venezuela and Brazil, and if Standard Oil is also in those countries, and if the CIA is there as well, then shouldn't they coordinate their activities? Of course, it will all come out right for the Rockefellers and for the country. It's a thick-as-thieves world he moves in and the cast of characters that assists him is fairly unchanging. His good friends Dillon and Kirkland were on the most recent CIA inquiry committee, just as, when Rockefeller was watching the CIA as a member of the President's Foreign Intelligence Advisory Board, he had good friends Johnny Foster (formerly in charge of research for the Defense Department and now a vice president of TRW Inc.) and Edward Teller (father of the H-bomb) to help him out. If they didn't get enough time to chat at committee sessions, they could always meet at the Commission on Critical Choices; and if that weren't enough, there were those dinners.

For instance, right smack in the midst of the CIA investigation, Joan sneaked in a secret dinner to show Helms a little support. Helms was the guy responsible for a lot of the CIA activity that Rockefeller was then supposed to be investigating. He was hurting no matter how much Rocky tried to protect him. You may recall his flipping out at CBS reporter Daniel Schorr, calling him "Killer Schorr" and what the papers the next day referred to as a "derogatory sexual expletive." Well, in the interest of historical accuracy, let me report that what I heard him say was "you cocksucker." They had to take Helms into another room to get composed.

So one can understand Joan's little private dinner of support. Only word of what was said there somehow leaked out onto the front page of *The Washington Post* and it was shocking, because the story had Robert McNamara, the head of the World Bank, offering a toast to Helms and saying, No matter what you did, I'm behind you. Which could be taken to mean condoning all sorts of violations of the laws of the land and old-fashioned decency as well. I asked Joan for her version of the dinner and was amazed to find out that her close friend Kissinger (they have a private lunch once a week when he's in town) was there, as well as Senator John Glenn, whose name had not appeared in the *Post* story. Joan conceded to me that the toast had been made but that the *Post* had gotten it wrong:

SCHEER: Was the toast at this party made by McNamara?
JOAN: They were made by McNamara, Averell [Harriman], and Stuart Symington.

SCHEER: But it was McNamara who was supposed to have said, I don't care what you did, but I support it.

JOAN: The only reason I don't want to talk about that is that I didn't at the time—it was wrongly reported . . . I think it's wrong when you have people for dinner to talk about it. I never gave the guest list—it's funny the way it happened, the way the story got out.

SCHEER: But it's part of history now, so why not set it straight?

JOAN: Well, I will—I tell you, as a matter of fact, because I think Bob [McNamara] had said, in fact, simply that Dick Helms did not act without the approval of the President of the United States and the Secretary of Defense. . . . His point was that whatever Dick Helms did was in the context of the decision by the President of the United States and the Secretary of Defense. . . . Basically, Bob McNamara is an unemotional man not given to this sort of thing, but this evening this guy was under attack, and they didn't come for that, but once here and realizing whatever you may think of Dick Helms or whatever he may have done, his own personal struggle over the last two years—being called back five, six times. . . . I had dinner with him and played bridge the night before he yelled at Daniel Schorr.

Which is a cozy enough understanding, but it obscures some basic points. Helms goes back to the Allen Dulles days at the CIA—he, more than anyone around, literally knows where the bodies are buried, and he is still the ambassador to Iran, whose leader, the Shah, was reinstalled in power by the CIA. This gathering of the Braden clan to give support to Helms, when Joan's close buddy Rockefeller is supposed to be trying to get information out of him, is quite suspect. But this is a club that makes its own rules.

One little footnote as to why hubby Tom left the CIA: Joan told me that it was not a matter of political disagreement with what it was doing but rather that it didn't pay enough: "If you have no money and your wife insists on having ninety million children, then you have to do something to make more money." What Braden did was have Rockefeller set him up in the newspaper-publishing venture. Helms stayed on, not being one of the direct beneficiaries of the Rockefeller largesse, at least as far as we know. But they are close friends, and in the midst of that investigation, there was yet another dinner with Helms, only this one was thrown by David Rockefeller at the Pocantico Hills estate. The occasion was the departure of the Shah of Iran; it was the last night of his May 1975 trip to this country.

At a somewhat less elaborate dinner, which he bought for me at Sans Souci, Morrow described that night with the Shah and Helms. We were a bit rushed, because Morrow had to stay up late to do the final edit on the CIA report. In fact, as we left his office, I jokingly offered to help with the editing, given my experience from the old *Ramparts* days. In response, he held up one of the many brown-paper bags around his desk that had the word BURN printed on them in big red letters.

He conceded that a great deal of thought goes into the selection of such a dinner list, and in this case it included David as host, Nelson, Dillon, the Shah of Iran, Helms, and Mrs. W. Vincent Astor. The discussion was serious and to the point. When it was completed, the Shah took a small plane down to JFK for his big flight home.

The point about dinners of this sort is not that any particular one can be singled out as the center of a particular conspiracy but, rather, that they are the normal way of doing business in this country. Rockefeller attends such a dinner virtually every night. There was one the night before with Kissinger and the Chief of State of Senegal, and one a few days later with James Cannon, who runs the Domestic Council, George Woods, who used to run the World Bank, and Robert McNamara, who now does.

It is so much the norm of this club, and certain individuals are so securely members, that it simply did not occur to Rockefeller that for all he had learned about the activities of the CIA (or, more accurately, had known about all along), he should not necessarily be meeting socially with Helms a few days before a report was due on him.

But what of the other ironies of such a gathering? The Rockefeller holdings in oil companies are substantial and are presumably in conflict with the Shah. Also, there was Dillon, of the big investment-banking interests, with holdings relating to Iran, and then, finally, Rockefeller in his other hat as Vice President, representing all of us gasoline consumers. But it has always been this way. The dinners merely reflect and cement the understandings among the powerful. The interests of the average citizen are assumed to be represented by the good intentions and public spirit of the gathered elite. And there is no real difference between this style of operation and the official mechanism of government, with the exception that with the latter, a million lower-level bureaucrats are on the fringes of the act to provide some democratic cover. They do make lots of little decisions, but in terms of planning the big shifts of policy—like, do we have a Cold War or détente? or how best to preserve the power of the multinational corporations—it's the business of the inner club, and Rockefeller provides the best illustration of that.

There is no question but that in terms of the current planning within the executive branch of government, Gerald Ford is a bystander—a small-town politician—and that Rockefeller's old club is running things. It is certainly spinning the big visions about where things should go in this country over the next forty years and making decisions that will very dramatically affect our world. And we are not, in any sense, participating in those decisions.

Rockefeller believes that American corporate capitalism is at a point of crisis in the world, and he is quite frank in stating that the working out of concrete plans for the survival of that system is the main contribution that he must make in what remains of his life. He believes that the system with which his family is connected is endangered and he speaks about it in such terms. He told me: "A lot of people don't want to be bothered or upset or disturbed by these awful things that are happening abroad, but more and more they are coming to realize that this is the fact, and I happen to be a great believer in Darwin's concept of the survival of the fittest, those who can adapt to their environment. Okay, that's the way I feel [and then he pulls you closer with those almost whispered tones of the Godfather]. This is a very exciting, open period, and if we are as smart and intelligent as I think we are as a nation, we'll work these things out, and if we get rid of the emotional things, I mean get them behind us . . . our emotional traumas are, I think, going to pass and we'll be able to settle down and sort this stuff out and approach it intelligently. I'm very optimistic about the future. I'm glad to see you. You really understand me."

By "awful things," he means poorer people in the world wanting a share of the pie; by "emotional issues," he means all of the resistance from Vietnam to Attica that people put up to his rule; and by being glad to see me, he means he thinks he's got me conned because I kept my mouth shut and nodded appreciatively every few minutes. But the real question in all of this Darwinian analysis is, Whose survival are we talking about—Exxon's and the Rockefeller family's? Isn't it about time that the idea that Rockefeller's interests and those of the average taxpayer are synonymous should appear ludicrous to us? How long can he get away with the notion that he is our neutral problem solver? Evidently for a while yet.

When Rockefeller gave up the New York governorship, it was ostensibly to devote full time to the Commission on Critical Choices, which was basically a gathering of his buddies such as Herman Kahn, George Woods, Jim Cannon, and Nancy Kissinger. He put up the first $1,000,000 and Laurance Rockefeller the second. They tried one session of elites under forty to get some youth into the act and it turned out to be a disaster—"too unstructured," said Rockefeller.

The purpose of the Critical Choices sessions was for a group of Rockefeller's choosing to figure out the long-run plans for the rest of us. The group includes old friends like Nancy Hanks; Robert Anderson, chairman of Atlantic Richfield Company; John Knowles, president of the Rockefeller Foundation; Clare Boothe Luce; Daniel Moynihan; Paley; and Bess Myerson. This private commission also involved Jerry Ford (as Vice President), Henry Kissinger, George Shultz, and the majority and minority leaders of both parties in both houses of Congress.

Remember, it was Rockefeller who said, "I'm a great believer in planning: economic, social, political, military, world planning." Does the question of class enter into this at all? "Not to me," he said. Which is awfully convenient if you happen to occupy the highest position of economic class power. It also allows the various commissions to proceed from the assumption that what's good for the Rockefellers, who are financing them, is also good for the nation. Therefore, they can serve their boss and the people as well. This becomes a more serious question when we realize that these studies are not meant to gather dust on library shelves.

Concretely, we do have Kissinger, who directs our National Security Council and our State Department, and his training for those positions was primarily in the Rockefeller employ. Rocky had been his boss for about fifteen years. And Nancy is still in the Rockefeller employ. She has been in charge of the foreign-policy studies of the Commission on Critical Choices, which has systematically studied the prospects for and requirements of U.S. policy throughout the world. That is to say that while Henry is taking care of the day-to-day affairs of foreign policy, Rockefeller has wife Nancy charting out the long-range plans for different sections of the world (the *ménages à trois* of Rockefeller are endless).

As an illustration of the complementary roles of Nancy and Henry Kissinger, take Cuban policy and the matter of Nancy's sending James D. Theberge, now ambassador to Nicaragua, down to Havana to interview Carlos Rafael Rodríguez, the Cuban vice-premier, on the prospects for improved Cuban-American relations. It was a detailed exploration of what conditions would have to be met in order to extend the "détente" with Russia to Cuba. As it turned out, Rodríguez was driving a hard bargain. He said that the United States had no right to impose an embargo on Cuba and that it must be lifted before there could be future talks. Although Theberge said that he had come as a private citizen, it was known to all that the wife of the Secretary of State, who also happened to be an employee of the Vice President, had sent him. It was a bargaining session and a typical Nelson-Henry show. Again, they were speaking for us. It was long-range planning being done for the U.S. government outside its normal channels. It was not at all under the purview of ordinary citizens. And again, this is not the exception but the rule.

On our flight to Virginia, the subject of Cuba and Castro came up. Rockefeller told me all about this unofficial contact: "Castro's a pretty smart guy. You've got to hand it to him; he's lasted. The Soviets have helped him, but he's lasted and he's shown the kind of flexibility that it takes to move with an evolving situation. As part of our work on Critical Choices, we sent a fellow down there to interview his minister of foreign affairs—it's under Nancy Kissinger . . . you ought to read this thing, because it's goddamn interesting, and this guy's talking to Castro. I mean the Minister of Foreign Affairs. It's a transcript and he says, Look, sure we want open trade relations, but don't kid yourself. We are part of the Communist bloc, we're going to stay there and the bloc's going to get bigger and the biggest mistake you ever made was allowing our government to exist. He just lays it, he just tells it like it is . . . this is a very open, frank—I read it with fascination . . . Remind Hughie that we ought to get you a copy of this thing."

But even with Hughie Morrow and Rockefeller trying to get me the document, it took three weeks, because Nancy and Diamond didn't want me to have it. The main reason for their reluctance was that it illustrates how Rockefeller and Nancy are making American foreign policy, even though the electorate has not authorized them to do so. Which is really how it works. You and I don't send scholars to foreign countries to explore the possibilities of détente. But Rockefeller and his staff have been doing just that for forty years.

More than any other single source, Rockefeller's various commissions have been feeding the basic data and training the key personnel for our foreign policy. But what is less noticed is that he has a Kissinger on the domestic side by the name of Cannon who came into the Ford Administration from Critical Choices.

The executive branch of the government is divided into two funnels that basically feed the President all the data on the choices he must make. Those members of the Cabinet who deal with defense meet with the National Security Council. Those concerned with all phases of domestic policy go through the Domestic Council. Just as Kissinger is central to the functioning of the NSC, Cannon is the executive director of the Domestic Council.

Rockefeller is, by virtue of being Vice President, a vice chairman of the Domestic Council; but in this case, Ford asked Rockefeller to take charge of the Domestic Council and, in particular, to "direct the staff." The measure of his power was his selection of his trusted cronies to run this body. As Richard Dunham, who is now a deputy director of the Domestic Council, explained it: "It's essentially the staffing system, coordinating system for domestic items, matters, development of policy for presidential determination and all the related decisions ranging from day-to-day decisions relating to more substantial questions, relating to fundamental or longer-range policies, but in the domestic area."

Rocky had become Vice President in mid-December, but it wasn't until March that he got Cannon into his job. One of his predecessors on the

Domestic Council had been John Ehrlichman. *The Washington Star* asked Cannon: "When John Ehrlichman had the job you have now, the council was used as a way for the White House to keep its finger in everything that was going on. Is that still the case?"

Cannon's answer was typical Ehrlichmanese: "Our purpose is to develop a very good staff system which manages a systematic determination of what is going on in all departments . . . to bring matters together on one memo to the President so that the President can focus on the central issues and evaluate the argument for and against each proposal."

But Ehrlichman was working for Nixon, not Agnew. And there's poor Jerry Ford playing at being President, while Rockefeller's man feeds him memos about the vital choices that have already been worked out by Rockefeller's Commission on Critical Choices, for which Cannon worked. Any sharp executive secretary knows that the power to define the choices in the last and only memo to reach the boss is the power to make the decision.

How close is Cannon to Rockefeller?

Dunham said, "He's close. He has worked on both the government side, as a go-between for the governor in New York and the federal government, and in the private payroll as a member of the staff of the Critical Choices commission. In that sense, they are close."

Dunham did not work for the Critical Choices commission, but his relation to Rocky is no less close. "We have worked together, well, it's now been over fourteen years. I've been at many social occasions with him." I asked Dunham if either he or Cannon was permitted to call Rockefeller by his first name and he said no. "The only ones who do are very close to him." It is possible for one to work closely for fourteen years with Rockefeller and still not be close in a personal sense. I was told by several confidants that only five people call him Nelson: Morrow, Woods, Kissinger, Oscar Ruebhausen, a prominent New York corporate attorney, and Bill Ronan. Family-retainer types say Mr. Nelson, because they are around more than one of the brothers. So it's Mr. David, etc. Longtime associates, except for the inside five, call him Governor. Recent arrivals call him Mr. Vice President. Cannon and Dunham aren't as important as Henry, so it's Governor to them. But they are loyal.

When one turns to look at what the Critical Choices commission does, it is clear that it feeds its recommendations directly into our government's policies. Recently, for instance, President Ford ordered the chairmen of the federal regulatory agencies to lay off the corporations. This had been a core idea of Rocky's commission.

The press was wrong to dismiss Critical Choices as just a platform for a Rockefeller candidacy. Rockefeller takes panels seriously and there is a direct connection between what was discussed at Critical Choices and the decisions that are currently being made by the U.S. government. Rockefeller had the money to buy the best brains in the country and bring them in for interminable meetings to hammer out a consensus for the rest of us. It's not the only private input into the executive branch, but there is no doubt of its strong influence.

As Vice President, Ford was invited to attend Critical Choices sessions— and an examination of the proceedings indicates they pursued one basic goal: developing a new politics in this country to usher in the new era of corporate operation. It is Rockefeller's view that we have gone too far with social legislation, that the corporations, his and others, are hamstrung, and that a new strategy has to be implemented that will "unfetter" the corporations.

It is now Ford's view that the government should give "maximum freedom to private enterprise." Speaking of Ford's recent curb on government regulatory agencies, *The New York Times* said that "in effect, the President called for a reversal of the nearly century-long trend toward federal supervision of key industries and national resources aimed at regulating competition and representing consumer interests."

As Rockefeller told me, the starting point is the greatness of the multinational corporation. "The multinationals, in my opinion, have got to be one of the great contributions of our system . . . but, hell, they've got the greatest system for taking technology, know-how, management, capital to any part of the world overnight; it's the most unbelievable program for diffusing knowledge."

Critics of the multinationals point out that they are extremely effective in exploiting cheap labor, ripping off resources, and generally making mockery of social legislation. Even Kirkland, who has been Rockefeller's token labor representative on the Critical Choices commission, has broken with him on this, because the top labor bureaucracy knows that the demands won by the unions (not to mention corporate tax reform, environmental controls, etc.) are being vitiated by companies' simply moving their production operations abroad and playing off one country against another. But Rockefeller the Godfather says Kirkland should not worry:

ROCKEFELLER: Well, Lane's worried about exporting jobs.

SCHEER: But he's saying that those corporations are escaping the progressive legislation.

ROCKEFELLER: Well, what he doesn't say is that the American people want all the social legislation, they want ecology, they want safety, they want all this stuff, but they want cheap goods, too.

SCHEER: But in the critical choices for Americans, are we now dealing with critical choices for different Americans—say, labor unions as opposed to multinational corporations? Are there different interests in America now that didn't surface before?

ROCKEFELLER: There seem to be, but in reality they are inseparable.

SCHEER: They're inseparable?

ROCKEFELLER: I don't think you can talk about the interests of one group without talking about the interests of the other—they see themselves in conflict, but they are part of a web or warp and it starts to unravel the rest. Now, how the balance is maintained between those sections is very important.

And Mr. Nelson has hit it right on the head. How the balance is maintained determines who gets screwed and who does the screwing. Or, if you like his image of the web, the question is who's going to be the big spider weaving it. But the image I like best is still that of a family—a world family built snugly around the worldwide corporate interests of the Rockefeller family— a Protestant *famiglia* far more ominous than any old-fashioned Italian Mafia.

The real power in this country is not in the gambling casinos of Reno or in the Presidency. Indeed, it doesn't even matter very much whether Rockefeller gets to be President—that's an ego trip. He doesn't need it. He already has the power and he should learn from the errors of the Mafia chieftains who got too much of a hankering for public recognition. If he would only hold back more and let Jerry Ford front for him a little more often, we could all go on believing that America is actually ruled by Midwestern congressmen. But Rockefeller is moving too fast, and in a time of economic recession, to have its richest and most powerful man pretend to be suffering equally with the rest of us and to be our neutral problem solver is so absurd that it is becoming obvious to the ruled.

As the plane began its descent, the Secret Service men cut out their poker game. Rockefeller's family collected their personal items for the short trek to the Pocantico Hills estate, and I pursued my interview with Rocky up to the last moment.

We finally landed in Westchester and Rockefeller and Happy, Morrow and I, and the Secret Service men struggled through the aisle. Happy for the last time said, "So good to see you."

Rockefeller said, "He doesn't miss anything."

Morrow said, "He does his homework, Nelson."

Rockefeller said finally, "Take care, my friend, I'm very optimistic about the future. I'm glad to see you. You really understand me."

(*Playboy*, October 1975)

Jimmy, We Hardly Know Y'All

The man himself is sitting, smile in place, in his studiously plain living room in front of a life-size portrait of his daughter, Amy, as though he were waiting for Norman Rockwell to appear. He is dressed in rumpled, down-home Levi's shirt and pants and is telling me and my *Playboy* editor that it would be a good thing to have a Southern Baptist as President, because it would be good for the young, the poor, blacks, women, and even those citizens who might be inclined to fornicate without the blessings of marriage. And once again, one wonders if Jimmy Carter is not too good to be true.

On one level, the man is simply preposterous. On another, he seems reasonable, sincere, and eminently sensible. It is difficult for me to believe that after four months of following him around the country, listening to the same speech five or six times a day, and after many hours of one-on-one conversation, I still nod in smiling agreement, like some kind of spaced-out Moonie, as another human being tells me he would never lie, would never be egotistical, doesn't fear death, would make federal government simple, workable, responsive to the average citizen, and that, in addition to doing away with the fear of death, he would do away with the fear of taxes.

As we stumble out into the muggy heat of Plains, Georgia, a movie-set hamlet of about eight buildings and what seem like two hundred photographers, all taking pictures of Jimmy's Central Casting mother, Miss Lillian, my editor tells me, "Hey, I really *like* the guy." Then, not thirty seconds later, he wonders aloud if we've been had. Which is how it always is with a James Earl Carter performance.

The ambiguity that one feels about Carter can be maddening. Is he one of the most packaged and manipulative candidates in our time or a Lincoln-esque barefoot boy who swooped out of nowhere at a time when we needed him? Is he a rigid proselytizer who wants to convert the country to his own vision of small-town, Sunday-school values or just a guy who believes in his personal God and will let the rest of us believe whatever the hell we want? Is he a true populist from something called the New South or yet another creature of the Eastern Establishment?

Hanging Out with Carter's Act

When Carter is a winner—and he seems to be as I write this in the fall of 1976—all these doubts emerge: his puritanism, his waffling on key questions, the sense that he and his campaign are an inexorable machine that have made us all cave in without really testing him. There is also at times an insufferable arrogance that seems almost patrician. But despite all that, when defeat threatened, back in the primary days, I was drawn to the man.

One night during the Oregon primary, the press people traveling with Carter were put up at a third-rate hotel and that fact seemed symbolic of what was then thought to be the coming disintegration of his campaign. The other candidates, Frank Church and Jerry Brown, were staying at better hotels. We were staying where we were because Carter had made a last-minute desperation switch in his schedule to spend an extra weekend in Oregon. He was running scared.

Brown had won handily in Maryland and Church seemed well ahead in Oregon. It looked as if Carter was facing a third-place finish in this Western primary. All of which seemed to portend the resuscitation of Hubert Humphrey's political corpse. Sam Donaldson, the ABC television correspondent, sat slumped in a sofa in the seedy hotel lobby and announced to anyone who would listen, "I smell blood in the water." We asked him to elaborate. "I smell a loser," he said. "I have a very sensitive nose and James Earl Carter is a *loser.*"

Donaldson is a good reporter and the judgment was so definitively stated that I mulled it over and was surprised to find myself suddenly depressed by the prospect of Carter's defeat. I say this with some objectivity, because, on the surface, the man was further from my own political beliefs than some of his more liberal opponents; but I didn't want him to leave the political stage. It was a sense that he did, in fact, represent some new, needed force that I couldn't yet define—but that somehow ought to have its day.

The feeling grew as I spent time with Carter, his family, and his aides in the months leading up to his nomination. To start with his aides, I found it increasingly difficult to think of them as possessing that cold-blooded uniformity of the Nixon gendarmes. Press secretary Jody Powell, campaign manager Hamilton Jordan, speechwriter Pat Anderson, and pollster Pat Caddell just don't fit the Haldeman, Ehrlichman, and Mitchell stereotypes. They *are* effective packagers, but worries about the palace guard throwing up the gates around the White House seem to fade as one stays up all night drinking with them in some redneck bar.

Maybe I'm just being suckered in by too much rural Southern exotica, but there is something raw, spontaneous, and physical about the people around Carter that puts a limit on their malleability and opportunism. It causes them to fuck up in ways I find reassuring. On one such occasion, I was riding with Jody and his wife, Nan, from Plains to nearby Americus. A car behind crowded us too closely and then passed, narrowly missing us. Jody shouted, "That fucking asshole!" and took off after the car. It would have made a fine wire-service story: Carter's press secretary, a former football player, wipes up the street with some local toughs. Nan managed to cool him down, but it was clear to me that in that moment Jody had stopped being a politician's aide. On another occasion, Jody and Pat Anderson got into a hassle with some locals over a rented car. Again, shouts and anger while the next President of the United States cooled his heels, waiting for Pat to show up with a draft of his acceptance speech.

One of Jody's more useful functions on the campaign is to serve as proof that one can have been born in a small Southern town, be a Baptist, serve for six years as Carter's closest aide, and still not be tight-assed. Add to that Anderson, who has written a novel called *The President's Mistress*; Caddell, hip and fresh out of Cambridge; Gerald Rafshoon, his media adviser and something of a carouser; Greg Schneiders, a one-time Washington restaurateur who is Carter's administrative assistant—and it becomes clear that Carter has not applied his concern with the Ten Commandments to the behavior of his staff. They are, at least some of them, as hard-drinking, fornicating, pot-smoking, freethinking a group as has been seen in higher politics.

Here's an exchange I taped with Hamilton Jordan:

SCHEER: Given the purity this campaign has projected, I find it odd that few of you guys go to church, that you all drink and mess around, and some of you even smoke dope. Isn't there a contradiction?

JORDAN: No. Jimmy's not self-righteous. He's very tolerant. If he weren't, he just wouldn't have people like me and Jody and Rafshoon around him.

SCHEER: So when you're with him, you don't feel as if you're with your Sunday-school teacher?

JORDAN: No, I don't feel that way. I'd never expect him to tell me how I should act. If people are concerned about his trying to foist his personal views on other people or that he somehow expects others to follow some rigid code he adheres to—well, that's just not him. He obviously hasn't made us change our way of living. He differentiates his personal and religious views from his actions as a political official. Look, all the same people who are so goddamned concerned about Jimmy's religion were early supporters of Martin Luther King, Jr. His forum was Southern Baptist, too, but it happened to be black. This thing of Jimmy talking about religion was a result of the press's always bringing it up, not him. If you're in Boston and you're a politician, you try to get your picture taken with Cardinal Cushing. If you're in the South, you're usually a Baptist and you go to church a lot. So?

Once, during the early stages of the campaign, a couple of his aides who were married had met two women in the hotel lobby and were taking them to their rooms. The elevator stopped at a floor below theirs, the door opened—and in walked Jimmy and Rosalynn. Not a word was exchanged. The aides stared nervously at the ceiling of the elevator as the two ladies giggled nervously and nudged each other. I was told later that Jimmy never mentioned the incident to either aide.

So much for reassuring anecdotes. At least these are anecdotes I've plucked out myself. But a modern campaign doles out anecdotes like a priest dispenses Communion wafers. The pack of reporters covering the candidate is always in a holding pattern of desperate anticipation, each waiting to be singled out for the blessing of an exclusive anecdote. This is because, during a campaign, a candidate is rarely going to say anything clear or provocative about anything important and, as a result, "color"—which is really just the plural for anecdote—becomes all-important. When we came out of our last interview session with Carter, a UPI reporter approached the assistant press secretary. The reporter was on the "body watch," which, as it was explained to me, means that the candidate might croak or fart and if the reporter's not there to record it, his ass is on the line. The newsman knew we'd been interviewing Carter and said, "Hey, what did those guys ask him? I need one crumb—anything for my lead this afternoon—because I've got nothing so far." The aide took an insignificant comment from our interview and doled it out.

So let's take the "oral sex" anecdote that Jody reserved especially for me. (Previously, I'd been given a Bob Dylan-meets-Jimmy Carter anecdote, but it slipped out and ended up being printed elsewhere.) It seems that on a trip to Washington, then-Governor Carter, Rafshoon, and a state trooper guarding the governor all went to a screening of the movie *Lenny*. During the performance, the trooper kept snorting and poking Rafshoon about the language and some of the steamier scenes. Carter just sat quietly, taking it in. When they got out, Rafshoon couldn't resist asking, "Say, Governor, do they have oral sex in Plains?"

Carter, after a pause, said, "Yep, but they don't call it that."

Which is a nice thing to know about Plains. But it's safe to say that the anecdote was reserved for a writer from *Playboy* and that Jody didn't offer it to, say, the people from *Reader's Digest* who preceded us that day. It served a purpose: to telegraph to the "typical" *Playboy* reader that Jimmy Carter is a regular guy. He may not use hip language, but he has hip thoughts. The same purpose was served when he dropped that Dylan quote into his acceptance speech at the convention—to do for the Dylan generation what a reference to Polish people did for those five million voters: tip them off that he was secretly one of them.

Well, compared with Ford, Carter *is* hip. And there's no doubt the people around Carter are good guys, quite the opposite from the cold technicians' image that has frequently been attached to them. I'd buy a used car from Jody or Hamilton—or from Jimmy, for that matter. After all, what he wants is for me to have a car as good and decent and as full of love as I deserve. I'm tired of cars and State Departments and CIAs that are lemons. But the trouble is that every time I feel good about the man, I can feel bad twenty minutes later when I remember that Jody wanted Wallace above all others to join Carter at the podium of the Democratic Convention and that, sure enough, there was Hamilton clapping politely for various Democratic politicians as they were called up to the podium, then clapping enthusiastically when Wallace's name was called. (From my conversations with Jody and Hamilton, I'm sure they were responding to a Southern outsider's having his day at the convention and not to Wallace's racist reputation. But it still made me nervous.)

So who is hustling whom? The problem is that one's judgments about Carter are necessarily fragmented because we have no sense of the depth of the man, of his experience and roots. He just came to us a winner. Carter's people are good at their business, so good that they've managed to cover the hard and interesting edges of the man. What we see is the packaging. The young men surrounding Carter let an occasional nugget drop for a particular constituency, then wrap him up again quickly. The manipulation of staged media events along with color results in lopsided opinion polls that will probably carry him to the White House, but when you look closely, you end up confused. His more liberal aides, such as Peter Bourne and Mary King, will tell you that he is a closet progressive, as Roosevelt was when he first ran, and that he has withheld disclosure of his full program: Once he's in

the White House—whammo! Others, such as Charles Kirbo, a more traditional politician, will confide to *his* friends that he's really a closet conservative.
And so speculation about Carter the man and Carter the President really
hangs on an appraisal of where his gut feelings are coming from.

Reporters covering Jerry Ford or Ronald Reagan or Scoop Jackson soon
stop looking for the "real" person behind the campaigner, because they realize
that if they should happen to find him, he would be boringly similar to the
one they've seen all along. But I have yet to meet a reporter who feels that
way about Carter. He is intriguing, baffling, and perpetually confounding.
Even to his family.

One afternoon, I was visiting with Carter's sister Gloria and her husband,
Walter Spann, in their farmhouse about five miles down the road from
Jimmy's home. Carter had remarked during the *Playboy* interview that he
felt closer to Gloria than to his evangelist sister, Ruth. The remark confused
me, because Gloria is loose and outgoing—as opposed to Jimmy—and supported McGovern, drives motorcycles, and doesn't seem to give much of a
damn about her image. I had first met Gloria when I was over at Miss Lillian's.
Carter's mother had told me that Gloria wasn't giving interviews. When Gloria
walked in, I asked her if she'd make an exception. She shot me a look and
said, "I'm not talking to any reporters unless they have jeans, boots, and a
beard." I had two of the prerequisites.

"Look," I said. "I'm only wearing this suit because I thought that's what
you do when you go calling on Southern ladies."

She laughed and said, "Well, I ain't no Southern lady, but you finish here
and come by and see me and Walter. I'll give you some bourbon, but no
interview."

At the Spann home, as the three of us sat drinking, my reportorial instincts
got the best of me and I started inquiring about Walter's political beliefs. He
was even blunter than Gloria: It was none of my business, he said, whom
he preferred for President or if he voted at all. He added, "I like it fine if
you're over drinking with us, but I don't want to be interviewed. I'm a farmer,
not a politician. Jimmy's the politician."

Later, they became more talkative and let me take notes. Gloria said that
she had always known Jimmy as a vibrant, adventuresome person. She said
that as a child, he was given the nickname Hot by his father and that his
sisters and brother still called him that privately. Hot seemed to fit Jimmy,
she said, because he felt deeply and was always in a fevered rush to do
significant things with his life. (The other family nicknames she mentioned
seem appropriate as well. Gloria, the family free spirit, was called Gogo.

Billy, the self-conscious redneck, was Buck. And faith healer Ruth was Boopy Doop.)

Gloria said it was "bunk" that Hot, or Jimmy, should be considered cold, ruthless, or unemotional. It was true that he had always taken himself seriously, but that the political life had made him become more guarded. At this point, late in the boozy evening, Walter broke in and said, "You reporters aren't going to get to know Jimmy, because he's onstage. He's been onstage ever since 1966, when he ran for governor."

To which Gloria added softly but with affection: "He's been onstage longer than that."

At one point during the interview with Carter, as I was fumbling with my tape recorder, I mentioned that my talk with Gloria had led me to believe he was a more relaxed and less mechanical person than he seemed on the campaign trail. Was there going to be any time in his life for the sort of openness that Gloria described?

"Sure," he said. "I've always lived that way. Listen, we're having a fish fry Saturday afternoon and you're welcome to come. We're not inviting many people. We're going to drain my little pond and get some of the bigger fish out of there and then have a fry afterward. I think it would be a good time for you to just see a typical incident in the life of the Plains community."

Two hours after I spoke with Carter, Jody invited the entire press corps to the fish fry. The typical scene in the life of the Plains community turned into yet another media event flashed around the world by television. It was a mob scene, with reporters outnumbering locals four to one. Carter looked about as relaxed as one of the flapping fish in the drained pond.

But Carter does come from a delightfully informal family. On one earlier occasion, Gloria and Miss Lillian had invited me to go along for supper at a local diner. Gloria had carefully prepared two jars of liquid refreshment—one filled with Early Times bourbon and the other with water—so I "wouldn't get thirsty" on the way to dinner. While we were there, they playfully felt under my coat to see if I was wired for sound and became totally relaxed as they sipped on the bourbon and talked irreverently about the foibles of people in Plains.

The shame is, they get uneasy when they see how friendly and natural they come off in print. I hope Miss Lillian doesn't react to my description of her the way she responded to some of what's been published about her—and, my God, she does get a wonderful press. Here is Miss Lillian talking to me about the media:

"Frankly, I don't like women interviewers. They're pushy, though one I had was just as sweet as she could be. Some of them, they freelance, and if what you say isn't interesting, they touch it up a bit. That one girl wrote an article and she said I had a drink in my hand and I waved it around in the air. I never had a drink with anyone who was interviewing me. Never. If I offered you a drink, I don't know whether you'd write it down or not, because I don't trust anybody. I know it's going to get worse and I'm prepared. I'm just kind of suspicious of a woman writer until I know where I stand. Most women are freelancers, did you know that? I'm besieged by publishers and I just tell everyone that Gloria is going to write my story. She's got all my letters and everything, isn't that right, Gloria?"

But the afternoon of the fish fry, another member of the family delivered an opinion of the press that was a bit less charming. I was on the porch chatting with Gloria and Walter. Jimmy had escaped from the other reporters and walked over to kiss Gloria on the cheek. He shook Walter's hand, too, but ignored my presence. We had recorded a number of conversations by then and it was an awkward moment for me, given the fact that he'd invited me over to see him in a "relaxed" frame of mind. But what made it even more awkward was that he began to speak about the press in unflattering terms to Gloria and Walter, as if I were not present.

"Guess it's hard for you to get away from all those reporters," Walter said. "They're like gnats swarming around."

Carter paused in his munching of a catfish and replied, "The press people are afraid I'm going to eat a fishbone and choke on it. They're afraid they won't have a picture when it happens." The tone wasn't bantering; it was more on the bitter side.

Now, it's true that the body watch doesn't want to miss anything and that that can get depressing for a candidate. But the press people hadn't climbed over any fences to get in—Carter had invited them because he wanted a folksy image of his fish fry beamed around the world. A part of Carter undoubtedly loves down-home fish fries. But another part of him wants to exploit the hell out of them.

And that's the dilemma: He uses the process and gets consumed by it. He cares for his mother, but, as the seventy-eight-year-old Miss Lillian told me, "When I came back from India [she was with the Peace Corps], Jimmy asked me to accept every single speaking engagement I could to help him get exposure." That's why he plays up Gloria, the motorcycle rider, to a bike-race audience in Oregon and sister Ruth to church folk in South Dakota. That's why his son Chip will be sent off to attend a gay function in San Francisco while Dad is addressing a meeting of black ministers (during which he pronounces homosexuality "a sin").

It is not that Carter is shallow or exploitative but rather that he and his staff have consciously decided to use—and thus to submit to—a process of campaigning that is inherently shallow and exploitative. One realizes that

Carter is capable of dealing with complicated thoughts. One also senses that he is a good man who cares for his family; that he has real roots; that he is serious about fairly representing the American people. But it is a fact that his life in these past two years—and perhaps longer, as his sister suggests—has been one staged media event after another.

Carter would probably admit to being onstage, to being packaged, and at times—when he becomes testy and stiff-necked—he seems to be grappling with the implications of this to his personality. When I brought it up with one of his aides, I was told that that was the precise reason Carter insists on returning to Plains every weekend during the campaign, even if only for one night. But, as a result, Plains itself has become a stage prop that he has prettified for us.

Offstage

The town of Plains has by now become sticky with media hype. It's what one Manhattan friend calls cracker chic. Residents and reporters alike have entered into a conspiracy not to disillusion visitors. Among the locals, "We wouldn't do anything to hurt Jimmy's chances" is the most common refrain. What we have are caricatures. There is a talkative old Miss Lillian, rocking on her porch, a lovable interview junkie; brother Billy, the redneck cracker; Rosalynn, the dutiful if uptight wife; cousin Hugh, the genial worm farmer; Jimmy's father, James Earl Carter, Sr., who died in 1953 and is rarely mentioned, except to say that he had Old South (i.e., racist and reactionary) ideas.

But, of course, as is the case with Jimmy himself, the scene is more complicated than that. Fewer solid colors; more gray. Southern rural life is no simpler than urban life. And if you throw in the extreme pressure of the civil-rights years, probably tougher. The folksy, innocent façade that surrounds Plains may be convenient to the Carter campaign, but it simply rewrites history.

Coincidentally, I had been through Plains sixteen years ago and felt the tension beneath the surface of this placid town. In 1960, I was driving through southwest Georgia with a group of people who wanted to integrate public facilities. I have a particular memory of a gas station in Americus where I stopped so a white companion could deliberately use the "colored" rest room. An ugly confrontation ensued.

Recently, I was riding around town with Walter and Gloria and I spotted what appeared to be the same gas station. I mentioned the 1960 incident to them and Walter said, "Did you do that? Hell, they should have blown your fool head off." I like Walter and I knew he was kidding. In fact, he's one of the few people around Plains who don't feel a need to ennoble the past.

And that's the point. Carter does. Just as the campaign packaging prevents one from seeing his complexities, his tolerance, and his tensions, so the whitewashing of the past prevents one from studying his real roots. His family have become town characters wtih stereotyped pasts, and his own past, though somewhat more closely examined, becomes a part of folklore. But to get a glimpse of the complexity of real life, there is no better case study than the crucible the Old South went through to become the New South: the civil-rights struggle.

There are two roads at the edge of Plains that meet at nearly right angles: One goes toward an integrated farm called Koinonia and the other leads to Americus. Both places were sources of the main shock waves from civil rights that reached the Carter family.

Americus has been much discussed in the press. It was once one of the meanest towns in the South, the scene of some of the ugliest demonstrations and acts of violence during 1963 and 1964. It was in Americus that Martin Luther King, Jr., was jailed and told to sweep the floors. Until not long ago, its bulletin boards displayed a letter from King "thanking" the jailers for their hospitality. What Carter did and did not do as a moderate and a supporter of Lyndon Johnson has been raked over the coals. He did not speak out forcefully during the sixties (and, indeed, took no position at all during the worst disturbances) but paid his dues as his family and he were taunted as "nigger lovers" during L.B.J.'s campaign. Americus is nine miles from Plains.

But Koinonia is something else. It is a raw nerve to both Jimmy and Miss Lillian. It has not been raked over the coals, because it is hardly mentioned. Koinonia was founded in 1942 by a progressive white couple named Clarence and Florence Jordan. It was a courageous attempt to show that an integrated communal farm run on Christian principles was a possibility in the Old South. It is seven miles from Plains.

When I questioned Miss Lillian about the Carters' relationship to the farm, I caught a rare flash of anger. "Why do you want to bring that up?" she snapped. "It's over with. You'd just stir up some of the wilder people around here, and then nobody knows what will happen."

The people who might stir things up around Plains are the same ones who gave Miss Lillian and Gloria a hard time back in 1964, when they worked for Johnson's election at the Americus headquarters. "Children yelled at me," Miss Lillian recalled, "and threw things at my car because Johnson was what they called an N-I-G-G-E-R L-O-V-E-R." Were they some of the same people who have turned to private schools to avoid integration? "Some of them," she admitted, "but they're not the nicest people in town."

Why Not the Best? is the title of Carter's autobiography. And the concept of the nicest, or best, people is the key to understanding Jimmy Carter, for it comes out of a patrician rural tradition of responsibility to which he is heir. The white elite who survived the civil-rights strife without losing their power either by overtly siding with the blacks or by taking racist stands formed the core of the New South that Carter personifies. It is moderate and pragmatic and, above all, patrician.

The Carters, after all, were patricians. Part of Jimmy's packaging includes reminiscences about his childhood in a home without electricity. Well, in the days before rural electrification, nobody much had it. But Earl, as Jimmy's father was known, owned four thousand acres, employed servants, and died with money in the bank. And to be patrician toward a radical experiment such as Koinonia meant to keep it at a proper distance without really siding against it.

Another personal coincidence: The period I spent nosing around Plains wasn't the first time I'd heard about Koinonia. I remember that when I left the gas station in Americus, I stopped to ask directions for the farm. I had read about it and stopped at a corner to naïvely ask a group of white men how to get to Koinonia. One of them sneered at me, "Why you want to go there, boy?" I chose to discontinue the dialogue. For the next few hours, there were many false starts up red-clay roads with flashlights shining on our California license plates and enormous dogs barking. I was about as scared as I've ever been, and to this day, I can't fathom the courage of blacks in Americus who decided to take a stand. Or the whites and blacks who dared to live together at Koinonia. That was the night I met Florence and Clarence Jordan, the founders of the farm.

Sixteen years later, on the Carter campaign, I met Hamilton Jordan and asked him if he was related to the Clarence Jordan I'd met years ago. Hamilton told me Clarence, who died in 1969, was his uncle and "one of the two people in my life I have respected most," the other being Carter. Hamilton and I discussed Koinonia and his uncle for quite some time.

Hamilton has his roots in this southwest Georgia clay and reached adulthood during the worst of the racial turmoil. He recalls that he was a segregationist until "after Kennedy," but he was always awed by the idealism of his Uncle Clarence. He visited Koinonia as a kid and remembers: "Clarence had a tragic life, but he was a great, great man—a straight shooter, at peace with himself."

Hamilton, like Jimmy, played the proper, white-sheep role in his family. A crusader like Clarence was therefore a "loser," but one who was a challenge to the rest of the family. As Miss Lillian admitted, "Clarence was twenty years ahead of his time."

Clarence Jordan was a Baptist minister with a Ph.D. who, quite literally, practiced what he preached. The Christianity and brotherly love about which he spoke so eloquently from the pulpit included blacks, and it didn't take the townspeople of Plains long to figure that out. In 1942, he formed a small community of farmers and workers, black and white, in what was essentially a commune. The Klan paid its first visit that year. By the fifties, the powerful White Citizens' Council had moved on to boycotts, bombings, and shootings. The farm became famous in the middle fifties, when an Atlanta newspaper printed a cartoon showing the Koinonia barn with a lightning rod on its roof.

How did Carter, back from the Navy after his father's death in 1953, respond to the farm? "I went there several times in the fifties and sixties," he told me. "They couldn't get anyone else to shell seed for them, and I did. I went down there a couple of times to talk to Clarence Jordan . . . I knew Clarence Jordan when we were going through the years of integration."

I checked his recollection with that of Clarence's widow, Florence, who still lives on the Koinonia farm. "It's not that I want to throw a monkey wrench into his campaign," she told me, "because most of us will probably vote for him. But it does seem kind of bad when a reporter calls here on the basis of Jimmy's having said he used to visit here and knew us. I have to say I'm sorry, but I don't even know the man. I've never met him, and we've been living down the road for thirty-four years. People came here from all over the world, but he hasn't come seven miles."

In that same conversation, she told me that there were people who had been friendly to the Koinonia folks, but that most of them had been forced to leave the area because of the social pressure. No one else in the county offered support. "They would lose their business or lose their friends," she said sadly, "and that was more important than their Christian beliefs. That was true of most people in the county and [Jimmy] was no different."

I went back to Carter and pinned him down on what stand he *had* taken when he heard about the shootings and bombings at Koinonia. "I didn't shoot at them or throw bombs," he replied, in what I believe was a sarcastic tone.

"I know," I said, "but did you speak out against it?"

"There was a general deploring of violence," he replied, "and the grand jury investigated it and I think everybody was embarrassed by it. It was done—if it was done—by a fringe element. This was a time, I'd say, of very radical elements on both sides."

If Florence wasn't lying to me about Jimmy's visits to Koinonia, then Jimmy was. Since the shootings are vastly documented, his hedge—"if it was done"—is chickenshit. And his answer to my question about whether he'd spoken out—"There was a general deploring"—indicates his embarrassment at any but the most heroic image of his past. And, to top it off, the grand-jury investigation Carter referred to as a presumably impartial force is known to have been a McCarthy-type witch-hunt directed *against* Koinonia.

When I considered Carter's promises never to lie, his sanitized version of events in his past, and his stubborn refusal to admit to imperfection, the implications of this exchange angered me—which comes easily and self-righteously to a Northerner. But it almost caused me to overlook what I was seeking out: complexity. I stumbled across another unknown incident involving an early member of Koinonia, and it softened the impact for me.

It was Gloria who told me to look up Jack Singletary. Singletary came from a patrician family like Carter's in another part of Georgia. He attended the Naval Academy at the same time Carter did (though they did not know each other there) and served in the Navy. But when the postwar draft came along, Singletary refused to register on religious grounds. He had already joined Koinonia when he was sent to federal prison; upon his release, he went back to the farm. After a couple of years, he moved to his own farm nearby, without giving up Koinonia's progressive ideas. He became, in Gloria's words, "the white nigger of Plains."

Chatting with this remarkable Georgian, who I thought would have little good to say about a man who did not support him through Koinonia's terrible years, I was surprised to find that his memories of Carter were positive:

"Jimmy came home from the Navy and I ran into him on the street and he and Rosalynn invited me to their apartment, which had never been done. That was in '53 or '54. He told me that night that he shared my views in regard to the race question. He told me about the incident when he was an officer on a ship and the crew was on shore leave and was invited to an official function. A black sailor wasn't invited, so the whole crew didn't go. He was proud. He wanted me to know this."

Singletary related the story of the boycott against his family. The White Citizens' Council in Sumter County decided that no merchant should sell goods to any member of Koinonia, and that included Singletary.

"There was a little store down here—Mrs. Howell's store—and they circulated stuff that me and Koinonia were buying our groceries from her. So the sheriff and the Georgia Bureau of Investigation agent went to see Mrs. Howell. They told her that if she didn't quit selling to us, something was going to happen to her. But the only contact I was having with Mrs. Howell was that my oldest child was dying with leukemia and we didn't have a telephone. Mrs. Howell's store had the nearest telephone. We had taken our son to Sloan-Kettering in New York for treatment and we were keeping in touch with them by telephone about his medicine. I'd go down and use Mrs.

Howell's telephone and I'd pay her telephone bill. Well, she told me that they had come to threaten her and that she was going to have to stop letting me use the telephone."

Singletary took his case to the local merchants' group, of which Carter was a member. The group decided to bend the boycott in Singletary's case, though it remained in force against the residents of Koinonia. They were good people, the merchants, and they weren't going to do something so inhumane as to deny help to a leukemic boy. It wasn't a great moment for Jimmy Carter, but it told the powerful White Citizens' Council where he and some of the best people stood.

There is even more to the Koinonia story that reflects on the Carter family and that invalidates the simple stereotypes we've been allowed to see. For instance, Singletary told me about a follow-up that changed my mind about Rosalynn, who doesn't get much credit for having taken courageous stands.

"Our little boy finally died of leukemia. It was when the boycott was on and we had our friends from Koinonia come over for the funeral. Rosalynn came the next morning and brought a ham. We invited her to stay and she did: we had a very informal Quaker-type service and put the body into a little box that Koinonia had made. We took it down to a little playground there where he had played and buried him without any remarks. Rosalynn left here, I'm told, really just all upset and went to Plains to see the Baptist preacher and bawled him out. He said he reckoned he'd be run out of town if he did it, but she made him come so we finally had a graveside service. Now, that's a little insight into the kind of person she is, and I'm sure that Jimmy was with her."

When I told Rosalynn that I had been talking to Singletary, she said quietly, "Yes, that's right—they were heroic people. It took people from the outside to shake us up into seeing what was right. I have a lot of respect for those people." I don't care what I read about Rosalynn in the *Ladies' Home Journal* from now on: I'm prepared to admire her without being cynical.

As I began collecting other bits of evidence, many of them favorable to the Carters, from sources that seemed impartial, I realized how superficially the press—with the connivance of the Carter campaign—had characterized these human beings. Earl Carter, for instance, turns out not to have been the hidebound racist he is made out to be. It was he, in fact, who first befriended Singletary, inviting him (on one occasion with a black friend) into the back of the store for a soda pop when such an act took courage. "Mr. Earl," as Singletary called him, also went into partnership with him to combine clover when no other farmers would even share equipment with Singletary. When Earl was dying in 1953 of cancer, Singletary was one of the two non-family members Earl asked to his bedside.

Billy Carter, the incorrigible cracker who still uses the word "nigger" when he's drinking with his old buddies at the gas station, took an unpopular stand against the church people in speaking out against the antiquated liquor laws. That much may not be surprising, but it was also he who financed a 1966 lawsuit against segregated private schools.

On the other hand, there is cousin Hugh, whom news people love to quote for bits of quaint philosophy. Hugh was the one who fought against the very desegregation initiative his cousins supported: he was also head of the board of deacons in the Baptist Church and in 1962 voted to keep blacks out of the church that Jimmy tried to integrate. And it wasn't just blacks he was opposed to. His board of deacons unanimously voted against admitting the Singletarys as church members, merely for associating with blacks. Singletary told me that the board had warned his family they weren't even welcome to visit the church. Needless to say, Jimmy and Rosalynn opposed Hugh's position on this and Jimmy stood up in church the following Sunday to plead unsuccessfully for the admission of the Singletarys.

Nor is Miss Lillian the Central Casting figure she likes to play. For instance, we've heard a lot about the fact that she entered the Peace Corps at the age of sixty-eight, but usually in the context of an old lady going off on a lark. In one of our conversations, she revealed some of that condescending but well-intentioned patrician spirit that now marks Jimmy (I have condensed a much longer monologue):

"I went to India, which is a dark country with a warm climate, because I felt the South had been so awful to blacks that I wanted to go where I could help people who had nothing . . . I did a lot of family-planning work and had to explain to those poor people why it was necessary for them . . . If a man had more than three children, he had to have a vasectomy, which was fair. It was the only way to handle it, because those people are ignorant and the only outlet they have is sex . . . I listened to one of the women at the clinic explain to one of the men why he needed a vasectomy. I had seen some of the men almost lose their minds. You know, they could not believe that if they had the operation they would still be men, so I would see a lot of scenes of broken men . . . I would see some of the attendants holding men down on the tables for their operation and I said, I can do better than that, so I must tell you what I did: I would stand at the man's head: he hadn't had a shot or anything, he had to stand it without anesthesia. I stood at his head and I got a pan of cold water and I would talk in a low, soothing voice and put rags on his head, and I would say, That's all right—I had a few words of Hindi that I could say to keep him calm . . . It hurts, you have to cut the thing in two, and, oh, that hurts. So that's what I did with the vasectomies."

My focus on the Carters' patrician spirit and on Koinonia and on civil rights isn't to raise the specter of intolerance or closet racism. It's pretty clear that Carter and most of his family were never racists—and were, on the whole, as courageous as any of the "best" families. But I do raise it to say that Carter and his family can't be capsulized as easily as they want to make us think. Despite Carter's acts of courage, he didn't *always* act courageously. He was caught in a terrible time and he was only human—which means he often didn't do the right thing. *But Jimmy Carter won't admit it.* The real heroes of the era were less than ten miles up the road in either direction from his home all his life, taking the most terrible punishment, and he won't admit that he shunned them like nearly everyone else. Like all of us.

Carter is addicted to the theory that we progress by stressing our virtues rather than by dwelling on failures; this is the major theme of his campaign speeches. There's undoubtedly some merit to this approach, but it seems to me that it excludes serious learning from past error.

The mythologizing of the past leads naturally to the prettification of present-day Plains. Right here, in brother Billy's fire-prone gas station and cousin Hugh's antique store, when the talking and drinking get going, one still finds considerable contempt for "niggers." I was with Billy when he pointed out a hulking, mean-looking local and explained, "He's a John Bircher—used to be in the White Citizens' Council. John Birch is real big around here. They've taken over from the Council and the Klan."

Plains and Americus are no better or worse than many other places, but hanging out in these towns makes you wonder where Jimmy gets off extolling the virtues of small-town living, as he often does. It merely leaves the rest of us feeling guilty, hankering for some sort of idyllic golden age that never existed. "Why not the best?" is a reasonable question if it is made clear that the best doesn't exist, that it's something we can only aspire to. And it is this self-righteous, sanctimonious, smily side of Jimmy Carter that gets to me, because it miseducates us about the real problems we face in trying to become the best. Carter frequently promises that he will never lie to us, but his power-of-positive-thinking stance is itself a lie. We are not all "full of love." We don't "all want the same things." His version of the good life, filled with churches and sermons, would bore a lot of people—including those in his hometown.

I remember one afternoon in a small town in Oregon during the primary campaign when there was a convention of barbership quartets. I didn't mind it until several of the quartets approached Carter and serenaded him with a syrupy rendition of "Dixie." Carter began to speak about how the scene was exactly the same in Plains, where people sit around on the grass and listen to music, and said that that was what the good life was really like. It was such a cloying performance all around that I began muttering incoherently about the need for a little perversity in everybody's life. I asked one of the singers whether he believed in all this small-town goodness that he represented, fully expecting to be punched out. His answer restored my faith in America much more than anything Carter said that day. "Hey, man," he said in a pleasing tenor voice, "this is *camp!*"

Kids are being busted right now in Plains for hard drugs. Carter's nephew is a hard-drug user and homosexual who is serving time in a California jail for armed robbery. Rosalynn told me that her friend's sixteen-year-old son is serving time in prison on a marijuana charge. In August, a twenty-eight-year-old puritan named Randy Howard was elected Sumter County sheriff on the basis of his record as a one-man narc squad, hassling half the younger population. Howard claims that organized crime has moved into the area with drugs, pornography, and gambling. He says alcoholism remains the number-one problem in the area.

The hypocrisy about booze is extreme. One hot night, when Carter and Walter Mondale were scheduled to speak at the Plains railroad depot, I went over to brother Billy's gas station to get a six-pack and then went back to the rally, only to be told by Buford Reese, a local Carter man, "Friend, would you put that away on behalf of the community?" We in the press giggled. But later I felt sorry for Buford and for Howard (who had told me that he never touches alcohol and doesn't think people need anything more than Coca-Cola), because their sincerity cannot possibly withstand their daily experiences with the reality of life in Sumter County. Hell, the next President's brother sells beer late into the night and his mother has been known, as are many older Southern ladies, to pick up a half-pint of harder stuff. (It always had to be bought in half-pint bottles or the liquor-store people, and therefore anyone else, might get the wrong idea.) But who *needs* this guilt?

Evidently it serves a purpose. The way Jody Powell explains it, life in these towns is so intimate and passions so close to the surface that certain fictions must be maintained as social restraints. There are just certain things that the "best people" ought not to be seen doing or everything else will fall apart. Although everyone knows that the contradictions are there, it is important to conceal them. And it is this principle that Jimmy Carter has made the mainstay of his drive for the Presidency. In the wake of Watergate and the myriad other revelations about the seamy side of government, Carter has proceeded to conduct himself as one of the best people who will not lie, cheat, screw around, gamble, or in any other way reflect a disheveled and chaotic spirit. Carter decided, as he states in his autobiography, to carry on "in the tradition of the best people," and that's just what he's been doing. His daddy had done the same and his momma took over after his daddy's death. They consciously attempted to publicly embody a high standard of morality as a playing out of their historic role as one of the leading families. It is therefore understandable that Jimmy has now extended that principle to national politics. What has startled everyone is that because of the particular disarray of American government, at this moment, that old style fulfills a national need.

The limit of this stance is that it is based on paternalism. It assumes that the best people are the source of cultural and moral wisdom. And although they have an obligation to help educate the rest of us, we don't stand much of a chance of getting educated. Hence, they will have to lead, cajole, and manipulate us sinners into being better than we are. That is why Jimmy appears fuzzy on the issues: he can't tell us too much or we might prevent his gaining power to do the right thing.

Will Carter Kick Ass?

If, after the inauguration, you find a Cy Vance as Secretary of State and Zbigniew Brzezinski as head of National Security, then I would say we failed. And I'd quit. But that's not going to happen. You're going to see new faces, new ideas. The government is going to be run by people you have never heard of.

—Hamilton Jordan

By the time I'd finished my Southern odyssey, it seemed to me that despite all the contradictions I'd found, most of the fears of Carter's liberal critics appeared unwarranted. A Carter Presidency will probably be strong on civil liberties and civil rights. Blacks and women will probably be amply sprinkled throughout the higher levels of his Administration (though it hasn't yet happened in his campaign staff) and freethinkers won't be thrown into jail. On the contrary: just as Nixon, secure in his right flank, was able to open relations with China, Carter's Bible base will probably permit him to extend our basic freedoms. If his current staff becomes the palace guard, it might even be fun.

But now that we have looked at Carter as a Southern patrician, what about his constant campaign cries against "political and economic elites," against "big shots"? Aren't successful Southern politicians part of the political elite?

And when they're backed by large Southern-based corporations, aren't they part of the economic elite? Carter has a particularly close relationship with Coca-Cola board chairman J. Paul Austin, who organized fund-raising and businessmen's groups for him. There was even some trouble when the press reported that Carter had taken a couple of trips abroad that were paid for by Coke. And while it's true that Coke is based in Atlanta and Pepsi is in Purchase, New York, both are huge multinational corporations with similar positions on foreign policy.

What got me thinking about all this was a campaign stop in Fayetteville, Arkansas. Carter was delivering his speech and I was chatting with Pat Anderson, his speechwriter, at the windswept airport. There was also a contingent of beauty contestants brought up onto the podium. I'd just interviewed Miss Poultry—honest to God—out of a fear that I'd go crazy if I had to listen to Carter's speech one more time.

SCHEER: Miss Poultry, I wonder if you could tell us your position on foreign policy?

MISS POULTRY: I'm sorry, we're not allowed to have positions. It's against the rules.

I turned to Anderson to ask him *his* position on foreign policy; I figured I'd have better luck with him, since he'd been jotting down notes for Carter's upcoming speech before the Foreign Policy Association in New York. Anderson waved me aside and said, "Later, I have to check this speech out with Brzezinski."

Check it out with Brzezinski? That was when I flashed back to the fact that the first time I'd ever really heard of Jimmy Carter wasn't over beers in some redneck bar with the likes of Jody Powell or Hamilton Jordan but in Mount Desert, Maine, with none other than Zbigniew Brzezinski.

It was the summer of 1975 and I was researching an article on the Rockefellers, who vacation on the coast of Maine. I'd met Zbig and his wife and they'd asked me over to their twenty-seven-room house just down the road from David Rockefeller's place. I found that Zbig had been sponsored by David Rockefeller in much the same way that Henry Kissinger had been sponsored by Nelson Rockefeller. ("With one important distinction," Zbig cautioned. "Henry worked for Nelson as an employee and I work with David as an associate.")

It was back then that Brzezinski told me that he favored a former governor of Georgia as the Democratic candidate. I was surprised. Why a Georgian peanut farmer who was supposed to be a grass-roots populist should have earned the enthusiasm of an Establishment intellectual like Brzezinski was a mystery to me.

Well, it turned out that Brzezinski and Carter had a relationship going back to 1972, when David Rockefeller asked the then-Governor of Georgia to join the new international-elite organization that he was forming called the Trilateral Commission. Carter told me he was never to miss a meeting of the Trilateral Commission during the next three years and that he received his basic foreign-policy education under its auspices. It is also clear that during this period, Carter was able to impress David Rockefeller, who is part of the group that runs things in this country. Carter had already decided to run for the Presidency, remember. Rafshoon, his media specialist, told me during the campaign that Carter's selection to the Trilateral Commission was "one of the most fortunate accidents of the early campaign and critical to his building support where it counted." It is also the source for the main foreign-policy ideas in the Carter program. Which should be enough of a build-up to justify the question: What is a Trilateral Commission?

Essentially, the Trilateral Commission is a group of political and financial bigwigs from Western Europe, Japan, Canada, and the U.S. formed to provide a common negotiating position for the industrialized capitalist nations. David Rockefeller was instrumental in its founding. It's as much of a political *and* an economic elite as you can find.

The Rockefeller family has long had a propensity for establishing foundations, commissions, think tanks, and study groups. These basically involve using tax-free dollars to buy up high-priced intellectual talent in order to develop social programs that ostensibly meet the public's needs while maintaining (a darker spirit might suggest "extending") the interests of the Rockefellers. The original Rockefeller Brothers Reports and, more recently, Nelson's Commission on Critical Choices for Americans, are examples of the process. David happens to have taken an interest in foreign affairs: The New York Council on Foreign Relations, of which he is the chairman, is one of his pet projects. The CFR was directed for twenty-five years by David's college roommate, one George Franklin, who left the CFR at David's behest to form the Trilateral Commission.

Franklin told me that he was the person who first hired an enterprising young Harvard professor to work for the council and, after eight years of heading up or participating in council studies, Henry Kissinger went on to do quite well in government service. Kissinger and Brzezinski were in the same class at Harvard Graduate School. Although both have been Rockefeller/Franklin protégés, they try to avoid speaking to each other, which is more of a reflection of their egos than of any serious policy differences between the two men. Franklin and David like them both and one suspects they don't really care which one is Secretary of State.

Carter has made an issue of his differences with Kissinger's foreign policy, but given his reliance on the Trilateral Commission and Brzezinski, he must have had to dig for differences. Since there aren't many, he decided to attack Kissinger's "Lone Ranger" methods. But it doesn't add up to much in the way of real dissimilarities.

Also, Jimmy Carter, the man who now says the war in Vietnam was terrible and racist, has chosen the Trilateral Commission's Samuel Huntington as one of his advisers. Huntington's main claim to fame is that he came up with the forced-urbanization program for Vietnam, which meant bombing the countryside to "dry up the sea of people" around the Vietcong. Carter is also relying on Paul Nitze, who, as nearly as I can tell, has been shouting, "The Russians are coming!" since the days of the last czar.

It makes you wonder if we aren't safer with Kissinger. Henry's balance-of-power ideas may be old-fashioned and dangerous, but are we better off with Brzezinski's slightly different notions of a gathering of the powerful—which is what the Trilateral approach is all about? When the Democratic Party elite return from exile with Carter (and they probably will: I saw most of them pop up while I traveled on the press plane during the campaign and we all know about the trek they took from Harvard to Plains after the nomination), they'll want to do something to outdistance Kissinger's mark. They'll want to be spectacular. So here we go again: the best and the brightest, part two.

Against that prognosis, all I had to go on as I pulled out of my odyssey was the assurance by sister Gloria and Carter's son Chip that they'd lead a demonstration if Carter got us into another Vietnam. That, and the assurance by Carter's young aides that our next President is a committed Georgia populist who will never cave in to the Eastern Establishment. And, to be fair, Carter himself has said that on principle he is against military intervention in foreign countries.

Still, if Brzezinski doesn't become Secretary of State, it's only because you can't have two accents in a row. As in Kissinger's case, he'll probably first do a stint as National Security Adviser. Zbig is better informed and more reasonable than most of the Establishment figures Carter has gone to, but when I talked with Zbig that summer in Maine, he made it clear that to him Carter was no Georgia populist who would rock any boats. He seemed to judge him an urbane thinker who had passed muster with the Establishment.

So which is it going to be—some fresh new faces or the old gang from Harvard? Or, put another way, can a millionaire from southwest Georgia who was raised to care about the poor and wants government to be returned to the people do so without kicking ass?

Is Jimmy Carter too good to be true? I still don't know, because I hardly know him. But I do have one more anecdote to throw into the hopper.

A couple of nights before he was to give his acceptance speech in New York, Jimmy Carter was sitting in his expensive suite with Anderson, Caddell,

Powell, and Rafshoon. He was reading his speech aloud and stopping every few sentences to get their reaction. When he got to the section blasting political and economic elites, one of his aides suggested it be cut: it was too controversial. (In fact, *The New York Times* attacked that portion of the speech a few days later as "demagogic" and "populist.") Up in his hotel room, Carter thought for a minute, looked around the room slowly, and said, "No. I have a very strong visceral feeling about that and I want to use it."

After all these months, after all the ambiguity and the packaging and the rewritten history, my visceral feeling is that Jimmy Carter has those visceral feelings.

It's also my favorite anecdote.

(Playboy, November 1976)

Reagan Country

It was Friday, so, according to the schedule, it must have been Augusta, Georgia—steamy, sultry, and dull—where we met the two ladies in the hotel lobby, wearing the current thigh-revealing, split-skirt fashion they were showing in New York. They sported the Reagan straw hats and buttons but also the pushed-up-cleavage look that one often finds at Republican dinners, a throwback to the forties tease who played opposite Ronald Reagan the actor. And it must be conceded that a REAGAN FOR PRESIDENT button pinned near the exposed portion of a woman's breast takes on a campy, rakish quality, making it less chilling when they flash that big smile and say they like Ronnie because he'll give us more bombs and throw the bums off welfare.

There was a contradiction here that one encountered in state after state, traveling with the Reagan campaign. On the one hand, the puritanical and aged warrior intoning a death chant against the godless Communists, permissive government, the immoral homosexuals, the welfare cheats, unrelieved and simplistic in its enmity but always self-righteous and pure. On the other hand, the people drawn to him tending to be more varied and hip than one would expect from the campaign rhetoric. It is as if they want Reagan to be something they no longer are.

That night in Augusta, the two attractive women, both divorcees in their late thirties, had imbibed a few drinks to prepare them for the meeting Reagan had planned with them and dozens of other hard workers in his local campaign. But as a result of their bar stop, they missed "the next President of the United States." They were left to the consolation of a flirting interview with a film crew sent South by TV producer Norman Lear to capture the essence of what Ronnie's campaign poster—the one with him in the cowboy hat looking twenty years younger—calls "Reagan country."

Earlier that day, in an interview with me on the plane into Augusta, Reagan had blamed the federal government for the breakup of the family by encouraging permissiveness. It therefore seemed appropriate to ask those women if they also were opposed to premarital sex. "I love it!" said one who'd worked for Reagan since her college days.

"But Ronald Reagan says the new permissiveness and the federal government are breaking up the family," I said, "and he would strongly disapprove of your engaging in sex without the blessings of marriage."

And then, with camera lights on and film presumably rolling, the aging cheerleader flashed that smile, tinged now with wisdom and cynicism, and issued her personal emancipation proclamation: "Well . . . fuck him."

Does that mean she won't support him? Hell, no. She'd still like Ronnie to be President and set everyone *else* straight. They've always liked Reagan because he's a strong moral leader who would bring the country closer together again. And they like his attacks on permissiveness: "I think we ought to have tighter controls."

Reagan can be magical on the stump, because he can convince even a cynical observer that he is a highly moral, honest, and purposeful man who has got his act together and can do the same for the country. His appeal is the nostalgic one—as in Reagan's movie roles—that of the good boy next door who will do right by the country, as he has for his family and friends. In that role, he effectively exudes an air of simple virtue that allows the audience to ignore serious gaps in his knowledge, his lackluster eight years as governor, and the reality that his own family life has been quite disorderly.

But people want the image more than the truth. The Reagan sermon is a throwback to the Jimmy Carter homilies of 1976—"Ah just want a country as good, honest, decent as are the American people"—and then some assurance about how wholesome everything was back home in Plains, Georgia. The people listening knew they weren't so pure, but they hoped Jimmy might be.

We rarely heard about Carter's nephew serving time in a California prison, or the widespread use of drugs by young people in the county, or the good ol' Carter boys checking out the latest crop of divorced women at the Best Western Inn near Plains, the closest they have to a night life down there.

Never mind—the voters wanted to believe that someone, somewhere in America, had a better life than they were experiencing, and Jimmy's con filled the void. Virtuous, Bible-studying Jimmy could make us feel good all over again and lead us to what Reagan now calls "the shining city upon the hill"—a phrase taken from the Puritans. But Jimmy's pristine image couldn't sustain him through the Presidency, even though he brought the image shapers—Pat Caddell, Jerry Rafshoon, Ham Jordan, Jody Powell, and company—right into the White House. It failed because we are not always so hardworking, selfless, and lacking in greed as Carter pretended. His mind ever on the polls, he would not tell us what we didn't want to hear or lead in an unpopular direction. So the image shrivels and the man himself ends up appearing weak and vacillating.

Well, let's just try again. Now, Ronald Reagan—there's a man who rides tall in the saddle; there's a man who can solve our problems the way we used to, who can take on the Russians and anyone else who gets in our way. Let's hear it for plain-speaking, two-fisted common sense. In an interview with me for the *Los Angeles Times* of March 6, 1980, he called the President of Panama "a pipsqueak dictator who hasn't got as much gross national product as Cincinnati, Ohio." And, as an indication of his presidential negotiating style, he said, "From the minute their dictator down there told us that we had to give up the canal or there was going to be trouble—he was going to make trouble for us—that's when we should have said to him, 'Look, Buster, you withdraw that threat or there's no more negotiation or sitting at a table with you, because we're not, in the eyes of the world, going to give this up in answer to a threat of violence.' "

Reagan's inherent promise is to solve our problems without additional sacrifice, without adding to our burdens—be they taxes or the draft. He is trusted the way a slicker like George Bush or John Connally wasn't—never to try any more newfangled governmental approaches or programs. Enough with change.

It is a mood well understood by Reagan's older daughter, Maureen, who campaigns for her father but is an advocate of change and disagrees with Reagan on the ERA. She is an attractive and strong-willed woman who has lived a bit, been divorced and has worked as an editor, a secretary, and an actress to pay the bills on her Los Angeles apartment. She is a delight to interview, because she keeps the Scotch coming and refuses to play the Goody Two-shoes role of a candidate's poster family. She can be brutal in her comments, as on the pro-lifers: "After dealing with those people for years, I'm convinced they are not anti-abortion, they are anti-sex." But she is also sympathetic to why people are disoriented by the changes that have occurred in this country and judges that apprehension to be the source of her father's greatest appeal: "You gotta understand that people are starting to fight change now because they're scared; they can only deal with so much; they can only handle so much that's different from the way it was supposed to be, and it isn't, and the way they were raised. Most of us are still part of a fairyland generation, and if we did it all right, Prince Charming was going to ride up on his white horse and we were going to go off into the sunset and live happily ever after. But it doesn't work that way. Maybe he's America's Prince Charming."

Maybe the Reagan phenomenon falls under what Erich Fromm called the escape from freedom. Maybe too much change, too fast, with too few good results. Then there's Iran, inflation, and the Russians, and not being able to believe in the dollar or working hard for the future. "They" just push us around and Jimmy Carter just takes it.

Traveling with the Reagan campaign, you hear it everywhere, and Reagan is the candidate best trained to play to that desperation. He has been railing against permissiveness, Big Government, and Communism for more than twenty years now and has become a creature of his one-liners. Jim Lake, his former press secretary, said in a conversation with me, "Ronnie just cannot resist throwing that red meat out to excite the audience and he sometimes forgets whether he really means it."

Lake, who intends to vote for Reagan, was referring to the fact that in private interviews one encounters a more reasonable Reagan, but on the campaign hustings he gets out of control and the crowds love it.

"Just who do they think they are?" he repeats over and over to a crowd in Greensboro, North Carolina, without ever making clear just who "they" are. The sad tale that day has to do with the government bureaucrats coming between a mother and her fifteen-year-old daughter, who is in "deep trouble." It's a story repeated in numerous other campaign stops, with the mother "hugging that child from birth on," only to suddenly lose control to the Feds. He has used it so often that in Greensboro he leaves out half the story. We never do learn the nature of the "deep trouble" and are left wondering whether she committed a crime or was knocked up by the New Deal. But the punch line—"Just who do they think they are?"—got big applause, anyway.

The best rouser is the one about the federal government's "destroying the American family." This last was even stated in the Republican primary debates, but no one had the presence of mind or the curiosity to ask Ronnie what he was talking about.

On the chartered campaign plane from Orlando, Florida, into Augusta, I finally got a chance to ask the governor to spell it out (this and all subsequent exchanges taken from the interview I did with him for the *Los Angeles Times*):

SCHEER: You speak of the breakdown of the family, the federal government's intrusion into life between the parents and the children. What do you have in mind?

REAGAN: There has been a constant effort on the part of government at almost every level to interfere with the family and make decisions with regard to children. For example, you've got a woman who has been appointed a judge by the President who has advocated that children should have the right to legal counsel in disputes with their parents. In California, they tried to get a bill passed that would allow underage children to go on their own, to a doctor, and get advice on contraceptives, and so forth, without the knowledge of their parents.

SCHEER: But isn't that one way to avoid the need for abortion, which you oppose?

REAGAN: But isn't that also government sticking its nose into the family?

SCHEER: But if you have an underage child, isn't it better that he or she get a contraceptive device and then thereby avoid what you have termed murdering a fetus?

REAGAN: What has ever happened to the teaching of a family . . .

SCHEER: What if the family has broken down, what if the parents aren't there, what if it's a grandmother or an aunt who's raising the child, and the child needs a contraceptive device or wants one; isn't it better to allow him or her to purchase it rather than to have an abortion or an unwanted baby?

REAGAN: Whatever happened to just saying no?

Is Reagan kidding? Does he not know what has been going on in this country, and does he really believe it's all due to government's "breaking up the family"?

Following that exchange with Reagan, I wandered back to my seat in the press section of the plane very much needing a drink. All I could think of was sound trucks cruising our communities, urging young people to just say no. "Hey, you, in the back seat of that car, whatever happened . . . ?" I wanted to say yes, to indulge some minor decadence. To sin in the pathetic way that one does covering a campaign, by heavy drinking. What world did Reagan live in? As in other campaigns, a number of the people around me on the plane, Reagan staff, press, off-duty Secret Service, would often spend their evenings near-drunk, just hoping that some woman or man would turn up to whom they could say yes. Many of them are divorced or actively behaving in such a way as to become so. And I'd never once on any campaign trip ever heard anyone speak in other than an approving way about extramarital sex. Nor was any of this permissiveness inspired by the federal government.

But what about Reagan himself? How had he managed to avoid the pitfalls of ordinary humans? Then suddenly I realized that I had accepted the sanctimonious Reagan stance at face value. I, in fact, knew very little about Reagan's family life, and neither did others in the press corps. His family life is a closely guarded secret. The Reagan staff barely concedes that the candidate has a family and keeps the press away from the two younger children.

But since Reagan has mixed up the personal and the political, it seemed necessary to take a closer look at his family life. After interviews with family and friends, it was possible to learn that Reagan does, indeed, live in the same messed-up world that the rest of us inhabit. And it hardly seems that the federal government caused the breakdown of his own family.

Was the government responsible for his divorce from actress Jane Wyman thirty-two years ago, or was it, as she testified in court, his attempts to subordinate her interests to his political preoccupations?

Was the government responsible for his younger daughter, Patti's, history of teenage rebellion and later running off to England with a member of a rock group—The Eagles—just prior to the 1976 campaign and not letting her parents know where she was? Or was it, as I hear it, Reagan's rigid refusal to allow the young musician into the house because they were living together without the blessing of marriage? Reagan makes the point repeatedly that a wholesome family life is the best and simplest counterweight to the ills of society spawned by a permissive government. He has also consistently led the hunt for scapegoats—hippies, radicals, lenient judges—which obscures the complexities of raising a family in a changing world. There is a smirking self-righteousness to the man—"Whatever happened to just saying no?"—which implies that he and other proper folks have been successful at coping with family problems.

The point is not to extend gossip but, rather, to observe that the Reagan family has experienced the same problems of divorce, generational revolt, conflicting morality, and dilution of sense of purpose as most Americans.

The campaign does not like to mention the Reagan children, because they do not conform to the plastic normalcy that Ronnie has been pushing all these years; but I was pleasantly surprised to find them far more interesting than the forties movie image of the family that he projects. True, all four Reagan kids dropped out of college over their parents' objections, but Maureen did so to become an actress and eventually an organizer for the ERA. Older son Michael races boats and sells gasohol, and Patti, twenty-seven, is now a rock musician. The youngest, Ronald, Jr., twenty-two, left Yale suddenly after his first year to become a ballet dancer. Maybe it doesn't fit Reagan's high-in-the-saddle image to have a son who's a ballet dancer, but his teacher's report is that he is a serious and talented student with the Joffrey Ballet who had worked extra hard to make up for his late start.

The Reagan children are an embarrassment to the campaign precisely because they are interesting. Reagan staffers cannot easily control the offsprings' comments or actions. The younger two are not currently campaigning for their father, and the older two, who are, must be kept at a distance, perhaps because they are bright and funny.

Aside from being outspoken and independent, Maureen, thirty-nine, and adopted son Michael, thirty-five (children of his first marriage), who strongly support their father's candidacy, are thought to be a liability because they sabotaged Ronnie's campaign simply by growing up. They both joked to me about the campaign staff's wanting to have some little kids sent over from Central Casting to complete the campaign portrait. They support Reagan because they judge him a very good man who will effectively lead the country. But he is a good man not because, as a father, he sat them down for prayer each night—he didn't. They lived mostly in boarding schools and occasionally got a weekend with Mom or Dad. It wasn't his fault; he and his ex-wife, Jane Wyman, were actors involved with the demands of their careers in Hollywood, and later, Ronnie was promoting General Electric and his own politics. Evidently, it is possible to be a good father even if you don't rush home from work to the suburban tract house to hug the wife and kiddies and take them to church on Sunday. But to hear Reagan's campaign speeches, you would never know that.

Wouldn't it be wild if Ronnie got up one day on the campaign trail and said, "Hey, even before *Kramer vs. Kramer*, I knew divorce wasn't the end of the world." Or, "My wife, Nancy, and I were so eagerly in love that we produced a seven-pound baby girl just seven and one half months after our wedding." Or, "I learned that kids can rebel against everything I stand for and still be in the human race." Or, "I got divorced because I was a male-chauvinist slob who was threatened by Jane Wyman's being a much better actor. So I went off to marry a woman who lives only through me and my career." Or, "After my divorce, I drank a lot and chased women and I still managed to come out of it okay."

In his autobiography, Reagan refers to his divorce only in the last four paragraphs of a chapter detailing how he and the House Un-American Activities Committee did in the Hollywood leftists. (Perhaps the Feds *were* responsible for his divorce, after all.) As he recalls, "I arrived home from the Washington [HUAC] hearing to be told I was leaving. I suppose there had been warning signs, if only I hadn't been so busy, but small-town boys grow up thinking only other people get divorced. The plain truth was that such a thing was so far from being imagined by me that I had no resources to call upon."

The question is whether or not he has since expanded those resources. For his campaign rhetoric still reflects—indeed, celebrates—the thinking of small-town boys, at least as they were pictured in the movies of the forties, following their father's example of hard work, pious living, and substantial success.

Reagan's real-life father, as he concedes, was something of an alcoholic who had trouble holding on to a job and was all but destroyed in the Great Depression. He and the entire Reagan family were saved from poverty only by F.D.R.'s New Deal. In fact, Reagan's father was one of those faceless bureaucrats, the "they" in the "Just who do they think they are?"—the guy who gave out the relief payments and then the jobs when they made him the head of the local WPA. The real-life older Reagan sounds as if he was terrific; and perhaps it reveals a hidden side of the son that he recalls his father's robust complexity so affectionately in his autobiography:

> I bent over him, smelling the sharp odor of whiskey from the speak-easy. I got a fistful of his overcoat. Opening the door, I managed to drag him inside and get him to bed. In a few days, he was the bluff, hearty man I knew and loved and will always remember.
>
> Jack (we all called him by his nickname) was a handsome man— tall, swarthy and muscular, filled with contradictions of character. A sentimental Democrat, who believed fervently in the rights of the work-ing man.

When Reagan wrote those words about his father, he had abandoned his own trade-union career with the Screen Actors Guild and gone off to preach the corporate message for General Electric.

Reagan recalls his father as "the best raconteur I ever heard, especially when it came to the smoking-car sort of stories." He claims that Jack "drew a sharp line between lusty vulgar humor and filth. To this day, I agree with his credo and join Jack and Mark Twain in asserting that one of the basic forms of American humor is the down-to-earth wit of the ordinary person, and the questionable language is justified if the point is based on real humor."

Privately, Reagan can use rough language both humorously and in occa-sional flashes of anger. He can also be one of the funnier candidates on the campaign trail. He likes to tell jokes, and that's why he told the ethnic joke that got him into some trouble. Perhaps if reporters didn't overreact to a politician's telling the very same joke they routinely hear and tell in the city room, we'd get more humor. Reagan seems inclined to that sort of jest, and he's even reported to have whispered an ethnic joke—about blacks and Chinese—at Jack Benny's funeral. But people who know Reagan deny that he's bigoted, and certainly not toward ethnic groups. He himself is the product of an ethnic joke—the cross of a hard-drinking Irish-Catholic father and a Bible-toting Scotch-English Protestant mother. His nickname, Dutch, derives from his father's referring to him at birth as a fat little Dutchman.

Reagan's humor may derive from his Irish father, but his puritanism bears the mark of his mother, who considered herself snatched by God from an early deathbed to stick around to convert sinners. Nelle Reagan's missionary work took her and her Bible in and out of the jails of the Midwest and later the hospitals of California. Maureen Reagan remembers her grandmother as a remarkable woman of near biblical strength and conviction, a woman of great social conscience and concern for the less fortunate. But it seems more a pie-in-the-sky, missionary's vow for the sinner to be saved than, as Jack would have had it, for the poor to organize to gain their just deserts. Those are two views of poverty, and Reagan seems to have traveled from the vision of the father to that of the mother in his march from early liberalism to late conservatism.

In any event, Reagan's mother was a strong figure and he seems to have looked for similar qualities in his wives, but their strengths differ markedly. In his marriages, he went from Jane Wyman, who exhibits a mocking independence, to his current wife, Nancy, a vassal of cold public virtue. The two women represent a startling contrast, and it is difficult to imagine his having been attracted to both, though each is strong-willed and possessed of a fiery temper.

I met Jane Wyman, who has shunned the press, by happenstance at a party for Ronald Reagan's daughter Maureen's dog. It was a party that was ripe for a snappy "conservative chic" dismissal, but that would have gotten it all wrong. Yes, there was a large red, white, and blue birthday cake and buttons saying, BARNAE FOR FIRST DOG (one guest offered—to considerable laughter—that it should be BARNAE FOR FIRST LADY), and the dog who received presents was one of those frisky little ones that rich people adore. But Maureen's apartment is modest and the crowd eclectic, a mix from the neighborhood including a *Los Angeles Times* pressman who belongs to Maureen's local Lutheran church and the local hairdresser, who doesn't. The party was an annual put-on for the little mutt who was found in the rain in Texas eight years ago, when Maureen was on tour. Brother Michael was happily telling ethnic and other jokes; he confessed he had told his father the one that got him into trouble, and he wasn't going to stop now. Actress Gretchen Wyler, who's involved in Actors and Others for Animals, talked about saving dogs, and Jane Wyman was challenging the role of multinational companies. It was L.A. at its best— an easy mix of immigrants from all over the country, featuring a variety of styles and obsessions, whose coexistence is made possible by an easygoing tolerance.

One could imagine the best part of Reagan (the one I've seen at moments in interviews and must confess to liking) enjoying this party with his two older children and his ex-wife, though Nancy would not welcome it. Nancy and Jane do not get along. And Nancy prefers socially important functions. She is a serious, no-nonsense social climber. In public, Nancy Reagan is the extreme opposite of open. She possesses the tightest smile in the land, and it can always be clicked exactly into place.

Nancy's chief mission in life appears to be to stick constantly to Ronnie's side to caution him when his momentary exuberance might lead him once again to put his foot in his mouth. I experienced her screening effect at one press conference in Sarasota in March 1980. In New Hampshire, Reagan had called marijuana "one of the most dangerous drugs." At the Sarasota press conference, he was asked for the factual basis for that statement. Reagan referred to an HEW study showing that one marijuana cigarette had a potentially greater carcinogenic content than an ordinary tobacco cigarette. I had read the same report, which also indicated that marijuana users need far fewer joints to get high than the number of cigarettes used by the average smoker. I broke through the babble of the press conference to point that out to him and thought I had him cornered. He was, as is his custom, about to compound the error by talking even more about a subject he knew nothing about. But Nancy swiftly moved her face next to his, looked up at him with her unwavering smile, and whispered loudly enough to be heard by a few reporters near her, "You wouldn't *know*." Reagan snapped to, suddenly relaxed, cocked his head back as if to ponder his answer, and said with a smile and on camera, "I wouldn't know."

But there is still some vestige of the preconservative, pre-Nancy Ronnie who is the old actor, who won't take himself too seriously, who is aware that the world is made up of many different types. Maureen says, "How could he be thought naïve and prudish when he worked so long in Hollywood? He met *all* types."

However, on the campaign trail, Reagan frequently rails against homosexuals. As governor, he got in a flap for his reported firing of two high-ranking staff members who were accused of being gay. Reagan's security man investigated the matter and could find no evidence, but they were fired anyway, on the basis of another staff member's accusation. The Anita Bryant people liked him in Florida; but on the other hand, it is Reagan who, more than anyone, gets credit for sinking the Briggs initiative in California in 1978 by publicly opposing the antihomosexual proposition. Yet his tolerance is ambivalent.

SCHEER: Why do you attack homosexuals, as you did at a recent rally?

REAGAN: I didn't attack them, I was asked a question. A fellow asked me if I believed that they should have the same civil rights and I said I think they do and should but that my criticism of the gay-rights movement is that it isn't asking for civil rights, it is asking for a recognition and acceptance of an alternative life-style that I do not believe society can condone, nor can I.

SCHEER: For religious reasons?

REAGAN: Well, you could find that in the Bible it says that in the eyes of the Lord this is an abomination.

SCHEER: But should that bind the rest of the citizens, who may not believe in the Bible? Don't we have the right to separation of church and state?

REAGAN: Oh, we do; yes, we do. Look, what other group of people demands the same things? Let's say here is the total libertarian—or libertine, I should say—who wants the right to just free and open sex.

SCHEER: That's the thing that's confusing me—it's the conservative who wants to keep government out of everything; why don't you keep it out of private morality? Why do you want the cops coming in, the government, the state, and telling people what their sex life should be?

REAGAN: No one is advocating the invasion of the private life of any individual. I think Mrs. Patrick Campbell said it best in the trial of Oscar Wilde. She said, "I have no objection to anyone's sex life, so long as they don't practice it in the street and frighten the horses."

California reporters who have long covered Reagan do not tend to judge him a mean-spirited man. He never seems the elitist and, indeed, conveys a sense of deference and concern to those who work for him or are just there to shake hands. Few people who have spent time with him dislike him, but there are far fewer people who will claim to really know him. He is a legendary loner who spends virtually all his free time in solitary activity—mending fences on his ranch or riding his horse. Solitary except for his ever-present mate, Nancy.

The ranch house near Santa Barbara, where they spend much of their free time, was built small with little room for guests. Ronnie has few if any close male friends, and one aide who worked with Nancy insists that she "simply does not like other women, she is threatened by their presence, including that of her own daughter." It was also said by one family member that "he is totally and devotedly in love with her and, for that reason, suffers her not infrequent tantrums." An associate said, "She is a force, a strong woman in the pre-liberation sense of strength. Her power derives from her association with and power over a male." First there was the famous neurosurgeon father, whose name and contacts gave her entree to Hollywood and her abortive starlet career prior to marrying Ronnie. Now she manages his equilibrium and has life-and-death power over his staffing decisions. In the weeks preceding the firing of former campaign manager John Sears, both Sears and his nemesis, Ed Meese, the governor's campaign chief of staff who won out, were compelled to make their case to the governor through the wife. And there is little doubt that she was instrumental in this and many other final decisions. This is no Eleanor Roosevelt or even a Rosalynn Carter, smart women with their own strong social values and insights. Her life is Ronald Reagan.

Which is how Ronnie wanted it in his second marriage. His first had come to an end when his movie career foundered and Jane Wyman's flourished. (She was nominated four times for Academy Awards and won once; he was never nominated.) Wyman clearly had ideas of her own and, perhaps, was ahead of her time. At their divorce trial in 1948, according to the account offered by the *Los Angeles Times*, "Miss Wyman told the court that she and Reagan engaged in continual arguments on his political views."

Reagan was then the gung-ho president of the Screen Actors Guild. It was when he came back from being a friendly witness at HUAC, testifying against Hollywood Reds, that Wyman first asked for a divorce. According to a report of their divorce, "Despite her lack of interest in his political activities, Miss Wyman continued, Reagan insisted that she attend meetings with him and that she be present during discussions among his friends. But her own ideas, she complained, 'were never considered important.' "

Those years of HUAC and the blacklist gave Reagan not only a new wife but also a new ideological commitment. To understand his persistent obsession with the Communists, one has to view history from his point of view rather than, say, from Lillian Hellman's. Reagan still believes that there never was a blacklist against Reds in Hollywood, as he revealed to me recently: "There was no blacklist of Hollywood. The blacklist in Hollywood, if there was one, was provided by the Communists. There were blacklists by our customers and clients who said to the motion-picture industry, 'We won't go to see pictures that those people are involved in.' "

In his view, it was war, as he stated back in 1951: "The Russians sent their first team, their ace string, here to take us over . . . We were up against hard-core organizers."

Some of Reagan's critics of the time suggested that the aging actor (he was forty then) was attempting to lay out a political string to compensate for a stalled acting career. But whatever the original motivation, there can be little doubt of the passionate hatred that Reagan developed for the people he considered Hollywood's hard-core Communists and their liberal fellow travelers. And the feeling was mutual. It was a civil war within a community that pretends to familial intimacy and even attains it at times, perhaps more than in any other industry. To hear each side tell it, the other had all the guns. There is now substantial literature documenting the fact that there was a blacklist and that many artists—actors, writers, directors—had their careers destroyed because people like Reagan could reach producers and theater owners and advertisers. But, as Reagan describes it, the Reds had the power of the pen and mouth—to besmirch reputations and to organize effective fronts to cloak subversion with the protection of the First Amendment. To be sure, both sides played hard ball, and Reagan, who was out in front for his cause, took his lumps.

It was similar to the ways in which one could view the campus disturbances at Berkeley over the Vietnam War when he was governor more than fifteen years later. The students saw that Reagan had the regents of the university and the cops, but he must have recognized that the students had grabbed the high moral ground and would win.

It is easy for Reagan to feel the aggrieved party. But then again, that's not unusual in an activist. The problem, however, is that Reagan's basic education for the Presidency—his world view—seems to have grown rather linearly and simplistically out of the Hollywood and Berkeley skirmishes with "Communism." To this date, a conversation with Reagan clearly indicates that he knows and cares less about the Sino-Soviet dispute in judging world events than he does about the battles within the Screen Actors Guild of the early fifties.

In fact, Reagan must now detest the Sino-Soviet dispute, because any such complexity, if accepted, would militate against the rage that still wells up in him at the memory of those Commies who first broke his liberal faith and led him on the long march toward a conservative Presidency. The new faith, steeled in combat, was simple, direct; Communism is godless and its practitioners are monsters. He believed that in 1951 in Los Angeles and in 1980 in Orlando, Florida.

SCHEER: You attacked "godless Communism" and I'm curious about the use of the word godless—why is that an important element there?

REAGAN: Well, because this is one of the vital precepts of Communism, that we are accidents of nature.

SCHEER: But is it the godlessness that makes them more violent, more aggressive, more expansionist?

REAGAN: Well, it is one that gives them less regard for humanity or human beings.

SCHEER: But here we have the Ayatollah in Iran, who certainly is not godless, and he seems to be—

REAGAN: A fanatic and a zealot—

SCHEER: But he's not godless.

REAGAN: No, not in his sense—and we have had that all the way back through history. We go back to the Inquisition in Spain. So there are people who, through their fanaticism, misuse religion. But the reason for the godlessness with regard to Communism—here is a direct teaching of the child from the beginning of its life that it is a human being whose only importance is its contribution to the state, that they are wards of the state, that they exist only for its purpose, and that there is no God, they are just an accident of nature that created a human being. The result is, this is why they have no respect for human life, for the dignity of an individual.

I remember one night, a long time ago, in a rally in Los Angeles, sixteen thousand people in the auditorium, and this was at the time when the local Communists, the American Communist Party—and this is all well documented—was actually trying, had secured domination of several unions in the picture business and was trying to take over the motion-picture industry, and with all of the rewriting of history today, and the stories that we have seen, and the screenplays and television plays, and so forth, about the persecution for political beliefs that took place in Hollywood, believe me, the persecutors were the Communists who had gotten into position where they could destroy careers, and *did* destroy them.

With Reagan, the categories get all mixed up and the Commies metamorphose into welfare socialists and the New Deal. Thus, in the appendix in his autobiography, under a section titled "Karl Marx," we find this tirade, not against the Russian Bolsheviks, but against the very Keynesians of the New Deal who kept his father from the gutter: "We are faced with the most evil enemy mankind has known in his long climb from the swamp to the stars. There can be no security anywhere in the free world if there is not fiscal and economic stability within the United States. Those who ask us to trade our freedom for the soup kitchen of the welfare state are architects of a policy of accommodation."

Is he talking about unemployment insurance and senior-citizen centers and Medicare? And why does that basic speech, now fifteen years old, still go over on the campaign trail? Because he's riding a crest of resentment toward overblown programs that don't work and bureaucrats who get paid even if they don't.

And just who do "they" think they are? If you can't afford the suburbs and must live in the inner city and get your child bused to a school with tough ghetto kids, you can get pretty pissed. Especially when they—the sociologists, the judges, the liberal scribblers, the HEW bureaucrats—send their kids to private schools.

There is pain out there among the employed taxpaying masses, and the brilliance of Reagan is that he can absolve his own politics of any responsibility while fixing blame on all past steps taken to solve any of the problems. Take tough blacks and white racists in the schools. Did the liberals invent racial hostility? Are they or their political ancestors responsible for slavery, the maiming of black culture, the persistence of segregation in the South, and discrimination in the North?

Reagan's own position on civil rights is of the "some of my best friends are" variety.

SCHEER: In 1966, you were quoted as saying you were opposed to the 1964 Civil Rights Act, as an example of federal intrusion.

REAGAN: I was opposed at the time, I can't remember the exact details, not for the idea of doing something against prejudice, certainly. I was opposed to certain features of that law that went beyond and infringed on the individual rights of citizens that are supposedly guaranteed by the Constitution.

SCHEER: Which features?

REAGAN: Well, they had to do with the, let's say the person who owns property, his right to do with his property what he wants to do.

SCHEER: Do you mean discriminate in renting it or discriminate in selling it?

REAGAN: At that time, this was what I thought was interfering with the right, particularly, with the idea of selling. I recognize that that could lend itself to the same prejudice that we're talking about, and I'm opposed to that prejudice. I said at that time that I felt that the President had a moral responsibility to use the powers of persuasion that the office has, to help cure us of the kind of bigotry and prejudice that made those discriminations possible.

SCHEER: But you would still be against the Civil Rights Act of 1964?

REAGAN: No, no, I wouldn't, because I recognize now that it is institutionalized and it has, let's say, hastened the solution of a lot of problems.

SCHEER: So why is that so difficult in an interview situation for a politician to say, "I was wrong in '66 and I've changed my mind and now I would have supported the Civil Rights Act"?

REAGAN: One reason is because, very frankly, you of the press—and not meaning present company—you of the press have a way of seizing upon a sentence and then distorting the view and presenting a political candidate or a political official as having some beliefs or prejudices that he does not have. Now, I will weigh my fight against bigotry and prejudice against that of the most ardent civil-rights advocate, because I was doing it when there was no civil-rights fight. I, on the air as a sports announcer years and years ago, was editorializing against the gentleman's agreement that kept blacks from playing organized baseball. I dealt with it in my football team alongside a black who's today my best friend, when this was not commonplace.

SCHEER: One thing that came up in the New Hampshire [Republican] debate was the question of the number of black people, the number of minorities on various people's staffs. I've been traveling with you for a few weeks now and I have yet to see a single minority person.

REAGAN: We've been traveling with a very small segment. When we talk about staff, we're talking about not only several hundred actual staff employees but even more, literally thousands of volunteers. I know we have a committee that is totally black. I don't know their exact numbers, but we're going to do an inventory and find out. But certainly there has been no effort to exclude.

Reagan is still against the desegregation of neighborhoods and affirmative action; and surely, having one black friend from college football days will not solve the problems. When Reagan was governor, he said jobs created by the private sector for hard-core unemployed blacks were the answer. And the answer turned out to be fewer than two thousand jobs in a state that has 40 percent black-youth unemployment, a state of twenty million people.

What Reagan added was a begrudging spirit—a contempt for those who had tried to do something. He loathed the civil-rights activists, whom he termed "irresponsible militants," and was later to embrace Nixon's Southern Strategy with equanimity. He made people on welfare feel even more forlorn and weak than they were. At the time of the S.L.A./Patty Hearst kidnapping, when the Hearst family provided food to the poor as a partial ransom, Reagan said, "It's just too bad we can't have an epidemic of botulism." He challenged the patriotism of those who would stop the war in Vietnam and had his own Strangelovian solution: "We could pave the whole country, put parking strips on it, and still be home before Christmas." He derided environmentalists by saying, "A tree's a tree—how many more do we need to look at?" He delighted in humbling the great public university system with inane comments such as "The state should not subsidize intellectual curiosity." He responded as governor to campus demonstrations by saying, "If it's to be a blood bath, let it be now."

Ironically, as governor, despite his vicious rhetorical stabs at programs for the poor and randomly heartless budget cuts, as in mental health, he ended up administering, indeed expanding, the liberal program of the most liberal state in the union. He did that begrudgingly—and only in his second term, when his back was against the wall—because of the pressures from Democrats and even liberal Republicans. As the editor of *Ramparts* then, I was among those who found much to criticize. But recently, I was surprised to find Reagan more reasonable on the "social issues" than one would have expected from his public pronouncements. He also can be quite genial, as in this exchange:

SCHEER: Why are you willing to talk to me? Why aren't you more uptight?

REAGAN: Well, because—why does a preacher preach?

SCHEER: It's an amazing encounter for me, because you seem relaxed, you don't seem like a zealot.

REAGAN: No, I'm not, but I remember this also: when I was a New Deal Democrat, I remember somehow that it was easier to dislike than to like. There seemed to be something about liberalism that worked better if you were kept angry and worked up.

SCHEER: And yet up on your public platforms, you convey a more hostile, nastier image than you do right now.

REAGAN: Well, let me give you a few things that I haven't mentioned up there on the platform to further confuse the image. As you know, I succeeded a very liberal governor, Pat Brown. As far as his record on minorities went, I found out that it was all talk. I appointed more blacks to executive positions than all the previous governors in California put together. And yet I was the conservative. Our divorce rate is 29.9 percent, while nationally divorces average 40 percent."

He also went on to point out that "Communism is infinitesimal in the motion-picture industry." Then, as now, Reagan was reassuring American businessmen that Communism could be stopped, that the moral fiber of the country was strong, and that all would be well if we kept the old family virtues intact.

It bothered none of his listeners that two weeks after that speech, the divorced actor married his second wife. Nor that he had his statistics wrong— the national divorce rate at the time was less than that in Hollywood, not more, as he claimed it was. Believe what I say, not what I do, and don't let's haggle over the facts. Then, as now, people loved it.

Reagan loves the sound of his own voice, and he works hard for the applause. During the 1980 campaign, he would continue to use erroneous information that worked with crowds, even after he had been told it was wrong. For example, his claim that a government study showed that Alaska had greater potential of oil than the known reserves of Saudi Arabia. Those of us traveling with him soon discovered that he had gotten the report wrong, and press aide Jim Lake conceded it. But Reagan had grown too fond of the line to drop it and claimed to his aides that it was based on a newspaper clipping that he had picked up somewhere but could no longer find.

The sloppiness is habitual, but it is dismissed by admirers as proof that he is his own man, not the carefully programmed product of advisers, as happened in the Carter phenomenon. There is a charming fumbling quality to Reagan's work habits, with his clippings stuffed into his pockets and anecdotes that he hears from those shaking his hand at receptions stuffed into his brain. The use of these "data" becomes less charming when it supports one scapegoat theory or another to explain the source of our problems. The bumbling septuagenarian then becomes the effective demagogue whipping up the passions of a public that is confused, frustrated, and ripe for the clarity of his positions, even when they are totally without foundation.

Reagan's sloppiness has caused him to be viewed with suspicion by the elite Northeastern wing of the Republican Party, probably less for what he did as governor than because they doubt his stability or fear that he may actually believe in some of his proposals for dismantling the federal government, which, after all, does serve the interests of big corporations. His proposal to return us to the gold standard must have been viewed as primitive by the economists at Chase Manhattan. Nor can the managers of multinational corporations, who have done quite well in a complex and changing world, be terribly sanguine about his sledgehammer nostrums for the world's problems. Those gentlemen are internationalists par excellence—world statesmen more interested in cutting deals with the Russians than in a holy crusade against them.

Unlike Carter and Nixon, Reagan has never made the journey back East to the centers of power to demonstrate his reasonableness. So the fear in those quarters persists that he may be a primitive isolationist.

Prior to the New Hampshire primary, David Rockefeller convened a secret meeting of like-minded Republicans aimed at developing a strategy for stopping Reagan by supporting Bush and, failing that, getting Gerald Ford into the race. Reagan heard about the meeting and was, according to one aide, "really hurt." This aide reports that Reagan turned to him and demanded, "What have they got against me? I support big oil, I support big business, why don't they trust me?" The aide suggested charitably that maybe it was because he was once an actor and that he attended too few important lunches in the East.

In any event, when Reagan scored his resounding triumph in New Hampshire in February, the overtures to the East began to work. New York Establishment lawyer Bill Casey, who became campaign director the day of the New Hampshire victory, began building bridges and promising that a more moderate Reagan would emerge after the Republican Convention.

The problem with the creation of a moderate Reagan after the convention will be with Reagan himself. His previous campaign manager, Sears, tried to do it during the primaries; and Reagan got so confused in the attempt to appear more restrained and reasonable that he became inarticulate. He fired Sears, went back to being his old outrageous self, and wooed them in the Southern states. William Buckley once likened Reagan to William Jennings Bryan, and there is something to that. He is far more effective as a demagogic speaker than he would be in the role of head of state. He is happiest with right-wing rhetoric and miserably plodding in any effort to express a more complex sentiment. I saw that one day in April 1980 when he went straight from a rousing rally in North Carolina, where he had them on their feet and seemed to know what he was talking about, to a stumbling performance before the American Society of Newspaper Editors, in which he might just as well have stuck his prepared speech into his ear. He was afraid of that crowd, not because they were more liberal than the electorate—they may not be—but because he feared them socially.

There is to Reagan a sense of great intellectual and social inferiority, born of the fact that he does not have the educational credentials or broad range of knowledge thought by some, including most editors, to be a prerequisite for the Presidency. He mispronounces the names of world leaders and gets countries in the wrong hemispheres. He prefers to stick to the simple slogans about the welfare state and godless Communism, because to venture into any greater complexity might prove acutely embarrassing, as it often has when he has tried it, be it in a discussion of his proposed blockade of Cuba or farm-price parity. He is painfully aware of the gaps in his knowledge and, for that reason, prefers to stick to his sure-fire one-liners. And the best ones—because he is a true believer on this—have to do with his attacks on the Russians.

The emotional high point of a Reagan campaign speech comes with his oft-repeated charge that détente is a failure and that we have been sandbagged by the Russians. To hear him, one would not know that our gross national product is twice that of the Soviets or that they have suffered immense reversals throughout the world, particularly with the loss of their influence in China and Egypt. Reagan's speeches about the threat of godless Communism are straight out of the fifties and would have an absurdly archaic ring to them were it not for the equally absurd positions that Jimmy Carter took to increase his standing in the polls—positions that have made Reagan seem suddenly credible.

Carter's overreaction to the Soviet Afghan intervention gave Reagan the opening he needed, and the elephant went charging through. Carter had said that Afghanistan represented the greatest crisis since World War II, implying that it was a greater breach of international etiquette than the Berlin blockade, the Korean War, the crushing of the Hungarian revolution, and the invasion of Czechoslovakia. That's all Reagan needed to hear to dust off his rhetorical guns and go blasting away at this détente business, which he always thought was a trick of some sort. If the Russians were as bad as Carter now had it, how could the President have pushed for the SALT agreement? How could he have abandoned trusted anti-Communist allies like the Shah in Iran or the government of Taiwan? How could he dwell on human rights and non-proliferation of nuclear weapons when he should have been backing any anti-Communist dictator he could find as a necessary ally for the future Armageddon? Carter had managed to shift some of the rage felt over the hostages in Iran to the Soviets in Afghanistan, and as we moved through the spring primaries, it almost seemed as if we were boycotting the Olympics in an effort to free the hostages. Suddenly the relative equanimity of détente was out and the old devil theories of Communism were in. And that, for Reagan, is a piece of cake—he never believed they were anything other than monsters, anyway, as he states in the following exchange with me:

SCHEER: The last time I talked to you, you said that no President of the United States should rule out the possibility of a preemptive nuclear strike in a potential confrontation [with the Russians] . . . Now, would that include the possibility of a preemptive nuclear strike by the United States?

REAGAN: What I'm saying is that the United States should never put itself in a position, as it has many times, of guaranteeing to an enemy or a potential enemy what it won't do. For example, when President Johnson, in the Vietnam War, kept over and over again insisting, "Oh no, no, no, we'll never use nuclear weapons in Vietnam." Now, I don't think nuclear weapons should have been used in Vietnam, I don't think they were needed; but when somebody's out there killing your young men, you should never free the enemy of the concern he might have for what you might do. See, you may feel that way in your heart, but don't say it out loud to him.

SCHEER: Do you believe that we could survive a nuclear war?

REAGAN: No, because we have let the Russians get strong and we have let them violate the agreement.

SCHEER: But let's say we get stronger than them again. Do you think we could survive a nuclear war? With the right underground shelter systems, with the right defense systems, could we survive one?

REAGAN: It would be a survival of some of your people and some of your facilities that you could start again. It would not be anything that I think in our society you would consider acceptable, but then, we have a different regard for human life than those monsters do.

SCHEER: How did the Chinese stop being monsters? I mean, they were on a par, at least, with the Russians in treachery and monstrous deeds, supposed to have killed twenty million of their people.

REAGAN: Fifty million.

SCHEER: Fifty million—I don't think the Russians have killed fifty million of their own people—when did the Chinese stop being monsters?

REAGAN: I don't know that they have.

SCHEER: And yet we're talking about having an alliance with them.

REAGAN: Because we're hoping that through time and through their animus and fear of the Soviet Union, maybe they'll become more like us. People who have gone there say there is indication—that they're trying to improve the situation and that they allow more human rights for their people.

SCHEER: Why couldn't the Soviet Union change in the way the Chinese have?

REAGAN: Have the Chinese changed? I don't know. The Chinese people are still the victims of tyranny.

In such private interviews, Reagan states his positions matter-of-factly, with no apparent sense that the future of civilization may hang in the balance. He comes on like a friendly but determined coach who says if we want to win in the second half, we've got to go all the way. But he does not tend to rave and rant, as he can in public appearances. This, some advisers will say, is the reassuring thing about Reagan—that he is more reasonable, even in foreign affairs, than his public rhetoric implies. And they also immediately add that his bark was worse than his bite as governor of California—and that, anyway, he was a "nine-to-five governor" who left running the state to a bevy of "reasonable aides."

But it was one thing to verbally shoot from the hip as governor, attacking welfare recipients and students, and quite another to dismiss one's international adversaries (and even one's friends, as in the case of China) as monsters. It may also prove scary. He savors making important decisions by himself, albeit based on his aides' one-page memos summarizing various options, and he prides himself on acting decisively. As Nancy once said, "He doesn't make snap decisions, but he doesn't tend to overthink, either." In California, that led to pronouncements of courses of action that had to be quickly reversed. But can sudden foreign-policy decisions be reversed so easily?

It's true that Nixon came in with a reputation not unlike Reagan's, as a hysterical Southern California anti-Communist, and he broadened contact with Russia and China. Perhaps Reagan would do likewise, though I cannot now imagine it. Nixon was always an opportunist, testing the winds of conventional wisdom; but Reagan has the marks of a true believer. He acts like a man who is captive of his own phrases, and it was not altogether reassuring to watch him nod solemnly when North Carolina Senator Jesse Helms introduced him one night by saying, "Perhaps God is giving us one last chance."

(*Playboy*, August 1980)

Sparring with Fallaci: The Playboy Interview

*T*o *the editors at* Playboy, *it must have seemed a natural: Robert Scheer and Oriana Fallaci . . . one tough interviewer takes on another . . . Turn the tables and see if the interviewer can take being interviewed. Fallaci is intelligent, well traveled and informed, and there was much in the way of profound and even occasionally brilliant commentary. But the mood was often hostile, and for the first time in my life, I found myself feeling sorry for the likes of Khomeini, Qaddafi, the Shah of Iran, and Kissinger—all of whom had been the objects of her wrath—the people she described as interviewing "with a thousand feelings of rage." I found myself feeling sorry not only for the subjects of her interviews but for mine as well, because the brute fact of the matter is that we do dish it out better than we take it.*

An interviewer must do many things to force a valid question that requires an answer. And Fallaci has her own well-practiced methods. She once said she stalks interviews as "pieces of theater with a story inside." Time quoted her as saying, "I make scenes, I yell and scream." That's fine as a technique for breaking through the obtuse answers of a hack politician. An interviewer can defend bad manners as an effort to get at a larger truth, but when the tables are turned and one becomes the subject of the exercise—and I have been there myself and made a mess of it—then screaming can be nothing more than an effort to avoid the point of a question rather than answer it.

All of the above is by way of an explanation for the combativeness one will find in this interview. But enough of such carping. While it is true, as Fallaci admits, that she lives life at a shout, and while that may make for brittle dinner companionship, she is rarely boring and always on. This last quality, along with huge globs of conviction about almost any topic—from the correct path to revolution to the correct path to the perfect pesto sauce—has made

her one of the world's most important journalists and a fascinating interview
subject. But I'm not going to say I loved it.

SCHEER: You're best known for the tough interviews you've published with some of the world's most powerful men and women. Let's start with possibly your most famous interview, the one with Henry Kissinger, in which he compared himself to a lone cowboy riding into a village by himself.

FALLACI: Don't let me speak about Kissinger again. It was in 1972, and they still persecute both of us because of it. I mean, even if we got married, we would be persecuted today over this point! But as to the interview, it's a pity. He lost an opportunity to become my friend. He should have had the courage to stand by what he said. Instead, he said he regretted doing it.

It was only fifty minutes, and I thought it was a very bad interview. *My worst interview!* I almost did not publish it. In fact, everybody was surprised at the indulgence and tolerance I demonstrated toward him during the interview. But I do these interviews to understand the person, to study how power takes place. And I had not the time with Kissinger. I think, though, if he had not been so concerned with immediate success during his four years with Nixon, he would have gone down in history as one of the greatest American Secretaries of State. I mean, the opening to China was real, historic, and it was he, not Nixon, who did it.

SCHEER: And his morality in the conduct of the Vietnam War?

FALLACI: Kissinger is beyond morality. The word would make him laugh. Men like him are amoral.

SCHEER: Who are other people like that?

FALLACI: Stalin. Nixon was *im*moral, a different thing.

SCHEER: What about your impressions of the Ayatollah Khomeini?

FALLACI: It may be a banal word, but the simple truth about Khomeini is that he is a fanatic. If you read my interview, you see that Khomeini is intelligent, unlike Arafat or Qaddafi. To me, a fanatic is *necessarily* an unintelligent person, but I must admit he is the one example that breaks the rule. I had thought to find an idiot, but I found a smart man. I began a question about Fascism, comparing the people of Iran to the Italians under Mussolini, and the more I said, the more I thought, Oh, damn, he's not even going to know what I'm talking about, this complicated concept of Fascism. But he knew. He answered me very well, he quoted Aristotle, he interpreted Fascism in the Western sense. But then, of course, when I interrogated him about executing women for prostitution, he got very, very angry.

SCHEER: Your most famous moment with him came when you threw off the Muslim veil, the *chador*, and offended him. Why did you do it?

FALLACI: Because *I* was angry! You know what he said to me? God! I was wearing the thing, all seven meters of it, pins everywhere, perspiring, and I began to ask him about the *chador* as a symbol of women's roles in Iran. By the way, Bani-Sadr was translating from Farsi to French for us. So Khomeini says, "If you don't like the *chador*, don't wear it, because the *chador* is for young, proper women." Bani-Sadr, the bastard, was laughing as he translated. I said, "Eeeeh! Will you repeat that?" I was reacting very strongly and Bani-Sadr was caught by surprise. "Ask him again!" I said. So Bani-Sadr whispers something to Khomeini, and he turns back to me and repeats the same thing. So I rip the veil off and I say, "This is what I do with your stupid medieval rag!" Khomeini had seemed so old and dignified, but when I did that, he jumped up like—have you seen those kung-fu movies, how quick they move?—like a cat, and disappeared. I remained sitting and called after him, "Where do you go? Do you go to make pee-pee?" Bani-Sadr was very frightened and said, "No, no, no, you must go. He has left."

I remained sitting there and said, "I don't go. I only have half an interview, I will not go." So I sat there for two or three hours—that was my strategy, I knew they couldn't touch me. When Bani-Sadr came to plead with me to go, I said, "You cannot touch me. You are Iranian, your religion says you cannot touch me. I'm going to stay until he comes back." Later, Ahmad, Khomeini's son, came in and said, "Please, madam, you must go." He came back four times, four times, and finally he was desperate. He said, "If he sees you again tomorrow, will you go now?" By then, I needed to go pee-pee myself. "Ahmad," I said, "if you get him to swear on the Koran, I'll get up." So Ahmad went away for the fifth time, then came back and said, "Return tomorrow." I said, "He swore on the Koran?" "Yes, yes! Tomorrow at five."

Well, the next day, Khomeini did come in. I look straight at him and say, "Now, Imam, let's start where we left off yesterday. We were talking about my being an indecent woman . . ." And Khomeini did something very interesting. You know, he never looks you in the face; he always looks at the floor, eh? Well, he looked straight back in my face with an amused smile! It was cute, because he couldn't laugh. So I continued, "Would you say that a woman like me, who had to sleep next to soldiers in combat in Vietnam, is an indecent woman?" And he says, "I don't know. *You* know what you did with the soldiers." It was so funny! Of course, I got angry again with him.

SCHEER: Of course. You also interviewed the Shah before he was overthrown. How would you compare the two men?

FALLACI: The Shah was not stupid, but he was less intelligent than Khomeini. Less politically shrewd. But in the matter of religious fanaticism, they were alike. I don't know why none of his other interviewers extracted this side of the Shah's character—except for me. His religious obsession.

SCHEER: Religious obsession?

FALLACI: Yes; the Shah entertained me for at least a half hour out of the five or six hours we spoke in telling me about his visions. He said he actually *saw* the saints and prophets, that he spoke with them. When I wanted to make fun of him and said, "You mean you could shake hands with them?" he said, "Of course." I said, "If I am there with you, can *I* see them?" He said, "Of course you cannot. I can, because I am the elected one"—and blah-blah-blah. Well, this kind of stuff was also in Khomeini. I remember thinking the two or three times that Khomeini raised his eyes to me—they were also the eyes of the Shah! They were opposite faces of the same coin.

SCHEER: After Khomeini, you were going to interview Bani-Sadr during the hostage crisis while he was still President of Iran, right?

FALLACI: Yes, he had interpreted for me and Khomeini and knew me well. I got a visa again, in spite of the fact that I was warned not to go. After the Khomeini interview, an Iranian newspaper had written something violent against me and published a photo of me that was torn in half. So, in a country where 50 percent are illiterate, all you have to know is that your photo has been published torn in half to be an enemy of the people. They know what it means. The people at *The New York Times*, who were sending me, were very nervous.

Well, I flew there and immediately was detained on the airstrip in Tehran. "You have no visa," they said. "What is that?" I said, pointing to my name. "That is *my* fucking name!" "So what?" they said, and started pushing me into a police room. So I started shouting, "You bastards!"—the kind of play I always do when I find myself in that situation. Usually, I count on the fact that my shouting will get them so tired they finally say, "Go away, go away."

Anyway, a man from the Italian embassy finally got me to my hotel. I keep myself hidden, because I don't want other journalists to know I'm in Tehran; otherwise, it happens, the same old story—Fallaci is here, etc. I finally get an official at the foreign ministry who ignores the fact that Bani-Sadr has promised me, in writing, an interview and calls me and the Italian government a nest of liars.

Then, a day later, I get a call warning that my life is in danger. It turns out that Bani-Sadr has given in to the militant students and is a total coward about seeing me. So I try to call Italy, to call the President of Italy, in fact, and they cut off all the lines. "Until when?" I ask. "Indefinitely," they say. So I went to another telephone and called London—which wasn't cut off. I dialed the first number in my telephone book, Ingrid Bergman's. I woke her up with the call and I said, "Ingrid. I call you from Tehran. Call Pertini [President of Italy at the time] and tell him I'm in trouble. *Ciao.*"

Ingrid was very smart. She got to the right people and they finally got me out and into London. Two days after I'm back, Bani-Sadr is in London for an economic meeting and he sends a message to me through my ambassador. "Pssst. Tell Miss Fallaci that I ask to be forgiven, I really couldn't do it. There will be a next time." I just said, "Fuck Bani-Sadr. There will not be a next time. I will never grant him an interview!"

SCHEER: Before that, there was your interview with Qaddafi, which you've already mentioned.

FALLACI: That one was truly scary. Qaddafi is clinically sick, mentally ill, a certifiable idiot. You cannot deal with him. He made me wait three and a half hours outside his offices in Libya. He sits in the center office of his palace, surrounded by four or five circles of protective barricades, like German check points. It's like entering a spiral. There are dozens of people standing around with machine guns. After the first hour, I wanted to go make the pee-pee, and I was stranded alone with my photographer in this huge library, but they didn't come to escort me to the bathroom. So I got infuriated—

SCHEER: Of course.

FALLACI: And I picked up this 1964 copy of Who's Who—the library was filled with books Qaddafi never read—and threw it against the wall to express my rage. Finally, Qaddafi came.

SCHEER: When did you become convinced he was insane?

FALLACI: You should listen to my tape. For ten minutes, ten full minutes, he is yelling, like a broken record, "I am the *gospel*, I am the *gospel*, I am the *gospel*." It's terrible, because he never stops, never stops. His face—his face is so out of this world while this is going on that I nudge my photographer to take the picture then. But the photographer was so scared he couldn't move his hands, and the interpreter was trembling, too. Finally, I interrupt him, which I almost never do, and I said, "Stop! Stop! Do you believe in God?" That was the most surprising question I could put to him, and he looked at me and said, "Of course; why do you ask that question?" I said, "Because I thought that *you* were God!"

He raised himself up and I thought, *Mamma mia*, goodbye, it's over. Whoever finds us again? Because he could do it. You know what happened to the manager of Alitalia in Libya? He just disappeared. Well, Qaddafi looked lost and confused for a moment, and then the interview went on and I knew I would not be arrested. But he *is* insane. He is obsessed with the color green, you know.

SCHEER: Green?

FALLACI: Everything around him is green. His handkerchief, everything is green. As we were sitting there, I picked up something—I forget what it was— that happened to be green, and something must have happened in his consciousness. He looked like he was going to strangle me. So I said, "Would you like it? Do you want this?" I gave it to him, and he took it. Immediately.

He wanted it *so* much. He should be under the care of a psychiatric doctor. Dangerous, dangerous, dangerous.

SCHEER: Qaddafi is a good-looking man, isn't he?

FALLACI: No. They had told me that he was a good-looking man. I don't know; in the photos he looks better. But when you see him, he has this very stupid face. No matter what are the features, when the person is stupid, stupidity shows. He has very little, little eyes. In the photos, they are bigger. Then he has this enormous chin, enormous! His head is very narrow, because he has very little cerebral inside, very little. He is repellent. I have a physical hate for Qaddafi.

SCHEER: The reason I asked about his looks is that when you interviewed Arafat, you made a lot of his being short and ugly and having an obese stomach. And I wonder whether that is fair.

FALLACI: I don't care if it was fair or not. I didn't like Arafat. I think Arafat is a phony!

SCHEER: Because he has an obese stomach?

FALLACI: No, no, no. That contributed to make his physical portrait.

SCHEER: You wrote about Golda Meir as if she were beautiful, yet by some standards she was ugly.

FALLACI: She *was* ugly, but I didn't *see* her ugly. Intelligence makes people beautiful.

SCHEER: But what is interesting is that when you talk about "ugly" Arafat, you say you are sympathetic to his cause. But Golda Meir, whom you describe sympathetically, is someone whose politics you reject.

FALLACI: Her Zionism, yes.

SCHEER: Why do you reject Zionism?

FALLACI: For the same reason that I reject the Catholic ideology and other ideologies. That is our fight in Italy against the Christian Democrats and the intervention of the Church. The theocratic state.

SCHEER: Why, when you interviewed Meir in your lengthy, friendly interview, did you not ask her one challenging question about Zionism?

FALLACI: You protest because I made *my* interview and not yours. I did not ask her the question *you* wanted, all right.

SCHEER: You wrote about the "fundamental justice" of Arafat's cause in the introduction to your interview with him. *Are* you sympathetic to his cause?

FALLACI: I understand his cause. Is it an answer? I understand his cause. And let's put it like this: I understand the cause of the Irish and I sympathize with the Irish. I understand the cause of the Palestinians. And I stop here because of several reasons that involve me, that mitigate the firmness of that judgment, for personal reasons and for political reasons. As everybody of my generation who is European, and particularly Italian, I cannot accept the blind hate and the contempt toward Jews. In the Resistance, we hid many of them. But it does not make me a crazy anti-Jewish person to say I am angry at the Jewish people for many things.

SCHEER: What are you angry at the Jews for?

FALLACI: For many things. If you want to take the example of America, how they hold the power, the economical power in so many ways, and the press and the other kind of stuff . . .

SCHEER: You say that Jews control the media in America?

FALLACI: Well, you see Jewish names as directors of TV and newspapers. The owners, the directors. I never realized how it happened and how they came to control the media to that point. Why?

SCHEER: That's not true. Jews by no means own the media.

FALLACI: But listen, at *The New York Times*, they are all Jewish.

SCHEER: *The New York Times* is owned by an old German Jewish family that was even anti-Zionist at one point. Sure there are some Jews who are prominent in some papers. But you can go to most newspapers or the networks and find that that doesn't hold up. That's a European perception and it's just not true.

FALLACI: It is not true?

SCHEER: No.

FALLACI: Okay.

SCHEER: Getting back to the subject of Arafat, what else didn't you like about him?

FALLACI: Arafat meets me with his automatic rifle, as if to say, "You know, with this rifle, I fight the enemy! I have just come from the combat." He didn't come from the combat! *Others* had been in the combat! And they were dead! . . . You know, I was told that he got married. I don't believe it.

SCHEER: In the preface to your interview with Arafat, you implied that he is a homosexual.

FALLACI: Yeah. Everybody knew it. Everybody would tell you. I don't imply it. He had at that time the most gorgeous young man I have seen in my life. He was a German. So handsome and so gorgeous, and he even behaved in a funny way with my photographer. He was a very handsome man and he never looked at me. He looked at my photographer. He was provoking him. He was doing things like that [*licking her lips*] and he was looking at him.

SCHEER: This smacks a little bit of character assassination. You admit that you couldn't come up with anything in the interview. You really couldn't get Arafat. So, in your introduction you get into personal attacks. You wrote: "His teeth are the teeth of a wolf."

FALLACI: What do you want to do? What do you want to do with me because I don't like Arafat? I don't like Arafat!

SCHEER: What if the introduction to this interview said Oriana has crooked teeth?

FALLACI: Let me see what I have written. [*Reads from her collection*] It is funny. It is amusing. It is amusing.

SCHEER: You wrote: "His fat legs and his massive trunk with his huge lips and swollen stomach." That's pretty tough stuff.

FALLACI: What do you care? Is he your friend?

SCHEER: I'm suggesting you didn't nail him in the interview, so you went a cheaper route. You wrote that it was an "unsatisfactory" interview because you couldn't get anything out of him.

FALLACI: Yeah, because he had nothing to say.

SCHEER: Not necessarily. For instance, he made contradictory statements. He said at one point, "We have to liquidate Israel!" Then, in another part of the interview, he said he has nothing against the Jews and he is *for* a democratic state.

FALLACI: Yeah.

SCHEER: Why didn't you ask him how he could be for both?

FALLACI: Because I had little time. You know how much it lasted? One hour. It was very short. When you have little time, you let them talk and you think you catch them later. But I never caught him later. I couldn't— he went away. He left with his beautiful, handsome German blond.

SCHEER: You sound as if you have contempt for Arafat *because* he is a homosexual. Is there something about homosexuals you don't like?

FALLACI: They don't like *me*.

SCHEER: Why?

FALLACI: Maybe because I'm more manly than they are. I irritate them— I don't know.

SCHEER: You're more manly?

FALLACI: I'm—if we get lost into that subject, I am going to say something which makes me very unpopular. I don't know if I should look for other enemies, I have so many already. But I'm not crazy about them, the homosexuals. You see them here in New York, for instance, moving like this [*makes a mincing gesture*], exhibiting their homosexuality. It disturbs me. It's . . . I don't know. Do you know the ones who have the high heels and put powder on and go to Bloomingdale's hand in hand, and they *squeak*?

SCHEER: It makes you nervous?

FALLACI: No, it doesn't make me nervous; I just can't stand them.

SCHEER: Heterosexuals can also be exhibitionists. They don't offend you in the same way?

FALLACI: Heterosexual means men that go with women?

SCHEER: Yes, or women with men.

FALLACI: Listen, here we get into the word "sex." It's so boring. Anybody who makes an exhibition of sex, who makes exploitation of it, disturbs me. With *Playboy*, I cut out the interview and sometimes other articles and I put them in the guest rooms of my country house because people are very happy to find them when they come in summer. It disturbs me to see all the nudity. It's like going to buy three pounds of steak. It is not puritanism, it's just a matter of aesthetics. Honestly, I mean, you at *Playboy* are so liberal on certain things and you are so illiberal in the use of the naked women. Sometimes, to clear your conscience, you include also some naked men, but that disturbs me just as much.

SCHEER: To find sex boring says something about you; most people find it exciting—and most men seem to like the pictures in *Playboy*.

FALLACI: It's boring for me. Listen, have you a *Playboy* magazine here? Please give it to me. I show you how boring it is. [*Begins thumbing through a recent issue*] It's always the same thing. I find *Vogue* much more interesting, because I like dresses. But this [*points to a picture of a Bunny*] is even aesthetically ugly. I shall never understand this uniform. I detest uniforms. Whether it is the military uniform, the uniform of the priest, or the uniform of the Playboy Rabbit-Bunny, okay? And it makes this woman ridiculous.

SCHEER: The way you find homosexuals at Bloomingdale's ridiculous?

FALLACI: Listen, I don't want to be unfair to my homosexual friends, because I have a couple who are friends, whom I like very much, as they are very pleasant people, they're intelligent persons. But there is a form of fanaticism in them, of dogmatism, of exhibitionism, of Mafia sense, all what I despise. I mean, why should I reject it in political parties and accept it in the homo-sexual party? They *are* a party.

SCHEER: How are homosexuals a party? Or a Mafia, as you put it?

FALLACI: Listen, I should say this in Italian. When I'm tired, my English becomes lousy. This sense of comradeship which exists among, for instance, certain sporting people, or certain followers of an ideology, like the Com-munists. The Communists among themselves, whatever language they speak, they feel brothers. It's the sense of the parties, the strength, the real sense of the party. The homosexuals are the same. But theirs goes beyond the com-radeship. It's kind of Mafia, and when they get together, for instance, in the artistic field, they are terrible, much worse than the members of a political party. Terrible, they use it, they're very strong. And I do not want to be obliged to love them. It's enough to let them live. I live my way, they live their way, to hell with it. But don't oblige me to love them.

SCHEER: The obligation is not to love homosexuals. But since you advance a conspiracy theory of homosexual life, and you liken them to the Mafia or to the Communist Party, you should be obliged to defend that.

FALLACI: It's a form of Mafia.

SCHEER: So defend that.

FALLACI: Tomorrow.

SCHEER: It's not to make you love them; it's making you be fair, making you be accurate.

FALLACI: Tomorrow I'll tell you.

SCHEER: You don't like being worn down in an interview?

FALLACI: I'm tired, I'm tired. Tomorrow I promise I'll do it. I'll elaborate tomorrow.

SCHEER: Have any of the people you've interviewed said to you, "Oriana, I'm tired of talking to you, I don't want to talk anymore"? Would *you* accept that?

FALLACI: I have never talked so long with the people. I never make an interview so long. Never!

SCHEER: Why is your journalism so consumed with politics?

FALLACI: I was always very political. You must understand that I made my first political rally when I was fourteen. I remember in Florence in the square outside the Palazzo Vecchio where the Medici lived, it was full of people and there was some rally, I don't know why, and they wanted to exploit me because I had been the key to the Resistance, etc. I remember very well how I was dressed. I had a dress in squares, red and white, and I remember this microphone and I remember the first words, because after, I was caught by terrible panic and I said, "People of Florence, it's a young girl who speaks to you! Listen to us young people!" And then I don't remember anything, nothing, nothing. I don't remember anything because I must have been talking or reading in the state of shock. I don't remember anything but "People of Florence"—and I loved it!

SCHEER: Who was exploiting you?

FALLACI: I was participating in the assembly of the Action Party, a kind of socialist party—an anarchist party that my father and brother belonged to. It was a very tiny party, where they were all generals, no soldiers. I guess I was the only soldier, I was so cute, and I wanted to stay with these people because they were all men and women of great culture, intelligent people, clean people, selected people who had been able to stand against Fascism in prison. So I was drinking their words.

SCHEER: How politically active was your father?

FALLACI: My father was a craftsman, and during the Resistance he had been the military chief of the Action Party for Tuscany. And he belonged to the Central Committee, he was one of the leaders. Then my father disappeared. He had been arrested and was under torture for many days.

SCHEER: Where was your mother?

FALLACI: My mother had the guts to face the head of the Italian SS, who was a very famous torturer. He received her and said, "*Signora*, you can dress yourself in black. He will be executed tomorrow morning at the parterre." And my mother raised her arm and said, "All right, I shall dress myself in black, but if you are born out of the womb of a woman, you'll tell your mother to dress *herself* in black." And he said, "*Signora*, get out of here, I will arrest you, too." And she got out, very dignified. She was pregnant and she took her bicycle and she started on the bicycle and she lost the child in the street. That was a very fantastic story of my mother; she was a very tough woman, very sweet, though. If you saw her, you would say, "Oriana, you call this woman a tough woman?" My God, she was the symbol of what you call femininity, yet she was so tough.

SCHEER: How old were you then?

FALLACI: Twelve or thirteen. I was already working in the Resistance; everybody gave me orders, you know, all these big people. I was like a messenger, you know, those boys who bring the coffee, and they yell, "You do this, go buy a Coca-Cola." The problem is, they didn't ask me for a Coca-Cola or for a coffee. They gave me, for instance, a hand grenade. "Take this hand grenade, go and take it to the group so-and-so." And I had to decide how to do it. For instance, for the hand grenade I had smart ideas; I was an intelligent kid. I hid the grenades in heads of lettuce.

SCHEER: How long was your father in jail before they let him out?

FALLACI: It was a few months.

SCHEER: They didn't kill him?

FALLACI: No, the Allies were coming up. It was clear the Fascists had lost, and they wanted to show some magnanimity; a certain lieutenant said to him, "I let you go, I know who you are; when the moment will come, remember that I let you go." I have seen so many things at that time. You know, when I speak in this country and they ask me, "What is the mark of your life?" and I say, "Resistance," I say it and I feel that they don't understand what I mean. But I really was a child of the Resistance.

SCHEER: The Resistance was a male environment; how did that affect your relationships with your mother and other women?

FALLACI: My mother was the *only* woman in my life. The influence that my father exercised on me was political in the full sense of the word, but also my mother, because she was a very good anti-Fascist, too. But in life itself, she influenced me much more. The talks with my father were political talks—democracy, socialism, Fascism, Nazism, liberalism, Christian Democrats, the Republicans—all that. The facts of life I discussed more with my mother, even indirectly. For instance, it was my mother who put it in my mind that I should go to work. All mothers said, "When will you get married?" My mother never cared about that. She said, "When will you go to work?"

I remember my mother, and I'm standing up in this bed, and she's crying and she says, "Don't do like me. Don't ever, ever, ever be a wife. Don't ever, ever, ever be a slave to a husband and children. Don't do it. I want you to go to work and I want you to travel the world and I want you to be independent. Go far away. Fly! Fly! Fly!" And she cried. That day was fatal to me, fatal, because I must have paid very much attention, maybe because she cried and her face was over mine; I have never forgotten those words. See? And she always pushed me in that sense. About marriage. When people ask me, "Why did you never get married?" I don't know how to answer, because it never occurred to me to marry anybody.

SCHEER: So you are a loner.

FALLACI: Oh yeah, no doubt about that.

SCHEER: And you're also not happy if you're not on the edge.

FALLACI: You're right, you're right.

SCHEER: You seem to impose this context of a world undergoing perpetual resistance on everything you do. Is your vision the only way to look at life? Must it *always* be within a resistance?

FALLACI: You are telling me—or are you accusing me—that I make a war out of peace in any circumstances of my life, including work? Well, there might be much truth in it. The fact is that I regard life as a war. If you read [my book] *Letter to a Child Never Born*, the very first page, it portrays me very well. I say to this embryo within me, "Life is war, dear child." I describe life to this embryo to make him decide if he wants to be born or not, and I do it in such a way that the poor kid says, "To hell with you, Mother, I'm not going to be born." Later in the book, there is this fantasy trial in her imagination, and she's condemned, and the one who condemns her is the child, who says to his mother, "How did you introduce life to me? Did you ever tell me that life can be sweetness and serenity and peace and the beauty of a kiss and an ice cream? You never did, you always told me terrible stories, fantastic stories, war stories, and why the hell should I be born to come into that?"

If I wanted to make me more sympathetic, I would try with all the politics I'm capable of to mitigate this, but then I would contradict myself. The truth would come out all the same, and so I am this. Besides, I'm always tired, I'm tired because I always live in tension. All I know is the war; I never knew the peace. I was born in the war, I grew up in the war, it was my school and here I am; it's a great limitation. I know at this point of my life to change is too late. I should have tried at least twenty years ago.

SCHEER: This insistence that life be lived on the edge runs through your latest book, *A Man.* Let's discuss the book's hero, Alekos. As an opponent of the Greek colonels' dictatorship in the sixties, he resisted torture bravely but died some years later. He was clearly a man of courage, but he seemed to care for nothing but his revolution. By your admiration for him, you seem to imply that anything other than the great drama of life is inconsequential—

FALLACI: Number one, the man in this book and who really lived is contrary to what you say. If you had that impression, you are one of a tiny minority. I don't take you seriously for one moment when you say that. Number two, since I respect even the opinions I don't agree with, then if I gave you—or two or three other people—that impression, then I'm ashamed. Because Alekos was the contrary. What he was—he could not be blackmailed. He could not be blackmailed! Now, *I* can be.

SCHEER: Because you care about someone.

FALLACI: He did, too, for Christ's sake. You are unfair to this man!

SCHEER: In the book, there's not a single moment in which he feels responsible for another human being—not even you. He seemed to say he had a nobler goal than most people and any means could be sacrificed to it.

FALLACI: Can I answer now?

SCHEER: All the answers you want. The magazine can't publish every word we say, of course.

FALLACI: One second. If you don't publish my answers, then it's not an interview.

SCHEER: No publication can print every word of every interview. They're edited, of course. Don't you edit your interviews?

FALLACI: I publish everything they tell me. Of course.

SCHEER: Every word?

FALLACI: That's why they're so long.

SCHEER: Then we'll have to direct this interview very tightly; we'll have to cut you off to stay on track.

FALLACI: You don't let *me* talk!

SCHEER: Go ahead.

FALLACI: I started to talk about repetitions in an interview. Obviously, sometimes you make people repeat something to be sure they meant it. For instance, when I interviewed [Polish Solidarity leader] Lech Walesa, he said if the government of Poland fell, Solidarity would go *into* the government. I was so shocked I asked him to repeat it. I said, Lech, I don't want to harm you, because what you said was dangerous, the Soviets will be reading this. By the way, he said more than that: he said not only would Solidarity go into government but he should become President. Since he is such a simple man, it was his way of expressing it. I said, Excuse me, Lech, I'm not going to write that you said you should become President, because you would be killed in a week. I'm not going to do that. And he said, Okay, don't write it. So I asked him twice again if he meant that Solidarity should govern, and he said yes. Now, of course, I didn't include my three interventions in the published interview.

SCHEER: Why not?

FALLACI: [*Angrily*] I'm not capable of doing it! Listen, you are—you are too tyrannical. I'm tyrannical, too. We cannot go on. We can't go on like this!

SCHEER: As you said in your interview with Walesa, "I ask the questions." You're not conducting this interview.

FALLACI: This is not an interview, this is a fight.

SCHEER: Let's establish that if we go off on a tangent, if it adds nothing, if it's boring, we'll edit it out. I certainly don't have the authority to say that anything that comes out of your mouth automatically will be published.

FALLACI: No, not all of it is good—not what I say and even less what I write.

SCHEER: Now, to get back to the theme of your book—

FALLACI: Yes, but you're hurting this man and it makes me very angry! You make me feel as if I give the wrong portrait of him. If I did, then I be damned.

SCHEER: What you say throughout this book is that his life defines the way a man should live. He resisted the dictatorship, he revealed nothing under torture. But at the same time, he considered bombing the Acropolis to dramatize his point, he talked about taking American tourists as hostages. And you seem to endorse that.

FALLACI: It is obvious that I admire that man, or, if you prefer, that kind of man. If I didn't, I wouldn't have spent three years of my life with him or the three additional years it took to write the book about him. I admired that kind of man before knowing Alekos—for me, it came during the Resistance to the Fascists in Italy. I like him, I like all men who resist. My father did it. Two others who were arrested with my father—one did, one didn't. When the one who didn't resist told me, ten years later, oh, I wanted to spit in his face. Oh, I do admire that kind of man. I do, I do, I do, I do! It is because of people like that that the world moves. I'm not a Marxist, you see. Marxism says it is movements, not individuals, who make the world move.

SCHEER: But to try to stay on the subject, what about the problem of means and ends? To consider kidnapping innocent American tourists in order to resist, that's a form of terrorism, and it's an important subject in the world today.

FALLACI: Okay. See, when talking like this with Americans, I feel a tremendous gap, something that divides us. I say this in sincerity and friendship, because I stay in the United States, nobody obliges me to; if I stay, it means I like it. But there is this void between us. We have different cultural perspectives. My concept of politics and everything is the experience I had as a human being, and the main experience I had in my life was the Resistance. I always go back to that. But you Americans don't *know* what that was, the Resistance. You see it in movies and in books, bad books, usually. So you will not understand when I say, "Yes, yes, under a dictatorship you can take hostages, yes, you *can!*" For you it is monstrous. For me it is not. The French would agree with me; a German, a Russian, a Belgian, a Dane; not a Swede, maybe. But *you* will not! So the dialogue becomes impossible. You could also ask me, Why kill an eighteen-year-old German in 1945? Why? Was he responsible? I say to you, No, he wasn't responsible. So you kill him? I answer to you: Yes, I kill him—crying, but I kill him. And this is monstrous to you.

SCHEER: First of all, you have a condescending view of Americans, and that comes out in the book as well. You write, "America is made up of the rejects of Europe." That isn't true. Many of the people who emigrated to America were the most adventurous, and it was an adventure to come to this country. It was the most energetic of the Chinese who somehow ended up in San Francisco, and to this day, it's the most energetic of the Guatemalans who crawl through barbed wire and somehow get to Los Angeles. But as far as the question of terrorism and hostages goes, I suspect the average Irish or French citizen would share my reaction to your view: it's not just that a hostage is different from a soldier, but there's a frivolousness with which revolutionaries consider taking hostages—and lives. It's as if the people to be used by revolutionaries weren't really living, human beings.

FALLACI: When I speak to you about this, I feel like when I speak to my little sister Elisabetta. And it makes me recall what Willy Brandt told me during our interview. He had the same problem with his children. They didn't care because they had not experienced what he had. So, in the same way, you are like the children of Willy Brandt and like my sister. You did not experience it, you do not have it in your consciousness. It is not an accusation. It is a fact.

You use the adjective "frivolous," and it is gratuitously offensive. There were *not* frivolous episodes, I tell you. For Alekos *was* concerned about those people. I am talking about one part of him, you about another. When I asked him, "What does it mean to be a man?" he gives me an answer and asks me, "And for you, what does it mean to be a man?" I say, "Well, something like you, Alekos." His answer, what he means, is he's just a man; a man is a man when he is human, with all his frailties and limits and guilts and mistakes—and also beauties.

SCHEER: But you don't present him as just a man; this was your lover, the man you admire, you hold up to the world—

FALLACI: My *brother!* I prefer the word brother more than lover. Lover makes you think something like *Playboy*, making jumps in the bed. No, he was my brother—

SCHEER: But he *wasn't* your brother.

FALLACI: Oh yes, he was.

SCHEER: With all due respect, he was a man you gave in to, you were used by—

FALLACI: No, I was his accomplice.

SCHEER: Because of him, you took risks you didn't believe in. You went along with things you thought were crazy; you wrote that you thought maybe he was mad. You went along like some teeny-bopper, some sorority girl. You did what lovesick groupies have always done: you went along with *his* plans, no matter what you thought for yourself.

FALLACI: Look, if tomorrow you have a plan to kill Qaddafi, I come with *you* and follow you in the same way. Following Alekos's plans to resist the dictatorship is the same thing I did when I was a little girl with pigtails. I entered the Resistance as a kid and was discharged as a soldier. Let me tell you this episode; it will explain to you why I was not the slave of Alekos.

My work during the war, as you will find in any book about the Italian Resistance mentioning my name—and my *nom de guerre* was Amelia—was to accompany American and English prisoners who had escaped from concentration camps in Italy. I guided them to the Allied lines because it was a bargain we made with the Americans. The Americans would supply us with ammunition and other things we needed, but they wanted their prisoners back. You know . . . it seems that has been the problem of the Americans for the past fifty years of history—they wanted the Americans back from Italy, they wanted the Americans back from Vietnam, they wanted the Americans back from Iran.

So . . . what I did countless times, all alone as a kid, was to accompany Americans on my bicycle for sixty miles, and we saved many Americans and English and South Africans in that way. There is no need to tell you how dangerous it was, because anyone found in contact with an escaped prisoner would be executed immediately. And my mother was always frightened by this. My father, who did not live with us, because he was hiding, didn't tell her after the first couple of times I went. It was crazy at the time—to go past German roadblocks with men who spoke only English. I'm used to participating in something that might be crazy or not! I didn't feel used by Alekos!

SCHEER: But the point you make in your book—

FALLACI: I was like a sergeant following the lieutenant.

SCHEER: The point you make in your book is that Alekos was an example of other men around the world who resist authoritarian power. It's like a prism for everything you believe about courage and politics and life itself. It seems as if you're saying that the real test of a man is the courage to resist torture, to resist institutional power. The test of a man is never being a reformer, making the world marginally better. It's never being a parent, diapering a baby. You seem contemptuous of anyone who takes *small* steps. That comes out in your interviews: the people you are interested in are big political figures, they make history. Anything else in human experience doesn't seem to interest you.

FALLACI: Okay, one thing at a time. About whether the test is diapering a baby—no, it is not the test, because that would be another book. I wrote *this* book, not another one. If you want that test, read my *Letter to a Child Never Born*, where the heroine is a woman and the test she has to face is of another kind.

SCHEER: Is that a test a man could face?

FALLACI: I let you talk when you put your very long question-accusation. Now you let *me* talk! I cannot do like this, because if you interrupt me, you do not want my answer! Why did you become a journalist and not a prosecutor-general?

Of *course* this book doesn't deal with the problem of diapers! I don't give a damn about the diapers of a child, because it was not the work of the character of the book. He had no children to wash anything for! The accusation, which was the real point you wanted to get to, is that I only deal—let's see if I understand it right—with exceptional people, I only care about people who do not belong to the crowd. Well, it is true and it is not true. It is objectively true, since all I offer to you is interviews with these people, and in this particular case, a book about such a man. It is not true if I recall to you that I do not make these interviews, or write this book, for those men—but for people who wash the diapers. To wake them up. To tell them, in the case of the interviews, who are the people who decide our life and death. Not necessarily bad people. Some are okay. Some are not. To tell them, in the case of this book, how much they are manipulated and how they are crushed in the preciousness of their individuality. How they must refind that individuality, because, as I say over and over, everybody is somebody. I don't know if it is good English.

In any case, I offer the extreme example of this man—extreme because I am not like him. I only write for the others as a moral commitment. I suffer when I write. It doesn't amuse me. I expose myself. I already told you I admire that kind of man; so what? Am I to be condemned? Yes, yes, I might be a little obsessed with courage. Something happened to me in my life— trauma—when I was a little girl. The trauma of Fascism and the trauma of Resistance. This has marked my life, morally and culturally, and I cannot change it. I must be taken for what I am.

SCHEER: Then because of that, we should accept everything you say?

FALLACI: No, you should not. If you accept everything I say, you do the contrary of what I preach.

SCHEER: So those of us who didn't participate in the Italian Resistance cannot challenge that view? What I am challenging is your view of courage. Individual acts of terrorism may be courageous, but don't they just alienate people and end up being self-defeating?

FALLACI: I feel helpless in talking to you, because even if you were a more tolerant interviewer, I feel as if I'm speaking Chinese. Take the Palestinians, for example. I feel they have no right to put a bomb in a bus with twenty-five schoolchildren—and I tell you that Alekos would never, no, never put such a bomb under a school bus. I would like you to recall that he never killed anybody, and the only violent act he did in his life was to put a couple of bombs that did not explode. What he did in Greece was to kill the tyrant, so to speak, which he did very well. And if I were courageous, I would do also. If I were courageous as he was, I would have killed Qaddafi when I interviewed him. I would have had the guts to die killing Qaddafi—but I didn't.

SCHEER: Who else among your interview subjects would you have killed?

FALLACI: Many others.

SCHEER: Which others?

FALLACI: I shall not mention anyone I have not yet been able to interview. I am not that stupid.

SCHEER: But which of the ones you *have* interviewed would you kill?

FALLACI: Let me think. Qaddafi for sure. I think it's a shame Qaddafi dies in his bed. Oh, God, if I had had the guts to do it! I should die with him, of course. Let me see . . . You asked me for names; I'm a serious person, I'm not going to shout names like that. You probably expect me to say Khomeini, but I shall not . . . Idi Amin, for sure, but I have not interviewed him.

SCHEER: That attitude may make good copy, but it also puts all journalists into question. Any time we interview someone, does that person have to fear he's going to be killed? Do you think we have the right to intrude this way?

FALLACI: To intrude in what sense?

SCHEER: To make history. You'll make history by killing Qaddafi.

FALLACI: No. I'll be protecting my life. He is a murderer. He is the man who helps the Red Brigades in Italy, who helps terrorists around the world, who wants a nuclear bomb for Libya. There are not many cases of absolute, personal dictatorships in our times like Qaddafi. I would say that was the case with Hitler. And I would think it was a tragedy for humanity that the attempt to assassinate Hitler failed.

SCHEER: But that doesn't really answer the question.

FALLACI: I didn't get a chance to *finish* answering! I never have the time to answer. Listen, *you* would make a very good dictator.

SCHEER: Calling me a dictator, what is that supposed to do? Make me say, "Sorry, I'll stop"? Is that to intimidate an interviewer so you won't get pinned down?

FALLACI: No, it's because I don't get a chance to answer. It's impossible! Let's just go have lunch instead of doing this interview.

SCHEER: Look, from the very start, you've taken offense that anyone should challenge this vision in your book of what courageous political action is all about. When I've raised questions about that, you've said it was because I'm an American, or I didn't live in the Resistance, or I'm an egomaniacal interviewer. The fact is, many people have profound questions about this topic, would agree with my challenges, and you're just refusing to meet the questions head-on.

FALLACI: You're not attacking me. You're attacking him, Alekos. And I'm thinking, Oh, God, Alekos is dead, he cannot answer—

SCHEER: But it's not he, it's the idea we are talking about—

FALLACI: Please! Please! Please! [*Screaming*] You see? He doesn't let me talk! *Dio mio,* he doesn't let me talk!

[*The interview was broken off at this point and resumed the next day in a more subdued atmosphere.*]

SCHEER: It seems as if some people need perpetual revolution . . . They need crisis, they need to think the world is falling apart; they're not happy if they don't think that Fascism is coming or we're on the barricades.

FALLACI: I don't belong to them. I am more moderate than you think. I do not think that everything must be destroyed. On the contrary, I think there is much to preserve, to renew, to remake, to try to make better, to change, but not to destroy, in any field. I'm not Attila. When I see that in New York, you destroy those old buildings—for instance, an old hotel—I suffer. If you translate it into politics, it tells you something.

SCHEER: Still, you seem always to live your life as a shout, as if you were still at a rally, crying, "People of Florence!" whether you're getting a taxi or demanding to change a table or complaining about the wine . . .

FALLACI: You're right—so what? You're right. I have nothing to answer. It's true. I've never been serene in my life. If you put me on a shore, of Acapulco or the Caribbean, beautiful shores, with this blue sea and the sky and the palm tree, and you say, "Okay, Oriana, now you rest, take a rest for a week, come on, stay there in the sun," I might stay half an hour and then I begin to think, What a bore, nothing happens here. You say, "What do you mean, nothing happens? You have the beautiful sea, the beautiful sky, and what else do you want, pineapple juice with the rum inside?" And you give me the pineapple juice, and when it is finished, I say, "What do we do now?" And you say, "Be quiet." I need things to happen.

SCHEER: Yes, you do. And it's obvious you love theatrics. You always make a scene at an airport or in a restaurant. You made a scene with Khomeini. But you know what you're doing and why, don't you?

FALLACI: I have a professional example which will please you a lot and which goes against me. When I was interviewing [Chinese leader] Deng Xiaping in Peking and he said something about Stalin, I let him talk a lot of time. But when it was over, I didn't take it. I felt the need to counterattack him. I said, "But Stalin"—and we got involved in a discussion so long about Stalin and it was such a waste of time, and Deng said at a certain moment, "Listen, let's do one thing." He was so cute; he said, "You remain of your opinion about Stalin and I remain about mine and we'll go on with this interview." And I said, "Yes, but that huge portrait of Stalin that you have in Tien An Men Square—why do you still have it up there?" That was around the end of our first encounter, which took place on a certain Thursday. I saw him again on Saturday and that morning, on our way to the Great Hall of the People, we passed through the square and I look up and there's no more Stalin! I couldn't believe my eyes.

When I entered again the Great Hall of the People, in this large room full of members of the government, I pulled another scene. My interview with Deng, it was not a private thing as we do now, or as I always do with the people I interview, but there were also TV people, newspaper people, photographers. I was *very* angry at Deng! I said, "I don't want them to stay here, the interview is mine, they are listening, they are going to steal it!" So he kept the government men and the photographers, but he sent away the newsmen. He was very nice, he was very cute.

SCHEER: By the way, do you think that a man could have gotten away with that?

FALLACI: Honestly, it might have helped, not only the fact that I'm a woman but that I'm a *small* woman. The point is that Deng, too, is very small; he's even shorter than I am.

SCHEER: You say it probably helped with Deng that you were a woman. What if a woman were interviewing *you?*

FALLACI: [*Refers to an unflattering article written about her by an American journalist*] When that fat woman reporter—do you want to know what is my problem when women interview me? If they are fat, be sure they will be nasty.

SCHEER: Why?

FALLACI: I don't know—maybe because I'm *not* fat. When they tell me how slim I am, I think, Oh, *mamma mia*, oh, *Dio, Dio,* now I know she's going to write something against me. It's the story of my life in every country.

SCHEER: You really have a problem with women, don't you?

FALLACI: You see, it's the fact that I grew up among men. The only women I was familiar with were my mother and sisters. But outside the family, in the intellectual world, it was all men. So in school, in the Resistance, as a reporter, there were no women at all, just men. I never learned the art of dealing with women.

SCHEER: How do you get along with feminists?

FALLACI: I'm sick and tired of them. I used to say in the past that the biggest revolution of our time was the feminist revolution. I said it for a couple of years. Until they started breaking my balls and became really unbearable. It is their victimization that disturbs me. I think it's like a dictatorship: if you accept it, you deserve it. A dictator never becomes one if the people are not scared, silent cowards.

SCHEER: How did they start breaking your balls?

FALLACI: They don't treat with me anymore, they ignore me, they punish me. When *Ms.* magazine received the manuscript of A *Man*, they said, "We are not interested." So now I'm exiled, which is good, because I don't want anything to do with that fanaticism. It's fanaticism once again. What feminists really wanted me to do was stand up and say, "Look what I have accomplished in spite of all the men who were so nasty to me." I mean, I am living proof of the contrary. When you choose a few examples of women who did it in our time, you have to choose me, too. I'm not Joan of Arc and I'm not Catherine of Russia and I'm not Golda Meir. But I am one of those who succeeded. And they wanted me to say I had done it through my own heroism, in *spite* of men. But I said, "No, it is not so. It *helped* me to be a woman. It helped a *lot!*"

Two things have helped me—to be born a woman and to be born poor. They were the things that pushed me, pushed me. I have said that if my name were Oriano, if I were a man and had been born the son of the Duke of Marlborough, I would probably be a fucking idiot, because I'd have nothing to fight for. Plus having the temperament I do, it has made more news that I was a woman. If I had been Oriano writing the same things, maybe I would have been more slowly or less known. So the fact is that being a woman has helped and the feminists got angry. I said that I was sick of their victimization, always crying, "This happened because I'm a woman." I say, "No, it happened because you are no good, not because you are a woman."

SCHEER: So you've never been held back by "male-chauvinist pigs"?

FALLACI: I have always been uncomfortable about that—there is much truth to the issue of male-chauvinist pigs, but *I* have not been experiencing it. I must say that I have received in my life, from any point of view—including those who write about me—much more nastiness by the women than the men. If you find a nasty article about me, be 98 percent sure it was written by a woman. Well . . . or by a homosexual.

SCHEER: That certainly brings up a familiar topic. What is it about you and homosexuals?

FALLACI: I remember once when I took my mother to London for the first time in her life. We were in front of Westminster Abbey and we saw these two workers, laborers, kiss each other on the lips. She almost fainted. She said, "Ccchhh. Is that what you always speak about, Oriana?" I said yes, so what? But no, I couldn't imagine two laborers kissing each other on the lips, making love. Those Bloomingdale's types that I cannot stand, or the homosexuals in Arab countries—it makes me sick. I can't imagine a homosexual in *any* position. When they swagger and strut and wag their tails, I can't bear them.

SCHEER: You, who claim to detest power and to root for the underdog, obviously associate homosexuality with weakness. You mentioned earlier that they don't like you because you're more manly than they are, so the implication is that they're weak and frivolous people.

FALLACI: No, I told you there are a few exceptions. I have very few friends among them, but as the Latins say, it is the exceptions that prove the rule. When they love me, they love me madly, but most don't at all. And I never understood why, but lesbians hate me much more. The only lesbian who is nice to me is Kate Millet. She always sends me unbelievable artworks—from pornographic or lesbian exhibits, all that kind of stuff. I said, "Kate, why do you send me those things?" She said, "It's good." "It's *ugly*," I said. Anyway, she's the only one who likes me. Yeah, they don't like me, thank God.

I'm very happy that lesbians don't like me. I'm not so happy that [male] homosexuals don't like me; because, after all, they are men, and I like men better than women. See? Eh. I live well with men, that's the problem. Of course, in the field of love, you can be hurt by men, but you hurt them *also*, for Christ's sake!

SCHEER: But why do homosexuals make you cringe? You were physically recoiling a moment ago.

FALLACI: No, don't exaggerate. I don't care. They can do what they want. It's their exhibitionism that disturbs me. There is a very nice homosexual here in New York and I see him rather often and he is cute. Polite, intelligent, and delightful. I would like to travel with him. Ooooo, I could go on holidays with him. How beautiful! You want to know why? So I have a man next to me and he doesn't bother me at night. He doesn't ask me anything. How cute. Cute.

SCHEER: Why don't you want to be bothered at night?

FALLACI: Because if you travel with a normal man, there is always a moment in which he may be attracted a little, make a gesture, and I say, "Oh, leave me alone." That will never happen with a homosexual.

SCHEER: You still haven't answered the question: Why are you so repelled by homosexuals, or by their exhibitionism, if you will?

FALLACI: I don't know. It's like seeing the beauty of the male body—and you will admit that the male body is much more beautiful than the female body—

SCHEER: No, I won't.

FALLACI: Oh, come on. There is no comparison! The Greeks understood that very well, for Christ's sake! And when homosexuals swagger—

SCHEER: You've never seen a female, a heterosexual female, swivel her hips?

FALLACI: I was trying to tell you, but you didn't let me say it! The male body has a different dignity than the female body. When the male swaggers, it breaks the harmony, it hurts the dignity. It disturbs me . . . You want me to think like you! You are doing to me what I did to Deng Xiaping, when he upset me and said I should remain of my opinion and he of his—and get on with the interview.

SCHEER: As long as you admit I'm not doing anything to you that you haven't done yourself as an interviewer.

FALLACI: But I was speaking of serious things when I fought with Deng. He liked Stalin! But you, you cannot bear that I am not in love with homosexuals.

SCHEER: Just rounding out the portrait, Oriana. You have a certain idea of maleness, and that connects to courage, to strength, to power—your field of study. Besides, you have a fascinating view of sex. What was it you said about it? That you found it boring?

FALLACI: Yes, it's boring. I have a friend, a very handsome and intelligent man who has many women. And he says, "Sex is an activity for porters."

SCHEER: For porters?

FALLACI: Yes, because all the blood goes down toward the legs, and the intellectuals, we need it in the head. It is not for us.

SCHEER: So assuming that even intellectuals occasionally have sex, what sort of man attracts you?

FALLACI: To love a man, it must be a courageous man. Once I was on NBC, doing the Today show to promote my book, and we got into a discussion of love, because Americans saw in the book a love story. So after a lot of talking, I became impatient and said, "Damn it! Don't you understand what I say? I'm saying I cannot love a Fascist!" It had a great success, this thing. They loved it very much.

SCHEER: What about sex with a man who is not a Fascist but whom you don't love, either?

FALLACI: That is my business. You will not come into my bedroom, I tell you.

SCHEER: You used the word "Fascist" in this regard. It strikes me, in thinking about the Moral Majority, that it was the Fascists—and today the Communists—who were the most puritanical, who suppressed "sinful" behavior and homosexuals—

FALLACI: Yeah, the Nazi leaders, the hypocrites—how often they were homosexual! My God, damn it, what hypocrisy!

SCHEER: But one of the reasons *Playboy* and others oppose the Moral Majority in this country is that those people equate their version of moral behavior with the good of the state—and that has elements of, if not fascism, authoritarianism.

FALLACI: Ah, you are putting up *Playboy* as an opposition paper, eh?

SCHEER: Well, what do you think of the trend toward mixing puritanical religion and politics?

FALLACI: Maybe in America, not in Europe, thank God. Churches are empty. Don't pay attention to those who go to St. Peter's Square—they are tourists.

SCHEER: But if America is where social movements start, Europe will catch up sooner or later and you'll find a similar revival of religion in state affairs.

FALLACI: That's not possible. History never goes back. No, no, no, no!

SCHEER: History is going back in America today.

FALLACI: Well, we make fun of you. I mean, in a country where the President of the United States, whoever he is, every time he opens his mouth, he has to mention God—well, my God! I mean, not even the Pope does that. It will never happen in Europe.

You know, Italy, in particular, is a pagan country. They are not religious. Maybe about half believe in God, but our Popes never believed in God. They forgot about it. You want to know how this new Pope, Wojtyla, was elected? When the other one died, all the Italian cardinals, they got together and said, "Hey! Any of us around here believe in God? Eh, Guido, you believe in God? No! Luigi, *you* believe in God? No! You over there? No! Well, we still got two countries where they believe in God—Ireland and Poland. Try Ireland first. Telephone lines all busy? Ho-kay, try Poland. Hallo. Wojtyla—you believe in God? You do? *Benissimo,* you come down to Rome, be our new Pope." This is a true story, Fallaci tells it to you.

SCHEER: Good story. When did *you* stop believing in God?

FALLACI: When I was twelve. I had very mixed feelings. What I said was "I *don't* believe in God. Oh, my God! What will God do to me if He finds out I don't believe in Him?" That was my approach. But over the years, I find out it was sincere. I have the test that I don't believe in God. When I was covering the student riots in Mexico in 1968, I was badly wounded and had those three bullets in me—one here, one here, and one here—

SCHEER: In your back, your side, and your shoulder.

FALLACI: Yes, and I was losing blood, and I was fainting, not knowing if the fainting was death coming. I remember two things very clearly. I remember seeing my country house in Tuscany, which is very beautiful, like a Leonardo da Vinci panorama, and from my house you see these hills and mountains and the cypress . . . I saw all that. And I remember that I never thought of God. The concept didn't come to me, I didn't ask for help from God.

SCHEER: Did you come to these thoughts on your own?

FALLACI: I told you that half of Italy is pagan. In our house, our anticlericalism was so profound that our dog, each time the town church bells did ding dong, he got angry and was barking. Once, the priest came to our house to reproach us. He says, "No one is coming to church." My mother was ironing. She put the iron down hard on the board and she said, *"Priore*, don't come here to teach me life. Teach it to others. My family will always sow the good seed, because it is what it is. Good morning, *Priore."*

SCHEER: When you mentioned nearly dying, you seemed almost resigned, fatalistic.

FALLACI: I love life. I mean, life is all, the only point of reference. So I am in love with life . . . but I'm very tired. I am tired inside. And when you see me do these things, you say, "That woman, how full of life she is!" But it is a kind of show I do with myself to fight the fatigue I have inside.

It started in 1976 and 1977, when they both died—Alekos and my mother. It was traumatizing. Something happened in my soul. You know, when you break a leg, the doctor comes, he puts the plaster on the leg, people come to visit and put the signature on the cast and say, "Poor Oriana, does it hurt?" Or you have a toothache: "Poor Oriana, did you go to the dentist?" But if you say, "God, I'm sad, I'm so depressed," people go, "Ahh!" They do not take you seriously. So I always try to hide this broken leg of my soul, this broken teeth of my soul. Because people wouldn't understand.

But the more I have it, the more I live with it. And if you ask me, "What is the word you think most about during your days and nights?" I will say, "Death." Always. I calculate how many years, how many days remain to live for me. Twenty? Twenty-five? I say, "Eeeh, my God, they are few!" And the more I think, the more I adapt to it. If people do something nasty to me, I get very, very depressed. I'm very vulnerable. My vulnerability is equal to my strength, my so-called toughness, and when I'm down, I sometimes say,

"Let death happen." But not suicide. It would be necessary for me to die in a decent way, with dignity—*for* something.

SCHEER: It's interesting that you admit to vulnerability, because the thing most people would associate with you is arrogance—as you've said, you sometimes use that professionally.

FALLACI: Yes, people think that I'm arrogant in a certain way. It is not arrogance. It's being uneasy—and not shy. It's a matter of uneasiness and a kind of . . . fear. Professionally speaking, it is, yes, yes, yes: fear, fear, fear. And this comes from being alone. My mother used to describe me as a very severe child—severe and isolated. I never played with the others.

SCHEER: It's hard to imagine you as a carefree child.

FALLACI: I wonder if I ever was. There is a story about my doll which will tell you. The Fascists in Italy would sometimes give out dolls to the kids, etc. I brought my doll home and my mother said, "Ahhh! What's that? A Fascist doll?" And she threw it out the window. Years later, when I was sixteen, I became a reporter. With my first paycheck, I gave most of the money to my mother, because there was need, but I reserved a small amount for myself. And with this money, I went to buy a very large doll. When I got it home, I gave it to my mother, because it was too late for me. She remembered my first doll and cried, and kept it for a long time. Today it is in my country house, dressed in red velvet.

SCHEER: Every time you mention your background as a sixteen-year-old girl, competing equally with men both in your profession and in the Resistance, you seem to be emphasizing how hard you had to fight to prove yourself. Is it too trite to suggest that is a battle you're still waging?

FALLACI: Well, with the Resistance, in particular, yes, it was my first great adventure. It was accompanied by fear, but it was a noble adventure. So I have been brainwashed, conditioned to love adventure, which explains so many things—including my encounter with Alekos, because he was the symbol itself of adventure. Today I make an adventure out of everything. And my interviews, which were once great adventures, are no longer a professional challenge. Let's admit it once and forever: I am more dedicated to my writing than to the interviews, because they are so easy for me. I *know* already what makes the interview—I don't know if I should say, because someone will try, stupidly. I cannot really explain it, except to say that they go beyond the tape recorder—it's the *way* I conduct them. They are pieces of theater. I prepare the questions, but I follow the ideas that come. I build the suspense, and then I have *coups de scène*, do you understand? But they are very fatiguing. Do you believe that in some two-hour interviews I have lost weight? And, as I say today, they are no longer the adventure, the challenge.

SCHEER: You say your book writing is more important than your journalism. Do you still consider yourself a journalist?

FALLACI: This book [A *Man*] took me away from journalism. It's been a psychological withdrawal from journalism. When Alekos died, I had to decide whether to be a candidate for the Italian Senate or get this book out of me. I chose to write this book. But for all that I've said, I don't consider myself out of journalism. I very proudly still consider myself a journalist. I love it; it's the greatest work in the world.

But what began to disturb me was that the journalism I fell in love with at sixteen was no more around me. I used to practice journalism as I had been told it should be done, as my uncle did. Like the doctors, you know, in the movies, old country doctors with the horse and buggy who deliver the children and the calves and the young horses and fix broken arms—do you remember? They still existed, those doctors, and they worked all day and night. And that was journalism, as I recalled it. Dedication! But around me, I saw instead the journalist becoming more and more pompous, with hours of work like people in the bank, you know—not on weekends, please. They don't give a damn, because they must go to ski. The more they become lazy, the more pompous they become, the more arrogant they become toward the world. They grew up with TV. I'll get into that later.

SCHEER: What do you mean by arrogance?

FALLACI: It is their lack of political commitment, and here I mean especially in America. I'm going to be hated, but it's what I really believe. The lack of political commitment is compensated by a kind of arrogance, which is the arrogance of the policeman. Journalists, especially the TV ones, address people as executioners: "Here I come, and I'm going to show you what I do to you, who you are," because they have the power, they have this tremendous pull in their hands, and they cannot be controlled. The press should control the politician, yes, but who controls the press? The old question, see?

There is this form of arrogance, which was particularly born in this country, which I remembered because I experienced it the first time as a little girl working with a reporter at the daily paper in Florence. One day Anita Ekberg stops at the Grand Hotel with her new husband. She had got married that very morning. She still had the white dress of the marriage with one sleeve and the other arm bared, very beautiful, all this blond hair, very sexy, this tremendous bosom, etc. Immediately, they were surrounded by journalists, and there is one, a half-American, working for *Time* magazine in Florence— so imagine what a little correspondent *he* was—and he says, "When do you plan to get divorced?" She was married that morning! I froze. I felt like crying for her. I said to the correspondent, "Why did you dare? Why did you do it?" He said, "Because I am a journalist. I can put *any* question I want!"

That kind of arrogance extends to politics. I mean, it is extraordinary how, lacking ideas, journalists serve ideologies without questioning them or being aware of them. Ideally, a journalist, more than an astronaut, more than a judge, should be the perfect man or the perfect woman. We are more or less in the position of the judges and the policemen. So what detached me more and more was this disappointment with what the journalist has become to-day—a form of power; therefore, an abuse of power. We write so much about the abuse of power, and we are among those who commit most abuse of power. You understand what I mean?

SCHEER: I think you're exaggerating the power of the journalist, at least in this country. Because in certain situations—not necessarily the most impor-tant—if there's a sex scandal or some document comes out, yes, journalists can make life miserable for someone. But as far as power to raise serious questions that citizens have a right to examine, I don't see any great power of the press. Politicians can play off members of the press against each other— I'll give you the interview, I won't give it to you—and cut off press conferences at will. In this last election, you could go through a whole compaign with Ronald Reagan, and the press never really challenged this guy's view of the world.

FALLACI: Listen, I do not know if you suffered as much as I did, on the night of the debate between Carter and Reagan. I would have given a finger of my hand to be one of the persons who put the questions. I would have done so much! I was in Los Angeles for the promotion of the book. I prepared myself to watch TV as you prepare for the theater: I ordered the drinks, and I put them next to me, and I had my cigarettes, my lighter, everything was— like a child, very excited. I couldn't believe! I shouted, "Ask him *that*—no, no, look what he answered! Why don't you ask? Why don't you do it?" The only one who said something, believe it or not, was Barbara Walters, because she tried, she said something. But the others—nothing, nothing. That day, if I were a citizen, I would have grabbed them and screamed, "You traitors! You were there for me, to represent me, and you betrayed me, as a citizen, you bastards! You parasite of powers, you are worse than them! At least *they* risk—you risk *nothing!*" Journalists don't risk. At least the leaders risk! Not only their life, because once in a while they get shot, but their reputation, all the shit that is thrown on them, the accusations, nothing is forgiven to them. For Christ's sake! And the journalists—who do what? Nothing!

But I have something to say more about the journalists and politics in your country, if you permit me. I followed very closely this last election. It was the first time I spent all the time in this country. Before, either I was in Vietnam or somewhere, I could never follow. And I looked very well what happened this time. It seemed to me that the campaign was not really done by the politicians; it was done by the American TV. The most important guy in America in those days was not Reagan or Carter—it was Cronkite. My God! The night of the results, I saw something that was so repellent to my democratic sense I couldn't believe it: They started calling the elections when people were still voting! I shall never understand it. I told it to everybody in Italy. I told it to my father, he said, "Come on, it's not true. It's one of your American paradoxes." He still does not believe me. But besides that, do you remember the deference that Ford, Reagan, all of them, had toward Cronkite? "Yes, Walter, thank you, Walter, Walter, Walter." I *like* Cronkite as a person. I like Cronkite, I know him. I've interviewed him, he's cute, very nice, he's a very decent person. But I'd die to tell him today, "Listen, Walter, it was *unbearable* to see you that night, because you were the real President of the United States!" He stayed solemnly there on the throne of TV—because it's true, you have a monarchy in America. You have TV. An absolute, tyrant monarch. And I remember, poor Reagan, he was so modest. He had not understood very well what had happened to him, that he had been really elected, until Walter Cronkite called him. So it seems to me that you have a system where journalists, who should be the bridge between the citizens and the power, become more powerful than the powers.

SCHEER: As someone who has interviewed some of the world's most powerful men, who do you think has more power—the President of the United States or the head of the Soviet Union?

FALLACI: The President of the United States. In foreign affairs, he can make the decision all alone. In the Soviet Union, decisions are made by a group, a collective. I know that Brezhnev did not decide on the invasion of Afghanistan all alone. The President of France probably has more power than the President of the United States, among nonautocratic regimes. He has more power on paper; he can take *any* decision. He is King of France for seven years. But he is questioned more in France on foreign things than the American President is.

SCHEER: And how do you see Reagan wielding that power?

FALLACI: It is too early to tell about Reagan. He is determined, he has a few simple ideas. In Europe, we do not know how much knowledge he really has. But I think maybe he will be a parenthesis in our life, a stasis. He is determined, whereas Carter was intelligent, but I agree with Kissinger that determination is a better quality of leadership than intelligence that is undetermined.

SCHEER: And you're not worried in Europe about someone with a cowboy mentality having his finger on the nuclear trigger?

FALLACI: Well, I don't believe the Third World War will happen in the next three or four years. I think it *is* inevitable—Deng Xiaping said that to me and he is right. The Third World War will take place. But we can skip it now and go in peace for a few years more.

SCHEER: You say it matter-of-factly, almost cheerfully.

FALLACI: I'm infuriated! We are all infuriated in Europe, because we will be the first ones to die! Because when you do your fucking Third World War, I doubt very much you will do it at home. You or the Soviets. You probably will not have to throw the nuclear bomb. Do you know why? Because you don't need it. You are going to make the war on our heads with conventional arms. The war will take place in Europe. You are preparing the genocide of Europe! Nixon's book *The Third World War*, that's what's going to happen. You are *already* making the war—by proxy! China and the Soviets are already fighting by proxy in Southeast Asia, and aren't your puppets fighting your war elsewhere—in the Middle East, in El Salvador? It's already there, the proxy wars, and the big war will burst in Europe. Darn right. Of course I'm angry. You ask if I'm cheerful. For Christ's sake!

SCHEER: Let's return to your critique of the American press. What do you know about the American media, anyway?

FALLACI: American journalism was one of my first loves, because it was an aspect of my falling in love with America. America was to me what Paris was to my parents. But I mistook the quality of the paper for the substance of American journalism—really. We came out of the war and didn't have this heavy, shiny paper and those marvelous photos—*Life* magazine, etc. But as for substance, *mamma mia!*

Today, domestically, perhaps, journalism in America is good. But on the international scene, it's more complicated, and American journalists don't have a very deep political culture. My impression is that American correspondents reporting from foreign countries know very little and understand even less. Usually they don't know the language. Why? Because of the imperialism, the arrogance of the English language: You go everywhere and everybody speaks English; why learn other languages? Well, I can at least say the U.S. journalist is not lazy. The Italian journalist abroad *is* very lazy. He usually copies the major daily papers, makes a summary, and that's it. Yes, he speaks the language because he has to read the newspapers and steal from them. The same goes for other European journalists.

SCHEER: What about journalism in Europe?

FALLACI: In France, with the exception of *Le Monde*—in spite of its pompousness and hypocrisy; it's easy to play the progressive abroad—the newspapers are the worst. As to English journalism, it would be stupid to ignore what *The* (London) *Times* has meant in the history of journalism. But the majority of English papers are shit. The most provincial of the whole world. You open the *Daily Express*, the *Daily Mail* and you see what there is. Nothing but stupidities about the royal family and that ridiculous wedding of Charles.

SCHEER: You're not much on royal weddings, is that it?

FALLACI: The horse who marries the blond girl? Who gives a damn if he gets married or not? Let me say I am not very sympathetic toward that family. I have nothing to say about the mother of the young horse, poor woman, but I have something to say of the father. When I was wounded in Mexico and I was in the hospital with three bullets in my body, Prince Philip was there, too, visiting. He was asked by a reporter what he thought about Fallaci being wounded in the riots. His answer was "What was she doing there?" So a reporter came to me in the hospital for an answer to Prince Philip's question, What was I doing in Mexico? I said to the reporter, "Tell Prince Philip that I was doing what he has never done in his life—working!"

SCHEER: Getting back to European journalism as compared with American journalism—

FALLACI: Yes, I was getting there. You must admit that in spite of this, *The* (London) *Times, Der Spiegel, Le Monde,* and several Italian papers are very well done. And in general, I would say the European press is better prepared to tell you the things of the world; the American press will give you abundance of information, of particulars, but never the full interpretation. At least in Europe, where newspapers have acknowledged political views, you know what you're reading.

SCHEER: Why should grinding an ideological ax be superior to trying to present the news factually?

FALLACI: If you insist on facts, then I insist that the choosing of facts is an opinion. I cannot imagine anything more arrogant than *The New York Times* motto, "All the news that's fit to print." Who decides what's fit to print? Who? There is much hypocrisy in this motto of the *Times,* and I don't buy it. I also say, if *The New York Times* is so proud of its objective stories and interviews, then why do they publish me and want me so much? For instance, they publish my interviews, which are the most opinionated on earth. Someday they will have to explain it to me.

SCHEER: You touched briefly on television journalism, which is, after all, where most people in this country get their news. Many people compare you to CBS correspondent Mike Wallace, since you're both known as tough interviewers. What's your response?

FALLACI: Ridiculous. I'm a *writer* who does journalism. In no case can you compare me to a person who *performs* journalism for TV. Oh, he might write the *Divine Comedy* tomorrow, but—

SCHEER: You're talking about Mike Wallace, right?

FALLACI: I'm not going to pronounce his name, not if you torture me, not even if you kill me!

SCHEER: Yes, well, why not?

FALLACI: He did an ugly thing and I'll tell you what it was. After Kissinger devoted two pages of his memoirs to my interview, admitting he had done it out of vanity but saying that he was quoted out of context, since I had never played the tape for anybody, I got infuriated. *Time* magazine published the Kissinger excerpts, so I wrote them a letter saying that someone *had* heard the tape—meaning Mike Wallace. *Time* then got an answer from Mike Wallace, in which he admitted he'd heard the tape but the tape was "fuzzy." What fuzzy? If he wanted to get Kissinger on 6o *Minutes* and be the servant of Kissinger, he's going to say a lie like this? The tape was far from fuzzy. He heard it when he was interviewing *me* for 6o *Minutes*. They showed a photo of me—it looked like a 123-year-old woman; I don't know where they got that ugly photo! For that show, Mike Wallace asked to hear the Kissinger tape, then tried to fool me by putting a microphone on after promising not to use it. I interrupted everything and said, "Out! Out!"—it was terrible. But, in any case, when he did hear it, Mike Wallace was very excited and danced around the room, saying, "Oh, oh! If I didn't hear that, I would never believe it!" Fuzzy tape!

SCHEER: Getting back to television journalism in general . . .

FALLACI: A TV journalist, first of all, he has to be a showman. Because TV is made of images—you watch more than you listen, and even when you listen, you are distracted by the image, which isn't even static, it is in movement, and the more movement the better. So TV can give the headlines. If I want to know if the Pope has been shot, I open the TV. But if I want to know *how* it happened, who did it and why, I've got to read the written page, damn it!

I would also say, though, if I wanted to work for television as a journalist, which I love for its images and its immediacy, I would be a cameraman. On TV, the real journalist is the cameraman, who writes through images, who chooses who and what to point the camera at.

SCHEER: A familiar complaint from TV journalists is that they can't cover a story after a while because they're too well known. What about your own fame?

FALLACI: Yes, it is a problem. In my interview with Walesa, I arrived in Poland a week before the meeting and a girl at the airport recognized me— then the TV got the news and there were photographers at my next stop. I was desperate because a photo would appear so far ahead of my first meeting with Walesa—the secrecy was gone.

SCHEER: But you say that with a lot of pride in your voice, even vanity.

FALLACI: Pride yes, vanity no. Very proud I am. I complain because to do this work you should be a transparent fly, and I am not that fly. I make news when I arrive. You have to admit it, sometimes it's the encounter of two celebrities, these interviews. But much as it disturbs me, I would be a hypocrite to say that I cry from despair. It is the result of a life of work.

SCHEER: But is it hurting your journalism?

FALLACI: It *is* hurting my journalism. Sooner or later, people recognize me, and not just in Italy or France or England or America, but in other countries, from Poland to Iran, from South America to Asia.

SCHEER: And it's not as if you haven't courted the fame. You speak at colleges, give interviews, you go on TV talk shows . . .

FALLACI: Yes, but don't forget the TV and the university offers come because I was *already* a celebrity . . . All right, I buy what you say for TV, but not for universities; that's not right. When I went to Yale—and now you can claim that I say it with satisfaction; okay, sure, damn it, yes! Ask anybody in Yale—I had crowds five or ten times as big as other people. The students didn't see me on TV; they had read my books, yes sir! I'm very proud of it, yes, yes, yes! The only degree that I have, I got here in America, and I never even finished the university.

SCHEER: Pride aside, how has fame—and success—settled on you?

FALLACI: I am totally incapable of dealing with success. It has been agonizing for me. I have never identified with stories of poor people from small villages who made it to New York or Paris—because I never said I wanted it. I was not even aware of the fame or success for a long time. I was traveling around the world, working. And then people began to stop me and say, "Are you a relative of *the* Fallaci?" And lately, *mamma mia!* In any city, I never make less than seven or eight hundred people for a speech; it's unbelievable. In Yugoslavia, they had to close the doors to the theater—and the screaming outside! The same in Helsinki. I remember a doctor from Fort Lauderdale coming to me to say, "Do you know why we love you?" And these were his words: "You are possibly the most famous Italian we have now in America"— which is doubtful, because Sophia Loren is that—"because we don't believe in anybody anymore. You have such credibility!" Now, you must admit that is the most beautiful compliment you can receive. Another time, an old concierge in France said, "Oriana, do you know why we love you? Because you have been teaching us courage." Oh, *mamma mia!* If I think of all the times in my life when I was scared to death—and he tells me I have been teaching courage. I felt guilty and confused.

SCHEER: Let's get back to your most recent book, *A Man*. You say it's your most important work, that it contains what you believe about power and courage and what an individual must do with his life. Why does discussing it get you so emotional?

FALLACI: The book haunts me. I have resurrected a dead man, and now he doesn't want to die anymore. My life is B.C. and A.D.—like before Christ and after—only it has to do with before and after this book which obsesses me. When I became known as a reporter and was traveling around the world and began to earn a little money, I began to feel like the Queen of England. It detached me from my political roots. I had been in Vietnam, in Cambodia, in Pakistan, reporting on wars and riots—and I had enough. *Basta!* I was fed up. Men are shit, they are garbage, they are bastards. What's the use? Then I met Alekos and it woke me up. He brought me back to political consciousness. And his death crystallized the message I tried to describe in the book: individual responsibility. It's the only answer. Ignore what the crowds say; if everybody is saying yes, you must say no. You are alone, okay. Tomorrow you will be two, then four and five and six. The one political message I have is the fight against indifference.

SCHEER: That message may be clear enough when there's a dictatorship, as there was in Greece, or a totalitarian state, as there is in Russia—

FALLACI: What I say about Russia is that for all we hear about solitary dissidents, they are such a tiny minority. There has been a dictatorship there for so long, with so little real resistance, you must ask yourself how much sympathy you can have for the Russian masses. Maybe they deserve what they have.

You know, I am reminded of the one interview I thought I won—but I was knocked out at the very last moment. I had interrogated [former CIA director] William Colby, putting to him some very hard questions. Just before we left the ring, I went down, because he said one very simple thing to me: Go speak with the head of the KGB and treat him as you have treated me. And he was right. No one resists, because there is no one there to confront.

SCHEER: This message of yours, about individual responsibility and the struggle against indifference is obvious enough in dictatorships, but how does it apply to a democracy?

FALLACI: As Alekos said, we are four billion people on this planet. If all those billions but one are oppressing one person, then we are all Fascists. In America, you are obsessive about individualism—thank God. All your epics— the epic of the cowboy, of the pioneers—all have to do with individuals, and it is charming. But when it comes to politics, to the participation of the citizen in politics, the individual is crushed. He can talk, he can write, he can even vote—but he does not participate in basic decisions.

SCHEER: So you dismiss town meetings, ringing doorbells for candidates, organizing to defeat or elect people? That's a pretty broad brush you're using to dismiss—

FALLACI: I was not dismissing. I was only speaking of the dramatic imperfections of democracy, and I agree with Churchill, who said democracy was lousy but we having nothing better. Remember in my book that it is Alekos who cries in front of the Acropolis, "Give me a bad democracy, a sick democracy, but democracy!" The only thing I would like is a democracy which is not bad or sick.

SCHEER: That takes us back to the problem we had earlier. When you admit that your hero, Alekos, in resisting dictatorship as an individual, considered taking hostages and blowing up the Acropolis, I have to ask you again: Is that moral? Is it correct?

FALLACI: Okay, you go back to that. Okay, I accept it, I let you go back. You are obsessed by it.

SCHEER: Because it goes to the heart of your beliefs, because it touches on courage and responsibility and terrorism—

FALLACI: I am not the one who wanted to take hostages. I tried to dissuade Alekos until I gave up and said, okay, let's try. But I *knew* he wouldn't do it! I have to admit that since this interview began, I have found other American readers who have asked about the same point. And if you have not understood, it is my fault. It is the fault of the author—the author of a *novel*, I remind you. I exaggerated a minor thing, perhaps, and it was much more in his imagination than I tell in the book. It was crazy, it could not happen.

SCHEER: He was trying a bluff, in other words.

FALLACI: Yes, a bluff. I mean, he did have this quality, which is a very dangerous quality, of being a leader who can lead by the force of charisma, who can make other people follow him—

SCHEER: All right, so for three weeks since we started this interview, *that* was the statement you didn't want to make.

FALLACI: Because you didn't let me talk.

SCHEER: Come on, Oriana, it's a hard thing to admit. You tried to give moral and political reasons why men like Alekos should be admired and followed, and it all comes down to the fact that certain people can have a dangerous seduction over the rest of us—yourself included—and sweep us up in actions that may, in fact, be crazy or immoral.

FALLACI: But I don't buy your word "immoral." Whether history recognizes them or not, yes, there are certain people who deserve to be followed. In Alekos's case, it never led to crazy things—that was just a fantasy—but there *are* occasions when violence is justified. Tyrants must be killed. But why must you persecute me for this? I remember when I did a story about the astronauts, I took a battery of intelligence tests and they were exhausting, they give me headaches. This is what you are doing to me. This is what you do with your fucking interview.

SCHEER: Poor Oriana, you never did this to anyone, right? What are your interviews if not a test of intelligence?

FALLACI: They're a test of force.

SCHEER: Now we're back on the topic of force, of power. It's interesting how much that term obsesses *you*. You dedicated your collection of interviews to your mother and to "all those who do not like power." In that collection, published in 1974, you wrote: "I see power as an inhuman and hateful phenomenon." Do you still?

FALLACI: That was written in 1973 and we are in 1981. Thank God, an intelligent person does not remain attached to something without thinking about it. A person moves, changes, that's life. Only the dogmatic—the Communists, the Catholics—would repeat the same thing eight years later. While I was waiting for this last interview session to begin, I was looking at *your* collection of interviews [*The Playboy Interview*] and I read what Bertrand Russell had to say: "Contrary to the customary pattern, I have gradually become more and more of a rebel as I have grown older." Well, for once in my life, I belong to the majority, to the "customary pattern." In aging, I became wiser rather than more radical. By wiser, I mean seeing things more rationally, more coldly.

So eight years from now, I don't know what I'd say—I might be a dictator in eight years—but in 1981, I would have to define power as an inevitable curse. Why inevitable? Because when you put together a community, as small or as large as it may be, it needs to be organized to survive. And to organize, the community needs to delegate power to someone. Sometimes people take the power, which is the essence of dictatorship. Sometimes they are given the power, which is the essence of democracy. Now, we don't even discuss dictatorship—we disqualify it. But to discuss the best situation, if there are twenty of us in the community, surviving together in a cave, we have to organize against the dinosaurs, provide ourselves with warmth and food. So we organize and say, "You go get the water, you tend the fire, you make the shoes, and you, over there, you make children . . ." I don't like very much that one has to make children, but one has to, right? Because once she makes the children, she has to give milk. And when she gives milk, she cannot do other things. So I will be the one who makes the *shoes*.

Anyway, so the cave must have a coordinator. That means the coordinator is the power, and once you admit that, you admit that power is a necessary curse. When the use of power is not only legitimate but reasonable, then you have to accept that power. But you also realize that the moment he rules the other nineteen people, without wanting to oppress them, he oppresses them all the same. Why? Because if he says that the rule is no one leaves the cave after 5 p.m., because otherwise the dinosaur eats you, he's right, because he protects my life.

But wait! I am Oriana. I am hysterical, I am an anarchist, I want to go out and see the stars! So when they stop me on my way out of the cave, I suffer and feel oppressed. I curse the coordinator. I say, "If the dinosaur eats me, that's my problem!" Then he says the terrible thing: "Oriana, you are not master of your life. You belong to this community, you make our shoes, we *need* your fucking shoes and can't afford the luxury of having you eaten by the dinosaur!" So I am admitting that freedom doesn't exist to begin with and that, to a certain extent, oppression is a necessity for the community. *Someone* has to be oppressed.

SCHEER: That's quite a change from the angry, shouting, anarchistic Oriana Fallaci of ten years ago. It makes one think you would be more tolerant of Kissinger today—

FALLACI: Yes, I am much more tolerant in 1981 of all the Kissingers—plural—than I was ten years ago.

SCHEER: Having admitted that, would it tend to make you less of an adversarial journalist if you had to interview those same people again?

FALLACI: No, it would make a more relaxed journalist.

SCHEER: And would it rob you of some of the passion and drama with which you confront people?

FALLACI: Yes, and for the better. Less dramatic and less theatrical but, in my opinion, better.

SCHEER: Nobody would guess it from this interview, but it almost sounds as if you're saying you've lost some of your fire—at least as far as journalism goes. That new tolerance of yours for power—

FALLACI: Eh, wait! All I said was "I *understand* you, Mr. Power. But I'm going out of the cave anyway, to look at the stars. To hell with you!"

SCHEER: That seems a good place to finish. Anything you want to add?

FALLACI: Yes, I would like to cancel what I said earlier about homosexuals. I'm sorry I touched that subject. When you talk hours and hours like this, you always make mistakes. Wipe it out, please.

SCHEER: Hold it. Here we have Oriana Fallaci, who has published comments from the high and the powerful they wish *they* could retract, asking us to erase something *she* said.

FALLACI: Because it makes me sound illiberal, and God knows I'm not.

SCHEER: We can't tailor the questions or the answers to what makes you sound liberal. The fact is, it's an issue in your life—you mentioned it prominently in your Arafat interview—

FALLACI: Because I just mentioned it! I touched on it! If you insist on publishing it, you are making a tyrannical, Fascist act!

SCHEER: It wouldn't be tyrannical; it would just be poor journalism not to publish it, something you'd never allow yourself. Besides, you didn't just touch on it—you expressed a series of opinions about male and female homosexuals.

FALLACI: Do you want this interview to educate people to intolerance, to lack of liberalism? In your magazine, you teach people to be more free, toward themselves and toward others. Why do you want to make propaganda for the other side?

SCHEER: Propaganda? Why? Because it turns out that Oriana Fallaci may be less than a perfect, 100 percent liberal?

FALLACI: I think of my homosexual friends. I'm ashamed of having said it. I think you shouldn't publish what I said, because if you publish one of my mistakes, you encourage the oppressors. Oriana is not perfect, no! She is the less perfect being on this earth. But I am a political animal. Oriana is a character, a personage, and she should not encourage intolerance. It is not I who will suffer; it is they, the homosexuals. And they are innocent.

SCHEER: Don't overreact. Confessing to a personal distaste, a chink in your armor, won't necessarily unleash the oppression you fear. You, of all people, shouldn't be involved in retracting statements.

FALLACI: So you will not erase it?

SCHEER: No.

FALLACI: *Mamma mia*, I tried. [*Shrugs*] Maybe it will be my Kissinger-cowboy statement. You got it from me, you got it! [*Laughter*] Well, it took you twenty hours to do it with me. It took me only an hour with Kissinger. So I still win, okay?

Now let's go out and have a good Italian meal.

(Playboy, November 1981)

THINKING
TUNA FISH,
TALKING
DEATH

※ ※ ※

Thinking Tuna Fish,
Talking Death:
Inside the Nuclear Establishment

I don't want to startle you but they are going to kill most of us.
—Kenneth Patchen

When the iconoclastic Beat poet wrote those lines back in the 1950s, it was largely in response to the new breed of nuclear strategists—on both sides of the Cold War—who had made a profession out of talking about nuclear deterrence and global death. In this country they were most notably represented by Herman Kahn, then of the Santa Monica-based Rand Corporation, whose book *On Thermonuclear War* argued that such a conflict was not only likely but also survivable and, indeed, winnable. Many of the scientists who had worked on the atomic bomb had been shattered by the implications of the destructive power they had unleashed. Their concern was summarized by Albert Einstein when he wrote: "The splitting of the atom has changed everything save our mode of thinking and thus we drift toward unparalleled catastrophe." But others, who styled themselves "new realists" (sociologist C. Wright Mills labeled them "crackpot realists"), insisted that nuclear weapons sooner or later would be used and that the nation ought to plan for that eventuality.

During the ensuing decades of great power negotiations and détente, Americans have been able to console themselves with the unfounded assumption that people no longer talk that way. But they do. Indeed, for some time now the "realists" have been gaining influence. The distance in time from the original Hiroshima blast, détente's failure to halt the nuclear-arms race, and the growing sophistication of the weapons themselves have contributed to a national mood in which thinking the unthinkable has become almost fashionable.

That's the way it was at a luncheon picnic held recently behind barbed wire and in the shadow of the Lawrence Livermore National Laboratory. The barbed wire was necessitated by the fact that Livermore, a division of the University of California, is, along with its sister lab in Los Alamos, New

Mexico, the main developer of America's nuclear weapons. The picnic was necessitated by the fact that even those who invent and deploy nuclear weapons must eat. The outdoor luncheon was an interlude in a conference on arms limitation. However, participants with close ties to the Reagan Administration soon made it clear that the topic was, for the near future, academic. Members of what has come to be known as the arms-control community—the people who gave us the Strategic Arms Limitation Treaties (SALT)—went about with long faces and gave sad speeches expressing a waning hope that the President, who had campaigned against the treaty they had helped negotiate and which they still fervently support, might yet endorse its ratification. Those close to the President acted as if they knew better, and talked instead of rapid increases in military spending as the surest path to safety in a nuclear world.

There was no mistaking the changing of the guard. The fifteen-year-old national consensus that accepted détente with the Soviets and the pressing importance of strategic-arms-limitation negotiations has been rudely shattered. Today's policymakers dismiss fears of an unbridled arms race as naïvely playing into the Russians' hands by holding back America's development of strategic weaponry. There is a sense, as the President stated recently, that critics of new weapons systems are, perhaps unwittingly, serving the needs of Soviet propaganda. In the current climate it is increasingly assumed that nuclear weapons may have to be used and that, when they are, they can be used in a limited and winning way.

At one of the Livermore picnic tables, former Secretary of the Navy Paul H. Nitze, who has since been appointed chief U.S. negotiator for theater nuclear force reductions, said that he thought "there could be serious arms-control negotiations, but only after we have built up our forces—in ten years." Nitze, who led the opposition to ratification of SALT II, uttered this prediction with the aplomb of one who, like the President himself, places his faith in hardware rather than treaties.

Cooled by a gentle breeze, the other picnickers sat munching tuna-fish sandwiches, as two fellows across the table from Nitze began making small talk, suggesting that a "city busting" nuclear strike on San Francisco might not devastate some surrounding areas—if the wind factor was right. But on that particular day, with its breeze, it seemed that Livermore might have gotten just a whiff of radiation from such a strike. City busting is intended to inflict millions of civilian deaths as opposed to "silo busting," in which enemy missile installations are the intended target. Some military strategists argue that it is not possible to engage in a nuclear strike against military targets without also hitting 100 million civilians. Those who think that nuclear war is fightable argue that the casualties could be kept down to a mere ten million. If the Soviets hit Livermore, for example, there would be substantial casualties in the San Francisco Bay area, but fewer than if San Francisco were the target. Livermore could be sacrificed and the war kept limited. Later in the conference, Herman Kahn would argue that a nuclear war could be contained even if a few major cities like San Francisco were sacrificed in what he termed a "city strip."

Nitze ignored the conversation on the other side of the table and concentrated instead on explaining how, as an experienced conference-goer, he alone had managed to acquire hot food while the rest of the participants were stuck with tuna. Nitze, now seventy-four, remains a dark, thin, intense fellow who seems wound up and competitive even when discussing lunch. But the matter of tuna fish provided a welcome relief from more grisly topics that in his circle have been overdiscussed and seem to lead nowhere.

In fact, the debate about waging war and peace in the nuclear age is most often restricted to the few who have mastered the arcane terminology of strategic weaponry. It's an interchangeable group of scientists, military men, and lawyers who move easily between stints at the Defense and State Departments, university think tanks, and the corporate defense contractors. At the Livermore conference, some were doves, but most leaned toward a more hawkish technocratic stance, perhaps reflecting the preferences of the bomb inventors who had handed out the invitations. But hawks or doves, they shared a common language and indeed a small, closed universe in which there is mutual understanding, though not often agreement. They spoke largely in the language of acronyms—MIRVs and MPSs and FERMs— harmless-sounding things that usually cost millions, if not billions, to make and which can kill millions, if not billions. At Livermore, the sponsors were considerate enough to provide a glossary of acronyms. One learned, for example, that a FERM is a "fast escape recoverable missile," which doesn't help much unless parentheses are added (ICBM-carrying airplane).

Soviet nuclear planners share this common language. Through twenty-five years of arms-limitation talks, the nuclear thinkers on both sides have spent many hours together and anecdotes abound of humorous toasts and tales of overindulgence at cocktail parties, as well as of hard bargaining. It is an oddly symbiotic relationship in which both sides must continually remind themselves of the bestial and aggressive motives they attribute to their counterparts across the table. On the other hand, they know that those who have attempted to negotiate arms limitations are by no means the most ghoulishly irrational or militant representatives of the opposing side. The problem with nuclear strategists is not, for the most part, one of a cold-blooded Strangeloveian eagerness to fight a nuclear war, but simply the occupational hazard of coming to accept insane calculations as normal. At the Livermore conference, this point was made one night at the Holiday Inn bar by the lab's former head of weapons testing, Gerald Johnson, the man who had set off more nuclear bombs than anyone else—fifty in all. Johnson, now with TRW, the huge missile contractor, was speaking over the din of the happy revelers attending the conference when he said: "The problem with discussions about nuclear war and arms limitations is that they are conducted without any feeling about what these bombs do."

That was the case during most of the Livermore meeting, where the participants seemed altogether too at ease with their bizarre subject matter, overly familiar with one another, and bored with their longstanding disputes. Bored, that is, until Herman Kahn inadvertently reminded one and all that the subject of their academic specialty is mass death. Kahn cheerfully told the conference audience that progress in SALT talks didn't matter very much because his Hudson Institute's projections of life in the twenty-first century showed it looking pretty good "even without arms control." He was doing fine with the one-liners and color slides that have made him a prized speaker on the military-industrial-complex lecture circuit. But he lost the audience when he predicted that a nuclear war would cease after Leningrad had been eradicated in retaliation for the Soviet elimination of New York City. Suddenly even the Livermore crowd was shocked by the glibness of it all. They had been talking about "taking out targets," and here was the 300-pound Kahn chortling happily over the destruction of real cities—places they had visited.

Perhaps it would have been less shocking if Kahn had limited his "targets of opportunity" to forlorn rural spots—the heartland where U.S. missiles are stored. The dialogue that ensued between the speaker and his audience of strategic thinkers provides some insight into what their field is all about.

QUESTION: I'm very uncomfortable with the idea of the eye-for-the-eye nuclear response, and I'm sure I'm not the only one. How are you going to overcome that revulsion of people thinking about that?

KAHN: Let me try the audience out, okay? Let's assume that the President was informed that New York City was destroyed by a five-megaton bomb, about thirty seconds ago. What's he going to do? He gets Brezhnev on the phone and Brezhnev says, "We did it deliberately, the Romanians push us around, the Afghans push us around, we got tired. After this event ain't no one going to push us around. As far as we're concerned the matter is closed." [*Laughter*] How many think the issue is closed? No, you're going to retaliate in some way. Now, you're not going to retaliate against his forces, because you don't have that ability. What do you think you're going to do? Leningrad— you're absolutely correct. Now let's say you're dumb and you took out Moscow. You'd get back a call, "Look, when we hit New York we knew Leningrad was going to disappear. Don't you read your own theories? What's the idea of hitting Moscow? It's more important than Chicago, Washington, and New York put together. We can't let you get away with it." There goes Philadelphia. [*Laughter*]) All right, what's next? It's even. Odds are rather high you'd quit at that point.

He then asked if the members of the audience would be in favor of striking back at the Soviets with an all-out attack if they knew that the entire American population would surely die in the Soviet counterstrike.

Walter Slocombe, former Deputy Under Secretary of Defense in the Carter Administration, criticized this hypothesis as "analytically a complete waste of time." Slocombe, a tweedy, George Will look-alike and former editor of the *Harvard Law Review* who is currently a Washington tax attorney, said he thought the President would not order an all-out attack but instead would "get the Air Force to target five cities." His point—one currently inscribed in official U.S. policy—was that the war could keep escalating on a limited tit-for-tat basis.

Kahn was gracious in defeat, conceding, "I think you've got the right solution. You hit five cities." Kahn then said that in 1960 he had asked the same question of a group of American leaders: "There were four congressmen present. They all said that the American President would press the button, and that they would press it, too. They happened to be Gerald Ford, Melvin Laird, Bourke Hickenlooper, and Henry Jackson. Two of them (Ford as President, Laird as Secretary of Defense) later had responsibility for this thing. That killed my briefing, because I couldn't make my next point, which was that if the President wasn't under drugs he wouldn't do it. Here were four congressmen who said they would press the button . . . to do what you [Slocombe] suggest, you do a city strip." That settled, Kahn soon tired of the subject and announced that he had "a sense of *déjà vu* about conferences like this with the same people arguing all the same old questions."

Kahn's point was well taken, for the setting for this exchange might just as easily have been the Carnegie Endowment for International Peace building in Washington, the Rand Corporation in Santa Monica, or any of the other watering holes in between where the small band of strategic thinkers work or periodically gather to compare notes on a subject that evidently bores the rest of us. Such gatherings of the nuclear initiates—those who pride themselves on thinking the unthinkable—have been occurring regularly since the first atomic bomb was dropped on Hiroshima. Given that in the event of war many of the scientist-diplomat participants have security passes to highly fortified shelters, it is likely that such conferences will continue up until the last bomb has fallen.

Concern about the horrors of nuclear war is not easily sustained and often seems like a 1950s issue. Thirty-five years have passed since Hiroshima, and attempting to comprehend nuclear war without experiencing it may have numbed us to its consequences. The Hiroshima explosion was caused by a primitive uranium bomb and yet managed to kill more than 75,000 people and injure another 100,000 out of a total population of 245,000. The collective power of the current world arsenal of nuclear weapons is more than one million times that of the bomb exploded in Hiroshima. The mathematics of misery implicit in these figures are not difficult to calculate.

Yet even at the conferences and think tanks of those who are paid to think about nuclear war, it is difficult to fully grasp its implications. Shortly before the Livermore conference, during a pleasant trip across the campus-like quad of the Rand Corporation a reporter was warned, almost surreptitiously, about the quicksand of strategic thinking. For days, the reporter's interviews at Rand had dealt with the macabre details of the comparative nuclear destructive capability of both superpowers—sort of a crash course in comparative death. On the way to lunch, Rand consultant Konrad Kellen, a refugee from Hitler's Germany and former associate of novelist Thomas Mann, started talking like the sane inmate in a lunatic asylum: "Don't let them get you sucked into this megatonnage and throw-weight business," he warned, "or you'll be lost and never be able to get back to what's important—which is that life as we know it could easily be destroyed over stupidities."

(*Los Angeles Times*, October 4, 1981)

With Enough Shovels

Ronald Reagan and George Bush had been in office less than a year when they approved a secret plan to provide the United States with the capability to win a protracted nuclear war. This plan, outlined in a so-called National Security Decision Document (NSDD), committed the United States, for the first time, to the idea that a nuclear war could be won—an idea that was first granted official respectability by Bush during his reign as director of the CIA.

"Nuke war," as Louis O. Giuffrida, whom Reagan had named head of the Federal Emergency Management Agency (FEMA), calls it, has come to be discussed not only as a war that can be won but as a war consistent with the preservation of civilization. "It would be a terrible mess, but it wouldn't be unmanageable," Giuffrida told ABC News. Or, as his assistant in charge of the civil-defense program, William Chipman, put it, when I asked him if democracy and other U.S. institutions would survive all-out nuclear war with the Soviet Union: "I think they would eventually, yeah. As I say, the ants eventually build another anthill."

The idea that "nuke war" is survivable begins with the assertion that an effective civil defense is possible. Proponents of this view in the Reagan Administration claim that civil defense can protect the Russian population and, therefore, that Soviet military planners think they can survive and win a nuclear war. According to Reagan and his people, this confidence is one important reason for the Soviet military build-up and for our own urgent need to close the "window of vulnerability"—Reagan's phrase to describe the presumed vulnerability of the United States to a Soviet first strike. Ergo, the renewed interest in America's civil defense, massive military spending, and new Pentagon plans for waging a protracted nuclear war—what Reagan calls "the rearming of America."

That attitude results in part from the growing sophistication of nuclear weapons in the arsenals of both superpowers: weapons that can do more than destroy heavily populated areas; weapons whose control and accuracy are, theoretically, so refined that they tempt their makers to think they can be detonated not only as weapons of genocide or countergenocide but as if they were conventional weapons, to take out selected enemy targets in a war that would be fought on a limited or, at least, a less than catastrophic basis. In other words, a war with winners as well as losers.

Combined with this view is the idea that détente has not served us well, that the Soviets have not accepted its terms but have, in fact, gained nuclear superiority. This argument was advanced by President Reagan, despite substantial disagreement among experienced people who had studied the question, as one justification for his $1.6 trillion five-year military program.

Whatever its inherent defects, as long as we lived in the era of détente, with its seemingly endless arms-control negotiations and other complex dealings between the superpowers, most Americans found it relatively easy to avoid thinking about nuclear annihilation. There was comfort in the knowledge that somewhere in the midst of the interminable SALT talks, our respective leaders were trying to cut whatever deal was possible in the interest of their, and our, survival. One assumption of the détente period was that no matter how awful the other fellow might be, he still didn't want to commit nuclear suicide; the instinct for self-preservation would win out over nationalist and ideological obsessions.

The notion that nuclear war means mutual suicide had for years been a basis of détente and arms-control negotiations. It became obvious, however, as Reagan installed his people in high places, that all this had changed as many of the highly vociferous critics of détente and arms control moved into positions of authority in Washington, and attempts to live with the Soviets became more scorned than honored.

As we shall see, a Cold War cabal of unreconstructed hawks and neo-hawks who had never been fully at ease with the arms-control efforts of the Nixon, Ford, and Carter Administrations suddenly came into its own. The members of this group categorically reject peaceful coexistence with the Soviet Union as that country is now constituted. They seek instead—through confrontation, through the use of political and economic pressure, and through the threat of military weapons—to alter radically the nature of Soviet society. They assume, as Reagan has stated, that "the Soviet Union underlies all the unrest that is going on. If they weren't engaged in this game of dominoes, there wouldn't be any hot spots in the world." Convinced that the nuclear-arms race is dangerous not in itself but only if the Soviets gain "superiority," they have shifted the emphasis of American foreign policy from the avoidance of nuclear war to the preparation for its possible outbreak.

If the extent to which this change occurred went widely unremarked at first, it was not because these men were secretive about their beliefs. As Eugene V. Rostow, Reagan's Director of the Arms Control and Disarmament Agency, had written before being selected for this important post: "We are living in a prewar and not a postwar world." Other statements by officials of the Reagan government have been just as direct. For example, we are now committed to what Deputy Secretary of Defense Frank Carlucci III, in his Senate confirmation hearing, called a "nuclear-war-fighting capability," a position that presupposes that nuclear war can be kept limited, survivable, and winnable.

In 1981, Secretary of Defense Caspar Weinberger told the House Budget Committee that the Reagan Administration would expand the U.S. capability "for deterring or *prosecuting* [italics mine] a global war with the Soviet Union." Halfway through Reagan's first year in office, Weinberger presented the President with a defense-spending plan by which the United States could gain nuclear superiority over the Soviet Union within this decade. The goal, according to senior Pentagon officials, was to build a capacity to fight nuclear wars ranging from a limited strike to an all-out exchange.

One of those who helped shape Reagan's war-fighting views was former Harvard historian Richard Pipes. In 1978, before he was appointed the senior Soviet specialist on Reagan's National Security Council staff, Pipes criticized the nuclear-war plans of previous Administrations, both Republican and Democratic, because "deeply embedded in all our plans is the notion of punishing the aggressor rather than defeating him." Or, as Secretary of Energy James B. Edwards put it, in a nuclear war, "I want to come out of it number one, not number two."

In a telephone interview with me in the fall of 1981, Charles Kupperman, a Reagan appointee to the Arms Control and Disarmament Agency, said that "it is possible for any society to survive" a nuclear war. He added that "nuclear war is a destructive thing but still in large part a physics problem."

Reagan's first year was continually marked by such comments about waging nuclear war in some form or other. The President himself claimed that it would be possible to keep a nuclear war on the European continent limited to a tactical exchange, thereby making Western Europeans more nervous than they had been in some time.

When word of the Administration's stance toward nuclear war began to emerge, it caused a powerful sense of alarm among the general public, both in this country and abroad. By the end of Reagan's first year, public-opinion polls were showing that proposals for a bilateral freeze on additional nuclear weapons were being approved by two-to-one margins. Demonstrations involving hundreds of thousands of people protesting the nuclear-arms race took place in Europe and the United States. Whatever else Reagan and his aides accomplished, they greatly stimulated the dormant peace movement in the free world and gave the Russians a fine opportunity to trumpet the fact that the United States was the more bellicose of the two superpowers, the greater threat to human survival.

By the spring of 1982, the Administration realized that it had got itself into deep trouble on this issue and began to alter its public posture. It was then that Reagan floated his so-called START proposal. START stands for strategic-arms-reduction talks and represents a replay of Reagan's successful ploy in his pre-election debate with Carter, when he called for bilateral arms reductions in an effort to counter Carter's portrayal of Reagan as a warmonger.

The Soviets were not likely to accept Reagan's proposal, because it would take from them half of their ICBM force while leaving ours relatively undisturbed. Former Secretary of State Edmund Muskie, in fact, suggested that START "may be a secret agenda for sidetracking *disarmament* while the United States gets on with *rearmament*—in a hopeless quest for superiority in these things." Even so, the proposal made for good public relations.

With the START announcement, the Administration showed that it had learned its lesson and thereafter would try not to alarm the public as it built up its strategic arms. From then on, there would be little public talk about nuclear-war fighting. The interviews by journalists with top Administration officials on nuclear-war fighting and survival would be harder to come by. At least, that was the plan; but such profound changes in U.S. defense strategy as were being conceived in the Defense Department and the White House were bound to leak out and would raise serious questions about the Administration's intent in the START talks.

In May 1982, a United Press International report by Helen Thomas stated: "A senior White House official said Reagan approved an eight-page national-security document that 'undertakes a campaign aimed at internal reform in the Soviet Union and shrinkage of the Soviet empire.' He affirmed that it could be called 'a full-court press' against the Soviet Union." (A full-court press is a basketball expression that describes an attempt to wrest the ball away from one's opponent in his own territory.)

That remarkable statement reflects the views of Pipes, who had said early in 1981 that "Soviet leaders would have to choose between peacefully changing their Communist system . . . or going to war." At the time, the Administration had sought to downplay Pipes's statement, but by the spring of 1982, his view seemed to have become official policy.

On May 30, a week after that UPI story, *New York Times* Pentagon correspondent Richard Halloran broke the story of the 1982 five-year Defense Guidance Plan. His article began with the following statement:

Defense Department policy makers, in a new five-year defense plan, have accepted the premise that nuclear conflict with the Soviet Union could be protracted and have drawn up their first strategy for fighting such a war.

The document was signed by Weinberger. It outlined the strategy to be pursued by the Pentagon for the next five years and was intended as a general guide for the next decade as well.

It would be difficult to exaggerate the implications of this strategy document, for it resolves a debate in the highest councils of government and places the United States, for the first time, squarely on the side of those extremists in this country and in the Soviet Union who believe in the possibility of fighting and winning a protracted nuclear war. As the *Times* put it:

> The nature of nuclear war has been a subject of intense debate among political leaders, defense specialists and military officers. Some assert that there would be only one all-out mutually destructive exchange. Others argue that a nuclear war with many exchanges could be fought over days and weeks.
>
> The outcome of the debate will shape the weapons, communications and strategy for nuclear forces. The civilian and military planners, having decided that protracted nuclear war is possible, say that American nuclear forces "must prevail and be able to force the Soviet Union to seek earliest termination of hostilities on terms favorable to the United States."

The nuclear-war strategy outlined in the document aims at the "decapitation" of the Soviet political leadership, as well as at preventing communication between the leadershp and the forces in the field. It specifies further that the Chinese would be granted military assistance to keep Soviet forces pinned down on Russia's eastern border. In addition, psychological-warfare, sabotage, and guerrilla-warfare operations would be improved. All of that presumably has to do with the full-court press on the Soviet empire.

Halloran underscored the significance of this Administration's departure from the attitudes of its predecessors on the matter of nuclear-war fighting when he wrote:

> In many parts of this document, the Reagan military planners started with a blank sheet of paper. Their views on the possibility of protracted nuclear war differ from those of the Carter Administration's military thinkers, as do their views on global conventional war and, particularly, on putting economic pressure on the Soviet Union.

The Defense Department's plan disturbed such experts as Nobel Prize–winning physicist Hans Bethe, who had headed the theoretical-physics division of Los Alamos National Laboratory during the Manhattan Project in World War II. Bethe and physicist Kurt Gottfried wrote that the plan "comes close to a declaration of war on the Soviet Union and contradicts and may destroy President Reagan's initiatives toward nuclear-arms control."

Nor did the professional military unanimously applaud these ideologically derived war-fighting plans. For example, *The Washington Post* reported on June 19, 1982, that General David C. Jones, who had retired as chairman of the Joint Chiefs of Staff, "left office yesterday with the warning that it would be throwing money in a 'bottomless pit' to try to prepare the United States for a long nuclear war with the Soviet Union." The newspaper said General Jones doubted that any nuclear exchange between the Soviets and the United States could be contained without its escalating into an all-out war. According to the article, " 'I don't see much of a chance of nuclear war being limited or protracted,' said Jones, who has pondered various doomsday scenarios. . . . 'I see great difficulty' in keeping any kind of nuclear exchange between the United States and the Soviet Union from escalating."

Despite the reservations of the general and of others in and out of the military, the Reagan Administration reaffirmed its commitment to programs in support of protracted nuclear war. In the summer of 1982, a Pentagon master plan to implement Reagan's strategic policy was drafted. It lays out military-hardware requirements and nuclear-targeting adjustments necessary to wage such a war.

Unlike the Defense Guidance Plan, which is an internal Pentagon document, the new master plan, as I reported in the *Los Angeles Times*, was drawn up in response to a secret White House directive, a National Security Decision Document—which mandated that the Defense Department provide a program for implementing Reagan's nuclear-war policy. Reagan's NSDD is the first policy statement of a U.S. Administration to proclaim that U.S. strategic forces must be able to win a protracted nuclear war. That goes considerably beyond earlier tendencies toward nuclear-war-fighting strategies.

All post–World War II Presidents, up to and including Jimmy Carter, have dealt with contingency planning. But the men around Reagan are not merely interested in "what if?" scenarios. This difference was acknowledged by Colin Gray, a leading advocate of the nuclear-war-fighting school and, oddly, now an arms-control adviser to the Reagan government. In 1980, before the election, Gray wrote in *Foreign Policy*:

> To advocate . . . targeting flexibility and selectivity [as Carter did] is not the same as to advocate a war-fighting, war-survival strategy. . . .

Victory or defeat in nuclear war is possible, and such a war may have to be waged to that point; and the clearer the vision of successful war termination, the more likely war can be waged intelligently at earlier stages.

In this article, titled "Victory Is Possible," Gray and his co-author, Keith Payne, complained that "many commentators and senior U.S. government officials consider [nuclear war] a non-survivable event." Instead, Gray presented the nuclear-war-fighters' alternative vision:

> The United States should plan to defeat the Soviet Union and to do so at a cost that would not prohibit U.S. recovery. Washington should identify war aims that in the last resort would contemplate the destruction of Soviet political authority and the emergence of a postwar world order compatible with Western values.

Gray proposed that "a combination of counterforce offensive targeting, civil defense and ballistic-missile and air defense should hold U.S. casualties down to a level compatible with national survival and recovery." The compatible level he had in mind would leave twenty million dead.

While there have undoubtedly been aggressive voices in previous Administrations, within the Reagan government the nuclear-war fighters are apparently unchallenged. The policies and the budget priorities of this Administration proclaim that the unthinkable can now be planned without hesitation. This development has alarmed many of the key architects of America's strategic-defense policy. One of those is Dr. Herbert York, a veteran of the Manhattan Project and a former director of California's Lawrence Livermore Laboratory, one of the nation's main developers of nuclear weapons. Dr. York, who was the director of Defense Research and Engineering under President Kennedy, told me in an interview in April 1982: "What's going on right now is that the crazier analysts have risen to higher positions than is normally the case. They are able to carry their ideas further and higher because the people at the top are simply less well informed than is normally the case. Neither the current President nor his immediate backers in the White House nor the current Secretary of Defense has any experience with these things, so when the ideologues come in with their fancy stories and with their selected intelligence data, the President and the Secretary of Defense believe the last glib person who's talked to them."

An alternative view in the Reagan Administration was offered by Richard Perle, Assistant Secretary of Defense for International Security Policy and an architect of the Pentagon's five-year war-fighting plan, who told me: "I've always worried less about what would happen in an actual nuclear exchange than about the effect that the nuclear balance has on our willingness to take risks in local situations. It is not that I am worried about the Soviets' attacking the United States with nuclear weapons confident that they will win that nuclear war. It is that I worry about an American President's feeling he cannot afford to take action in a crisis because Soviet nuclear forces are such that, if escalation took place, they are better poised than we are to move up the escalation ladder."

Perle strongly believes that we can stockpile nuclear weapons and threaten to use them without increasing the risks of nuclear war. When I asked him about the fear of the nuclear-arms race expressed by such groups as Physicians for Social Responsibility, he replied: "I am as aware as [the anti-nuclear-weapons advocates] are of the presence of nuclear weapons in the world. I'm more confident about our ability to deter war, nevertheless, than they are, and that is based partly on some judgments about history."

Perle's judgments about history begin with the assumption, as he told me, that the Soviet Union is much like Hitler's Germany—inexorably bent on world conquest unless an aroused West intervenes. Like many others in the Administration, Perle fears that the danger of appeasement far exceeds that of nuclear escalation.

Eugene Rostow, Reagan's chief disarmament man, echoed Perle's fear that we are up against another Hitler. In 1976 he wrote: "Our posture today is comparable to that of Britain, France and the United States during the thirties. Whether we are at the Rhineland or the Munich watershed remains to be seen." When I interviewed Rostow in 1981, he told me, "I do not think the real danger of the situation is nuclear war and mass destruction; I think the danger is political coercion based on the threat of mass destruction. . . . And that is very real. You can smell it."

What Rostow, Perle, and others who insist on this analogy ignore is that neither the Allies nor Germany possessed nuclear weapons at the time of Munich. Would even such a madman as Hitler have attempted world conquest—would his generals have allowed him to?—if French and British missiles had been holding Berlin hostage? Nor would Perle find much support outside his own tight cabal of anti-Soviet hard-liners for the idea that Soviet leadership is driven by the same furies that possessed Hitler. As for the Soviets themselves, who have their own memories of Hitler, the analogy can only be enraging.

There are two possible inferences to be drawn from this recent intensification of U.S. rhetoric. Either the Reagan Administration, while believing that nuclear war is catastrophic, has chosen to play nuclear chicken with the Soviets, with the intention of changing their political system and challenging their empire, or the United States really has abandoned the view that nuclear war is inevitably cataclysmic and that nuclear weapons can be detonated as viable instruments of policy.

Although I have spent much of the past three years reporting for the *Los Angeles Times* on our drift toward nuclear war, there are still times when I lose my sense of the devastation that lies behind the sterile acronyms by which these modern weapons are described. The words have grown stale after nearly four decades of so-called strategic development. We hear about SLCMs and MIRVs or of that weird hodgepodge of nuclear-war-fighting strategies—the window of vulnerability, the first-strike scenarios, the city strips—and after a while, the mind doesn't react with the appropriate horror.

The question of universal death grows stale partly because the arguments are often unnecessarily complex, rely on an insider's lingo, and use terms that mute just what it is these bombs will do—which is, to start with, kill the people one loves and nearly everyone else as well.

I came to appreciate this fully only during a conversation with a former CIA analyst who had been responsible for evaluating Soviet strategic nuclear forces. He has spent much of his adult life concerned with the question of nuclear war and has heard all the arguments about nuclear-war fighting and survival. But an experience from his youth, he told me, remains in his mind and, he admits, may yet color his view.

This man had conducted some of the most important CIA studies on the Soviets and nuclear war. Now in his middle years, still youthful in manner, clean-cut and obviously patriotic, the father of a Marine on active duty, he recently left the CIA to join a company that works for that agency, so I cannot use his name.

He told me about this experience of his youth because he was frightened by the Reagan Administration's casual talk about waging and winning a nuclear war and thought it did not really comprehend what kind of weapon the bomb was. As an illustration, he recalled having seen, as a lieutenant in the Navy, a bomb go off near Christmas Island in the Pacific. Years later, at the CIA, he had worked with computer models that detailed the number of fatalities likely to result from various nuclear-war-targeting scenarios. But to bring a measure of reality to these computer projections, he would return in his mind as he did now to that time in the Pacific.

"The birds were the things we could see all the time. They were superb specimens of life . . . really quite exquisite . . . phenomenal creatures. Albatrosses will fly for days, skimming a few inches above the surface of the water. These birds have tremendously long wings and tails, and beaks that are as if fashioned for another purpose. You don't see what these birds are about from their design; they are just beautiful creatures. Watching them is a wonder. That is what I didn't expect . . .

"We were standing around, waiting for this bomb to go off, which we had been told was a very small one, so no one was particularly upset. Even though I'd never seen one, I figured, Well, these guys know what is going to happen. They know what the dangers are and we've been adequately briefed and we all have our radiation meters on . . . No worry."

He paused to observe that the size of the bomb to be exploded was ten kilotons, or the equivalent explosive power of 10,000 tons of TNT. The bombs dropped at Hiroshima and Nagasaki were thirteen and twenty-three kilotons, respectively. Now such bombs are mere tactical or battlefield weapons. Some of the ones to be used in any United States–Soviet nuclear war are measured in megatons—millions of tons of TNT.

He continued his account: "So the countdown came in over the radio, and I could see all these birds that I'd been watching for days. They were now suddenly visible through the opaque visor of my helmet. And they were smoking. Their feathers were on fire. And they were doing cartwheels. And the light persisted for some time. It was instantaneously bright but wasn't instantaneous, because it stayed and it changed its composition slightly. Several seconds, it seemed like—long enough for me to see birds crash into the water. They were sizzling, smoking. They weren't vaporized; it's just that they were absorbing such intense radiation that they were being consumed by the heat. Their feathers were on fire. They were blinded. And so far, there had been no shock, none of the blast damage we talk about when we discuss the effects of nuclear weapons. Instead, there were just these smoking, twisting, hideously contorted birds crashing into things. And then I could see vapor rising from the inner lagoon as the surface of the water was heated by this intense flash.

"Now, this is a primary effect of the weapon; it is an initial kind of effect that precedes other things, though it is talked about and you can see evidence of it in the Hiroshima blast and in Nagasaki—outlines of people on bridges where they stood when the bomb was dropped. But that initial thermal radiation is a phenomenon that is unlike any other weapon I've seen."

The men who now dominate the Reagan Administration and who believe that nuclear war is survivable would surely wonder what those reflections have to do with the struggle against the Soviet Union. But what my CIA friend was telling me was that those birds are us and they never had a chance.

"It's the Dirt That Does It"

Very late one autumn night in 1981, Thomas K. Jones, the man Reagan had appointed Deputy Under Secretary of Defense for Research and Engineering (Strategic and Theater Nuclear Forces), told me that the United

States could fully recover from an all-out nuclear war with the Soviet Union in just two to four years. T.K., as he prefers to be known, added that nuclear war was not nearly so devastating as we had been led to believe. He said, "If these are enough shovels to go around, everybody's going to make it." The shovels were for digging holes in the ground, which would be covered, somehow or other, with a couple of doors and with three feet of dirt thrown on top, thereby providing adequate fallout shelters for the millions who had been evacuated from U.S. cities to the countryside. "It's the dirt that does it," he said.

After parts of my interview with T. K. Jones ran in the *Los Angeles Times*, a subcommittee of the Senate Foreign Relations Committee demanded that Jones present himself to defend the views that Senator Alan Cranston said went "far beyond the bounds of reasonable, rational, responsible thinking."

Meanwhile, Senator Charles Percy, the Republican Chairman of the Foreign Relations Committee, had confronted Jones at a town meeting in the senator's home state of Illinois and had been sufficiently troubled by his relatively complacent views of nuclear war to pressure the Pentagon for an accounting.

But by then, the Administration had muzzled Jones, and he missed his first three scheduled appearances before the Senate subcommittee. It was at this point that a *New York Times* editorial asked, "Who is the Thomas K. Jones who is saying those funny things about civil defense?" Elsewhere, Jones's espousal of primitive fallout shelters was dismissed by editorial writers and cartoonists as a preposterous response to what nuclear war was all about. However, what these dismissals ignored was that Jones's notions of civil defense, odd as they may seem, are crucial to Reagan's strategic policy.

Reagan's nuclear-arms build-up follows from the idea that the United States is vulnerable to Soviet nuclear weapons, an idea that rests in part on calculations made by this same Jones before he joined the government, when he worked for the Boeing Company. It was his estimates of the efficacy of Soviet civil defense that provided much of the statistical justification for the view that the Soviets could reasonably expect to survive and win a nuclear war while we, without a comparable civil-defense program, would necessarily lose.

And it was his celebration of the shovel and of primitive shelters that helped call into question the Administration's claim of U.S. vulnerability. In fact, it was from the Russians that he had borrowed the idea of digging holes in the first place. He had become fascinated with the powerful defensive possibilities of dirt only after he had read Soviet civil-defense manuals that advocated such procedures. If his evacuation and sheltering plans were absurd for the United States, how, then, could any observer take the Soviet civil-defense program seriously? And if the Soviets were not capable of protecting their society and recovering from a nuclear war, how could anyone genuinely believe that they were planning to fight and win such a war?

I had first interviewed T.K. at his Pentagon office in the fall of 1981. I was interested in his views because of his extensive testimony five years earlier before congressional committees and because of articles he had written on the need for civil defense and the possibilities for surviving nuclear war. The interview took place in an office hung with pictures of the atomic devastation of Japan. Jones, as in his barely reported congressional testimony, was reassured by the familiar scenes of destruction and pointed to the few surviving structures in an otherwise barren wasteland of rubble to support his analysis that, indeed, there are defenses against nuclear war. He praised the resilience of the Japanese, noting, "About thirty days after the blast, there were people in there salvaging the rubble, rebuilding their houses." Jones acknowledged that modern nuclear strategic weapons are hundreds of times more powerful than the devices exploded in Japan and that a large U.S. city would receive not one but perhaps more than a dozen incoming warheads. Yet he insisted that the survival of more than 90 percent of our people was possible.

I asked Jones about the Administration's vision for civil defense for Los Angeles in the eighties: "To dramatize it for the reader, the bomb has dropped [in Los Angeles]. Now, if he's within that two-mile area, he's finished, right? If he's not in the two-mile area, what has happened?"

Jones replied, "His house is gone, he's there, wherever he dug that hole . . . You've got to be in a hole . . . The dirt really is the thing that protects you from the blast, as well as the radiation, if there's radiation. It protects you from the heat. You know, dirt is just great stuff."

He told me that he had been deeply impressed with what he claimed was the Soviet plan to evacuate the cities and protect the urban population in hastily constructed shelters in the countryside. He also referred to his studies at Boeing to show that the Soviet method of piling dirt around factory machines would permit their survival even if nuclear bombs fell close by.

These studies, he explained, were not universally admired. Some critics, for example, did not share his enthusiasm for the Soviet civil-defense program and scoffed at the prospect of millions of Soviet citizens digging holes during the freezing winter in order to cover themselves and their machinery.

The day after the interview, I saw Attorney General William French Smith and his entourage. It was a reassuring sight—they all looked so solidly adult, sober, respectable; surely, they had too much going for them to accept the prospect of giving it all up for a hole in the ground or even for one of the fancy but ultimately no more effective government blast shelters. And just as surely, Reagan and George Bush were solid and responsible. Or were they?

How much, I wondered, did the views of men such as Jones reflect the thinking of our new heads of state? Had they all gone mad in their obsessive fear of the Russians? Or was Jones an aberration, a solitary eccentric who had somehow found his way into the Pentagon?

Reagan and Bush

Reflecting on Jones's startling remarks, I thought back to the time in January 1980 when I had interviewed presidential candidate Bush aboard a small chartered plane en route from Houston to New Orleans. Bush was then seen as a moderate Republican alternative to Carter, and it was for this reason that what he told me startled me so, though at first I barely caught its implications.

The question that had provoked Bush's reply derived from the conventional wisdom of the previous twenty years that there was a limit to how many nuclear weapons the superpowers should stockpile, because, after a point, the two sides would simply wipe each other out, and any extra firepower represented overkill. This had been the assumption ever since former Defense Secretary Robert McNamara had conceived the mutual-assured-destruction policy. But Bush had faulted Carter for not being quick enough to build the MX missile and the B-1 bomber, and I asked, "Don't we reach a point with these strategic weapons where we can wipe each other out so many times and no one wants to use them or is willing to use them, that it really doesn't matter whether we're 10 percent or 2 percent lower or higher?"

Bush bristled a bit and replied, "Yes, if you believe there is no such thing as a winner in a nuclear exchange, that argument makes a little sense. I don't believe that."

I then asked how one won in a nuclear exchange.

Bush seemed angry that I had challenged what to him seemed an obvious truth. He replied, "You have a survivability of command and control, survivability of industrial potential, protection of a percentage of your citizens, and you have a capability that inflicts more damage on the opposition than it can inflict upon you. That's the way you can have a winner, and the Soviets' planning is based on the ugly concept of a winner in a nuclear exchange."

Did that mean, I asked, that 5 percent would survive? 2 percent?

"More than that," he answered. "If everybody fired everything he had, you'd have more than that survive."

The interview with Bush seemed internally inconsistent at the time. But later, when I learned about an organization that called itself the Committee on the Present Danger (of which more later), I discovered the source of this dangerous, if muddled, line of thought.

The organizers of the committee had formed the center of opposition to détente. They had introduced the idea that the Soviets are bent on nuclear superiority and believe they can be victorious in a nuclear war. As I would learn, those men were influential not only with Bush but even more so with his campaign opponent, Ronald Reagan.

A month after I interviewed Bush, I was in another airplane, and the man beside me was talking. He said that, assuming we had a Soviet-style civil defense, we could survive nuclear war: "It would be a survival of some of your people and some of your facilities, but you could start again. It would not be anything that I think in our society you would consider acceptable, but then, we have a different regard for human life than those monsters do." He was referring to what he said was the Soviets' belief in winning a nuclear war despite casualties that we would find unacceptable. And he added that they are "godless" monsters. It is this theological defect "that gives them less regard for humanity or human beings."

The man telling me all this was Ronald Reagan, as I interviewed him on a flight from Birmingham to Orlando, where he was headed to pick up some votes in the upcoming 1980 Florida Republican primary. By mentioning the Soviets' low regard for human life, he meant to validate the view that he confided to me later—that the Russians have for some time been preparing a preemptive nuclear war.

"We've still been following the mutual-assured-destruction plan that was given birth by McNamara, and it was a ridiculous plan, and it was based on the idea that the two countries would hold each other's populations hostage, that we would not protect or defend our people against a nuclear attack. They, in turn, would do the same. Therefore, if both of us knew that we could wipe each other out, neither one would dare push the button. The difficulty with that was that the Soviet Union decided sometime ago that a nuclear war was possible and was winnable, and they have proceeded with an elaborate and extensive civil-protection program. We do not have anything of that kind, because we went along with what the policy was supposed to be."

As President, Reagan set out to get something of that kind. The goal of the Reagan–Bush Administration has been to emulate what Reagan claimed was the Soviet program by developing the ingredients of a nuclear-war-fighting capability. And the key ingredient, even more than the number and power of the nuclear weapons themselves, is the ability of a country's leadership to control a war in the midst of massive nuclear explosions. This is what Bush had in mind when he told me that nuclear war was winnable by having "survivability of command and control." And when Reagan, in the fall of 1981, announced his strategic package, he singled out an $18 billion program for enduring command, control, and communications (C^3) as the most important element in his program.

But the calm and understated former Secretary of State Cyrus Vance had this to say when I asked him, in an interview in March 1982, what he thought of the Reagan Administration's plans to improve C^3 in order to attain a nuclear-war-fighting capability: "I think it is sound and proper to have a command and control that could, hopefully, survive a nuclear attack. However, to take the next leap—that it is important to have a command and control that is survivable so that you can fight a nuclear war—is a wholly different situation. I happen to be one of those who believe it is madness to talk about trying to fight a continuing nuclear war as though it were like fighting a conventional war and that one could control the outcome with the kind of precision that is sometimes possible in a conventional war situation."

That the Administration had begun moving in a direction that Vance called madness was made abundantly clear by Lieutenant General James W. Stansberry, commander of the Electronics Systems Division of the Air Force, as reported in *Aviation Week & Space Technology*:

> Stansberry said there is now a shift in strategic-warfare philosophy in the U.S. and that the country must be prepared to fight and to keep on fighting, and that an eight-hour nuclear war is no longer an acceptable concept.

The main reason that an eight-hour nuclear war is no longer acceptable is that the Administration has adopted the view, once held by only a fringe group of strategic analysts, that the Soviet Union is bent on acquiring nuclear superiority so as to win a nuclear war, as Bush had said. This was the point of Colin Gray and Keith Payne's controversial article "Victory Is Possible," referred to earlier. They argued not only that nuclear war is winnable but also that the United States should be prepared to *initiate* it.

Two years after that article appeared, Gray was appointed by the Reagan Administration as consultant to the Arms Control and Disarmament Agency. He was also named a member of the General Advisory Committee to the Arms Control and Disarmament Agency and a consultant to the State Department.

If the Russians had appointed a man with Gray's views to a high and visible government post, our own hawks would surely say, "We told you so" and demand vast new categories of armaments. Nor did Reagan appoint such men as Gray and T. K. Jones inadvertently. Their views and those of the other hard-liners were well known to the Reagan people who selected them, and they were compatible with the strategic policy pursued by the Administration. For the views of these hard-liners, in fact, permeate the present Administration. They are views that had been espoused for years by men languishing in the wings of power, waiting for one of their own to move to center stage. With Reagan, their time had come.

The Committee on the Present Danger

It was the fall of Reagan's first year in office, and Charles Tyroler II, the director of the Committee on the Present Danger, was boasting a little. Five years before, he and a small band of Cold Warriors had set out to reshape American foreign policy, which they felt was too soft on the Russians, and suddenly they had succeeded beyond their wildest dreams. One member of their group was now the President of the United States, and he had recruited heavily from the committee's ranks for his top foreign-policy officials.

Committee members were ensconced as heads of the CIA and the Arms Control and Disarmament Agency and in top State and Defense Department and White House positions. Paul Green, the committee's public-relations director, told me that Eugene Rostow, a founding member of the committee and the new head of the Arms Control and Disarmament Agency, had just that week written part of the President's speech on arms control. It was in that speech that Reagan had for the first time referred to START as the alternative to SALT. Green was proud that it had been Rostow who had come up with the acronym START, and both Green and Tyroler were obviously pleased that SALT II, which had taken three Presidents and six years to negotiate and which the committee had strenuously opposed, now seemed securely buried.

"The leaders of the government," Tyroler boasted, "the Secretary of Defense, the President of the United States, and the Secretary of State, the head of the Arms Control and Disarmament Agency, the National Security Adviser—when they give a speech, in general terms, it sounds like what we said in 1976. Yes, I think that is a fair statement." He then offered a self-satisfied laugh and added, "And why wouldn't that be? They use the same stuff—and they were all members back then."

The same stuff, of course, was the committee's persistent and shrill criticism of the SALT II treaty in particular and of détente with the Soviets in general. What emerges from the committee's literature is the view that the Soviet Union is as unrelentingly aggressive as Nazi Germany: "The Soviet military build-up of all its armed forces over the past quarter century is, in part, reminiscent of Nazi Germany's rearmament in the thirties. The Soviet build-up affects all branches of the military: the army, the air force, and the navy. In addition, Soviet nuclear offensive and defensive forces are designed to enable the U.S.S.R. to fight, survive, and win an all-out nuclear war should it occur."

Committee founder Paul Nitze later added, "The Kremlin leaders do not want war; they want the world. . . . The Soviets are driven to put themselves into the best position they can to achieve military victory in a [nuclear] war while assuring the survival, endurance, and recovery of the core of their party."

This last notion, later embraced by candidates Bush and Reagan, originated with the men who founded the committee and who have since become key players in the Reagan campaign and Presidency. It is they who have given us the language and the imagery of limited nuclear war and who claim that we can survive and even win such a conflict. It is they and their allies within the Administration who have pushed most strenuously for a rapid arms build-up. And it is they who are responsible, along with their Soviet counterparts, for dragging the world back into the darkness and the danger of the Cold War.

The committee's ideologues couldn't have done it alone. Their rhetoric fed on the continued Soviet military build-up and the wasteful civil-defense program that accompanied it, to say nothing of the violent statements of various Soviet military leaders and the outrageous suppression of their own and their satellites' people, as well as the invasion of Afghanistan. Yet the Soviet build-up does not, as we shall see, justify the committee's program or that of the Administration it now so profoundly influences. As Paul Warnke, Carter's arms-control director, says, "If you figure you can't have arms control unless the Russians are nice guys, then it seems to me that you're being totally illogical. If the Russians could be trusted to be nice guys, you wouldn't need strategic-arms control. And you wouldn't need strategic arms."

But Soviet behavior did alienate much American opinion that might have favored arms control and, thus, provided the emotional context and the minimal plausibility that were essential for the revival of a Cold War mood. The hawks on both sides of the superpower confrontation have a long history of feeding on each other's rhetorical and strategic excesses. In particular, both sides tend to exaggerate the technological success of the opposing side's defense program, meanwhile denying that the enemy can do anything else right. The hawks on both sides, including the Committee on the Present Danger, are threat inflaters who dourly predict every success for the forces of evil and nothing but trouble for the side of virtue unless that side adopts the methods and programs of its opponents.

The founding members of the committee included, among others, veterans of what came to be known as Team B, a group of hawks whom Bush had brought into the CIA from outside its ranks when he was that agency's director in 1975–1976. The aim of Team B was to re-evaluate the agency's own assessment of the Soviet menace, which Team B found too moderate. Team B's chairman was Richard Pipes, Reagan's top Soviet expert on the National Security Council. And one of its most active members was former Secretary of the Navy Paul Nitze, who has since become Reagan's key negotiator on European strategic weapons. To no one's surprise, Team B concluded what it had originally hypothesized: that the CIA had seriously underestimated the Soviet threat. In November 1976, Nitze, along with Rostow, formed the Committee on the Present Danger and asked several hundred prominent individuals, including Pipes, to support them.

"The committee's philosophy is dominant," said PR director Paul Green, who had joined Tyroler and me in the committee's offices. Green's cherubic demeanor and pleasant smile promise something far less threatening than the group's dire warnings about the strategic balance. Yet what he was about to outline suggested the end for serious efforts at arms control during the Reagan Administration.

"So the committee's philosophy," Green went on, "is dominant in the three major areas [in which] there is going to be United States–Soviet activity." He was referring to the various arms-control negotiations that were being resumed with the Soviets and that were directed by committee members Reagan had appointed to his Administration—all of whom had been strident critics of SALT II. The implications of Reagan's victory, not only for arms control but for relations in general with the Soviets, became starkly clear as Tyroler continued his inventory of the powerful posts then held by members of his group.

"We've got [Richard] Allen, Pipes, and Geoffrey Kemp over at NSC. We've got the people most intimately involved in the arms-control negotiations for the Defense Department: [Fred] Iklé [Under Secretary of Defense for Policy]; his deputy, [R. G.] Stillwell; and Dick Perle. At the Arms Control and Disarmament Agency, there are Rostow, the head of it; [Edward] Rowny, the SALT negotiator; and Nitze, the TNF [Theater Nuclear Forces] negotiator. And [William] Van Cleave on the General Advisory Committee. Well, that's the whole hierarchy."

Special-interest groups tend to exaggerate their influence, but in this instance, we have the word of Ronald Reagan himself to confirm the committee's importance. After his election, he wrote in a letter to the committee: "The statements and studies of the committee have had a wide national impact, and I benefited greatly from them." He added that "the work of the Committee on the Present Danger has certainly helped to shape the national debate on important problems."

These unremitting Cold Warriors seem almost to miss the Stalinist era, those black-and-white years when the Soviet Union, with its alleged timetable for world conquest, seemed to hold the unchallenged leadership of a monolithic international Communist movement arrayed against a united free world content within its own borders. They seem uncomfortable with events as they have evolved since then; the Sino-Soviet split, West Germany's increasingly close ties to Russia, and the Eurocommunist movement independent of Moscow apparently annoy them by having introduced troublesome complexity into that world view. For them, Communism is evil, and that's all there is to it.

Lest I be accused of exaggeration, I should report that when I interviewed Rostow in the spring of 1981, just after Reagan had appointed him Director of the Arms Control and Disarmament Agency, and asked him whether or not he believed that the Soviet Union had any legitimate grievance against the United States, he replied, "None whatever."

Ironically, committee leaders, who had for decades supported the U.S. nuclear-weapons build-up, offered the Soviet counterparts of their own hawkish position as proof that the two nations do not share a common perception and fear of nuclear war. Of course, it would be splendid news for everyone if the Soviet Union agreed to unilateral restraints in the arms race. Ever since their humiliation during the Cuban Missile Crisis, the Russians have piled missile upon missile. However, the committee wants the United States to pile weapons systems upon weapons systems, and as long as that is so, the cheering will have to wait. The committee's leaders must be aware that the United States did not hesitate to develop each new weapons system it thought workable and useful as the Soviets pursued their own build-up in the seventies. Thus, we have the Pershing II and cruise missiles, the Trident submarines and missiles, and the technological basis for the MX missile, each of which exceeds Soviet development by a good five years, jeopardizing the expanding Soviet array of land-based missiles—the basket into which the Soviets have put most of their nuclear eggs.

Much of what we know, or think we know, about Soviet intentions and strength is based on estimates inferred from U.S. intelligence data, though during the SALT talks, both sides did provide details on their strategic systems. The Soviets do not reveal many details of their defense budget or force structure, and they alone seem to take seriously the relatively low annual defense-budget figure that they publish. The Western countries, however, possess a great deal of highly accurate information of the specifics of the Soviet-force makeup gleaned from constant and increasingly precise satellite surveillance as well as from old-fashioned spying. But this vast amount of material has to be submitted to intelligence analysis before its meaning becomes clear. To do that, however, involves interpretation based on the skills and the experience of U.S. intelligence agencies, particularly the CIA, which has traditionally attempted to evaluate Soviet strength in an objective manner.

One reason for the current confusion is that this objectivity was seriously compromised under the administration of CIA Director George Bush, with the help of some key founders of the Committee on the Present Danger. Those events occurred in 1976, and they were to have a profound effect on our evaluation of the Soviet threat and on the course of presidential politics. I am referring to the creation of Team B, the group of outside analysts whose leaders were permitted by Bush to re-evaluate the CIA's own estimates of Soviet strength and intentions. The objective procedures by which the CIA formerly evaluated the scope and the nature of the Soviet threat may thus have been the first casualties of the new Cold War.

Bush's Team B

Until 1976, the CIA did not believe that the Soviets were militarily superior to the United States or were aiming at nuclear superiority. Nor did agency analysts believe that the Soviet leadership expected to survive and win a nuclear war. Then George Bush became head of the CIA, and the professionals at the agency were told to think otherwise.

Bush was appointed CIA Director during the last year of Gerald Ford's Presidency and took the unprecedented step of allowing a hawkish group of outsiders to challenge the CIA's own intelligence estimates of Soviet strength. In a break with the agency's standards of secrecy, Bush granted this group access to the most sensitive data on Soviet military strength, data that had been culled from satellite photos and reports of agents in the field, defectors, and current informants. Never before had outside critics of government policy been given such access to the data underlying that policy. Bush did not extend similar privileges to dovish critics of prevailing policy.

This intrusion into the objective process of CIA analysis greatly inflated the existing estimate of U.S. vulnerability to Russian forces and would eventually be used to justify an increased U.S. arms build-up. As *The New York Times* noted in a strongly worded editorial at the time: "For reasons that have yet to be explained, the CIA's leading analysts were persuaded to admit a hand-picked, unofficial panel of hard-line critics of recent arms-control policy to sit at their elbows and to influence the estimates of future Soviet military capacities in a 'somber' direction."

The group that Bush appointed was called Team B, to distinguish it from Team A, the CIA professionals who were paid to evaluate Soviet strength in an unbiased fashion. Thanks to Bush, Team B was successful in getting the

U.S. government to alter profoundly its estimates of Soviet strength and intentions, though critics charged that Team B had seriously distorted the CIA's raw data to conform to the political prejudices of its members.

Those prejudices were described in a *New York Times* report as follows: "The conditions [for Team B members] were that the outsiders be mutually agreeable to the [foreign intelligence] advisory board and to Mr. Bush and that they hold more pessimistic views of Soviet plans than those entertained by the advocates of the rough-parity thesis."

The Team B report helped bolster and may even have been the source for Bush's and Reagan's assertions in the 1980 campaign that the Soviets had betrayed the hopes of détente and were bent on attaining nuclear superiority. It was the Team B study that led to charges during the campaign that Carter had allowed the Soviets to gain nuclear superiority and that the United States must "rearm."

The *Times* account of what followed the introduction of Team B was based on nonattributable interviews that suggested a civil war within the intelligence community. One intelligence officer "spoke of 'absolutely bloody discussions' during which the outsiders accused the CIA of dealing in faulty assumptions, faulty analysis, faulty use of intelligence and faulty exploitation of available intelligence. 'It was an absolute disaster for the CIA,' this official added in an authorized interview. Acknowledging that there were more points of difference than in most years, he said, 'There was disagreement beyond the facts.'"

Another outspoken critic of Team B was Ray S. Cline, a former deputy director of intelligence of the CIA, who, according to *The Washington Post*, is "a leading skeptic about Soviet intentions and a longtime critic of Kissinger." The article continued: "He [Cline] deplored the experiment. It means, Cline said, that the process of making national-security estimates 'has been subverted' by employing 'a kangaroo court of outside critics all picked from one point of view.'"

Team B was hand-picked by Bush, and as noted by *The New York Times*, a "pessimistic" view of the Soviets was a prerequisite for inclusion on the team. The committee's chairman was Pipes, the same hard-liner who, in 1981, announced that the Soviets would have to choose between peacefully changing their system and going to war.

According to Jack Ruina, professor of electrical engineering at MIT and former senior consultant to the Office of Science and Technology Policy at the White House, "Pipes knows little about technology and about nuclear weapons. I know him personally. I like him. But I think that on the subject of the Soviets, he is clearly obsessed with what he views as their aggressive intentions."

Pipes is the intellectual godfather of the thesis that the Soviets reject nuclear parity and are bent on nuclear-war fighting, a thesis later advanced by Bush and Reagan and now permeating the Reagan Administration. Pipes clarified his position and that of Team B in a summary of the classified Team B report that he provided in an op-ed piece in *The New York Times*. The article criticized the view that each side had more than enough nuclear weapons and that the notion of nuclear superiority between the superpowers no longer made sense. Pipes wrote: "More subtle and more pernicious is the argument, backed by the prestige of Henry A. Kissinger, that nuclear superiority is meaningless. This view was essential to Mr. Kissinger's détente policy, but it rests on flawed thinking. Underpinning it is the widely held notion that since there exists a certain quantitative level in the accumulation of nuclear weapons that, once attained, is sufficient to destroy mankind, superiority is irrelevant: There is no overtrumping total destruction."

Pipes's alternative to Kissinger's view of strategic policy was the one embraced by Team B. His article continued: "Unfortunately, in nuclear competition, numbers are not all. The contest between the superpowers is increasingly turning into a qualitative race whose outcome most certainly can yield meaningful superiority."

Five months after his piece in the *Times*, Pipes argued, in a *Commentary* article titled "Why the Soviet Union Thinks It Could Fight and Win a Nuclear War," that the Soviets do not agree that nuclear war is fundamentally different from conventional wars, a viewpoint that he himself seems to share as more realistic than the prevailing American idea that nuclear war would be suicidal. Pipes noted that, at first, the U.S. military had held what he claims is actually the Soviet view, that "when it came to horror, atomic bombs have nothing over conventional ones," a point he attempted to prove by reference to the devastation of Tokyo and Dresden by conventional weapons. He argued that this sound thinking on the part of the military was "promptly silenced by a coalition of groups, each of which it suited, for its own reasons, to depict the atomic bomb as the 'absolute weapon' that had, in large measure, rendered traditional military establishments redundant and traditional strategic thinking obsolete."

Pipes complained that "a large part of the U.S. scientific community had been convinced as soon as the first atomic bomb was exploded that the nuclear weapon, which that community had conceived and helped to develop, had accomplished a complete revolution in warfare." That conclusion, he wrote, "was reached without much reference to the analysis of the effects of atomic weapons carried out by the military and, indeed, without consideration of the traditional principles of warfare." Instead, Pipes argued, this misguided notion was the result of psychological and philosophical distortions by the scientists themselves. "It represented," he wrote, "an act of faith on the part of an intellectual community that held strong pacifist convictions and felt deep guilt at having participated in the creation of a weapon of such destructive power."

Thus, Pipes dismissed the anguished concern of many of the scientists who knew these weapons best, as if their feelings of guilt and their wishes for peace were absurd or decadent or, perhaps, even anti-American.

The Soviets, by contrast—according to Pipes, who in a perverse way seems to revel in the heartlessness he assigns to them—were not so sentimental. They believed, instead, that Clausewitz was right: Nukes or no nukes, war was still the pursuit of politics by other means. And because the hardheaded Soviets believe that nuclear weapons can be used just as successfully in war as conventional weapons can, the Americans must prepare to emulate the Russians.

The principal Team B analysts, Nitze and Van Cleave, shared this view. They had already held discussions for months with Rostow and others to plan the formation of the Committee on the Present Danger even before those gentlemen, acting as Team B, had entered CIA headquarters at Langley, Virginia, to re-evaluate the agency's data. Thus, their decision to form an activist organization based on the notion that the United States was losing out to the Soviets and to press for greater arms expenditures predated their look at the CIA's material. So much for pretensions of objectivity.

Team B's conclusions were based on three points: a depiction of Soviet strategic intentions; the claim that the Soviets were engaged in a massive military build-up; and the idea that the Soviets' civil-defense program made credible their expectation of surviving a nuclear war with the United States.

Those same three points would later form the core assumptions of the Reagan Administration's strategic policy, including, of course, T. K. Jones's shovel-based plan for protecting the civilian population. Yet, while the Team B study is still classified, enough of it has leaked to raise serious questions about the credibility of its analysis.

When Bush accepted the Team B conclusion that the Soviet build-up was much greater than had previously been assumed by the CIA, he did so, he told *The New York Times*, because of "new evidence and reinterpretation of old information [that] contributed to the reassessment of Soviet intentions." Yet the new evidence to which he referred, in fact, actually *refuted* the conclusions of Team B and the subsequent assumptions of the Reagan-Bush Administration.

The new evidence available to Team B was the CIA's revised estimate of Soviet defense spending, published in October 1976, which held that Soviet military spending as a percentage of GNP had increased from the 6–8 percent range to the 11–13 percent range. That was Team B's proof that the Soviets were building a bigger military force than the United States had thought.

However, as former CIA analyst Arthur Macy Cox pointed out in an article in *The New York Times*, the revised CIA estimates of 1976 tell us, in fact, nothing of the sort. As Cox observed in another article, in *The New York Review of Books*, "While Team B's report . . . remained classified, the CIA's own official report on Soviet defense spending of October 1976 had contradicted Team B's conclusions, not supported them. The true meaning of the October [CIA] report has been missed. A gargantuan error has been allowed to stand uncorrected all these years."

Cox then cited the same CIA report on which Team B had relied and to which Bush had referred as the new evidence: " 'The new estimate of the share of defense in the Soviet GNP is almost twice as high as the 6–8 percent previously estimated,' the CIA report said, but then added, 'This does not mean that the impact of defense programs on the Soviet economy has increased—only that our appreciation of this impact has changed. *It also implies that Soviet defense industries are far less efficient than formerly believed.*' "

It was exactly wrong, then, for Bush to have suggested that the CIA had doubled or even measurably increased its estimate of the size of the actual Soviet defense program, for what it had revised was only its evaluation of the efficiency of Soviet production—in other words, the amount the Russians were paying for what they got. What the CIA showed was that the Soviets were having a harder time punching out the same number of tanks and missiles as the CIA had formerly projected for them; that they were, in other words, paying more for the same level of production. As Cox noted, "What should have been cause for jubilation became the inspiration for misguided alarm."

As for increases of actual Soviet defense spending during the seventies, the CIA, in its official estimate published in January 1980, concluded that for the 1970–79 period, "estimated in constant dollars, Soviet defense activities increased at an average annual rate of 3 percent." This is higher than the U.S. increase during the seventies and lower than the U.S. rate from 1979 through 1983. For the seventies, NATO expenditures exceeded those of the Warsaw Pact. A 3 percent increase in Soviet military spending is actually no higher than the overall increase of the Soviet GNP during the seventies, which is put at between 3 and 5 percent by experts on the subject.

There is much more to be said about the increases that have occurred in the past two decades in the Soviet-force posture relative to that of the United States and of its allies. My purpose here is simply to emphasize the serious error that underlay Team B's assertion that U.S. intelligence had underestimated the Soviet build-up and that a new spiral in the arms race was therefore in order.

Team B's somber estimates of Soviet intentions, accepted as the national intelligence estimates under Bush's prodding, were to alter the climate for détente and arms control that the incoming Carter Administration would face from the time of its inauguration. According to *The New York Times* in December 1976, "President-elect Carter will receive an intelligence estimate of long-range Soviet strategic intentions next month that raises the question whether the Russians are shifting their objectives from rough parity with United States military forces to superiority." The *Times* account added that "previous national estimates of Soviet aims—the supreme products of the intelligence community since 1950—had concluded that the objective was rough parity with United States strategic capabilities." It then quoted Bush as saying that the shift in estimates was warranted because "there are some worrisome signs" and added that "while Mr. Bush declined to discuss the substance of the estimate, it can be authoritatively reported that the worrisome signs included newly developed guided missiles, a vast program of under-ground shelters and a continuing build-up of air defenses."

The Team B report remains classified, but retired Lieutenant General Daniel O. Graham, who had participated in that group's challenge to the previous intelligence estimates of Soviet strength, told *The Washington Post,* when the Team B report was filed at the end of 1976, that there were "two catalytic factors" that had caused this re-evaluation of Soviet intentions. One was the recalculation of the percentage of Soviet GNP going to defense—the meaning of which, as we have seen, was distorted in the Team B report. And, according to the *Post,* "The other major force in changing the official U.S. perception, Graham said, has been 'the discovery of a very important [Soviet] civil-defense effort—very strong and unmistakable evidence that a big effort is on to protect people, industry and to store food.' "

But this big effort, as much as it may have impressed and alarmed General Graham, is simply the primitive-shelter-and-evacuation scheme that T. K. Jones had advocated in his interview with me. When Jones told me that the United States could recover from general nuclear war in an estimated two to four years, he meant that we could do so with a "Soviet-type civil defense." But if digging a hole and covering it with doors is a preposterous defense for Americans, by what logic does the same procedure become "a very important civil-defense effort" according to Team B? Why do Soviet manuals telling their people to dig holes in the tundra become a serious problem for American strategic planners? Yet it is these very holes in the ground that are meant to justify the assertion that the Soviets think they can win a nuclear war.

Window of Vulnerability

When you first hear it, the term window of vulnerability sounds an elusive but unquestioned alarm.

It was a favorite of Republican candidates during the 1980 election, and while neither my colleagues in the press corps nor I understood exactly what it meant, it sounded provocative enough to keep us listening. What we were told was that this window would open up sometime in the mid-eighties and in would fly thousands of "heavier" and more accurate Soviet ICBMs in a first strike capable of wiping out our own intercontinental missiles. Indeed, as candidate Reagan frequently asserted, the window would be open so wide that "the Russians could just take us with a phone call." He meant that Soviet superiority would be so obvious to our leaders that the Russians could blackmail us into surrendering merely by threatening a first strike.

This claimed vulnerability is the major justification of the massive nuclear-arms build-up called for by the Reagan Administration. It was also the basis for Reagan's attacks on the SALT II treaty and for his opposition to a nuclear freeze, both of which, he insists, would lock the United States into a position of strategic inferiority. According to Science magazine, "The scenario [of U.S. vulnerability to a Soviet first strike] did not achieve wide circulation until it was taken up by the Committee on the Present Danger."

Whatever its degree of plausibility, the window of vulnerability was scary stuff in a political campaign, echoing as it did the missile gap of John F. Kennedy's presidential campaign, which, while no more accurately describing an impending real crisis, offered the same kind of simple slogan that voters might buy. In 1960, Kennedy scored heavily with his accusation that the Republicans had left open a missile gap between us and the Soviets. Once he was elected and read the intelligence data, he discovered that the Soviets had only a few missiles compared with our one thousand. But no matter. By the time he discovered the error, he was President.

So, too, the window of vulnerability became a successful election ploy for Reagan and for the other Republican candidates who succeeded in scaring voters into believing that our country's strategic posture had been seriously damaged by Carter's policies of "disarmament." But the analogy with Kennedy ends here, for Reagan became addicted to his campaign rhetoric and as President continued to invoke the window of vulnerability to justify his massive arms build-up. At the October 1981 press conference in which he outlined his strategic program, Reagan once again warned that "a window of vulnerability is opening," and he added that it would "jeopardize not just our hopes for serious, productive arms negotiations but our hopes for peace and freedom." Yet he was not clear about just what this vulnerability entailed. Christopher Paine, who is on the staff of the Federation of American Scientists, described the press conference in *The Bulletin of the Atomic Scientists:*

> "Mr. President," inquired one reporter, "when, exactly, is the 'window of vulnerability'? We heard yesterday the suggestion that it exists now. Earlier this morning, a defense official indicated that it was not until '84 or '87. Are we facing it right now?"
> The President appeared confused by the question. He responded, "I think in some areas we are, yes." As an example, he cited the longstanding "imbalance of forces in the Western front—in the NATO line, we are vastly outdistanced there." And then, in an off-the-cuff assessment that must have touched off a few klaxons in the Navy, the President added, "Right now, they [the Soviets] have a superiority at sea." What did any of this have to do with silo vulnerability?

Referring to the President's observation about Soviet naval superiority, Roger Molander, a former National Security Council member and founder of Ground Zero, told me that Reagan's comment "demonstrated how poor the President's grasp of this issue was. If there's one area in which the United States has acknowledged superiority, it's the Navy—submarines, antisubmarine warfare, aircraft carriers, naval armaments, across the board."

In any case, to link a presumed Soviet naval advantage with the vulnerability of our land-based nuclear weapons to a Soviet first strike was a startling non sequitur. But this sort of exaggeration worked for Reagan as a rhetorical device both during the campaign and in the Presidency. In a speech to the Veterans of Foreign Wars in August 1980, he said, "We're already in an arms race, but only the Soviets are racing." Reagan is convinced that the United States disarmed unilaterally during the seventies while the Soviets barreled ahead in weapons development and deployment; that we accepted parity in nuclear weapons while the Soviet Union pushed forward to attain superiority.

One problem with that argument is that few experts on strategic matters agree that the United States is inferior. While it is possible that the United States may be inferior to the Soviets in specific areas of conventional military power, such as the size of land forces or the number of tanks, it is difficult to understand the charge that the United States is inferior to the Soviets in nuclear weaponry. Perhaps the kindest thing that can be said for such assertions, to quote Gerard Smith, President Nixon's chief negotiator on strategic-arms-limitations talks, is that they "raise questions about the Administration's common sense and, worse, its credibility."

Reagan's campaign rhetoric confused a threat to U.S. land-based missiles with a threat to overall U.S. ability to deter a Soviet first strike. While there is much disagreement among experts as to the percentage of U.S. missiles that would be destroyed by a Soviet attack, no one doubts that the increased accuracy of Soviet missiles has made U.S. land-based missiles more vulnerable to such attack. While U.S. observers were surprised by the speed with which the Soviets caught up to the United States in land-based missile accuracy, no one had seriously doubted that this would eventually occur.

It was precisely because of this expectation that land-based missiles would become more vulnerable that the United States decided to concentrate instead on the other legs of the defense triad—submarine-launched missiles and the bomber fleet. The Soviets have not been able to develop the technology to match this development, and as a result, the survivability of the U.S. nuclear force is unquestionably far greater than that presumed of the enemy.

This last point is important, since Reagan's literal definition of the window of vulnerability is the prediction that at some point in the near future the Soviets will have a strategic advantage of such magnitude that they can launch a first strike sufficient to prevent a devastating U.S. response. This prediction, however, rests on a distortion of elemental facts about the makeup of the U.S. deterrent force and the nature of nuclear war—a distortion so transparent that the prediction of U.S. vulnerability has the hollow sound of deliberate fabrication.

For the window-of-vulnerability argument to work, its proponents must simply ignore America's submarines and bombers, most of which are on alert at any given time and cannot, therefore, be taken out in a first strike. Most experts believe that these two legs of the triad of U.S. defense forces would survive a Soviet first strike and, given their firepower, that their use in retaliation following a Soviet first strike would mean the end of Soviet society. As Harold Brown, Carter's Secretary of Defense, noted in his last statement on the defense budget, "The retaliatory potential of U.S. forces remaining after a counterforce exchange is substantial even in the worst case and would increase steadily after 1981, with or without SALT."

During the campaign, Reagan was fond of offering sad-eyed descriptions of "our aging B-52s," punctuated with his inevitable anecdote about encountering a B-52 pilot whose father and grandfather had flown the same plane. The implication was that the plane—part of our deterrent forces against a Soviet first strike—was all but falling apart, hopelessly old-fashioned, and in every other way inadequate to the grand defensive task at hand. Carter had disarmed us, or so the Reagan argument went, in part by refusing to fund the B-1 bomber to replace those presumably derelict B-52s.

Reagan ignored the fact that the Soviet bomber fleet is a poor shadow of our own. Most modern Soviet bombers lack the range to reach the United

States, and the airplanes that *can* reach us are slow and are used mostly for reconnaissance. Nor did Reagan mention the air-launched cruise missiles that the Carter Administration had brought into production at great cost to the taxpayer. One argument against the B-52s is that they are supposed to be increasingly vulnerable to Soviet antiaircraft fire. Yet when cruise missiles are installed on those B-52s, the aging planes become very effective launching platforms far outside Soviet territory, beyond the range of Soviet antiaircraft power. No matter who had won the 1980 election, those air-launched cruise missiles would have been installed beginning in 1982.

This fact prompted Hans Bethe, who dismissed Reagan's charge that the Carter Administration had somehow "disarmed" America, to note, "On the contrary, the most important progress in weapons in the past decade, I would say, was the cruise missile, which was developed under Carter."

Now seventy-six, Bethe has continued working on U.S. strategic-weapons systems, from the hydrogen bomb through anti-ballistic-missile defenses, and helped design the heat shield to protect ballistic missiles as they re-enter the atmosphere. It was, therefore, from a position of some authority that he challenged Reagan's vulnerability argument last winter, telling me: "I don't think that either country is going to make a first strike, because it is absolutely crazy to do so. But suppose there were a first strike from the Russians, and suppose they could destroy all our Minuteman missiles. It wouldn't make the slightest difference. Would we be defenseless? Not at all. We have the submarine force with an enormous striking power."

Bethe, as is his custom, referred to careful notes he had made in preparation for our interview. "I would like to state that there is no deficiency in armaments in the United States, that we don't need to catch up to the Russians, that, if anything, the Russians have to catch up to us. The Russians have their forces mostly in ICBMs, a type of weapon that is becoming more and more vulnerable. I think our military people know this, but they always talk about the vulnerability of our nuclear ICBMs and never talk about those of the Soviets. The Russians are much more exposed to a possible first strike from us than we are to one from them."

One who agrees with Bethe is McNamara. I asked him how it was possible to argue that the Soviets could now contemplate a first strike when the United States was not able to pull that off at a time of massive nuclear superiority, and he replied: "They no more have a first-strike capability today than we had then. No one has demonstrated to me that the Soviets have a capability of destroying our Minutemen. But even if they could destroy our Minutemen, that doesn't give them a first-strike capability, not when they are facing our Polaris submarines and our bombers. The other two legs of the triad are still there . . . The argument is without foundation. It's absurd."

Postscript

I have referred to some of the men now running our government's foreign policy as neo-hawks, because they are more ideological, more complex, and better informed in their advocacy of a hard military line than the traditional "nuke 'em" crowd. These men came to their militarism not through a love of battle or of the gadgetry of war, or even through a belief in the robust cleansing effect of rough physical contact. They are intellectuals who in their personal demeanor hardly bring to mind Achilles or Hector but, instead, reveal a fussy, polemical, hairsplitting intellectual style that becomes only verbally violent.

Eugene Rostow, Paul Nitze, Richard Perle, Richard Pipes, who initiate policy for the Reagan Administration—who write the position papers and the policy options that are then funneled up the chain of command that sets the bounds for the major decisions—most of those men are academics or at home in academic settings. As I have come to know them, I have been struck by this curious gap between the bloodiness of their rhetoric and their apparent inability to visualize the physical consequences of what they advocate.

These neo-hawks refuse to acknowledge that reality. They want to threaten the use of nuclear weapons at a time of nuclear parity, when such a threat jeopardizes not only the enemy but one's fellow citizens. For the significance of parity is that both sides will be destroyed if we really do get high enough up the escalation ladder. To climb that ladder, as Perle, for example, would like to do, requires a fundamental alteration of the most common view of nuclear war: that it is an unspeakable disaster that would reduce both sides to ashes and destroy civilization for longer than anyone cares to contemplate—maybe forever.

These true believers in nuclear-war fighting, including the President of the United States and most of his key advisers, tell one another what they want to hear: that playing a game of nuclear chicken with the Soviets is not as dangerous as it might seem, for even in the worst case—even if the Soviets don't back off, even if they don't submit to our nuclear pressure—the resulting war will not be so bad; it can be limited and civilization can bounce back sooner or later.

But it is one thing to talk oneself into accepting that the nuclear-arms race and the game of threat escalation are not so dangerous and quite another to convince ordinary voters to go along with this madness. This is why in a time of nuclear parity, when both sides are totally at risk, our hawkish leaders invoke the chaste vocabulary of vulnerability and deterrence rather than the blunt language of death and disaster.

Early in this report, I described a former CIA analyst who has never forgotten the birds that turned to cinders as he observed them through the pulsing thermal effect of a nuclear explosion many years ago. This man has a son, and this is what he thinks about when he thinks of that young man:

"You know, my son just joined the Marine Corps. I don't know why he did it. He went out and joined the Marine Corps. And I think about him. He's a very enthusiastic kid. Goddamn, he's full of life, energy. And he really wants to be a Marine. He wants to be a good Marine. He's seriously involved in that stuff. He's an expert marksman. He does hundreds of push-ups, runs miles in a very few minutes. And I think of him in a nuclear war. I try to personalize what that is like according to the calculations that we do. I think of my son in a foxhole and what he's experiencing as this nuclear weapon goes off. And I'm comparing what he's experiencing with what I've seen of a nuclear weapon. Only he's up close—not like me, far away . . . He's right there; he's on the front lines. And I'm saying to myself, He's in serious trouble. I can see a variety of things that are going to happen to him, either quickly or afterward, that are not pleasant. And then I put myself back in this theoretical, strategic stuff, where these guys just calculate megatonnage. But my son is fried."

(*Playboy*, December 1982)

The Shambles of Star Wars

1

Secretary of State George Shultz was perplexed and turned to the aerospace executive next to him to ask what the President was talking about. Shultz said the President's plan sounded worrisome. The executive wasn't quite sure just what the President had in mind, but he assured Shultz that it would never get off the ground. They were guests at a hastily arranged and secret White House dinner gathering of about fifty top government officials, weapons contractors, and scientists dramatically summoned on very short notice from throughout the country to be briefed on a speech the President would soon be making to the nation. Between their main course and dessert, the President left them to face the television cameras to speak of "changing the course of human history" with a bold new program aimed at rendering "nuclear weapons impotent and obsolete." A scientist in attendance that night reports that most of his colleagues were stunned by the President's pitch, "except Edward [Teller]—he was just beaming. This is his baby. He's been pushing defense for years, but everybody else I talked to thought the speech was just off the wall."

So it went, back in March of 1983, when Reagan—in what is most commonly referred to as his "Star Wars" speech—proposed building a defensive system that would protect the United States against attack by intercontinental ballistic missiles. It was a flyer, a gambit, an impulse totally outside mainstream thinking on national defense. There was even something pixieish about how the President just stuck it into the end of a speech calling for more spending on offensive nuclear weapons, such as the MX missile. "I've been having this idea," the President explained at a press conference a few days after the speech. "It's been kicking around in my mind for some time here recently . . . And since we don't know how long it will take . . . we have to start."

Now the whole world is discussing what is officially termed the President's Strategic Defense Initiative (SDI), a name that suggests a carefully conceived, well-thought-out, and meticulously planned proposal. It is none of those things, and Administration insiders concede that the program it spawned is in disarray. "There was no one in the Administration who had thought through the consequences," a key White House scientific consultant told me, "and so it was natural when that bombshell hit for people to scramble around and figure out what they are going to do next." The consultant, who requested anonymity, still works on the project but expressed concern that the office set up in the Administration to run this program is "in a shambles . . . everyone's scrambling for contracts, but it's not at all clear what we're after."

But shambles or not, Star Wars has become a major fact of life in the nuclear-arms negotiations between the United States and the Soviet Union. The President had hoped to shift the discussion away from traditional arms control and onto defensive strategy. Both sides agree that efforts to construct defensive weapons are a serious obstacle to reaching agreement on a comprehensive test ban treaty, a ban on weapons in space, and perhaps any far-reaching arms control at all. The President has repeatedly said he would not halt development and testing of a Star Wars system in exchange for deep cuts in the number of Soviet offensive missiles.

However, despite its immediate impact, one point about the Star Wars debate can be made bluntly: neither side seems to know exactly what they are talking about. As yet, neither superpower has even the recognizable beginnings of a defensive system that could render nuclear weapons "impotent," as the President has proposed. Most experts agree that this particular goal will never be met. Thus, most proponents of SDI are resigned to accomplishing something far less significant, and the talk in the trade is now most often about new anti-satellite weapons or some increased measure of protection for missile silos. And even Star Wars's most enthusiastic boosters never claimed that the system could thwart attack by nuclear-armed cruise missiles, manned bombers, or low-trajectory missiles.

However, that night in March, Reagan clearly had more in mind. For years before he became President, he had been getting enthusiastic briefings from members of the political right—such as physicist Edward Teller and retired Army Lieutenant General Daniel Graham—urging development of a defensive shield to protect America against incoming missiles. Theoretically, this shield would protect civilians as well as missile silos. Teller and Graham were preaching to the converted. Reagan was predisposed to believe in a scientific fix to the threat of nuclear weapons. Back in 1980 on a campaign flight Reagan told me of the following experience: "NORAD is an amazing place—that's out in Colorado, you know, under the mountain. They actually are tracking several thousand objects in space, meaning satellites of ours and everyone else's, even down to the point that they are tracking a glove lost by an astronaut that is still circling the earth up there. I think the thing that struck me was the irony that here, with this great technology of ours, we can do all of this yet we cannot stop any of the weapons that are coming at us. I don't think there's been a time in history when there wasn't a defense against some kind of thrust, even back in the old-fashioned days when we had coast artillery that would stop invading ships if they came."

This belief that nuclear weapons could be treated as conventional weapons once were has long had appeal to those like Reagan who put their faith more in weaponry than treaties as a means of dealing with the Soviet threat. Like Teller, Graham, and other members of their circle, Reagan had opposed the Nixon Administration's treaty with the Soviets limiting deployment of anti-ballistic missiles and other defensive systems. Like them, Reagan looks with dark suspicion upon what they all see as the Anti-Ballistic Missile Treaty's aftermath—an unwarranted Soviet build-up permitted by the flawed Strategic Arms Limitation Treaties (SALT) negotiated by the Nixon, Ford, and Carter Administrations.

In the months preceding the President's speech, this lobbying had intensified, buttressed by selective leaks to the media about alleged technological breakthroughs. But few members of the defense Establishment—Republicans or Democrats—were converted to the concept of defensive shields. In fact, according to White House insiders, the President deliberately avoided the normal channels for clearing a new defense program because he anticipated that his government's own experts would summarily reject the proposal. Reagan wrote the relevant portions of the speech himself, while at Camp David, consulting only Robert McFarlane, his then National Security Adviser, and George Keyworth II, his chief science adviser. No advice concerning the speech was asked for or received from the Joint Chiefs of Staff, the State or Defense Departments. Defense Secretary Caspar Weinberger, who was traveling in Europe the week of the speech, had to be told by phone that something big was up.

All of this suggests that the President's impulsive proposal was a response to something other than strategic or technical necessity. That impression was confirmed by Gerold Yonas, the project's chief scientist and acting deputy director, who recalled that, during those months, the White House felt increasingly under siege: "The opposition to MX and the freeze movement were very close to succeeding; [there was] the Catholic bishops' pastoral letter, which at one point said nuclear weapons were immoral. All of us working in the weapons game were aware of that whole business, including the anti-nuclear movement in Europe. There was a lot of frustration." According to Yonas, there also was concern over public response to the television movie *The Day After*, which graphically portrayed the effects of nuclear war.

The factors Yonas cited have all but faded from the scene, and even critics now concede that Star Wars has been an enormous political achievement for the President, permitting him to capture the moral high ground at a time when his defense build-up was under increasing attack. Civil defense as the underpinning of the Russians-are-coming nuclear-war-fighting scenarios had become a bad joke. But in Star Wars Reagan found an up-to-the-minute alternative to digging holes in the ground.

While Star Wars the speech was an immediate political success, even SDI proponents agree that Star Wars the program has proved at best to be vague and contradictory. The speech was a mixture of "hope and hype," says George Smith, an expert on nuclear-war fighting at the Lawrence Livermore National Laboratory—one of two facilities where America's nuclear weapons are developed. "The hope is getting rid of nuclear weapons, which we all want. The hype is thinking it can be done with these new exotic weapons."

What originally caught the public's imagination was the President's notion of an umbrella that could prevent nuclear missiles from hitting this country's population as well as its military targets. "Let me share with you a vision of the future which offers hope . . ." Reagan said that night. "What if free people could live secure in the knowledge that their security did not rest upon the threat of instant U.S. retaliation to deter a Soviet attack, that we could intercept and destroy strategic ballistic missiles before they reached our own soil or that of our allies?" As James Schlesinger, who served as defense secretary in two previous Republican Administrations and as an arms control adviser to Reagan's, said recently, "The heart of that speech was the promise that some day, American cities might be safe from nuclear attack. . . . That is the political appeal. That is what the American public hopes is going to occur. . . . [But there is] no realistic hope that we will be able ever again to protect American cities."

The President himself soon learned that there was hardly anyone around who thought such a goal realistic in the foreseeable future. Certainly not William Perry, a hard-liner who, as Under Secretary of Defense in the Carter Administration, presided over a $1-billion-per-year defensive weapons research program. "I was incredulous," Perry told me. "My first question was who in the world was advising him [Reagan] on this. It's a very attractive idea. Too bad it's a fantasy." Perry added that "there were no breakthroughs in technology nor, in my opinion, in the [Soviet] threat" to warrant an expanded SDI program. That view was echoed by Richard Delauer, Reagan's former Under Secretary of Defense for Research and Engineering. "They were going to make nuclear weapons obsolete," Delauer said. "But those of us who knew what was really going on couldn't support that."

"Nobody believes in 100 percent leakproof defense," Yonas told me. "Nobody believes in 100 percent anything that's ever worked on military systems." His view was echoed by another SDI proponent, Paul Brown, Livermore's assistant associate director for arms control: "When you consider what the President intended, which was a leakproof umbrella, I think that that's something that very few scientists think is going to be possible."

Yet there has been no shortage of scientists lining up to attempt the impossible. The SDI office recently reported that it has a stack of 1,000 proposals from universities hoping to work on Star Wars. Major aerospace contractors already have been given substantial commitments for research. Even SDI's critics have doubts about halting a program that has developed such a substantial constituency of scientists and contractors. "There's a tipping point on any weapons system," notes physicist Sidney Drell, deputy director of the Stanford Linear Accelerator Center. "Once a certain amount of money is committed, even if the weapon makes no sense, it's not going to be easy to change course. What's happening now is that all of the industries and many scientists are being brought into this, and that creates a constituency of support that, up the road, becomes impossible to turn off."

The Soviets' shrill criticism of Star Wars, which Drell regards as hypocritical in light of similar programs in that country, has also served to confuse the debate. "Once the Russians started bleeding so much about this, it made it easy to lump criticism of SDI with being soft on the Russians, which I am not," Drell said. "This is just not a good way to defend the country. There are better, more workable, and cheaper ways to improve our defenses. In fact, it's distracting us from real problems we have on defense."

One of the most distracting things about SDI is that even its most fervent proponents are divided over what they are proposing. Even before the President's speech, for example, Teller and Graham—who had influenced Reagan to make his proposal—had fallen out over just what it meant. Teller had resigned from the advisory board of Graham's High Frontiers organization, which lobbies for defensive weapons, because they are committed to diametrically opposed solutions to the problem. Graham and his group favor using what he claims is existing, off-the-shelf technology that could be deployed rather swiftly and relatively cheaply. Graham also looks to non-nuclear weapons. Teller, on the other hand, favors a massive, high-tech research program that would take at least a decade, require massive funding, and feature work on a device called a nuclear-pumped X-ray laser under his sponsorship at Livermore.

Reagan's speech appeared to favor Teller's approach in stressing the long-term research aspect of the program. But a month later, reports from the White House indicated that the program was to be non-nuclear, which would cut out Teller's pet project. Nor was the matter made any clearer earlier this year, when Energy Secretary John Herrington, whose department funds Livermore, issued a joint statement with Weinberger stating that the program would be non-nuclear, although research on the nuclear part would continue as a backup if all else failed. More significant is the Administration's broad retreat on the stated purposes of the program. The emphasis now is increasingly on adding to deterrence rather than replacing it as a national strategy. In the process, the Strategic Defense Initiative has come to look more and more like an expanded ABM program.

Confused though the program's objectives may be, the Administration plans to spend $26 billion on it over the next five years. During the program's first year, the money could not be spent fast enough to use up the yearly appropriation. The size of such funding requests comes as no surprise to Delauer, who until recently was Weinberger's top assistant on weapons technology. He is a weary veteran of lobbying efforts by Teller, Graham, and other proponents of a crash program on SDI, and he feels that they seriously underestimate the cost of eventually deploying a system. "Everybody still underestimates the cost. The Secretary [Weinberger] gets mad at me about that. I was never against SDI. I just said it was going to cost a lot of money, and it wasn't going to do what everybody thought. But I didn't think it had to." Delauer's testimony before the Senate Armed Services Committee produced the $26-billion price tag for the program over the next five years, a figure that Delauer now says he just pulled out of the air, although it was used by the Administration as a realistic projection. As Delauer remembers it, his improvisation came under pressure from the Senate committee's ranking Democratic member: "I tried to figure out what the hell we're talking about. Sam Nunn (D-Ga.) wanted a number and kept insisting on having a number . . . okay . . . first year was $2.4 billion, and I figure, okay, best we could handle is maybe a 20–25 percent per year growth. It's not small potatoes," ventured Delauer with the air of one accustomed to shopping markets where items are routinely rounded out to the nearest million and sometimes billion for convenience of calculation. Moreover, he emphasizes that his cost estimates are for research only and have nothing to do with the expense of actually developing a Star Wars system, if one eventually is developed.

Serious proponents of SDI tend to promise nothing and instead focus on the desirability of research. After all, something may work, they say, and anyway, we have to be certain that the Soviets do not surpass us with any surprise successes. In this scenario, all problems raised by the program's critics become opportunities for research. What has been called the technological imperative for change has driven all modern weapons programs, but it is particularly powerful in pushing SDI, because the science and engineering involved are so complicated and undeveloped. William Lowell Morgan, a Livermore physicist working on the X-ray laser weapon, has grave doubts about the possibility and wisdom of deploying SDI but concedes that the science is "very interesting." This is particularly true in comparison to "just going on building warheads for missiles, which had gotten very predictable and boring."

While the vast majority of the project's scientific proponents tend to be similarly cautious in their hopes, a sense of adventure often seems to overwhelm them. Yonas, for example, was somewhat euphoric as he ticked off the proposal's challenges: "Look, we don't have a guarantee at this point. This is still a risky venture. And we're going to continue to bill it as a research program . . . There's an awful lot of program breakthroughs we have to make if we're going to do it. What we're doing in the SDI is trying to make the twenty-first century happen a lot faster than it would have ordinarily. We're going to pull it forward by making a technology thrust." Yonas would not rule out any of the techniques that have been proposed, except to note lightly that "we've dropped all emphasis on the crossbow—trying to pull that string tight is really a bitch, particularly when you're under attack." One hears jokes like that all the time from proponents and critics of the program, suggesting that they are not quite sure what they are looking for, but it's fun getting there. "I think that the great majority of the lab's technical people view the President's speech as somewhat off the wall and the programs being proposed as being, in the end, intrinsically rather foolish," notes Livermore physicist Hugh DeWitt. "But obviously the lab is benefiting right now and will continue to benefit, and everybody's rather happy with the marvelous new work."

However, other scientists have resisted the temptation. In June 1985, computer scientist David Parnas quit an appointment that paid him $1,000 a day for service on a high-level advisory panel convened by the SDI organization to evaluate the computer part of the system's battle management. "Most of the money spent will be wasted; we wouldn't trust the system if we did build it," charged Parnas, a professor who previously worked full-time at the Naval Research Laboratory on computer applications to weapons systems. Parnas said he had no ideological objection to the defensive weapons program but had concluded that a computer program of such complexity and accuracy could not be completed. Citing the challenge of the President's speech asking scientists to work toward making nuclear weapons impotent and obsolete, Parnas wrote to the SDI organization: "It is our duty, as scientists and engineers, to reply that we have no technological magic that will accomplish that. The President and the public should know that." Parnas, who will continue with the Navy on other weapons, conceded in his report that "I am quite certain that you will be able to find software experts who disagree with my conclusions." He also noted that other scientists and defense contractors see SDI as a "pot of gold just waiting to be tapped."

2

"But is it a bomb?" Defense Secretary Weinberger wanted to know one day walking through the halls of the Pentagon with his then-undersecretary Richard Delauer. Weinberger was inquiring about the X-ray laser, a key weapon in the President's Star Wars program.

"I had to tell him," Delauer recalled recently, "you're going to have to detonate a nuclear bomb in space. That's how you're going to get the X-ray."

But Weinberger repeated his question: "It's not a bomb, is it?"

No, Delauer said tactfully, it would be a "nuclear event."

Weinberger seemed satisfied and, as Delauer later told me, he concluded that the defense secretary "didn't understand the technology. Most people don't."

As Weinberger's "tell-me-it-ain't-so" question indicates, the X-ray laser, initially expected to carry much of the load for SDI, has turned out to be a seriously flawed defensive weapon. It requires a substantial nuclear explosion to generate the laser, a fact now judged inconvenient in a program defined by the President as a "non-nuclear" effort to make nuclear weapons "impotent and obsolete." Critics of SDI have made much of the prospect of thousands of nuclear bombs circling in space set to launch their X-rays but—regrettably—also subject to other misfortunes. "A bomb in space is a bomb in space," said Abraham Szoke, a physicist at the Lawrence Livermore National Laboratory, "and we wouldn't be too happy if the Russians had them up there." Worse, the consensus among scientists is that the X-ray laser—if it ever really works—will be useful first as an anti-satellite weapon and then, much later, as a limited part of a defensive system. If it also is developed by the Soviets, it could be used to quickly eliminate what critics refer to as the "sitting ducks" of Star Wars—the huge mirrors, battle stations, spy satellites, and sensors that would have to be deployed in space at a cost of billions of dollars as part of the President's proposed shield against enemy missiles. Thus, the weapon that more than anything else may have inspired the optimism of the President's initial Star Wars speech is now treated as something of an embarrassment by the Administration.

The Administration is well aware of the political vulnerability of this weapon. Keyworth, the President's science adviser, at one point all but dismissed the X-ray laser as a defensive weapon when he said: "I think it is unlikely that the American people will maintain full and enduring support for these [Star Wars] systems if they continue to rely upon nuclear weapons as defensive means, when there is no assurance that the defense weapon is not potentially as damaging as the threat that they confront." But the Administration continues to fund the X-ray laser to the tune of an estimated $100 million a year and the tale of its persistence forms a curious and important part of the Star Wars story. As with much of the rest of the tale, it is difficult to tell without conjuring up the stooped, somewhat enfeebled but always feisty figure of Edward Teller, ever alert to the problems of national security and their potential nuclear solutions.

A good place to begin is one day three years ago at the Lawrence Livermore National Laboratory, which is funded by the Energy Department and nominally managed by the University of California regents. It was the scene of Teller's past triumphs. Teller had come to mark the lab's thirtieth birthday by speaking against the nuclear freeze and for construction of "a third generation" of nuclear weapons.

"The first generation," Teller explained with mounting enthusiasm, "was the fission [atomic] one. The second was the fusion [hydrogen] bomb. The third, I would describe as the kind of bomb that uses the nuclear explosion only as a starting point to accomplish something else." The something else was the X-ray laser—that well-publicized example of Star Wars exotica. "What this laboratory can accomplish now," Teller told his audience, "is more important than what we ever have accomplished before. The third-generation efforts give us every expectation of an effective nuclear defense," he said. "And if defense by nuclear weapons is possible, we must have it." He also warned that the Russians were at work on a defensive system and that if we didn't build one, they would.

Seven months later, after much prodding by Teller, Reagan echoed those sentiments in his Star Wars speech. Teller had been talking anti-ballistic-missile defense with Reagan and many other politicians for decades. But this time he had brought something new to the table: persuasive talk of a bold new weapon—the X-ray laser—which, he claimed, for the first time made defense of the U.S. population feasible. Initially dubbed the Excalibur, after King Arthur's legendary sword, the X-ray laser is now called the Super Excalibur, indicating a progression of sorts. According to SDI's proponents, an important step in that progression occurred on March 23, 1985, during the explosion of an experimental nuclear device at the government's Nevada test site. The test's code name was "Cottage."

That the Cottage test involved the X-ray laser should have been a tightly guarded secret. But within a short time the press was flooded with leaks from pro-SDI sources proclaiming the experiment a success. Civilians living near the Nevada test range are routinely warned about the size of impending tests, and on March 23 they were told to expect a blast in the 20–150 kiloton range. Thus, the fact that Cottage involved the X-ray laser is a critical bit of intelligence. It indicates that the explosion needed to pump the X-ray laser was not "small," as leaked reports had claimed. It was at least 20 kilotons, possibly as large as 150 kilotons. The bomb that devastated Hiroshima was 13 kilotons. Leaks about the Cottage test alarmed those charged with administering SDI. As a result, the FBI in May began a major investigation at Livermore to determine just how it all happened.

One possible leak occurred soon after the Cottage test in a speech Teller gave in April at U.C. Irvine. It was reported in the Orange County edition of the *Los Angeles Times*, but not picked up elsewhere. In an upbeat report on Star Wars progress, Teller said the X-ray laser weapons "exist not on paper" but in reality. "Three weeks ago, I couldn't have said that," he said. Teller's statement apparently referred to the Cottage test, which had occurred two weeks earlier, and as such, the speech may have violated classification guidelines. On his way home to Palo Alto, after giving the Irvine speech, Teller ran into me at the San Jose airport. When I told him I was working on a Star Wars story and was on my way to see Sidney Drell, Teller said: "Make sure Drell tells you of the latest developments."

Half an hour later, Drell, a cheerful Ed Asner look-alike, greeted me with an impish smile and the words: "I know, you met Edward at the airport. He called me to make sure I knew of the latest test results so that I could tell you." Drell, a veteran of many defense science projects, who has been briefed extensively on SDI but remains critical, said he did not share Teller's assessment of the results but felt bound by classification restrictions not to say anything further about the subject. In fact, some critics suggest that proponents of SDI have misused classified data to present a far too promising picture of the work done on the X-ray laser, but that classification rules prevent their responding in kind.

The most disturbing example of that, they claim, was a front-page article in *The New York Times* a month after Teller's Irvine speech. "What appears to be an important advance in developing an X-ray laser space weapon powered by a nuclear bomb," the paper reported, "has been made by scientists at the Lawrence Livermore National Laboratory." The article, by William Broad, reported that, according to information supplied by "federal scientists," the work at Livermore "has increased the brightness and thus the power of the X-ray device by focusing its rays."

The appearance of that story propelled the FBI into its investigation. Lab classification rules had even prevented use of the word "focusing" in the non-classified titles of talks or papers. The identification on the focusing process and a report of its success were more serious. One White House science adviser said of the *New York Times* article that "it was a press release. The Livermore guys saw the President's policy moving away from their favorite toy, so they began a counter campaign." This same adviser also would not comment on the test results because of classification, but he believed that the reports of its success were exaggerated. "As a piece of basic research in physics, they have done some clever stuff, but to go from there to a weapons system is a tremendous leap." He added that "the public is being whipped around by selective leaks of highly classified information."

In Livermore, the *New York Times* article evoked a pithier response from physicist Ray Kidder, who has "worked on more different weapons projects than I can remember" during twenty-nine years at the lab. Sitting in a Chinese restaurant, Kidder—a big, ruddy-faced, mustachioed man, dressed in blue jeans and a broad-checked, open-neck sports shirt—sucked on a Budweiser and concluded, "It's just baloney. The public is getting swindled by one side that has access to classified information and can say whatever it wants and not go to jail, whereas we [SDI's critics with access to classified information] can't say whatever we want; we would go to jail, that's the difference. It's so frustrating to me, because nearly everybody around here [Livermore] agrees with what I've said except two guys who are the world's biggest BSers, and they're goddamn good at it, and that's Teller and Wood." (Lowell Wood is a Teller protégé who has been instrumental in pushing the X-ray laser program at Livermore.)

Kidder has worked with Teller, including consulting recently on a problem related to the X-ray laser, and he is at great pains to indicate respect for Teller as a physicist. It is a respect he does not extend to Wood, whom he refers to only as "that salesman." Kidder, who ran the lab's laser program for its first decade, has written scathingly critical internal technical memoranda on the lab's nuclear-pumped X-ray laser. "If the X-ray laser works, and it might," Kidder wrote in a declassified version of his critique, "space-based weapons will become no more than provocative sitting ducks," because the laser will be first and foremost an anti-satellite device.

In his speech at U.C. Irvine, Teller seemed to confirm Kidder's charges about the X-ray laser's uses. Teller said it "could be, and probably will be, used in destroying [Soviet] satellites."

But, unlike Teller, Kidder thinks that that is its only use, and that it cannot fulfill the role it was expected to play in a Star Wars defense. This is because the X-rays themselves cannot penetrate deeply into the atmosphere. "The atmosphere is equivalent to a wall of water thirty feet thick," Kidder observed, "and X-rays can't go through that wall of water, no matter how desirable that may be to politicians."

This is no minor limitation, because Star Wars proponents originally hoped to down Soviet missiles in the initial stage of their flight, in what is known as "boost phase." But if the Soviets redesign their missiles to complete their boost phase within the atmosphere—as they're now expected to do—they will be invulnerable to X-ray lasers. A missile in the first stage of its flight can be likened to a huge bus carrying fuel, warheads, and decoys disguised as warheads to fool the enemy. It is easier for satellites to detect at this stage because of the heat it emits on takeoff. And it is easier to destroy in this phase because the bus missile is made of more fragile material than the warheads that it will eventually release. Most important, if the missile is hit in boost phase, all its warheads and decoys are destroyed with one shot. After boost phase, the warheads and decoys will disperse, and there will be hundreds, if not thousands, of targets to contend with. For all of these reasons, it is widely assumed that the ability to knock out enemy missiles in their boost phase is essential to the success of SDI.

But four months after the President's March 1983 speech, a panel commissioned by the Administration to look into SDI heard disquieting testimony from the Martin Marietta Corporation, considered to be expert on rocketry. Company scientists estimated that it was a relatively simple matter for the Soviets to adopt a so-called fast burn that would cut their boost phase from five minutes to fifty seconds. The significance of this was twofold—the time in which the missiles could be hit would be prohibitively short, and their boost phase would be completed within the atmosphere, which would protect them from the X-rays.

Formerly, it was thought that the Soviets would be in boost phase for five minutes, permitting an X-ray laser bomb to be "popped" from the ground into space, where it would explode, directing its X-rays down at the Soviet missile. ("Pop up" was thought to be a politically acceptable alternative to leaving the X-ray bomb permanently in space.) It is generally accepted that the fifty-second boost phase would be prohibitively short for interception by pop up. "You're talking about something that might have to work in a minute. That's just too short a time to make decisions to make something like this work," said Paul Brown, Livermore's assistant associate director for arms control.

Knowledge about the fast-burn option came as a considerable shock to SDI proponents. According to Kidder: "Teller almost certainly didn't know about fast burn when he pushed the X-ray laser on the President, and now he's caught out on a very thin limb with a weapon that can't do the job." Teller was not available for comment on this question, but Yonas confirmed that "X-rays cannot penetrate the atmosphere."

Yonas stressed instead that the X-ray lasers might play a role in intercepting missiles in mid-course or at least in exploding balloons and other decoys unleashed by the Soviets along with their missiles to confuse the defense. But George Smith discounts the efficacy of the X-ray laser as an intercept weapon, even in mid-course, because of another technical limitation. Because it is generated by a nuclear explosion, the whole weapon is destroyed quite suddenly and there is a limit to how many warheads, or balloons disguised to look like warheads, it can take out in that time. "You only get one or, at best, a few shots off from the weapon," Smith claimed, "before the thermal effects of the bomb's explosion destroy the whole works. It would be very expensive to pop these things up to take out a few decoys."

No survey exists of what people at Livermore think about the Kidder-Wood controversy, but it is not difficult to encounter expressions of skepticism about some of the grander goals set for SDI. And on an off-the-record basis, it is often made quite clear that Teller and Wood are considered a bit wild in their optimism.

"I would characterize it slightly differently," commented George Miller, Livermore's deputy associate director for nuclear design, when asked about Kidder's assessment of the mood at the lab. "I think that most of the people at the working levels are skeptical, but they understand enough of technological innovation and that the potential for defense is so important that we should spend the effort trying to find out."

Yonas, who is respected by the program's boosters and critics for his sense of balance, falls squarely into that camp. In fact, while discussing the project's hopes and potential pitfalls, he catalogued the obstacles in what sounded almost like a Hasidic chant of scientific ecstasy: "We need tens of millions of elements . . . more sensors in a focal point arrangement that doesn't exist. Can you do it? Yeah, I think you can do it. Have we done it? No, we haven't done it. Optics, large optics, cheap large areas. Do we have it today? Now, we don't have techniques for manufacturing optics. But if you say that the first light bulb and the 10 millionth light bulb are gonna be the same, I don't agree with you."

But when it comes to the X-ray laser, there is general agreement that the weapon is in the infancy of its development. The "success" of the Cottage test proved only that some slight focusing of the X-rays was possible. Proponents think this may be improved upon after years of further testing, but critics are doubtful. Both sides agree that at this point neither the Soviet Union nor the United States is even close to deploying such a weapon.

William Lowell Morgan decries the failure of some of his Livermore colleagues to acknowledge the device's real status and limitations: "The public holds scientists in awe and has implicit trust in them. Scientists, consequently, have an obligation to level with the public. To lie to the public because we know that the public doesn't understand all this technical stuff brings us scientists down to the level of hawkers of snake oil, miracle cleaners, and Veg-O-Matics."

Critics and supporters of the X-ray laser also agree that neither the United States nor the Soviets could develop the weapon if a comprehensive test ban treaty or even one banning tests below the level of ten kilotons were in force. "To get an X-ray laser requires an awful lot of data," Yonas said, "and when you have to get the data with underground tests that we don't fire very often, it's a long and tedious process."

Miller and Brown agree that even a low threshold test ban would stop the Soviet and American programs on the X-ray laser. But they claim that Livermore opposes a test ban for other reasons, particularly that of maintaining the reliability of the stockpile of weapons. DeWitt insists that the lab's objections to a test ban are largely motivated by the fact that government contracts for the third-generation nuclear weapons have given the lab "a new lease on life."

Soon after the President's Star Wars speech, Cornell University physicist Kurt Gottfried predicted that the desire to push ahead with anti-missile weapons was the real reason for the Administration's resistance to a test ban treaty. After noting that "every President from Dwight D. Eisenhower to Jimmy Carter has sought a comprehensive test ban," Gottfried added, "the Reagan Administration surprised everyone with its refusal to follow through on this. Now we know why: A limit as low as ten kilotons would kill the X-ray laser ABM program." Thus, the argument over the X-ray laser, like the Star Wars controversy itself, ends up being less over science or technology and more a disagreement about the value and possibility of arms control itself.

3

The two septuagenarian geniuses of nuclear physics and war sat in uneasy peace, obviously more aware of each other than of the young men who talked on about the wonders of their new laser and beam weapons. One of the young weapons makers confessed to a sense of awe in the presence of Nobel Laureate Hans Bethe, a giant of modern physics, who had journeyed to the Lawrence Livermore National Laboratory to be briefed on their work. They were more used to the other legend present, Edward Teller, often called the father of the hydrogen bomb and the spiritual patron of their efforts.

The briefing was designed to gain Bethe's support for Star Wars. But Bethe, who has played a key role in U.S. nuclear weapons development since the first A-bomb, remained critical. And Teller, seated across the table during a luncheon break, began to glower. Suddenly Teller could no longer contain his anger at the man with whom he had once shared the heady and secret intimacy of making the world's first atomic bomb. In those days of innocence, they had even double-dated. Later, they worked together on the hydrogen bomb, for which Bethe did much of the important theoretical work, though he doubted the wisdom of creating an even bigger weapon. But now, Bethe was not simply a doubter but the enemy.

"You fought me on the hydrogen bomb forty years ago," Teller's voice rose, breaking the studious decorum of the luncheon, "and now you're fighting me on defensive weapons. Let's have it out once and for all."

The two-day briefing almost came to an end, but Livermore Director Roger Batzel rose to move the agenda, and Teller calmed down. Throughout the incident, Bethe would not respond, telling a colleague later that "it's no use on these matters. It's political for Edward, and he cannot change."

Asked about this incident a week later, during a chance airport encounter, Teller told me that he agreed "the arguments about SDI are primarily political and philosophical, not technical." Teller believes that America is "under a propaganda attack from the Soviet Union, aided by misinformation from our own media and many of our own scientists."

Bethe insists that his objections to SDI are both technical and political. Star Wars cannot "provide a comprehensive defense," he has written, "against a determined adversary who could overwhelm it with warheads and decoys or circumvent it with cruise missiles and bombers." It will simply lead to building more offensive weapons to overwhelm the defense. "Star Wars," Bethe wrote, "is a guaranteed recipe for another ratchet in the nuclear competition."

The Teller-Bethe incident is illustrative of a civil war that has been tearing apart the defense Establishment ever since Reagan's Star Wars speech. The feuding has revived old disputes, made bitter enemies of longtime colleagues and friends, and introduced a note of rancor not often encountered in such circles. Both sides feel that the stakes are terribly high and that, for better or worse, SDI represents a major shift in the politics of the nuclear age. At issue is deterrence, the time-worn, some say twisted, notion of "mutual assured destruction" (also known by its acronym MAD), a policy of preventing nuclear war that has dominated Soviet-American relations since the Russians also obtained the bomb. The idea of deterrence is as simple as it is grisly: each side holds the other's population hostage. Should one be foolish enough to launch a nuclear attack, he must do so with the knowledge that his own cities will be destroyed.

The premise of Star Wars proponents is that it may be possible to find a technological means to free us of the nuclear threat quite apart from what the Soviets do or think about things. Proponents of SDI do not tend to fear the arms race itself but, rather, the prospect of the Soviets winning it. They view Star Wars as an opportunity to make high technology—in which America has a major edge—the decisive competitive factor.

Star Wars opponents argue that the nuclear competition is not in the interest of either superpower, cannot be won, and will lead inevitably to their mutual demise. "All our technological genius and economic prowess cannot make us secure if they leave the Soviet Union insecure," Bethe stated in a recent article that he co-authored with former Secretary of Defense Robert Mc-Namara. Post-Hiroshima history, they argued, has demonstrated that "the nuclear arms race is a burden to both sides." Critics view SDI as an attack on the arms control process because it threatens existing treaties, such as the one limiting anti-ballistic missiles (ABM), and may prevent conclusion of new ones, such as a prohibition on weapons in space and a comprehensive test ban treaty. "SDI is a way of killing arms control by people like Reagan, who always thought it was a Soviet trick," says John Pike of the Federation of American Scientists. "It is a technological and military solution as opposed to a political one on the part of people who do not believe you can deal with the Soviets."

The President insists that he favors arms control, but he has also defended Star Wars as an alternative route to peace. "There is another way," the President said in a press conference two days after his Star Wars speech, and that is if the scientists who gave us these weapons "could turn their talent to the job of perhaps coming up with something that would render these weapons obsolete." That he took this to be a major break with past strategies of deterrence was made clear in the closing refrain of his Star Wars speech, when he said: "My fellow Americans, tonight we're launching an effort which holds the promise of changing the course of human history." The President asked for prayers "as we cross this threshold."

Crossing the threshold is just what troubles some longtime defense experts. Defining it as "the issue of the decade," Sidney Drell charges that SDI is a cover for abandoning a policy of deterrence that has kept the peace. "I'm not afraid of Star Wars working. Technologically, I don't see the system going anywhere. The emperor has no clothes. The limits of X-ray lasers and lasers in space are clear. What I am afraid of is that we'll lose deterrence—mutual survival by recognizing our mutual vulnerability. That concept has been under attack by the moralists, who say it's immoral to threaten people, and the nuclear-war fighters, who want to go back to treating nuclear weapons like any other weapons." Drell refers to people's "fatigue" after decades of living with the bomb. "The world is stuck with deterrence for as long as we live, and people don't want to hear that."

Defense Secretary Weinberger disagrees. In a 1984 television interview he said, "I've never been a proponent of the ABM treaty. I've never been a proponent of the mutual assured destruction, the MAD theory, the idea that if both sides stopped doing anything about their defense and let themselves be tremendously vulnerable, everything would be all right."

For both sides, the Star Wars proposal has put a fresh sheen on a much older debate about the nature of nuclear weapons that surfaced more than fifteen years ago in the ABM fight. Those who defended MAD then and now insist that it is simply a statement about the unique power of nuclear weapons. "The capability for mutual assured destruction," physicist Richard Garwin argues, "is not a theory but a fact of life."

Teller challenges that view and its implications for defensive systems: "If defense cannot eliminate the horrors of nuclear war," he wrote during the ABM debate, "it can accomplish a lesser purpose. It can make it probable that enough Americans will survive and will be able to act that the United States will continue to exist as a nation and as a power. That the ideas and ideals which are the essence of our nation should survive is certainly worthy of a great effort." Thirteen years later, Teller used the same argument in attempting to enlist Reagan's support for Star Wars. In his speech at Livermore in August of 1982, a month before he met with the President to urge a commitment to third-generation weapons, Teller charged, "That the old MAD policy of mutual assured destruction is nonsense should be clear to everybody."

It is not at all clear to the people who gave us MAD as a doctrine and still believe in its utility. Some of the toughest critiques of Star Wars have come from those former defense officials and scientists who are largely responsible for the nation's past military strategy and who consider SDI a dangerous distraction. In a joint statement, McNamara, former National Security Adviser McGeorge Bundy, former Ambassador to the Soviet Union George Kennan, and Gerard C. Smith, Nixon's arms-control negotiator, wrote that they shared "the gravest reservations about this undertaking." They concluded that Reagan's Star Wars speech "represented an explicit expression of the President's belief that we should abandon the shared view of nuclear defense that underlies not only the ABM treaty, but also all our later negotiations on strategic weapons." A similar charge was leveled by James Schlesinger, who served two Republican Presidents as Secretary of Defense, and who has said that the protection of America depends on "the forbearance of those on the other side, or [on] effective deterrence. And it is for this reason that cries of the immorality of deterrence are premature and pernicious."

Some proponents of SDI, however, argue that these pillars of the American defense Establishment are attempting to hold on to an untenable system of deterrence simply because they helped create it. "It's the same crowd of critics—the same two dozen people who opposed the ABM and now oppose Star Wars," Yonas charges. Like Drell, Yonas cites "frustration with arms control" as a major impetus behind Star Wars, though he feels the emotion is justifiable. In Yonas's view, the ABM treaty assumed that the Soviets would exercise restraint in producing offensive weapons and they have not. Yonas also disagrees with those he calls the "minimum deterrence people," among whom he numbers most SDI opponents. Those people, he says, believe "that we don't really need very much to deter the Soviets. They tend to believe that the Soviets don't really mean us any harm."

Yonas argues that the Soviets have built more land-based missiles than they need to deter and that the U.S. ability to retaliate is in question. The President took an identical position when he proposed SDI: "This strategy of deterrence has not changed," he said. "It still works. But what it takes to maintain deterrence has changed. It took one kind of military force to deter an attack when we had far more nuclear weapons than any other power; it takes another kind now that the Soviets have enough accurate and powerful nuclear weapons to destroy virtually all of our missiles on the ground."

Critics of SDI deny this assertion and cite as proof the conclusions of Reagan's own Commission on Strategic Forces, headed by retired Air Force Lieutenant General Brent Scowcroft. The commission's report, issued one month after the President's Star Wars speech, denied Reagan's claim that a "window of vulnerability" had opened in the U.S. deterrent. The Scowcroft Commission also denied the value of a crash program to build defensive systems: "No ABM technologies appear to combine practicality, survivability, low cost and technical effectiveness sufficiently to justify proceeding beyond the stage of technology development." Moreover, as the critics note, one side's defensive system—no matter how limited or incomplete—could be perceived as an offensive weapon by the other side. As former President Nixon said of SDI in an interview with me, "Such systems would be destabilizing if they provide a shield so that you could use the sword."

Some SDI proponents agree, but go on to argue that the initiative could still facilitate arms control, since a Star Wars system cannot be made to work unless negotiated agreements make deep cuts in enemy weapons. "The claim by the critics of Star Wars that active defense is an impossible and dangerous illusion is as mistaken as the Administration's claim that the SDI is useful regardless of the arms control context," wrote physicist William Barletta, a Star Wars proponent who directs the beam-research program at Livermore. "All technical approaches [to Star Wars]," he wrote, "share the limitation that if the offense is unconstrained and unlimited, the defense faces impractical odds and unacceptable expense."

"The only way you can make any case for SDI," says DeWitt, "would be if the number of attacking warheads is very small, and that would require a drastic reduction in the arms of both nations through arms control." The paradox is that the Soviets say they will not negotiate such reductions if the Administration goes ahead with Star Wars. They have, in fact, said that if the United States deploys a defensive system, they will simply expand their offensive forces enough to overwhelm it. The Administration charges that the Soviets' shrill opposition to the President's program is hypocritical, given their own history of working to develop defensive weapons. Just what the United States knows about what the Soviets are doing in this area is highly classified information. Defenders of SDI privy to such information claim it is a great deal. Teller, for example, has said that the Soviets are ahead in space-based defensive technology. Critics of SDI who also have seen these data claim that the Soviets are behind the United States. Both sides generally agree that, at the moment, the Soviets are far behind in the computer technology needed to actually deploy a Star Wars system. "In most of these areas," George Keyworth admits, "we have a substantial edge."

Both sides also agree that neither superpower could develop a comprehensive defense system if nuclear testing and space-based weapons were banned by treaty. They also agree that research on defensive systems can't be stopped and that the Soviets' demand for such a prohibition is unreasonable because it is unverifiable. One thing is clear: SDI is already a reality—not as a weapons system but as an idea with powerful advocates at home and an impact abroad.

Given that reality, Schlesinger, for one, believes Star Wars ought to be used as a bargaining chip at the negotiating table: "If we are able, through Soviet fears of American space technology, to achieve a breakthrough in arms control in an unpromising era, the development of this new initiative will have been rewarding." However, Reagan has ruled out just such a negotiating strategy. For better or worse, Star Wars, once just a gleam in the eye of diehard arms-control opponents, has now become the very foundation of the President's thinking on the nuclear threat. According to White House sources, it is the thing he plans to offer the Soviets as a substitute for the traditional arms-control treaties whose worth he has long denied.

But to McNamara and Bethe, that course is perilous: "We must not forget Winston Churchill's warning that 'the Stone Age may return on the gleaming wings of science,' and we must learn to shed the fatalistic belief that new technologies, no matter how threatening, cannot be stopped."

(*Los Angeles Times*, September 22–24, 1985)

And Then Came Gorbachev

1

And then came Gorbachev. As I watched him at a reception in the Palace of Congresses at the Kremlin, where my outstretched hand had been pushed aside by Yoko Ono's mad charge to present the top Bolshevik with some memento of John Lennon's music, while off to the side Gore Vidal sought to engage Andrei Sakharov, newly released from his exile in Gorky, and Andrei Gromyko wanly smiled at Norman Mailer, it seemed as if we had all just stepped through the looking glass. Unbelievable: a pragmatic and appealing Soviet leader replacing the septuagenarian hacks who seemed destined to run that nation into the ground. Before him, there seemed little hope for altering the collision course of the superpowers. After him, the Soviet Union and the Cold War would never be the same.

How did it happen? What playwright would have dared to introduce a character of such immense distinction from what came before? Who is Gorbachev, what does he represent, and will he last? For three months in the spring and fall of 1987, the year of *glasnost* and *perestroika*, I talked to the new Soviet elite—leading editors, Central Committee and Politburo members of the Communist Party, and high government technocrats—that had been swept into power by this new man and his program. I talked with the new crew running Chernobyl after the disaster that more than any other single factor jolted the Soviet leaders into a full appreciation of the futility of nuclear weapons. And I talked with the people who went to college with Gorbachev to examine the roots of this modern Peter the Great, who would attempt once again the modernization of Mother Russia. Over seemingly endless trays of cookies and tea served in the spartan Politburo offices of Aleksandr Yakovlev, the more pretentious quarters of *Izvestia* editor Ivan Laptev, and the downright dingy and cluttered cubicle of cinematographer and pacifist Alex Aleksandrov, the theme and the spirit were similar. The message was a replay of Lenin's old question: What is to be done? Once again, it was a call for a revolution within the revolution rendered more urgent now that much of the post-Lenin programs have been judged a failure. What is to come? What kind of economy? How much pluralism? What about bureaucracy and human rights? Questions are raised in a constant and urgent pecking at the once forbidden. The spirit, with few exceptions, has been brash and open; the answers, elusive.

This uncertain chapter of Soviet history with its vast implications for the world took most people by surprise. But if you listened closely, you could hear the sound of change coming even before the Reign of Gorby, back in the last days of the dying Andropov, the dour KGB chief who, in his brief fifteen months as head of all the Russias, managed to set in motion the process now called *perestroika*. Georgi Arbatov, the director of the U.S.A.–Canada Institute, was the first to sing Andropov's praises to me. "He is a modern man, and if he lives, you will see big changes," Arbatov had said when I first encountered him in 1983 at the Amsterdam Conference of International Physicians for the Prevention of Nuclear War. Andropov didn't get his chance, but he was to have his impact. As head of the KGB, Andropov had learned the full truth of the sorry state of the Soviet economy and the degree of corruption that ran rampant through its political life. Rather than join in sharing the spoils, it seems that he began plotting the demise of the Brezhnev era by pushing the careers of uncorrupt cadre like Gorbachev. While Andropov certainly had the blood of KGB crimes on his hands, he seems, by his own brief actions as General Secretary and by the company he chose to keep, to have been committed to a better way.

During one late-afternoon rumination in his nineteenth-century merchant's house-cum-office in Moscow, Arbatov showed me a poem that Andropov had sent him in the last weeks of his life, which contained the line: "It is said that power corrupts men, but I have learned that it is men who corrupt power." Later that day, I sat with Arbatov and three of his top aides watching a videocassette of the once-banned movie *Repentance*, which in a chilling fashion excoriates the crimes of Stalin and Beria, his secret police chief. When the movie ended, Arbatov asked me for my reaction. I replied that after watching the movie I could not understand why he or the others in the room remained in the Communist Party. There was an awkward pause and he answered: "That is the challenge."

It is ironic that the battle to limit arbitrary power should have been advanced by one of Beria's heirs in the secret police, but in the land of the czars, one takes what one can get. Andropov's enduring legacy is that, from his deathbed, tied to a kidney dialysis machine, he somehow had managed to nudge into place a new elite, which, although stalled by Chernenko, his immediate successor, has now come to the fore. It is this new elite that is remaking Soviet society in a way not predicted by a single Kremlinologist, most of whom had developed an emotional as well as a professional stake in the continued obscurity and repression of a Soviet Union administered inevitably by corrupt and brutal gangs of aging and unyielding Bolsheviks.

This new elite need not be a matter of immense mystery, as I discovered in months of interviews. Its members crisscross America in waves, pursuing contacts that serve a domestic Soviet economic and social need more than they do foreign-policy objectives. In January 1988, for example, I was in Gettysburg, Pennsylvania, at a small retreat hosted by the Eisenhower World Affairs Institute and the United States Information Agency. Our side included the woman who runs the Soviet desk at the National Security Council, who assured me that her rank was higher than Ollie North's and of her faith in the politics of Richard Perle. Also in attendance were the head of the USIA-Soviet exchange program, various cultural impresarios, and a hawkish congressional aide. Our side, despite some less rigid people from the art world, was generally stodgy and unyieldingly careful that it not betray the cause. A dialogue with Soviets was perceived by most of us as yet another battle of Cold War politics. We acted like Russian delegates used to, determined in the eyes of our colleagues to adhere to the party line.

The Soviets, by contrast, were freewheeling and often divided. At one moment, the director of the Taganka Theater denounced a high official from the Ministry of Culture for never answering his phone calls and went on to argue that private exchange programs were better than official ones. He wanted to be free to take his theater to Chicago or Madrid, based on the highest bidder. At which point a leading Soviet cosmonaut pointedly observed that the theater was government-financed and that the director had no business just running off anywhere he desired. The director, nonplussed, shot back that cosmonauts are overpaid and know nothing of the economic hardships of actors. Two top guys in the Soviet book-publishing world then sharply disagreed over where they stood on the director's lament, the top Soviet hockey goalie muttered that this was a fight about nothing and we should go eat, and a columnist for *Izvestia* summed up the Donnybrooks by declaring, "Well, this is *perestroika*." Even more startling was the happy willingness of the Soviets to have me write all this up and the demurrer of the Americans that it was, after all, a private retreat.

The debate now unfolding in the Soviet Union has its limits, of course, but it is charged with a fervency and relevance that makes much of our own discourse seem tepid. It is still largely a debate within elite ranks, and it is dependent upon the continued ascendancy of the new elite that desperately welcomes this spirit. The obstacles are real—the reformers will not have an easy time of it, but they are very much on the scene, and it is difficult to imagine all of this just blowing away. Too many people—from Gorbachev on down—have made too public a commitment to the new course.

The new Soviet elite is a post-World War II class of highly educated people determined to make some variant of their system work, and work according to world standards of efficiency and quality. I find members of this elite quite accessible, ever since I first met some of them in Amsterdam in 1983. I had been invited to attend a conference to discuss the prevention of nuclear war. I almost decided not to go, upon learning the Soviets would participate. Why go and hear the old rhetoric? I had given up on the prospects for profound change in the Soviet Union after the second of two previous visits. On the first trip, in 1963, when Khrushchev was in power, I was a beatnik who sold books at Lawrence Ferlinghetti's City Lights bookstore and wandered into the confusion that then marked Russia. Stalin was dead, his crimes partially revealed, but what policies would come in his wake was still unclear. My mission, other than bumming around Europe, was to collect poetry from the likes of Yevgeny Yevtushenko and Andrei Voznesensky. Ferlinghetti had called them "Red Cats" when he published a book by that name of their poetry—not a bad title given the zaniness of that ever-uncertain moment when the "liberator" was as intellectually and physically disheveled as was Khrushchev. The rules of change were far more tenuous than they are today. The Léger exhibit at the Pushkin "is on," shouted a poet acquaintance passing in the street. "No, it's off," a *babushka* informed as she pushed me down the museum's stairs.

My unofficial guide in Moscow was Heberto Padilla, the Cuban writer, whom I had met in Havana three years earlier when I took a Volkswagen bug down to Key West and from there a boat to Havana to witness that revolution at first hand. The hot item in Havana in those days was a weekly cultural supplement, *Lunes de Revolución*, carried in the official daily news-paper, *Revolución*. In those first heady months of the revolution, *Lunes* printed Allen Ginsberg and Ferlinghetti, and it looked as if Cuba might escape the dead hand of that parody of "scientific socialism" that has come to dom-inate socialist revolutions elsewhere.

Now, three years later, *Lunes* was gone and Cuba had tightened up con-siderably and Padilla was worried. He was in Moscow as a correspondent for *Revolución* and the Spanish edition of the Soviet paper *Moscow News*. But his main work was to send back dark but alas accurate reports of the sorry state of Soviet socialism, despite Khrushchev's reforms, to Carlos Franqui, his paper's editor. Both Padilla and Franqui would later flee Castro's ship, with ample cause. But in 1963 Padilla still retained some hope for socialism with a human face. He was particularly close to the young Soviet poets to whom he introduced me, and seemed to share their wary enthusiasm for the changes then underway.

When I returned to the Soviet Union seven years later, none of that hopeful optimism was left. As I would tell Yegor Yakovlev in an interview that he ran in his *Moscow News* in the spring of 1986: "In 1970 this was a dead society. There was no point talking to politicians. You knew in advance what they would say. I wanted to get out as fast as I could." But I added that by 1985 I had known that change—although not this much change—was coming. The first inkling of what the future might hold was given to me in Amsterdam by Arbatov. Not everyone in the United States who has dealt with Arbatov likes him. I do. He was open to argument, spoke on the record, and was capable of controversial comments. But the best thing he did for me at that meeting was to point out a chubby fellow down the hall of our hotel whom he suggested I interview on scientific and nuclear weapons issues.

I went up to Yevgeny Velikhov. Remember that the time was not so long ago that no top Soviet would consent to an interview without his own eyewitness or KGB guide accompanying the reporter and the answers all came out as party-line static. But here was a top Soviet physicist and member of the Central Committee quite willing to disappear with me into his hotel room to face several tape recorders and some barbed questions. Velikhov would later confess that one of his remarks to me that "of course" we do have our crazies who might also want to build a Star Wars system caused him some moments of discomfort. Andropov had died before the interview ran in the *Los Angeles Times*, and in the new uncertain days of Chernenko it was judged by some that Velikhov had misspoken.

But Velikhov is a brave man, as he would later show when he risked at least some years of his life flying in a helicopter over Chernobyl, desperately seeking a way of containing the smoldering disaster below him. And, as is well known to a large number of American scientists who have dealt with him on many sensitive intelligence matters (including getting the supersecret Krasnayarsk radar installation open to Western inspection), he is driven by an urge for honesty. It is an urge born early in his student days, when he sought to master the rigors of the scientific method at a time when the madman Lysenko controlled Soviet science. Velikhov would tell me later that the computer gap and other failures of modern Soviet technology stem precisely from the heavy hand of such political interference. Nevertheless, the physical sciences always fared better than the social sciences in the Soviet Union. The physical scientists were better positioned to defend their turf, because the preservation of scientific method was vital for national defense. As Velikhov put it: "The social scientists just started to repeat or illustrate the political development, and after this, it was not science at all. Science is very demanding; if you are not honest with science, you lose very fast."

The revolt of the scientists is basic to the coming of the Gorbachev revolution, and they had their first success with the rehabilitation of Sakharov. I was at the February 1987 Moscow peace conference that Sakharov attended upon his return from Gorky. I caught up with him at the cloakroom as he was bundling up to go out into the cold. He granted a short interview in which he made the same critical remarks about the Soviet presence in Afghanistan and the lack of human rights that he had tried to make from internal exile. Sakharov's unrepentant presence at that conference was one of the more striking moments in recent Soviet history. At the closing session, he was seated in the grand hall of the Kremlin, about thirty rows back from the stage. Gorbachev was on the dais, listening intently, while Frank Von Hipple from Princeton, summarizing the work of the scientists' group, ended by saying, "We were especially pleased to be able to have the participation of Academician Andrei Sakharov . . . [who] stressed the particular importance of openness and democratization . . . the theme for which he was awarded the Nobel Peace Prize." And I looked, and there was Gorbachev on the stage and Sakharov in the audience and the system didn't crumble. It became stronger.

Velikhov, as vice president of the Academy of Sciences, was instrumental in the opening to fellow Academician Sakharov. But his goal is larger: to free Soviet science and scientists from the restraints of all political cant. Although he is a close adviser to Gorbachev and has accompanied him on all his foreign trips, Velikhov insists on the need for a science independent of politics. When we talked after a lecture he gave at Moscow State University on the history of nuclear weapons, in which he admitted being disgusted at having to use American statistics because Soviet statistics are still secret, he recalled an old peasant proverb: "Hair is a good thing, and soup is also a good thing; but when you mix the two, what you get is not good."

Peasant maxims notwithstanding, the fact is that for much of its history the Soviet Union has been ruled by a politics that is stylistically and substantively out of joint with the requirements of a modern society. Thus, many influential technocrats like Velikhov and Roald Sagdeyev, the head of the Soviet Space Research Institute, believe that a profoundly different politics is required if economic and technological reconstruction is to proceed. As Gorbachev himself said in 1987, in a major address defining *perestroika* for the Central Committee: "Reorganization is a decisive turn to science, the businesslike partnership of science and practice to achieve the best possible end results, an ability to ground any undertaking on a sound scientific basis."

But scientific openness is not compatible with a society driven by political paranoia. For that reason the push for domestic reform is inextricably tied to a re-evaluation of the Soviets' foreign-policy agenda.

At the heart of this "new thinking" is a challenge to the siege mentality built up over decades to ensure the survival of Soviet state power. It recognizes that forty years of Cold War confrontations with the developed West and deep entanglement in Third World politics have drained Soviet resources, without a commensurate addition to Soviet security. "What is your interest to have a war?" asks Arbatov, who argues that the historical identification of land, people, and resources with power has been turned on its head. "The Germans fought for *Lebensraum*, and now they have the smallest *Lebensraum* in their history and they are better off than ever. The Japanese have less territory with fewer resources than ever, and they are the fastest-growing economy in the world."

The Soviets have come to realize that a muscle-bound nuclear state makes no sense, that the stockpiling of ever more sophisticated and dangerous weapons is a prescription for a nation's economic enfeeblement. "The whole meaning of force changes now," Arbatov observes. "You can have a lot of military force and you cannot use it. The only size of war where you can be successful is a Grenada-size war; anything bigger creates great problems. If you really analyze the fundamentals, all of the intricate military strategies are built on a foundation of illusions. How can the weapons be used, where does the present trend lead, and what is your interest to have a war?" This view is shared by Marshal Sergei Akhromeyev, chief of the Soviet General Staff, who, in a reply to one of my written questions, said, "Today the use of nuclear weapons is meaningless. No nation at present can strengthen its security by nuclear weapons. Mountains of nuclear weapons continue to grow. However, the security of the nuclear powers decreases." Akhromeyev also denied the plausibility of any fighting strategies for limited nuclear war, saying that "the use of not only strategic but also operational-tactical and tactical nuclear weapons is not possible." The result of any use of nuclear weapons, he argued, would mean that "the entire humanity and the whole life on our planet would be annihilated."

Whatever the previous consideration given to notions of surviving and winning a nuclear war among some Soviet Herman Kahns, the experience of Chernobyl was the turning point. "With Chernobyl we had to mobilize the resources of the entire country," Velikhov told me upon my return from a visit to that ghastly area where, for centuries, one will be afraid to pick a flower, adding, "But a nuclear war involves many more frightening incidents, including the more devastating effects of blast and heat. So what could you do? Nothing." Velikhov, the theoretical nuclear physicist, had come up against the reality of the destructive power of his science, and although he never had given much credence to nuclear-war-fighting scenarios, after Chernobyl he was filled with contempt for such notions. "After two weeks of discussion with the Army Corps, I asked how you wish to survive a nuclear war if you have no possibility to clear this small piece of nuclear garbage. Here we had no panic, but in nuclear war you would have much. We had full access to support from all over the country, and only because of such access, we had tens of thousands of people working here. A soldier can be used for only ninety seconds in the hot place. After that, he is free for life from any [nuclear-related] duty; the same with pilots of the helicopters. It cost [us] thousands of people who are no longer able to work in this industry. Without this possibility to use the nation's resources, it would have been impossible to save the 135,000 people who were relocated. It didn't change my thinking about civil defense because I never believed in it. But it opened the eyes of all people that civil defense is nonsense."

The impact of Chernobyl on Soviet nuclear thinking was profound. More than any other single event, Chernobyl prompted grave doubts within Soviet policymaking circles over the wisdom of continuing to put faith in technological fixes. Nuclear science had somehow seemed pure and logical. Suddenly Chernobyl had opened a window through which could be glimpsed a vision of what nuclear war would bring. Visiting Chernobyl was a shock for me. Particularly disturbing was the sight of a collective farm complete with white farmhouses with blue trim, tractors and other farm tools, clothing hanging on a line, children's toys, everything except people. The Soviets, as a whole, suffered a similar shock. Chernobyl sparked an intense debate between those who thought you could have limited nuclear-war options and those who thought that the nuclear-arms race was very dangerous, that it was never ending, that having to gear up to defeat high-tech specters like Star Wars would exact intolerable economic costs, that it was a fool's game. There was, of course, the additional fear, given the Reagan Administration's fevered rhetoric, that adults were no longer minding the American store. Combined with the sagging Soviet economy, a serious re-examination of what power means in the modern world was in order. There is today a growing realization that being a modern nation is not contingent on having a certain number of troops in the field and certain kinds of weapons. That it is possible to be a nuclear Gulliver and an economic Lilliputian.

How widespread is this view? In the West you hear much talk among Soviet experts about the opposition to Gorbachev from hard-liners. Perhaps. Who knows? It's still a closed society, and neither I nor the Kremlinologists are privy to the inner debates of the Politburo. But I tend to accept the assessment offered by Politburo member Yakovlev when he told me, "I cannot recollect any divergence on foreign policy; there is a very firm consensus, including the military." The military people whom I interviewed agree. In one session that took up the better part of an afternoon, a generally genial discussion about arms control was shattered by some table thumping after I had insisted once too often that the Soviet military brass must, deep down, desire a continuation of the self-importance and perks conferred by a heightened state of international tension. Surely, I argued with as much impertinence as I could muster, your very way of life as a military man would be threatened if peace were to break out, surely you believe that there are risks in the new peace proposals. "Our security," General Yuri Lebedev of the Soviet armed forces General Staff told me in no uncertain terms, "depends on our people finding the same quantity and quality of goods in the stores as your people find." Lebedev, whom Soviet intellectuals regard as a hard-liner, said that arms-control agreements with the United States are part of *perestroika*. "I am always surprised when I am asked such questions. I am deputy chief of the department of the General Staff concerned with the elaboration of our position in arms reduction talks. The military in our department were the authors of these new approaches [to arms control]. And, moreover, during recent times we have to take into account that we have very major problems to resolve: the food problem, reconstruction of our economy . . . We certainly understand that to carry out this task we need resources, and these resources can be obtained through reducing military expenditures. We also have a problem with needing more workers, and in reducing weapons systems we will have more workers to be hired in civil enterprises. We have to give the people an example that something is being changed, and the first sign of something being changed for a man in the street is goods in the stores—goods that are available in the West. So we have a big job to do. But in waging *perestroika*, we are winning in a political and moral sense, and we are gaining our supporters in the West." Deputy Foreign Minister Vladimir Petrovsky echoes the sentiment: "Nowadays, the initial Leninist concept that we could prove the triumph of socialism only through our domestic policies is now installed as an official policy."

While Soviet reformers see a reduction of military competition with the West as a necessity of their domestic reconstruction, they do not foresee an end to competition on other fronts. There is, for example, a strongly stated position among these officials that improvements in the quality of Soviet life and a move to a more flexible and pragmatic foreign policy will expose certain weaknesses in the U.S. model of development. For instance, Yegor Yakovlev, editor in chief of *Moscow News*, one of the liveliest publications to emerge in the Gorbachev era, is convinced that the U.S. military-industrial complex will seek actively to prevent an end to the arms race and that the more reasonable the Soviet posture, the more obtuse and warlike will seem the American response. This view was defended by Anatoly Dobrynin, the former Ambassador to the United States, one night in a lengthy and informal discussion in his imposing office at the Central Committee headquarters. Dobrynin, now a Secretary of the Central Committee, speaks a Washington columnist's insider English and noted, "You know, this idea of a military-industrial complex was invented by General Eisenhower, not by us." When I replied that surely such a comparable complex must exist in the Soviet Union, Dobrynin, who spent more than twenty-five years in Washington, smiled and said, "When our generals retire, they go fishing. They don't become vice presidents of aerospace companies or lobbyists to the Kremlin. As to the military industry, instead of tanks they can make cars. We need cars, and the profit will be the same because we set the profit."

"Our intention is to have a period in which we would be able to concentrate on domestic affairs," Deputy Foreign Minister Petrovsky told me, adding, "This is the categorical imperative of our time. The best way to prove which system and which way of life is better is by putting your own house in order. Sometimes some people here thought that foreign policy could compensate for domestic shortcomings, and this is wrong. The roots of foreign policy are at home; for foreign policy to be effective, it must rely on a well-organized domestic order." Such an order, according to Dobrynin, must include democratization of decision-making. But he concedes that the institutionalization of public restraint on government is a novel question for modern Soviet society.

Ivan Laptev, editor of *Izvestia*, considers democratization the main problem for the Soviet Union. "The people must know everything," he says. "It's the main measure of control, of monitoring official activities to prevent mistakes, and this is the main value of democratization and openness in our society, so that the whole party will be prevented from making mistakes and people's eyes will be open." Toward that end, the Soviet press has been printing the results of Politburo meetings for the first time, publishing information from critical ministerial reports, muckraking journalism, and some foreign observations. In one startling article recently carried by *Izvestia* and titled "Where Did the *Nyets* Come From?" the author listed dozens of prohibitions ranging from dress codes to ideas. The answer offered was that the official *nyets* were the result of mindless bureaucratic imperatives. Laptev refers to this problem as a "disease of thoughtlessness" and says that "this disease is a heritage from those days when it was considered a rule that whoever was the boss knew the truth, and this disease took hold of our psychology. Now we are trying to change this mindset. We stand for open discussion—different opinions and effective solutions." The tough-looking product of a Siberian orphanage,

Laptev, both of whose parents died in World War II, is one of this country's new men. He started his professional career as a crane operator, while studying in the evening to graduate from the Automobile Institute. Eventually he came to Moscow as a champion bicycle racer and entered the Moscow State University School of Journalism where he finished by writing a doctorate on the social and political problems of ecology. He has gone on to write several books, one of which, he claims, predicted the rise of the Greens in West Germany. After a stint working for the Central Committee, he went to *Pravda* and ended up head of the editorial board. After eighteen months he was "unexpectedly brought here to edit *Izvestia*," where he has been for the last two years. Asked about the prospect of *Izvestia* criticizing Gorbachev, Laptev replied, "We haven't had him for long, but I think that if this atmosphere of *glasnost*, of openness, is established, you can expect this criticism to occur."

Guys like Laptev leave one feeling optimistic about the future of the Soviet system, not only because they want what's right, but because that system, even in its worst days, nonetheless produced Laptev . . . and Gorbachev.

(*Playboy*, August 1988)

2

Chopped liver was served, pickles and shredded cabbage were passed around, a few toasts with vodka were drunk, and the reminiscing about Mikhail Sergeyevich Gorbachev's college days began. Photos and anecdotes from the old days were once again exchanged over dinner in a small Moscow apartment last month [November 1987], as they have been each year since this small group of about fifteen of Gorbachev's classmates graduated from the Moscow State University law school in 1955. For five years, these people had taken the same courses, shared the same dormitories, and waited in the same lines for tickets to the ballet and theater. They have kept in touch over the years, and Gorbachev and his wife, Raisa, had joined them at previous reunions, though this time other duties intervened. These friends knew the Soviet leader during the formative years of a new Russia as well as a new Gorbachev. It was the period during which Stalin died and Khrushchev began his rise to power; a period during which a rube harvester driver from the grain regions of southern Russia came to Moscow with his one good suit, learned as much as he could about the larger world, and returned home five years later—still in that same suit—to launch a political career that has brought him face to face with the President of the United States.

Just how did the stagnant, conformist Soviet society produce a leader apparently committed to reform? Is Gorbachev's preoccupation with change a public-relations device designed to woo Western audiences and lull the Soviet public, or is it real? Definitive answers are elusive. Soviet leaders traditionally are secretive about their private lives. But talks with Gorbachev's classmates provide a rare glimpse of the Party chief's personality during an important period of his life. Their firsthand knowledge of his subsequent career is, of course, limited to occasional personal contacts.

On one point, however, his college mates—not all of whom agree with every aspect of his current program for restructuring Soviet society—are unanimous: the guy is the same guy they knew back then. Their only surprise is that someone with Gorbachev's qualities could make it to the top. And some fear he may not be able to stay there. The people who lived with Gorbachev in his youth are not surprised by his bold behavior now. They recalled his toughness in openly criticizing the professor in their class on Stalin's writings, his tendency to scoff at official propaganda's overblown claims, and his loyalty to friends under political suspicion during Stalin's last years.

One of those friends was his closest, Vladimir Lieberman, a Jew eight years his senior, who came under attack during the anti-Semitic hysteria generated when Stalin fabricated charges that a group of Jewish doctors had conspired to poison him. Lieberman, a former Red Army colonel and decorated war veteran, was a member of the same Party unit as Gorbachev. He recalled the incident this way: "Some comrades, sniffing the wind, tried to criticize me. I was the only Jew at the law school's Communist Party meeting. Gorbachev had entered the Party right before this event, but it was he who tried to prevent the attack on me and did so very sharply, using some unparliamentary words. He called one of our old and respected ex-soldiers 'a spineless animal.' That just stopped them."

Is a Western reporter permitted to hear all this because of Gorbachev's policy of *glasnost,* or is he being fed a line by people who remain fearful of the next turn of the wheel of state power? "It's *glasnost,*" concluded Zdenek Mlynar, who has no need to fear. Mlynar, a Czech national, had lived across the hall from Gorbachev during college and regarded him as his closest friend. He is now in exile in Vienna, one of those who tried to reform Czechoslovakia twenty years ago as, in his view, Gorbachev is attempting to do now in the Soviet Union.

"I can remember the day when it was reported in the papers that the Jewish doctors had been arrested," Mlynar said during a recent interview in Vienna. "I was walking with Gorbachev and some others, and they were talking about it. Somebody from the group said, 'Today, I don't want to be in Lieberman's shoes.' Gorbachev said to be silent. Gorbachev and I had a very high opinion of Lieberman. He wasn't a Jew for him, but somebody to look up to as a typical Communist." According to Mlynar, he also personally benefited from Gorbachev's personal loyalty. "It was important that you could depend on him as an individual. For example, I can remember in the year '51–'52 there were the political trials in Prague and I was criticized in the Czech Moscow Party group as a potential Party enemy. When the General Secretary of the Party in Prague was arrested, there was a rumor that I would be arrested, too. I remember that I could talk openly with Gorbachev about these matters but that it never affected him and we stayed friends. Gorbachev didn't withdraw from me, and that wasn't simple in those days. If I had been called back to Prague, it could have been unpleasant for Gorbachev as well."

But for Mlynar, Lieberman, and others from their university circle, Gorbachev's formative years were not simply the bad old days. In fact, Westerners are surprised to hear that their recollections of that time center not on purges but on the joys of friendly political debates, exploring Moscow, and learning ballroom dancing. Gorbachev met Raisa at such a dance class, where he had gone to heckle Lieberman, an enthusiastic student of the waltz. In the fading photos from that time, Gorbachev is handsome enough, with thick hair covering the now famous red birthmark on his forehead. His secret weapon with women was that he was, in the words of an English-speaking friend, "nice—not the typical Russian domineering male." Some who were present at his marriage to Raisa in 1954 remember that she was considered quite a catch, and Mlynar says she was attracted to Gorbachev by his "lack of vulgarity." "A real Russian man is authoritative, domineering, and the woman is partially an object for him," said the former Czech official. "Gorbachev was never that type of person. Their relationship was always a partnership, which would be normal elsewhere."

Gorbachev's other college friends clearly are proud that Gorbachev, who also holds a degree in agriculture, is the best educated Soviet leader since Lenin. They also recall that Raisa, who has a doctorate from Moscow's Lenin Pedagogical Institute, played a key role in broadening Gorbachev's interest in Moscow's cultural life. "Raisa had a much stronger grounding in literature and Misha was very eager to become familiar with that world," said Nadezhda Mikhaleva, who herself went on to teach law. "Raisa would take him to plays and concerts, and we all thought she complemented him perfectly," Mikhaleva said. "Raisa was very smart, as well as being very pretty, and she's still both. So why shouldn't she play a leading role?" Mikhaleva said, with the air of one who had a score to settle with a few male-chauvinist Russians she had met in her day.

Gorbachev himself was no slouch as a college student. He was, Mlynar recalled, "exceptionally intelligent, open, curious about everything." Mlynar recalls that he felt closer to Gorbachev than to any of the other students.

Both men fell in age and experience somewhere between the two groups of students then most typical at their elite university. One was a hard-drinking group of war veterans, who seemed preoccupied with their combat experience and their vodka. Another was the incoming younger generation that seemed apolitical and otherwise untouched by the devastating experiences of the previous decade. Gorbachev had lived in the shadow of the advancing Nazi Army, which was stopped just short of his hometown, Privolnoe, near the larger city of Stavropol. He was fourteen when World War II ended and by that time had been pressed into service running harvester machines. He was decorated for his work and that, along with his natural intelligence, brought admission to Moscow State University's prestigious law school.

At the recent reunion here, however, a friend recalled that Gorbachev "never wore his worker's medal to exams as some of the others did to curry favor with the instructors. Misha just wasn't like that. He wanted to make it on his own." Unlike so many of his classmates, the young farmer had no high-level political connections, though his grandfather had been chairman of a collective and may, some believe, have suffered during Stalin's purges. Last spring, in a private meeting with Soviet newspaper editors, Gorbachev pointed to two of his Politburo colleagues—Aleksandr Yakovlev and Yegor Ligachev—and said that all three had family members who had suffered under Stalin. In fact, Gorbachev's college chums all had family members touched by Stalin's tyranny. Yet they remember the postwar years as a period not just of austerity but of idealistic pride. "Stalin had saved the world from Fascism, and the repression of the 1930s seemed a dim memory," said Mlynar. "We were more idealistic than the young generation today," said Mikhaleva, "maybe because we didn't have much. I had one pair of shoes with wooden soles, one dress for everyday wear." According to Lieberman, Gorbachev himself had a single pair of everyday pants, which he went on wearing even after they were torn in his sophomore year.

All agree that the future Party chief was a high-spirited though never wild participant in their school's life. "Misha never liked to drink," confided one of Gorbachev's former roommates. "Once in a while he did, but it was not important to him," he said with a thirty-year-old touch of wonder at this deviation from national tradition.

And though the reunion crowd was made up largely of sedate, Establishment people, they also made it clear they could live without the long liquor lines that Gorbachev's anti-alcohol campaign has produced. They were similarly wary of the threatened price increases so basic to Gorbachev's new economic campaign. "If Gorbachev had taken over ten years from now, he'd be greeted by everyone as the Messiah because things would be visibly falling apart," observed Lieberman, who strongly supports Gorbachev's program. But he is now a professor of industrial management and knows a great deal about the harsh facts of the Soviet economy. Some of the others may be ambivalent about the new ways, as befits middle-aged graduates of the Moscow law school who have found their niche and feel they have something to lose in the strong winds of change. But there are no vocal opponents among them. Nor do they seem the least bit surprised with the open style of the man who is now their leader or that he is dramatically shaking things up. He is remembered as the very popular leader of their school's Komsomol—the Communist youth organization—who was, in the words of one, "never pompous, he was always down to earth, with a good sense of humor."

"The thought that Gorbachev might sit in the Kremlin instead of Stalin, that would have been an absurd concept back then," said Mlynar. "But it would have been absurd back then to think that I would be in the Hilton in Vienna as an immigrant giving an interview to the *Los Angeles Times*. Everything is absurd. But I can say that Gorbachev belonged to those who stood apart from everyone else. He was never an average person."

And, for a Komsomol leader and a Party member, he was independent in judgment. One classmate recalls that Gorbachev publicly scoffed at propagandistic documentaries about the achievements of Soviet agriculture, having himself recently experienced the deprivations of life in the countryside. Gorbachev, Mlynar agreed, detested "that colorful propaganda that made everything look so good. He always confronted it with reality and spoke about it ironically, especially the films of Stalin's period. There was a film about the success of the *kolkhozes* [collectives] in the north Caucasus, and Gorbachev said in reality it's not at all like that. In the film, the tables were full of foodstuffs, and Gorbachev, who came from this particular area, said it's not like that at all. So he was always an opponent of the typical propaganda of that period that made everything look much better than it really is."

"One of the most striking features of Gorbachev," said Lieberman of their student days, "was that he was on the verge of nonconformity." Lieberman went on to recount an incident attendant to the publication of a new work by Stalin. Extra class hours were ordered for the study of this extremely dry work, which among other things meant the loss of the students' lunch hour. The additional class was taught by an expert brought in from the outside, who proceeded to simply read aloud from page after page of the new tome. Gorbachev and Lieberman penned an anonymous note to the lecturer pointing out that all the students present had been admitted to the Moscow law school and, therefore, presumably could read. The visiting lecturer was incensed at the note, read it aloud to the class, and pronounced its author an obvious opponent of all things socialist. At that point Gorbachev rose to take responsibility for the act, observed that he was a dedicated Communist and the leader of the Komsomol, and that the problem was not with socialism but rather with pedantry. In the ensuing brouhaha, Gorbachev was chastised by higher officials, but the lecturer was replaced by one who was more open to classroom discussion. Gorbachev survived, became a full member of the Communist Party in his second year, and returned home after graduation to begin his career as a Party organizer in the grain-rich rural region of Stavropol. It proved a time of uncertain change.

A year later, at a meeting at Stavropol Party headquarters, the Party faithful were summoned and under the tightest security, heard a reading of the speech that Khrushchev had delivered to the Twentieth Party Congress on the crimes of Stalin. That speech, soon published in the West, is still not publicly available in the Soviet Union. But its effect on the Party faithful, by most accounts, was devastating. It detailed a pattern of madness and repression that they had tended to discount as aberrational. The conclusion seemed inescapable that something was rotten with the system that had permitted all that. Gorbachev subsequently told Mikhaleva that he was shaken by the revelations of the Twentieth Party Congress. "I remember he admired greatly Khrushchev for raising the issue of the victims of Stalin," she said.

But, as Gorbachev has recently pointed out, Khrushchev himself failed to grasp the obvious, that democratization of the political process was the essential barrier to a return of Stalinism. "But the failures of the reforms undertaken in that period were mainly due to the fact that they were not backed up by a broad development of democratization processes," Gorbachev stated in his recent speech on the seventieth anniversary of the Bolshevik Revolution. Khrushchev failed in another way, perhaps of more immediate concern to a young Party official such as Gorbachev trying to make the system work as he moved up through its ranks. Instead of overhauling the whole economy, as Gorbachev is now attempting to do, Khrushchev contented himself with a hysterical and contradictory barrage of directives for change in day-to-day operations, particularly in agriculture.

When Khrushchev was deposed in 1964, Gorbachev, who by then was traveling periodically to Moscow for Party congresses and other meetings, would confide to his friends his hopes for thorough reform as opposed to the crazy patchwork of the Khrushchev era. He was to be bitterly disappointed with the rise of Brezhnev to power. He told Mlynar, who visited him socially in 1967, that he considered the Brezhnev appointment an interim one; he must have been deeply chagrined to witness it endure for eighteen years.

Mlynar had returned home to Czechoslovakia upon graduation and became a top academician and leader in the ruling Communist Party. He was prominent during the reform period known as the "Prague Spring" and visited Gorbachev in Stavropol in 1967, one year before Brezhnev dispatched Soviet tanks to crush the Czechs' experiment in socialist reform. Gorbachev met him at the airport and Mlynar chuckled that his old friend clearly was an important Party bureaucrat because he had begun to wear the wide-brimmed, old-fashioned hat made famous by the likes of Khrushchev and Gromyko, then the Soviet Foreign Minister. By then, Gorbachev had attained the important rank of Stavropol Party leader. Two years later, he would be deputy director of the entire region and, two years after that, a member of the Soviet Union's Communist Party Central Committee. He was clearly doing well. After their visit, Mlynar came away convinced "that Gorbachev belongs to the group of people in the Communist Party in the Soviet Union who are interested in reforms." How did he know Gorbachev was reform-minded? They spoke about the problems after the period of Khrushchev's rule and what was being done in Prague by Mlynar and others. "And we both understood that reforms were necessary, that the Party couldn't continue the way it was," Mlynar said.

Although Gorbachev referred to Brezhnev as a weak man who would be out in a few years, he was proved far off the mark. Brezhnev's tanks crushed Mlynar's reforms the next year and Gorbachev went back to minding his business in Stavropol for the next decade. Mlynar remains convinced that, up to then, his old friend "was not interested in attaining power for its own sake but as a means of achieving something." Again, how can a system of such monumental corruption permit the rise of one whom Mlynar refers to as a "man of integrity"?

"Thousands of people with these characteristics have been destroyed precisely because they had these qualities, and yet one manages to survive," Mlynar mused. "It can happen. This is a typical situation for societies that have a crisis situation." Not at all naïve about the ways of Communist Party power struggles, having been destroyed in one himself, Mlynar added, "For sure, the help through Andropov was a condition."

Andropov, a native of Gorbachev's region who liked to vacation there, had become head of the KGB in 1967 and began building a base of those who were opposed to the emerging corrupt life-style within the Party elite. Gorbachev fit the bill, and they struck up a close friendship that was to prove decisive in the young Party official's final rise to power. Gorbachev was getting good economic results in his region. He had established a reputation for economic experimentation, honesty, and hard work that became an increasingly rare commodity as the Brezhnev years unfolded, and Andropov let other reform-minded people know it. Thanks largely to Andropov's assistance, according to Party insiders interviewed in Moscow, Gorbachev was brought to Moscow in 1978 as the Central Committee's Secretary for Agriculture. Whether through the luck of the weather or skillful innovation, his first year was an enormous success: the harvest of 1978–79 was the biggest in Soviet history. His reward was an appointment as candidate—or non-voting—member of the ruling Politburo.

Unfortunately, the next year's harvest proved disastrous, but Gorbachev managed, as he often has, to turn adversity to his advantage. Rejecting Soviet agriculture's traditional wild schemes to till virgin land and divert rivers, he emphasized the nuts-and-bolts problems of storage and road construction, and the Politburo endorsed his approach. That was in the spring of 1982. Six months later, Brezhnev was dead and Andropov came to power. Though in failing health, the dour former KGB chief nonetheless represented a boon for the reformers, particularly in the economic sphere. Gorbachev found himself in the middle of the action. But then came Andropov's death after fifteen months in office and, as one current Gorbachev confidant put it, "the disaster of Chernenko."

Konstantin Chernenko, chosen to succeed Andropov, seemed to confirm Western Kremlinologists' predictions of a self-perpetuating gerontology of Soviet leaders that would leave no room for the reformers of Gorbachev's generation until they, too, were sufficiently infirm that they would not threaten the established order. According to Moscow insiders, Chernenko represented a compromise in a power struggle between the old Brezhnev forces and the group that had assembled around Andropov. Chernenko got the top post, but the Andropov people augmented their strength, and when Chernenko died thirteen months later, Gorbachev was able to win out.

"Who would have thought," observed a slightly bewildered Mlynar, "that I would be an émigré in Vienna for espousing the same ideas that have now brought Gorbachev to the top of the Kremlin—namely, to change the system in such a way that you have an economic reform, which is accompanied by political change and democratization and that society cannot be modernized in any other way?"

(*Los Angeles Times*, December 4, 1987)

3

The Soviet Union is now in the grip of a new realism about its domestic crisis and world priorities. Gorbachev's top foreign policy advisers are convinced that the "new thinking" of *perestroika* in foreign affairs has permitted a breakthrough on arms control beyond the signing of a ban on intermediate range nuclear force (INF) missiles. They speak openly of a dramatic deal to halve each side's strategic missile force in return for continued strict observance of the existing Anti-Ballistic Missile (ABM) Treaty. Whether or not such a breakthrough occurs, Gorbachev has tried to build an image of his *perestroika* as a domestic policy whose foreign policy postulate is an end to the Cold War as we have known it, thus providing a much needed period of peace for the remaking of Soviet society.

Perestroika, or restructuring, is based on a profound criticism of the "stagnation" of Soviet society and an insistence on radically reordering its essential economic mechanisms. But *perestroika* requires for its success a breeze of *glasnost* blowing through the country's stultified intellectual and political life. If *perestroika*—for now a top-down movement with all of the limitations thus implied—succeeds in cutting through the morass of bureaucratic inefficiency and stupidity to ignite a grass-roots support, it will represent a second Soviet "revolution." Or so Gorbachev claims.

"*Perestroika* means initiative," Gorbachev writes in his remarkable manifesto, published with great fanfare in the East as well as the West, "and creative endeavor, improved order, and discipline, more *glasnost*, criticism, and self-criticism in all spheres of our society. It is utmost respect for the individual and consideration for personal dignity. . . . The essence of *perestroika* lies in the fact that it unites socialism with democracy. . . ." Reading those bold words in the historic National Hotel up the hall from Room 107, where Lenin sat in 1918 looking out at the walls of the Kremlin where his Party inexplicably and suddenly held power, leaves one wanting to dash out into the streets, like John Reed in the movie *Reds*, to witness the change.

Reinforcing the Hollywood image of revolution is the presence of actress Vanessa Redgrave, in Moscow for the celebration of the seventieth anniversary of the Bolshevik Revolution, who sits each morning in the hotel restaurant huddling with her British Marxist adviser, speaking as if nothing has changed since 1917. But it's not that sort of revolution. When tanks move here as they did dramatically one recent night, sweeping through Red Square, it's not for the seizure of power but rather practice for a parade.

This is a settled-in society, and nobody knows this better than Gorbachev does. He must now manage a society that he admits was, when he took power, close to "unmanageable" and yet quite comfortable for the people whose privilege and power might be lost in his reform. As he puts it, "The atmosphere in our society has grown tense as the *perestroika* effort has gone deeper. We have heard some people say: 'Was there any point to starting this at all?' "

What has Gorbachev to start with in the way of ideology or indeed mere example? Every leader other than Lenin has been discredited. Lenin's portrait hangs everywhere virtually alone, since Gorbachev frowns on the display of his own picture, fearing a cult of personality, and all of those who came in between him and Lenin are not favorably recalled, to put it mildly. Unfortunately, there are precious few prescriptions left over from the founder to tell a modern leader what is to be done. "The classics of Marxism-Leninism left us with a definition of the essential characteristics of socialism," Gorbachev writes; "they did not give us a detailed picture of socialism." Instead, what evolved over the years after Lenin's death and through Stalin's madness were forms that "were canonized, idealized, and turned into dogma. Hence the emasculated image of socialism, the exaggerated centralism in management, the neglect of the rich variety of human interests, the underestimation of the active part people play in public life, and the pronounced egalitarian tendencies."

So what is to be done? What Gorbachev holds out is unprecedented for the leadership of an authoritarian state. Questions more than tasks "have to be tackled, with no ready-made answers. Nor are there such answers today. Social scientists have not yet offered us anything cohesive. The political economy of socialism is stuck with outdated concepts and is no longer in tune with the dialectics of life." The trouble is, it was easier to seize power than to use it to accomplish the nobly expressed aims of the Revolution, as Lenin well knew and recorded in his last writings. Life is not a movie like *Reds*. It is more often dull, complex, and undramatic. It is the waiter at the National Hotel simply disregarding the fact that Vanessa Redgrave—beautiful, famous, and imperious—wants another cup of coffee, because there isn't a damn thing she or anyone else can do for or to him if he moves far slower than his customer's desire. In a weird way, he is the master of his fate, but the end result for society is what has become a favorite word around here to describe the Brezhnev decades: "stagnation."

What is to replace the motives of fear and greed—derided as they are by Marxists—that make waiters and everyone else in capitalist societies hop to it? How is any leader to move a society in which full employment is a birthright and in which the price of essentials is so artificially low that differences in ruble earning mean little? Oddly enough, intellectual freedom has been easier to develop than a new work ethic. Writers tear into taboos as if taking another swig of vodka. For them, freedom of thought is intoxicating.

But for others, the long lines for real vodka, caused by Gorbachev's curtailment of alcohol sales, may be more pressing. There is more grumbling among ordinary people about that deprivation than there is outrage about the newly exposed crimes of Stalin or the continued investigative reports in the press about inefficiency and corruption in high places.

Gorbachev's criticism of the system he inherited is as devastating as anyone's: "In the last fifteen years the national income growth rates had declined by more than half and by the beginning of the eighties had fallen to a level close to economic stagnation." "An absurd situation was developing," he continues, "the Soviet Union, the world's biggest producer of steel, raw materials, fuel and energy, has shortfalls in them due to wasteful or inefficient use. One of the biggest producers of grain for food, it nevertheless has to buy millions of tons of grain a year for fodder. We have the largest number of doctors and hospital beds per thousand of the population and, at the same time, there are glaring shortcomings of our health services. Our rockets can find Halley's comet and fly to Venus with amazing accuracy, but side by side with these scientific and technological triumphs is an obvious lack of efficiency in using scientific achievements for economic needs, and many Soviet household appliances are of poor quality." Nothing new in this for those of us in the West except that it comes from a book by the Soviet nation's top leader in a country grown used to celebrating failure as success.

Perestroika is an attempt to unleash individual human economic energy, and to date, its results are not obvious. There have been few real successes on the economic front, although the grain harvest is big for the second year in a row, and that is significant, given the recent unusually harsh winters. The more dramatic changes revolve around the other magic word of Gorbachev's revolution: *glasnost*. Here, too, there are still serious limits. The granting of the Nobel Prize to émigré poet Joseph Brodsky was only belatedly and briefly noted in the avant-garde publication *Moscow News*.

The connection between *glasnost* and *perestroika* is nonetheless vital. Gorbachev writes: "Today our main job is to lift the individual spiritually, respecting his inner world and giving him moral strength." And, he adds, in italics no less, *"in short we need broad democratization of all aspects of society."*

The reason for this is obvious. *Perestroika* means replacing a command economy, or administrative society run from the top, by planners setting quantitative goals for production, with a decentralized economy of individual production units and contract labor teams free to respond to market forces and earning profit by producing goods of sufficient quality as to attract consumers: "The present economic reform envisages that the emphasis will be shifted from primarily administrative to primarily economic management methods at every level, and calls for extensive democratization of management, and the overall activization of the human factor." And that requires freedom.

So much for intentions. Not a single person I have interviewed in several months of such efforts, ranging from dissidents to Politburo members, from Sakharov to Yakovlev, doubts the sincerity of Gorbachev's intentions. Indeed, the fear that is most often expressed is not that he will betray his program or that he is anything but sincere in connecting *glasnost* with *perestroika* but, rather, that he will be worn down by the opposition of a society's inertia— not, as is often suggested in the West, by the opposition of the KGB or the military, both of which, Gorbachev points out, are firmly under the political control of the Party. This remains an authoritarian one-party state without any serious political opposition; but as with the divisions of the Pope, inertia has many troops.

"Will it last?" was the question posed by the head of the national Union of Writers, speaking a few feet in front of the assembled leadership at the recent celebration of the seventieth anniversary of Soviet power. It is a question not easily answered. On this occasion, the speaker said it would, because the time for change is ripe. Echoing Gorbachev's own speech of that same day, he said that an economic crisis is at hand, that everyone knows it, and that the leadershp is boldly dealing with it.

But this urbane and suavely dressed writer had been preceded by a stocky Uzbekistani harvester driver who offered a perhaps more realistic appraisal. In dress, she was a caricature from a Wendy's ad about Soviet fashion, but, in speech, a poet of moving proportions. Yes, the Revolution had done much for her, the daughter of a peasant, who was now an alternate member of the Party's all powerful Central Committee. But she still was responsible for getting the cotton in; and cotton, as she warned them, responds to its own rhythms. Cotton, she told this audience of the Party elite and invited dignitaries, who tend to spend their lives drunk with abstractions, is like a small child whose growth and very survival is at constant issue. Each day she ventures out into the field to look into the face of this cotton as a mother into a child's face and ask how is it doing. Is it getting enough nourishment from the soil, is its growth stunted, what more does it need to be healthy? Will it be harvested in time and with a care that will not damage what has been so carefully nurtured? For twenty-three years she has operated a cotton harvester, which she described as a woefully inadequate machine. And for twenty-three years she has witnessed a parade of experts who have come to inspect this problem of the harvester. But, despite one hundred different scientific dissertations written on this subject, she is still driving the same lousy harvester. *Perestroika*, she stated in a booming voice, will not work if the top leaders do not leave their offices and get out into the fields and look that cotton in the face. And it will not work unless people are free to criticize the top leaders and elect new ones when they fail to improve the harvester despite so much talk.

Gorbachev, himself a harvester driver in his youth and the son of a harvester driver, knows this all too well. He has seen claims of reform come and go. In *perestroika*, Gorbachev is a kind of agent provocateur, not because he tells the Soviet people what to think, but because he calls on them to think in the first place. Centuries of political oppression and authoritarian rule have left this people, despite its formal education, without the habit of thinking and, more important, acting independently. Gorbachev writes:

> The greatest difficulty in our restructuring effort lies in our thinking which has been molded over the past years. Everyone, from the General Secretary to worker, has to alter his thinking. And this is understandable, for many of us were first formed as individuals and lived in conditions when the old order existed. We have to overcome our own conservatism. . . . Many decades of being mesmerized by dogma, by a rule book approach, have had their effect. Today we want to inject a genuinely creative spirit into our creative work. This is difficult but it must be done.

He admits that "We do not yet have enough ethic of debate . . . but there is a steadily growing understanding that democracy is incompatible with excessive bureaucratic regimentation of social life." Tough talk, but will the commitment to *glasnost* continue when that openness threatens, as it now does, to spawn new groupings and even militant demonstrations that portend at least a limited plurality of power?

Gorbachev's answer is quite clear; and by personnel changes and example, he is imposing his answer on the Party leadership more with each passing month: "It is no longer a question of whether the CPSU Central Committee will continue the policy of *glasnost*. . . . We need *glasnost* as we need the air. . . . There is no present-day socialism, nor can there be, without democracy." Laws implementing this principle are supposedly being drawn up now, and their public codification and enforcement could go a long way to making *glasnost* a permanent feature of Soviet society. Laws, and—a subject not addressed by Gorbachev in his book—an independent judiciary to enforce the laws.

Can there be legality without the separation of powers and without pluralistic political power? And to what degree is the Soviet Communist Party now prepared to march down that road of power sharing? If *glasnost* is as necessary as air, they had better march pretty far and pretty fast. As Gorbachev concedes, "Law and legality are not just concomitant of the deepening of our democracy and acceleration of social progress. These are working instruments in the restructuring and a reliable guarantee of it being irreversible." But we shall have to wait to see, for starters, how far the new laws go in the direction of guaranteeing rights of *habeas corpus* and independent counsel.

Gorbachev's call for "new thinking" is not always mirrored in his public pronouncements or writings. After reading his sensitive discussion of the strains on family life brought on by both parents working and the double price paid by Soviet women who are generally expected to be both disciplined workers in the field and homemakers at home, one hoped for a plea to men to take on more of the burden. Instead, he writes of "the question of what we should do to make it possible for women to return to their purely womanly mission." Was Lenin's Revolution fought to bring the views of Phyllis Schlafly to power?

He also writes that "it is a tradition of our party to combat any manifestation of nationalist narrow-mindedness and chauvinism, parochialism, Zionism and anti-Semitism, in whatever forms they may be expressed." This is simply not true. Anti-Semitism, sometimes in the guise of anti-Zionism, has been a consistent feature of life in Mother Russia from the time of the czars to the present, and it has to be dealt with forthrightly if the spirit of *glasnost* is to be observed.

Ironically, Gorbachev endorses Zionism, if by that is meant the right of the Jewish people to a secure homeland of their own. "Nonexistent anti-Israeli prejudices are ascribed to the Soviet Union, although our country was among the first to promote the formation of the state of Israel." After reiterating the Soviet plan for a Mideast peace conference involving the Soviet Union as a precondition for restoration of full diplomatic ties, Gorbachev adds: "I want to stress in this connection that we do not bear any hostility toward Israel in principle. . . . We have no complexes here. As for the contacts already existing between our countries, we will not abandon them."

According to interviews with high Soviet foreign ministry officials, those contacts are substantial, though generally with the Labor wing of the Israeli government. The sticking point now is the matter of the emigration of Soviet Jews desiring to leave, and this topic is simply avoided in his book. This stagnant approach to Israel stands in sharp contrast to Gorbachev's fresh "new thinking" on most other outstanding international questions.

Basically, Gorbachev argues that the time of the Cold War is over and that the Soviet Union and the United States no longer have a military avenue for pursuing their differences. It is a point not very different from that made by President Nixon in his book *The Real Peace*, which holds that war, either nuclear or conventional, isn't any longer an option. "Peace is the only option," Nixon wrote. Gorbachev puts it somewhat differently: "Having entered the nuclear age . . . mankind has lost its immortality." He adds: "Clausewitz's dictum that war is the continuation of policy only by different means, which was classical in his time, has grown hopelessly out of date. It now belongs to the libraries. . . . Security can no longer be assured by military means— neither by the use of arms or deterrence, nor by continued perfection of the 'sword' and 'shield.' Attempts to achieve military superiority are preposterous."

The economic impetus for the Soviets' "new thinking" in foreign policy is equally clear to Gorbachev: "We are saying openly for all to hear: We need lasting peace in order to concentrate on the development of our society and to cope with the tasks of improving the life of the Soviet people. Ours are long-term and fundamental plans. That is why everyone, our Western part-ners-rivals included, must realize that our international policy of building a nuclear-weapon-free and nonviolent world and asserting civilized standards in interstate relations is equally fundamental and equally trustworthy in its underlying principles." Gorbachev has steadily advanced his theme of the interdependence of the modern world and the need for a much higher level of cooperation centering on the United Nations, an institution to which the Soviets have been devoting increasing attention. But he has also thrown a challenge that cannot be ignored: which side needs the Cold War, and why?

(*Los Angeles Times*, November 15, 1987)

Robert Scheer was born in the Bronx, New York, on April 4, 1936. He attended City College in New York and did graduate work in economics and Chinese studies at the University of California at Berkeley, where he was a fellow at the Center for Chinese Studies. He was managing editor and later editor-in-chief of *Ramparts* (1964–1969); he was also an editor of *New Times*. Scheer has written extensively for *Playboy* and *Esquire* magazines. Since 1976, he has been a national correspondent for the *Los Angeles Times*. He is also Adjunct Professor in Social Sciences at U.C. Irvine.